D1330954

OBSERVER MECHANICS

OBSERVER MECHANICS

A Formal Theory of Perception

BRUCE M. BENNETT
Department of Mathematics
University of California
Irvine, California

DONALD D. HOFFMAN
Department of Cognive Science
University of California
Irvine, California

CHETAN PRAKASH
Department of Mathematics
California State Univeristy
San Bernardino, California

ACADEMIC PRESS, INC.
Harcourt Brace Jovanovich, Publishers
San Diego New York
Berkeley Boston London Sydney Tokyo Toronto

ACADEMIC PRESS, INC.
San Diego, California 92101

United Kingdom Edition published by
ACADEMIC PRESS LIMITED
24-28 Oval Road, London NW1 7DX

LIBRARY OF CONGRESS CATALOG CARD NUMBER: 89-6737

ISBN 0-12-088635-9 (alk. paper)

PRINTED IN THE UNITED STATES OF AMERICA
89 90 91 92 9 8 7 6 5 4 3 2 1

To our parents

CONTENTS

CHAPTER 10. RELATION TO QUANTUM MECHANICS

PREFACE

Observer Mechanics is an inquiry into the subject of perception. It suggests an approach to the study of perception that attempts to be both rigorous and general.

A central thesis of *Observer Mechanics* is that every perceptual capacity (e.g., stereovision, auditory localization, sentence parsing, haptic recognition) can be described as an instance of a single formal structure: viz., an "observer." The first two chapters of *Observer Mechanics* develop this structure, resulting in a formal definition of an observer. The third chapter considers the relationship between observers and Turing machines. The fourth chapter discusses the semantics of observers. Chapters 5–7 present a formal framework in which to describe an observer and its objects of perception, and then develop on this framework a perceptual dynamics. Using this dynamics, Chapter 8 defines conditions in which an observer may be said to perceive truly. Chapter 9 discusses how stabilities in perceptual dynamics might permit the genesis of higher level observers. Chapter 10 comments on the relationship between the formalisms of quantum mechanics and observer mechanics. Finally, the epilogue discusses the philosophical context and implications of observer mechanics.

We want the ideas and principles in *Observer Mechanics* to be accessible to a wide audience; this dictates a rather informal style. On the other hand, we want to introduce a new formalism; this requires a fairly technical language and thereby restricts the audience. We have been advised to do one or the other but not to attempt both. We have chosen, perhaps foolishly, to ignore this advice. We want to communicate to the nonmathematical reader as well as to the mathematical reader without seriously offending the sensibilities of either. Here, in outline, is how we have attempted this.

In Chapters 1–6, when mathematics is necessary to develop a point, we intersperse liberal explanations for nonmathematical readers. Chapters 2, 5, and 6 each have a section presenting basic mathematical notation and terminology. We intend these sections to be helpful references for readers having many different levels of mathematical sophistication. Chapters 7–10 are primarily mathematical; they are intended to give rigor to the intuitive discussions of the first six chapters.

For convenience in reference, we number in one sequence all definitions, terminology, figures, equations, propositions, and theorems. For example, "Definition 5-2.1" refers to the first numbered item in section two of Chapter 5. Figures are numbered in sequence with all other numbered items. For instance, a figure immediately following Proposition 6-3.8 would be numbered "Figure 6-3.9," even if it were the first figure in the third section of Chapter 6. At the top of each page we display the chapter and section. For instance, a page in section three of Chapter 4 would have the display " 4-3."

For suggestions and critical comments we thank N. Ahuja, G. Andersen, J. Arpaia, R. Black, M. Braunstein, V. Brown, R. Carmona, T. Cornsweet, D. Estlund, D. Glaser, C. Glymour, H. Hironaka, D. P. Hoffman, L. Hoffman, X. Hu, T. Indow, A. Jepson, R. Kakarala, M. Kinsbourne, P. Kube, D. Laberge, Lê D.-T., A. Lewis, E. Matthei, L. Narens, A. Nelson, J. Nicola, R. Olson, D. Revuz, S. Richman, R. Reilly, J. Sarli, W. Savage, B. Skyrms, D. Smith, B. Teissier, W. Uttal, D. Van Essen, P. Williams, P. Woodruff, and J. Yellott. We thank especially J. Koenderink, H. Resnikoff, and W. Richards for reading substantial portions of the manuscript and for making many suggestions. We thank A. Mendez, J. Nicola, and J. Sinek for proofreading and J. Beusmans for writing a computer simulation of the participator dynamics. We thank the Westview Press for permission to use materials from their 1988 book *Cognition and Representation*.

Work on this book was supported in part by National Science Foundation grants IST-8413560 and IRI-8700924, and by Office of Naval Research contracts N00014-85-K-0529 and N00014-88-K-0354. We are grateful for their support.

B. M. Bennett
D. D. Hoffman
C. Prakash

CHAPTER ONE

PRINCIPLES

In this chapter we discuss the principles that underlie our definition of observer. We then illustrate the principles by two examples of observers, one fabricated and one realistic.

1. Introduction

Science seeks, among other things, unity in diversity. One goal of the theoretical scientist is to find unifying structures and causal laws which encompass, as special cases, the explanations accepted for specific phenomena or or properties of individual systems. Behind (e.g.) the diversity of atomic and subatomic phenomena, from the gravitational attraction of atoms to the chromatic properties of quarks, theoretical physicists seek a unity, a unified field theory, which encompasses as special cases the explanations accepted for these phenomena. Similarly, behind the diversity of possible algorithms, from the recognition of primes to the scheduling of traveling salesmen, computer scientists have found a unity of structure, the Turing machine, which encompasses as special cases all algorithms.

But behind the diversity of perceptual capacities (e.g., stereovision, auditory localization, sonar echolocation, haptic recognition) no such unity has been found. The field of perception has no unifying formalism remotely approaching the scope and precision of those found in physics and other natural sciences. This is perhaps not surprising. Before one can unify one first needs something to unify. In the case of perception one first needs theories of specific perceptual capacities that (1) are mathematically rigorous, (2) agree with the empirical (e.g., psychophysical) data, and (3) work. And these have, until recently, been in very short supply.

But there is now reason for guarded optimism. The last few years have witnessed the genesis of just such theories. We now have theories of (e.g.) stereovision that are mathematically rigorous, that are not too comical to the psychophysicists, and that actually (sometimes) work when one implements them in computer vision systems. Theories with similar salutary properties are on offer for aspects of visual-motion perception, the perception of shading and texture, object recognition, and light source detection. With this growing collection of rigorous theories comes a growing temptation: viz., the temptation to wade around in this collection of theories in search of structural commitments that are common to them all. If such we find, from these we might fashion a unifying formalism which encompasses each theory, perhaps every perceptual theory, as a special case.

We have succumbed to the temptation. And, as you might have guessed, we think we have found something. This book records where we have looked, what structural commitments we have encountered in theory after theory, and what unifying structures we have, in consequence, constructed.

Perhaps the most fundamental is a structure we call an "observer."[1] An observer is, roughly, the *static* structure common to all theories of perceptual capacities we have so far studied. Much of this chapter and the next are devoted to the explication of this structure, so we shall not dwell on it here. Instead we shall enter claims and disclaimers regarding this structure.

First a disclaimer. There are, of course, many perceptual capacities whose theories we have not yet studied, and far more capacities, e.g., in the modalities of taste and smell, for which there simply are no adequate theories. Our own training is in visual perception, with the consequence that the examples adduced throughout this book are primarily visual.

Now for a claim. To make things more interesting, we shall stick out our necks and advance the definition of observer as a unifying structure not simply for some capacities in vision but, rather, for all capacities in all modalities. Accordingly, we propose the following *observer thesis*: To every perceptual capacity in every modality, whether that capacity be biologically instantiated or not, there is naturally associated a formal description which is an instance of the definition of observer.

---

[1] The term "observer" is, we have found to our dismay, already used extensively in the theory of linear dynamical systems. It was introduced by David Luenberger (Luenberger, 1963; O'Reilly, 1983). An observer, in Luenberger's theory, infers the state of a linear dynamical system, with the purpose of using this information for feedback control. We do not yet know what relationship, if any, exists between our observers and Luenberger's.

This thesis is vulnerable to disconfirmation by counterexample. As new capacities are studied, or as the structure of existing theories of specific capacities are reexamined, capacities may be found whose formal structures are not instances of the definition of an observer. And given the definition's foundation in a somewhat small collection of specific theories this eventuality is, despite our efforts to the contrary, not impossible. If it happens, then the definition will be, in consequence, further refined or entirely replaced by a more adequate structure.

After defining an observer in chapter two, we set it to work on several problems in perception and cognitive science. One problem is to define the concept *transduction*. Some relevant intuitions here are that transduction involves the conversion of energy from one physical form (say light) to another (say neural impulses); that transduced properties are, in a certain sense, illusion free; that in the case of vision it is properties of light that are transduced and the transducer is the retina; and that in the case of audition it is properties of sound that are transduced and the transducer is the cochlea. But turning such intuitions into a workable definition has proved difficult; it is a remarkable fact about the field of perception that such a basic concept is as yet ill-defined. It indicates, perhaps, that not all the relevant intuitions can simultaneously be granted. Indeed, some get sacrificed in the observer-based definition we propose.

We also employ observers in an effort to define the *theory neutrality* of observation. Philosophers still debate about the proper intuitions for this term: some argue that to say observation is theory neutral is to say that the truth of observation reports is independent of any empirical hypotheses; others argue that it means that scientific beliefs do not "cognitively penetrate" perception, i.e., roughly, that the beliefs one holds do not alter one's perceptual apparatus—the intuition here being that if observation is in this sense theory neutral then two scientists could hold competing theories and yet agree on the data that they observe in critical experiments. We employ observers not to settle the empirical issue (viz., is observation *in fact* theory neutral) but, rather, simply to define it. To this end we first propose relational definitions for the terms *cognitive* and *cognitive penetration*. We then formulate the claim that observation is theory neutral to be the claim that the relation *cognitive* is, in the appropriate context, an irreflexive partial order. This development, together with the definition of transduction mentioned above, leads to a novel functional taxonomy of the mind. This taxonomy is discussed briefly in chapter two and more extensively in chapter nine.

Observers capture, so we claim, the static structure common to all perceptual capacities. But perception is notably active: it involves learning, updating perspective, and interacting with the observed. To account for these aspects of perception an entity other than the observer—a dynamical entity—is needed. We propose one, viz., the *participator.* Participators are developed in chapters six through nine, so we content ourselves here to make two comments. First, the relationship between participators and observers is particularly simple: collections of observers serve as state spaces for the dynamics of participators. So one might say that participators, not observers, turn out to be the real stars of the show. Observers simply serve as states in the state spaces of participators. Second, the dynamics of participators is stochastic, and its asymptotic behavior, in particular the stabilities of its asymptotic behavior, can be used to define conditions in which the perceptual conclusions of observers are "matched to reality." This is the topic of chapter eight.

Observation is of interest not only to philosophers, perceptual psychologists, and cognitive scientists, but also to physicists studying the problem of measurement (see, e.g., Greenberger 1986). The problem of measurement is roughly that, contrary to the assumptions of classical physics, it now appears that one cannot ignore the effects of the measurement process on the system being measured, especially if the system is very small or moves very fast. Indeed, it is widely held that elementary particles behave one way when they are not being measured, viz., according to the Schrodinger equation (in the nonrelativistic case), but behave another way when they are being measured, viz., according to von Neumann's "collapse" of the wavefunction. Perceptual psychology has heretofore had little to offer the measurement theorists, because its insights and advances have not been expressed in a language of the requisite generality and mathematical precision. One purpose of this book is to advance the exchange of ideas between these two disciplines. To this end, chapter ten presents some preliminary thoughts on the relationship of observer mechanics and quantum mechanics.

2. Principles

Our wading about in current theories of specific perceptual capacities has led us to conclude that three principles are crucial to understanding the structure of these theories. These three principles underlie our definition of observer:

1. Perception is a process of inference.
2. Perceptual inferences are not, in general, deductively valid.
3. Perceptual inferences are biased.

These principles have been discussed before, in one form or another, many times in the literature on perception.[2] We consider them in turn.

Perception is a process of inference.

The term "inference" has, particularly among psychologists, connotations we want to avoid. To some the claim that perception is a process of inference implies the view that consciousness is an essential aspect of perception; to others it implies the view that perceptual processing is "top down" as opposed to "bottom up." By using the term we mean neither to imply nor to deny either view.

An *inference,* as we use it throughout this book, is simply any process of arriving at conclusions from given premises. The premises and conclusions of an inference together constitute an *argument*. For example:

Premise: A retinal image has two dimensions.

Premise: A cup has three dimensions.

Conclusion: A retinal image of a cup has fewer dimensions than a cup.

Premises and conclusions are *propositions.* Just what propositions are is the subject of debate among philosophers. For our purposes, however, a proposition is that which can be true or false. A proposition may be expressed, as in the example above, by a declarative sentence of English; it may be expressed by a well-formed formula in, say, the standard propositional calculus; it may also be expressed by a probability measure on some space. In this latter case one can, for example, interpret the measure as a set of statements, one statement for each event in the space; each statement specifies the probability (e.g., the relative frequency) of its corresponding event. So interpreted, a probability measure expresses a set of statements, each either true or false; it therefore expresses a proposition. We note this because, as we shall see, probability measures conveniently represent the conclusions of perceptual inferences.

Figure 1.1 illustrates the inferential nature of perception. This figure contains two sets of curved lines lying, of course, in the plane of the page. However, what one perceives is not simply curved lines in a plane, but a pair of curved surfaces ("cosine surfaces") in three dimensions. Only with effort can you see the curved lines as simply lying in a plane, though the fact that they are printed on paper makes this unquestionable.

[2] Some examples are Helmholtz (1910), Gregory (1966), Fodor (1975), and Marr (1982).

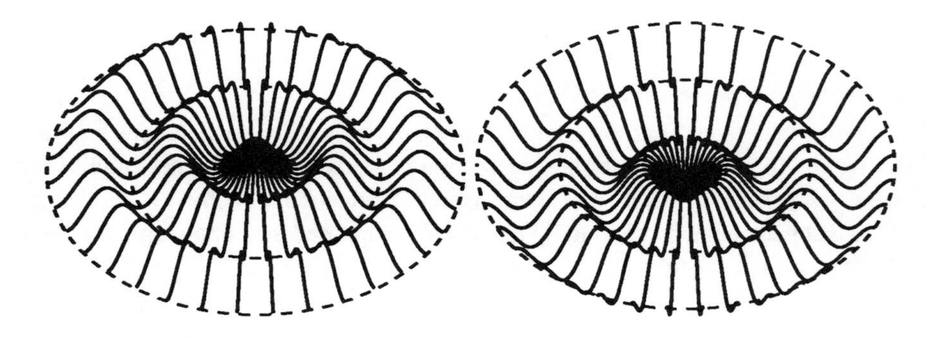

FIGURE 1.1. *Two cosine surfaces. Even though this figure is in fact planar it appears three-dimensional. This suggests that a failed inference underlies your perception of this figure, an inference whose premises derive from the two-dimensional arrays of curves on the page and whose conclusion is the three-dimensional interpretation you perceive. Indeed, the conclusion of your inference is not just one three-dimensional interpretation, but two. To see the other interpretation, slowly rotate the figure and observe the behavior of the raised "hills."*

To a first approximation, we can describe one's perception of Figure 1.1 as an inference with the following structure: the premise is the set of curved lines in a plane, and the conclusion is the set of perceived surfaces embedded in three dimensions.[3] Or we can give a finer description in terms of a series of inferences, inferences first about patterns of light and dark in two dimensions, then about line segments in two dimensions, then about extended curves in two dimensions, and finally about a surface in three dimensions. Vision researchers argue, as they should, over the details of a proposed sequence of inferences, but this is irrelevant to the point made here: perception is a process of inference.

Another illustration of this point is stereovision, a perceptual ability sometimes exploited by movie makers in the creation of "3-D" movies. These movies superimpose two slightly different images in each frame and, by wearing special glasses, the viewer is shown one image in the left eye and the other in the right. If all is done

[3] To avoid cumbersome language, we sometimes fail to distinguish between a proposition and its representation. However, a premise must be a proposition—and a set of curved lines in a plane is not a proposition but a representation. Similarly, a conclusion must be a proposition—and a perceived surface is not a proposition but a representation.

correctly, the viewer does not perceive two separate and flat images, but one image in three dimensions. The resulting perception of depth can be striking.

Perception in stereo can be described as an inference with the following structure: the premises are the disparities between two, slightly different, flat images, and the conclusion is the perceived depth. Again, one can give a more detailed series of inferences, inferences first, say, about light and dark in two dimensions, then about two-dimensional line segments, then about disparities in the positions of line segments between the two images, and finally about depth. But our conclusion is the same: perception is a process of inference.

Other examples abound. Consider our ability to recognize individuals by listening to them talk. The premise here is, say, certain vibrations at the eardrum, and the conclusion is the identity of the individual. Consider our ability to localize a sound source. The premise is a difference in intensity and in phase of the sound wave at the two ears, and the conclusion is the position of the source in three dimensions. Consider a child's acquisition of a language. The premise can be taken to be a finite set of sentences in the language (presented by parents and friends), and the conclusion to be the grammar of the language. Or consider one's structural comprehension of a spoken sentence. The premise is, say, a finite sequence of phonemes, and the conclusion describes the syntactic structure of the sentence. The same inferential structure underlies face recognition, haptic recognition, color perception—in fact, we suggest, it underlies every conceivable act of perception, whether biologically instantiated or not.

Perceptual inferences are not, in general, deductively valid.

A natural question to ask about an inference is this: What is the evidential relationship between the premises and the conclusion? Do the premises support the conclusion or not?

One can judge the evidential relationship between the premises and the conclusion of an inference by two standards: deductive validity and inductive strength. An argument is *deductively valid* if the conclusion is logically implied by the premises; equivalently, but more intuitively, it is deductively valid if the conclusion makes no statement not already contained, at least implicitly, in the premises. An argument is said to be *inductively strong* if it is not deductively valid, but the conclusion is probable given that the premises are true.[4] The following arguments are deductively valid.

---

[4] For a lucid discussion of this, we recommend Skyrms (1975).

Premise: John is a boy.
Premise: John has brown hair.
Conclusion: John is a boy with brown hair.

Premise: All cars have wheels.
Premise: All wheels are round.
Conclusion: All cars have round wheels.

Premise: Bill is a boy with brown hair.
Conclusion: Some boys have brown hair.

Premise: All emeralds are green.
Premise: Everyone has an emerald.
Conclusion: My emerald is green.

We display these arguments not simply to give concrete examples, but also to counter a common misconception, namely that deductively valid inferences have general premises and specific conclusions whereas, in contrast, inductively strong inferences have specific premises and general conclusions. Of the four arguments given, the first has specific premises and a specific conclusion, the second has general premises and a general conclusion, the third has specific premises and a general conclusion, and the fourth has general premises and a specific conclusion. All four arguments are deductively valid. The distinction between deductive validity and inductive strength lies not in the generality or specificity of the premises and conclusions, but rather in the evidential relationship that obtains between them.

The following argument is not deductively valid.

Premise: John is 93.
Conclusion: John will not do a double back flip today.

This argument is not deductively valid because the conclusion, though very likely to be true given the premise, is not in fact logically implied by the premise. John could surprise us, even though the odds are very long.

Now back to perception. It is widely acknowledged, among those who take perception to be a process of inference, that the inferences typical of perception are not deductively valid. Consider again the cosine surfaces of Figure 1.1. We found that one's perception of this figure could be described as an inference whose premise is the set of curved lines in a plane, and whose conclusion is a pair of surfaces embedded in three dimensions. Now this premise in no way constrains one by logic to conclude that the lines lie on any particular surface. One could conclude, as the visual system does, that they lie on cosine surfaces; or one could conclude, as is in fact the case, that they lie on a planar surface. With little imagination, one could concoct many different surfaces on which the lines might lie. Since one is not required either by the rules of logic or the theorems of mathematics to conclude that they lie on any particular surface, the inference here is not deductively valid.

Consider the example of stereo perception. We said that the premise is a set of two slightly different, flat images and that the conclusion is some perceived scene in three dimensions. As in the previous example, the premise in no way compels one by logic to accept any particular conclusion about the structure of the scene. Although the visual system arrives at one conclusion, there are many other conclusions which are logically compatible with the premise. One could conclude, for instance, that the scene is flat, a conclusion that is correct but overlooked by the visual system when one views a 3-D movie.

Once again, other examples abound: the inferences involved in voice recognition, auditory localization, face recognition, haptic recognition, language acquisition, and color perception are not deductively valid. This is typical of perceptual inferences.

Perceptual inferences are biased.

The conclusions reached by our perceptual systems are not logically dictated by the premises they are given; this fact does not stop them. When, for instance, one views Figure 1.1 one's visual system reaches, as we have seen, a unique conclusion about a surface in three dimensions. When one views a stereo movie, one's visual system again reaches a unique conclusion about depths.

In the absence of logical compulsion, people systematically reach certain perceptual interpretations and not others; their perceptual inferences are biased. We consider later (chapter eight) what it means for such biases to be justified; for now we simply illustrate them. We start by considering again our perception of Figure 1.1. We have said that the premise of the inference here is the curved lines lying in the plane of the page, and that the conclusion is a pair of cosine surfaces. All normal human viewers reach the same conclusion, even though logic compels none to do so, and even though there are many other plausible conclusions; in this way our inferences here all share a common bias.

Another feature of the figure also exposes this bias. Consider the cosine surface to the left in the figure. Observe that it appears organized into a set of raised concentric "hills," one circular hill meeting the next along the dashed contours. Now slowly rotate the figure so as to turn it upside down, and watch the behavior of the hills. The hills remain intact until you rotate the figure through a quarter turn, then suddenly the entire surface appears to change, old hills vanishing and new hills appearing. Observe that the new hills no longer meet along the dashed contours; these contours now lie on the crests of the hills. We find, then, that our perceptual inference is biased toward one interpretation when the figure is upright, and toward a different interpretation when the figure is inverted. One might maintain that rotating the figure alters the premises presented to the visual system; one is not surprised then that it reaches different interpretations. We agree. However, if one says this then one must admit that each small rotation of the figure also alters the premises. But note: one's bias about the hills remains unchanged for most such rotations; one's inference sticks to a single bias through one range of rotations, and then shifts to another bias for the remaining rotations, indicating that the observer's bias, not just its premises, determines the perceptual interpretation.

Our perception in stereo provides another example of perceptual bias. The premise, in the case of 3-D movies, is a pair of planar images. The conclusion is typically not planar, but is some particular assignment of depth to the various elements of the images. Since no particular assignment is favored by logic, the only way to avoid reaching a biased conclusion would be to reach no conclusion (or stick to the given images).

As another example, consider the following demonstration. Place two dozen small black dots on a clear plastic beach ball. View the ball with one eye at a distance of about three meters. If the lighting is such that there are no specular reflections from the ball, you will perceive the dots to lie on a single plane, not on a sphere. Now spin the ball at about eight revolutions per minute. View the ball as before and you will see clearly the spherical arrangement of the dots. If you continue to watch you will see the ball appear to reverse its direction of spin. This visual ability to recover the three-dimensional structure of objects from their changing two-dimensional projections onto the retina is called "structure from motion."[5]

The inference here has the following structure: the premise is a sequence of images of dots in two dimensions, and the conclusion is the pair of spherical interpretations in three dimensions (one with the correct direction of spin, one with an incorrect direction). The inference is not deductively valid: there are infinitely many interpretations in three dimensions one could give for the sequence of images without violating the rules of logic or the theorems of mathematics. However, our visual systems reach the two spherical interpretations. To explain this, some perceptual psychologists have suggested that our visual systems are biased toward rigid interpretations, namely interpretations in which all points maintain fixed rela-

[5] There is a vast literature on this subject. We suggest the discussions found in Ullman (1979) and Marr (1982).

tive positions in three dimensions over time.[6] Other psychologists have suggested a bias toward planar or fixed-axis interpretations. Still others suggest that the bias cannot be simply described. These are issues of great interest to vision researchers, but the details are irrelevant here. What is relevant is the need for some bias.

Where do these biases come from? Why does an observer exhibit one bias instead of some other? How are they justified? These are difficult questions which we discuss throughout the book.

3. Bug observer

In this and the next section we consider two examples of visual observers, examples designed to illustrate the principles that underlie our definition of observer. The examples are chosen for their perspicuity and their mathematical simplicity. They are not intended to be a representative sampling of all the work done in perception. In fact, the first example is fabricated. However, in chapter two we consider seven real examples, all of which are drawn from recent work in perception.

Imagine a world in which there are bugs and one-eyed frogs that eat bugs. The bugs in this world come in two varieties—poisonous and edible. Remarkably, the edible bugs are distinguished from the poisonous ones by the way they fly. Edible bugs fly in circles. The positions, radii, and orientations in three-dimensional space of these circles vary from one edible bug to another, but all edible bugs fly in circles. Moreover, no poisonous bugs fly in circles. Instead they fly on noncircular closed paths, paths that may be described by polynomial equations.

The visual task of a frog in such a world is obvious. To survive it must visually identify and limit its diet to those bugs that fly in circles. How does the frog determine which bugs fly in circles? First, the frog's eye forms a two-dimensional image on its retina of the path of the bug. If the path is a circle, then its retinal image will be an ellipse.[7] The contrapositive is, of course, also true: If the retinal image is not an ellipse, then the path is not a circle. Therefore the frog may infer with confidence that if the retinal image of a path is not an ellipse then the bug is poisonous. In this case the frog does not eat the bug.

The frog needs to eat sometime. What can the frog infer if the retinal image is

[6] Again the literature is extensive. We suggest Wallach and O'Connell (1953), Gibson and Gibson (1957), Green (1961), Hay (1966), and Johansson (1975).

[7] For simplicity, we assume parallel projection from the world onto the retina.

an ellipse? It is true, by assumption, that if the path is a circle then its retinal image will be an ellipse. But the converse, viz., if the image is an ellipse then the path is a circle, is in general not true. For example, elliptical paths also have elliptical images. With a little imagination one can see that many strangely curving polynomial paths have elliptical images. In fact, for any unbiased measure on the set of polynomial paths having elliptical images, the subset of circles has measure zero. So the converse inference, from elliptical images to circular paths, is almost surely false if one assumes an unbiased measure. Putting this in terms relevant to the frog, if the image is an ellipse then the bug is almost surely poisonous, assuming an unbiased measure. If the image is not an ellipse then the bug is certainly poisonous.

This situation presents the frog with a dilemma each time it observes an elliptical image. It can refuse to eat the bug for fear it is poisonous, in which case the frog starves. Or it can eat the bug and thereby risk its life. Regardless of its choice, the frog will almost surely perish.

This is a world harsh on frogs, but one which can be made kinder by a simple stipulation about the paths of poisonous bugs. Stipulate that poisonous bugs almost never trace out paths having elliptical images. So, for example, poisonous bugs almost never trace out elliptical paths. (This is not to say, necessarily, that poisonous bugs go out of their way to avoid these paths. One can get the desired effect by simply stipulating, say, that there are approximately equal numbers of edible and poisonous bugs and that all polynomial paths are equally likely paths for poisonous bugs. Then only with measure zero will a poisonous bug happen to traverse a path having an elliptical image.) This is equivalent to stipulating that the measure on the set of paths having elliptical images is not unbiased, contrary to what we assumed before. In fact it is to stipulate that this measure is biased toward the set of circles. With this adjustment to the world frogs have a better chance of surviving. Of course it is still the case that each time a frog eats a bug it risks its life. The frog stakes its life on the faith that the measure on bug paths is biased in its favor. But then the frog has little choice.

Presumably the frog makes visual inferences about things other than bugs, so we will call its capacity to make visual inferences about bugs its "bug observer." This bug observer is depicted in Figure 2.1. The cube labelled X is the space of all possible bug paths, whether poisonous or edible.[8] An unbiased measure on this space will be called μ_X. The wiggly line labelled E denotes the set of circular bug paths. E has measure zero in X under any unbiased measure μ_X. This is captured pictorially by representing E as a subset of X having lower dimension than X. A

[8] This cubic representation implies no statement about the dimensionality of the space of all closed curves (in $\mathbf{R}^3$) represented by level sets of polynomials.

biased measure on X that is supported on E will be called ν. The square labelled Y is the space of all possible images of bug paths, whether poisonous or edible. The map π from X to Y represents orthographic (parallel) projection from bug paths to images of bug paths. An unbiased measure on the space Y will be called μ_Y. Y is depicted as having dimension lower than X because the set of all paths in three dimensions which project onto a given path in the plane is infinite dimensional (by any reasonable measure of dimension on the set of all paths). The curve labelled S represents the set of ellipses in Y, i.e., $S = \pi(E)$. S has measure zero in Y under any unbiased measure μ_Y. This is captured pictorially by representing S as a subset of Y having lower dimension than Y.

We now interpret Figure 2.1 in terms of the inference being made by the bug observer. The space Y is the space of possible premises for inferences of the observer; the space X is the space of possible paths. Each point of Y not in S represents abstractly a set of premises whose associated conclusion is that the event E of the observer has not occurred. Each point of S represents abstractly a set of premises whose associated conclusion is a probability measure supported (having all its mass) on E. To each point of S is associated a different probability measure on E. This probability measure can be induced from the probability measure ν on E and the map π by means of a mathematical structure called a conditional probability distribution, to be discussed in chapter two. We call π the "perspective" of the bug observer.

In summary, a lesson of the bug observer is this: the act of observation unavoidably involves a tendentious assumption on the part of the observer. The observer assumes, roughly, that the states of affairs described by E occur with high probability, even though E often has small measure under any unbiased measure μ_X on X. (More precisely, the observer assumes that the conditional probability of E given S is much greater than one would expect under an unbiased measure.) This is to assume that the world effects a switch of event probabilities such that the observer's interpretations have a good chance of being correct. The kindest worlds switch the probabilities so that an observer's interpretation is almost surely correct. In this case the measure in the world is not unbiased; it is completely biased towards the interpretations of the observer.

One can put this another way. The utility of the bug observer depends on the world in which it is embedded. If it is embedded in a world where states of affairs represented by points in $\pi^{-1}(S)$ are all equally likely, then it will be useless. Put it in a world where states of affairs represented by points of E occur much more often than those represented by all other points of $\pi^{-1}(S)$, and it is quite valuable. An observer must be tuned to reality. And no finite set of observers can ever determine if

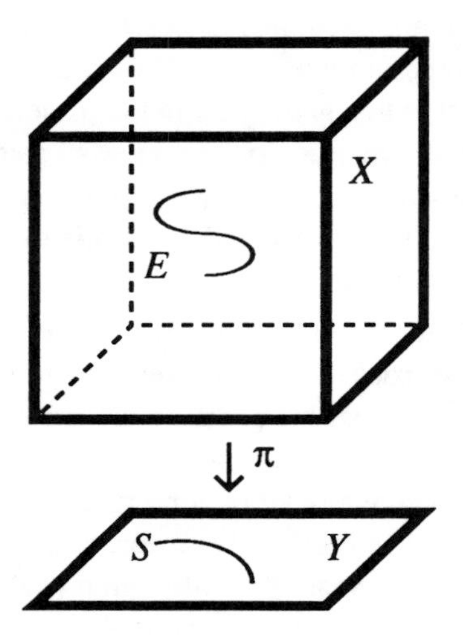

FIGURE 2.1. *Bug observer.*

the world in which they are embedded effects the necessary switch from the unbiased to the biased measure. They must simply operate on the assumption that it does; perception involves, in this sense, unadulterated faith.

4. Biological motion observer

The bug observer discussed in the previous section was chosen primarily for its simplicity; it permitted the examination of some basic ideas with minimal distraction by irrelevant details. In this section we construct an observer that solves a problem of interest to vision researchers.

The problem is the perception of "biological motion," particularly the locomotion of bipeds and quadripeds. Johansson (1973) highlighted the problem with an ingenious experiment. He taped a small light bulb to each major joint on a person (ankle, knee, hip, etc.), dimmed the room lights, turned on the small light bulbs, and videotaped the person walking about the room. Each frame of the videotape is dark except for a few dots that appear to be placed at random, as shown in Figure 3.1. When the videotape is played, the dots are perceived to move, but the perceived motion is often in three dimensions even though the dots in each frame, when viewed statically, appear coplanar. One often perceives that there is a person, and that the person is walking, running, or performing some other activity. One can sometimes recognize individuals or accurately guess gender.

To construct an observer, we must state precisely what inference the observer must perform: we must state the premises, the conclusions, and the biases of the inference. Now for the perception considered here, the relevant inference has, roughly, this structure: the premise is a set of positions in two dimensions, one position for each point in each frame of the videotape; the conclusion is a set of positions in three dimensions, again one position for each point in each frame of the videotape. Of course, this is not a complete description of the inference for we have not yet specified how many frames of how many points will be used for the premises and conclusions, nor have we specified a bias.

A bias is needed to overcome the obvious ambiguity inherent in the stated inference: if the premises are positions in two dimensions, and the conclusions are to be positions in three dimensions, then the rules of logic and the theorems of mathematics do not dictate how the conclusions must be associated with the premises; given a point having values for but two coordinates there are many ways to associate a value for a third coordinate. We are free to choose this association and, thereby, the bias.

If we wish to design a psychologically plausible observer, we must guess what bias is used by the human visual system for the perception of these biological motion displays. To this end, let us consider if a bias toward rigid interpretations will allow us to construct our observer.

When we observe the displays, we find that indeed some of the points do appear to us to move rigidly: the ankle and knee points move together rigidly, as do the knee and hip points, the wrist and elbow, and the elbow and shoulder. Our perception does indicate a bias toward rigidity. We observe further, however, that not all points move rigidly: the ankle and hip do not, nor do the wrist and shoulder, the wrist and hip, and so on. It appears, in fact, that our bias here is only to see some *pairs* of points moving rigidly.

This suggests that we try to construct a simple observer, one that has as its premises the coordinates in two dimensions of just two points over several frames, and that associates the third coordinate in such a way that the two points move rigidly in three dimensions from frame to frame. We assume that each point can be tracked

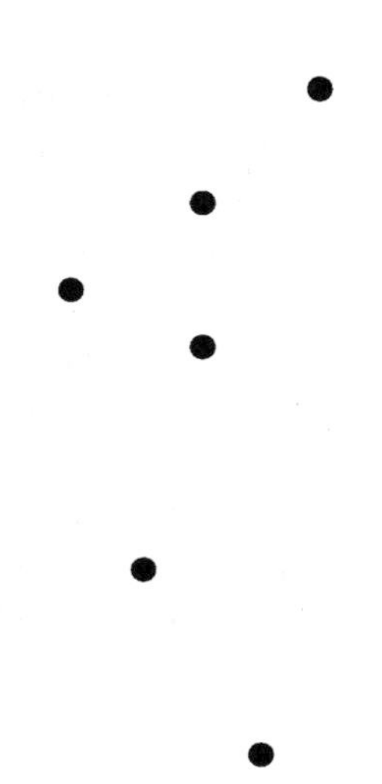

FIGURE 3.1. *One frame from a biological motion display.*

from frame to frame. (This tracking is called "correspondence" among students of visual motion and is itself an example of a perceptual bias, namely an assumption, unsupported by logic, that a point in a new position is the same point that appeared nearby in the preceding frame.)

Now this inference must involve distinguishing those premises that are compatible with a rigid interpretation from those that are not, for as we noted above, we see some pairs of points as rigidly linked and others as not. This is to be expected: of what value is an observer for rigid structures if its premises are so impoverished that they cannot be used to distinguish between rigid and nonrigid structures? This suggests what is, in fact, an important general principle, the *discrimination principle*:

3.2. An observer should have premises sufficiently informative to distinguish those premises compatible with its bias from those that are not.

We shall now find that it is not possible to construct our proposed observer so that it satisfies this principle. To see this, we must first introduce notation. Denote the two points O and P. Without loss of generality, we always take O to be the origin of a cartesian coordinate system. The coordinates in three dimensions of P relative to O at time i of the videotape are $p_i = (x_i, y_i, z_i)$. We denote by $\hat{p}_i = (x_i, y_i)$

the coordinates of P relative to O in frame i that can be obtained directly from the videotape. This implies that $\hat{p}_i$ can be obtained from p_i by parallel projection along the z-axis. If the observer is given access to n frames of the videotape, then each one of its premises is a set $\{\hat{p}_i\}_{i=1,\ldots,n}$.

We will find that no matter how large n is, all premises $\{\hat{p}_i\}_{i=1,\ldots,n}$ are always compatible with a rigid interpretation of the motion of O and P in three dimensions over the n frames. That is, there is always a way to assign coordinates z_i to the pairs (x_i, y_i) so that the resulting vectors always have the same length in three dimensions. Therefore this observer violates the discrimination principle.

To see this, we write down a precise statement of the rigidity bias using our notation. This bias says that the square of the distance in three dimensions between O and P in frame 1 of the tape, namely the distance $x_1^2 + y_1^2 + z_1^2$, must be the same as the square of this distance in any other frame i, namely the distances $x_i^2 + y_i^2 + z_i^2$, $1 < i \leq n$. We can therefore express the rigidity bias by the equations

$$x_1^2 + y_1^2 + z_1^2 = x_i^2 + y_i^2 + z_i^2, \qquad 1 < i \leq n.$$

This gives $n - 1$ equations in the n unknowns $z_1, \ldots, z_n$. Clearly this system can be solved to give a rigid interpretation for any premise $\{(x_i, y_i)\}_{i=1,\ldots,n}$ $(= \{\hat{p}_i\}_{i=1,\ldots,n})$. Therefore the observer contemplated here violates the discrimination principle and is unsatisfactory.

Ullman (1979) has shown that one can construct an observer using a bias of rigidity if, instead of using two points as we have tried, one expands the premises to include four points. He found that three frames of four points allow one to construct an observer satisfying the discrimination principle. This valuable result can explain our perception of visual motion in many contexts. Unfortunately we cannot use Ullman's result here, for in the biological motion displays only pairs of points move rigidly, not sets of four.

Perhaps we could resolve the problem by selecting a more restrictive bias. Further inspection of the displays reveals the following: pairs of points that move together rigidly in these displays also appear, at least for short durations, to swing in a single plane.[9] The ankle and knee points, for instance, not only move rigidly but swing together in a planar motion during a normal step. Similarly for the knee and hip. The plane of motion is, in general, not parallel to the imaging plane of the videotape camera. All this suggests that we try to construct an observer with a bias toward rigid motions in a single plane. We will find that we can construct an

[9] For some discussion on this, see Hoffman and Flinchbaugh (1982); Hoffman (1983).

observer with this bias, an observer that requires only two points per frame and that satisfies the discrimination principle.

Equations expressing this bias arise from the following intuitions. If two points are spinning rigidly in a single plane then the points trace out a circle in space, much like the second hand on a watch. (The circle may also be translating, but by foveating one point such translations are effectively eliminated.) The circle, when projected onto the xy-plane, appears as an ellipse. Therefore if two points in space undergo rigid motion in a plane their projected motion lies on an ellipse. If we compute the parameters of this ellipse we can recover the original circle and thereby the desired interpretation.

To compute the ellipse, we introduce new notation. Call the two points P_1 and P_2. Denote the coordinates in three dimensions of point P_i in frame j by $p_{ij} = (x_{ij}, y_{ij}, z_{ij})$. Denote the two-dimensional coordinates of P_i in frame j that can be obtained directly from the videotape by $\hat{p}_{ij} = (x_{ij}, y_{ij})$. If the observer is given access to n frames of the tape, then its premise is the set $\{\hat{p}_{ij}\}_{i=1,2;j=1,\ldots,n}$.

The x_{ij} and y_{ij} coordinates of each point $\hat{p}_{ij}$ satisfy the following general equation for an ellipse:

$$ax_{ij}^2 + bx_{ij}y_{ij} + cy_{ij}^2 + dx_{ij} + ey_{ij} + 1 = 0. \tag{3.3}$$

Each frame of each point gives us one constraint equation of this form, where the x_{ij} and y_{ij} are known and a, b, c, d, e are five unknowns. Note that (3.3) is linear in the unknowns. Two frames give four constraint equations (one equation for each point in each frame), but there are five unknowns. Therefore each premise is compatible with an interpretation of rigid motion in a plane.

Three frames give six constraint equations in the five unknowns. For generic choices of x_{ij} and y_{ij} these six equations have no solutions, real or complex, for the five unknowns.[10] This is exactly what we want. To say that for a generic choice of x_{ij} and y_{ij} our constraint equations have no solutions is to say that, except for a measure zero subset, all premises are incompatible with any (rigid and planar) interpretation. Furthermore, the constraint equations are all linear, so that if the equations do have solutions then generically they have precisely one solution for an ellipse.

---

[10] Remarkably, one can prove this by finding one concrete choice of the x_{ij} and y_{ij} for which the six equations have no (real or complex) solutions. Proof by concrete example is possible in this case since, for systems of algebraic equations, the number of solutions is an upper semicontinuous function of the parameters. This fact often allows one to determine the number of interpretations associated to each premise rather easily. For more on this, see Hoffman and Bennett (1986).

This ellipse, in turn, can be the projection of one of only two circles, circles that are reflections of each other about a plane parallel to the xy-plane. So if a premise is compatible with at least one interpretation then generically it is compatible with precisely two interpretations (the two circles). Thus to each premise in S is associated, generically, a conclusion measure supported on two points of E (where E is the set of rigid planar interpretations).

It is not true that if the premise is compatible with at least one interpretation then it *always* has precisely two interpretations. Within the set of premises that are compatible with at least one rigid-planar interpretation there is a subset of measure zero that is compatible with infinitely many such interpretations—namely, those $\{\hat{p}_{ij}\}_{i=1,2;j=1,\ldots,3}$ for which the Equations 3.3 give infinitely many solutions.

The abstract structure of the biological motion observer is the same as that of the bug observer shown in Figure 2.1; the meaning of the sets X, Y, E, S, and of the map π is different, but the abstract structure is the same. In fact, we propose that all observers have this same abstract structure, and capture this proposal formally in the next chapter where we define the term observer. For the biological motion observer the space X is the space of all triples of the three-dimensional coordinates of the second point relative to the first point, i.e., $X = \mathbf{R}^9$. This space represents the framework for expressing the possible conclusions of the biological motion observer. Each point in X represents some motion over three units of time of two points in three-dimensional space, where one of the two points is taken to be the origin at each instant of time. The space Y is the space of all triples of the two-dimensional coordinates of the second point relative to the first, i.e., $Y = \mathbf{R}^6$. This space represents the possible premises of the biological motion observer. Each point in Y represents three views of the two points. The map π is projection from X to Y induced by orthographic projection from $\mathbf{R}^3$ to $\mathbf{R}^2$. E is a measure zero subset of X consisting of those triples of pairs of points in three-dimensional space whose motion is rigid and planar. S is the image of E under π, $S = \pi(E)$. Each premise in S consists of three views of two points such that the motion of the points is along an ellipse. To each premise in S is associated a conclusion, viz., a probability measure on E. This structure, represented abstractly in Figure 2.1, can also be represented as follows:

$$\begin{array}{ccccl} X = \mathbf{R}^9 & \supset & E & = & \textit{rigid planar motions} \\ \downarrow \pi & & \downarrow \pi & & \\ Y = \mathbf{R}^6 & \supset & S & & \end{array} \tag{3.4}$$

CHAPTER TWO

DEFINITION OF OBSERVER

In this chapter we define the concept *observer*. The previous chapter introduced this notion by concrete examples. We now abstract from these examples a formal definition. We discuss the definition, discuss under what conditions an observer is ideal, and give an example.

1. Mathematical notation and terminology

The definition of observer given in the next section makes use of several mathematical concepts from probability and measure theory. In this section we collect basic terminology and notation from these fields for the convenience of the reader.[1]

Let X be an arbitrary abstract space, namely a nonempty set of elements called "points." Points are often denoted generically by x. A collection $\mathcal{X}$ of subsets of X is called a *σ-algebra* if it contains X itself and is closed under the set operations of complementation and countable union (and is therefore closed under countable intersection as well). The pair $(X, \mathcal{X})$ is called a *measurable space* and any set A in $\mathcal{X}$ is called an *event*. If $(X, \mathcal{X})$ is a measurable space and $Y \subset X$ is any subset, we define a σ-algebra $\mathcal{Y}$ on Y as follows: $\mathcal{Y} = \{A \cap Y \mid A \in \mathcal{X}\}$. This measurable structure on Y is called the *induced measurable structure*. A map π from a measurable space $(X, \mathcal{X})$ to another measurable space $(Y, \mathcal{Y})$, $\pi: X \to Y$, is said to be *measurable* if $\pi^{-1}(A)$ is in $\mathcal{X}$ for each A in $\mathcal{Y}$; this is indicated by

[1] For more background, beginning readers might refer to Breiman (1969) or Billingsley (1979). For advanced readers we suggest Chung (1974) and Revuz (1984).

writing $\pi \in \mathcal{X}/\mathcal{Y}$. In this case the set $\sigma(\pi) = \{\pi^{-1}(A) \mid A \in \mathcal{Y}\}$ is a subσ-algebra of $\mathcal{X}$, called the *σ-algebra of* π. It is also denoted $\pi^*\mathcal{Y}$. A measurable function π is said to be *bimeasurable* if, moreover, $\pi(A)$ is in $\mathcal{Y}$ for all $A \in \mathcal{X}$. A measurable function whose range is $\mathbf{R}$ or $\bar{\mathbf{R}} = \mathbf{R} \cup \{-\infty, \infty\}$ is also called a *random variable*; the symbol $\mathcal{X}$ also denotes the random variables on X. (The σ-algebra on $\mathbf{R}$ or $\bar{\mathbf{R}}$ is described in the next paragraph.) A *measure* on the measurable space $(X, \mathcal{X})$ is a map μ from $\mathcal{X}$ to $\mathbf{R} \cup \{\infty\}$, such that the measure of a countable union of disjoint sets in $\mathcal{X}$ is the sum of their individual measures. A measure μ is *positive* if the range of μ lies in the closed interval $[0, \infty]$. A measure μ is called *σ-finite* if the space X is a countable union of events in $\mathcal{X}$, each having finite measure. A property is said to hold "μ almost surely" (abbreviated μ a.s.) or "μ almost everywhere" (μ a.e.) if it holds everywhere except at most on a set of μ-measure zero. A *support* of a measure is any measurable set with the property that its complement has measure zero. If X is a discrete set whose σ-algebra is the collection of all its subsets, then *counting measure on* X is the measure μ defined by $\mu(\{x\}) = 1$ for all $x \in X$. A *probability measure* is a measure μ whose range is the closed interval $[0, 1]$ and that satisfies $\mu(X) = 1$. A *Dirac measure* is a probability measure supported on a single point. If ν and μ are two measures defined on the same measurable space, we say that ν is *absolutely continuous with respect to* μ (written $\nu \ll \mu$) on a measurable set E if $\nu(A) = 0$ for every $A \subset E$ with $\mu(A) = 0$. A *measure class* on $(X, \mathcal{X})$ is an equivalence class of positive measures on X under the equivalence relation of mutual absolute continuity. Given a measure space $(X, \mathcal{X}, \mu)$ and a mapping p from $(X, \mathcal{X}, \mu)$ to a measurable space $(Y, \mathcal{Y})$, one can induce a measure $p_*\mu$ on $(Y, \mathcal{Y})$ by $(p_*\mu)(A) = \mu(p^{-1}(A))$. Then $p_*\mu$ is called the *distribution of p with respect to μ*, or the *projection of μ by p*, or the *pushdown of μ by p*.

If X and Y are two topological spaces, a map $f: X \to Y$ is *continuous* if $f^{-1}(U)$ is an open set of X whenever U is an open set of Y. A continuous f is a *homeomorphism* if it has a continuous inverse. A *basis* for a topology is any collection of sets that are open and such that any open set is a union of sets in the basis. A topological space is called *separable* if it has a countable basis. The smallest σ-algebra containing the open sets of a topology (and therefore also the closed sets) is called the *σ-algebra generated by the topology* or the *associated measurable structure of the topology*. A *metric* on a set X is a function $d: X \times X \to \mathbf{R}_+ = [0, \infty)$ such that for all $x, y, z \in X$, $d(x, y) = 0$ iff $x = y$, $d(x, y) = d(y, x)$, and $d(x, y) + d(y, z) \geq d(x, z)$. Given $\epsilon > 0$, the set $B_d(x, \epsilon) = \{y \mid d(x, y) < \epsilon\}$ is called the *ϵ-ball centered at x*. A topological space is *metrizable* if there is a metric on the space such that the open balls in the metric are a basis for the topology. A *standard Borel space* is a separable metrizable topological space with a σ-algebra generated by the topology. The topology on $\mathbf{R}$ or $\bar{\mathbf{R}}$ is here taken to be that generated by the open intervals. The associated measurable structure constitutes the *Borel sets*. *Lebesgue measure* λ is the unique measure on the Borel structure such that $\lambda((a,b)) = b - a$ for $b \geq a$. The *Lebesgue structure* is the smallest σ-algebra containing all Borel sets and all subsets of measure zero Borel sets. Lebesgue measure λ then extends to a measure with the same name on the Lebesgue structure.

Let μ be a finite measure on X. Let $\mathcal{M}$ denote the set of functions from X to $\bar{\mathbf{R}}$. The relation $\sim$ on $\mathcal{M}$ defined by $f \sim g$ iff $f = g$, μ-almost everywhere, is an equivalence relation. Let $\bar{\mathcal{M}}$ be the collection of equivalence classes of $\mathcal{M}$ under $\sim$. $\bar{\mathcal{M}}$ is a vector space which has a distinguished subspace $L^1(X,\mu)$ and a linear function

$$L^1(X,\mu) \longrightarrow \mathbf{R}$$
$$f \mapsto \int f d\mu$$

with the following three properties (by an abuse of notation we do not distinguish between functions and their equivalence classes):

(i) $L^1(X,\mu)$ contains all indicator functions 1_A, for $A \in \mathcal{X}$;

(ii) For all $A \in \mathcal{X}$, $\int 1_A d\mu = \mu(A)$;

(iii) If $\{f_i\}$ is an increasing sequence of nonnegative functions in $L^1(X,\mu)$ and if $f(x) = lim_{i\to\infty} f_i(x)$, then $f \in L^1(X,\mu)$ iff $lim_{i\to\infty} \int f_i d\mu < \infty$. In that case $\int f d\mu = lim_{i\to\infty} \int f_i d\mu$.

Let $(X,\ \mathcal{X})$, $(Y,\ \mathcal{Y})$ be measurable spaces. A *kernel on X relative to Y* or a *kernel on* $Y \times \mathcal{X}$ is a mapping $N: Y \times \mathcal{X} \to \mathbf{R} \cup \{\infty\}$, such that

(i) for every y in Y, the mapping $A \to N(y,\ A)$ is a measure on X, denoted by $N(y,\ \cdot)$;

(ii) for every A in $\mathcal{X}$, the mapping $y \to N(y,\ A)$ is a measurable function on Y, denoted by $N(\cdot\ ,A)$.

N is called *positive* if its range is in $[0,\infty]$ and *markovian* if it is positive and, for all $y \in Y$, $N(y,X) = 1$. If $X = Y$ we simply say that N is a *kernel on* X. In what follows, *all kernels are positive* unless otherwise stated. If N is a kernel on $Y \times \mathcal{X}$ and M is a kernel on $X \times \mathcal{W}$, then the *product* $NM(y,A) = \int_X N(y,dx)M(x,A)$ is also a kernel.

Let $(X,\ \mathcal{X})$ and $(Y,\ \mathcal{Y})$ be measurable spaces. Let $p: X \to Y$ be a measurable function and μ a positive measure on $(X,\ \mathcal{X})$. A *regular conditional probability distribution* (abbreviated *rcpd*) of μ with respect to p is a kernel $m_p^\mu: Y \times \mathcal{X} \to [0,\ 1]$ satisfying the following conditions:

(i) m_p^μ is markovian;

(ii) $m_p^\mu(y,\cdot)$ is supported on $p^{-1}\{y\}$ for $p_*\mu$-almost all $y \in Y$;

(iii) If $g \in L^1(X, \mu)$, then $\int_X g d\mu = \int_Y (p_*\mu)(dy) \int_{p^{-1}\{y\}} m_p^\mu(y, dx) g(x)$.

It is a theorem that if $(X, \mathcal{X})$ and $(Y, \mathcal{Y})$ are standard Borel spaces then an rcpd m_p^μ exists for any probability measure μ (Parthasarathy, 1968). In general there will be many choices for m_p^μ any two of which will agree a.e. $p_*\mu$ on Y (that is, for almost all values of the first argument). If $p: X \to Y$ is a continuous map of topological spaces which are also given their corresponding standard Borel structures one can show that there is a canonical choice of m_p^μ defined everywhere.

2. Definition of observer

Definition 2.1. An *observer* is a six-tuple, $((X, \mathcal{X}), (Y, \mathcal{Y}), E, S, \pi, \eta)$, satisfying the following conditions:

1. $(X, \mathcal{X})$ and $(Y, \mathcal{Y})$ are measurable spaces. $E \in \mathcal{X}$ and $S \in \mathcal{Y}$.
2. $\pi: X \to Y$ is a measurable surjective function with $\pi(E) = S$.
3. Let $(E, \mathcal{E})$ and $(S, \mathcal{S})$ denote the measurable spaces on E and S respectively induced from those of X and Y. Then η is a markovian kernel on $S \times \mathcal{E}$ such that, for each s, $\eta(s, \cdot)$ is a probability measure supported in $\pi^{-1}\{s\} \cap E$.

A five-tuple $((X, \mathcal{X}), (Y, \mathcal{Y}), E, S, \pi)$ satisfying the first two conditions is called a *preobserver*. An observer $((X, \mathcal{X}), (Y, \mathcal{Y}), E, S, \pi, \eta)$ *completes* the preobserver $((X, \mathcal{X}), (Y, \mathcal{Y}), E, S, \pi)$. The constituents of an observer have the following names:

X — *configuration space*
Y — *premise space*
E — *distinguished configurations*
S — *distinguished premises*
π — *perspective*
η — *conclusion kernel,* or *interpretation kernel*

We also say that, for $s \in S$, $\eta(s, \cdot)$ is a *conclusion measure.*

Discussion

In what follows, we sometimes write X for $(X, \mathcal{X})$ and Y for $(Y, \mathcal{Y})$ when the meaning is clear from the context.

Fundamentally, an observer makes inferences with one notable feature: the

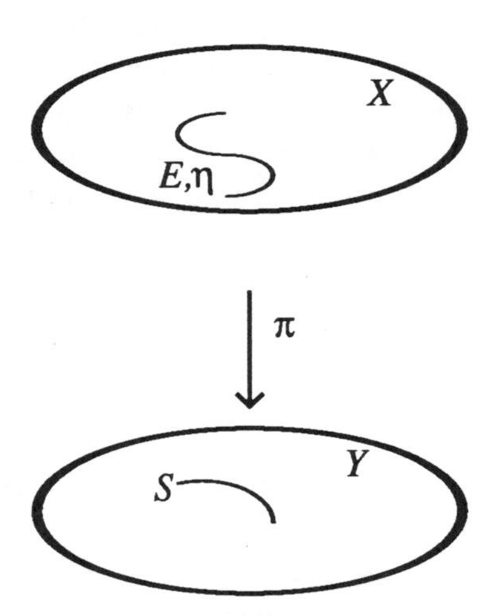

FIGURE 2.2. *Illustration of an observer.*

premises do not, in general, logically imply the conclusions. In the definition of observer, the possible premises are represented by Y and the possible conclusions by the measures $\eta(s, \cdot)$.

An observer O works as follows. When O observes, it interacts with its object of perception. It does not perceive the object of perception, but rather a representation of some property of the interaction. X represents all properties of relevance to O. Suppose some point $x \in X$ represents the property that obtains in the present interaction. Then O, in consequence of the interaction, receives the representation $y = \pi(x)$, where $y \in Y$. Informally, we say that y "lights up" for O. If x is in E, then y is in S; if x is not in E and not in $\pi^{-1}(S) - E$, then y is in $Y - S$. All O receives is y, not x. O must guess x. If y is not in S, then O decides that x is not in E and does nothing. If y is in S, then O decides that x is in E. But O does not, in general, know precisely which point of E. Instead, O arrives at a probability measure $\eta(s, \cdot)$ supported on E. This measure represents O's guess as to which point of E is x. If there is no ambiguity, then O's measure is simply a Dirac measure supported on the appropriate point of E.

From this description we see that an observer deals solely with representations: x and y are elements of the representations X and Y respectively, and $\eta(s, \cdot)$ is a measure on X. What these representations signify we discuss in chapter four. In these discussions we use the term preobserver to refer to sets of observers having the same $(X, \mathcal{X})$, $(Y, \mathcal{Y})$, E, S, and π, but having different conclusion kernels.

One notes at once that the definition of observer is quite general. The class of observers is large, almost surely containing observers for which there is no human, even no biological, counterpart. Given this, of what use is observer theory to those interested in human perception?

Roughly, it is of the same use as formal language theory is to those interested in human, or "natural," languages. That is, formal language theory provides a framework within which one can formulate precisely the question, "What are the human languages?" Similarly, observer theory provides a framework within which one can formulate precisely the question, "What are the observers of relevance to human or, more generally, biological perception?" And just as the answer in the case of language has not come from formal language theory alone, so one would expect that the answer in the case of perception will not come from observer theory alone. In both cases the theory provides not an answer but a framework within which to seek an answer.

The framework should, of course, allow one to describe concrete instances of relevance to human perception. Therefore in section five we present several such examples. Moreover the framework should guide one in the construction of new results. Therefore in **5–6** and **9–4** we present an example of this.

The conditions on observers

We discuss the three conditions listed in the definition of observer.

Condition 1: *$(X, \mathcal{X})$, $(Y, \mathcal{Y})$ are measurable spaces. $E \in \mathcal{X}$ and $S \in \mathcal{Y}$.*

X is a representation in which E is defined. X itself is not the real world, but a mathematical representation. Y represents all premises from which the observer can make inferences. We stipulate that X and Y are measurable spaces because this is the least restrictive assumption that always allows us to discuss the measures of events in these spaces. It would be unnecessarily restrictive to specify that X must be, say, an Euclidean space or a manifold.

Condition 2: *$\pi: X \to Y$ is a measurable surjective function with $\pi(E) = S$.*

π must be surjective, for otherwise there would be premises in Y unrelated to the configurations in X: the observer would have premises that were gratuitous. π must be measurable for the premises Y must, at the very least, be syntactically compatible with the configurations X. $\pi(E) = S$ is a necessary condition for the distinguished premises to be good evidence for the conclusion measures.

Condition 3: *η is a markovian kernel on $S \times \mathcal{E}$ such that, for each s, $\eta(s, \cdot)$ is a probability measure supported on $\pi^{-1}\{s\} \cap E$.*

η represents the conclusions reached by an observer for premises represented by S. For each $s \in S$, η assigns a probability measure whose support is $\pi^{-1}\{s\} \cap E$; the measure has this support because, from the perspective π of the observer, only the distinguished configurations in $\pi^{-1}\{s\}$ are compatible with the premise represented by s.

Morphisms of preobservers and observers

Definition 2.3. Let $P = (X, Y, E, S, \pi)$ and $P' = (X', Y', E', S', \pi')$ be two preobservers with completions $O = (X, Y, E, S, \pi, \eta)$ and $O' = (X', Y', E', S', \pi', \eta')$ respectively. A *morphism between preobservers* P and P' is a pair of maps f and g which make the following diagram commute.[2]

$$\begin{array}{ccc} X & \xrightarrow{f} & X' \\ \downarrow{\scriptstyle \pi} & & \downarrow{\scriptstyle \pi'} \\ Y & \xrightarrow{g} & Y' \end{array}$$

If, moreover, the maps f and g make the following diagram commute, they are a *morphism between observers* O and O'.

$$\begin{array}{ccc} \mathcal{X} & \xleftarrow{f^*} & \mathcal{X}' \\ \downarrow{\scriptstyle \eta} & & \downarrow{\scriptstyle \eta'} \\ \mathcal{S} & \xleftarrow{g^*} & \mathcal{S}' \end{array}$$

Here we interpret the spaces $\mathcal{X}$, $\mathcal{X}'$, $\mathcal{S}$ and $\mathcal{S}'$ to consist of random variables on X, X', S and S' respectively. Then if $h \in \mathcal{X}'$, f^*h is the function $h \circ f$ on X; similarly for g^*. If $k \in \mathcal{X}$, ηk is the function on S given by $\eta k(s) = \int_X \eta(s, dx)\, k(x)$. If the maps f and g are bimeasurable bijections, each morphism is called an *isomorphism*.

[2] To say that this diagram commutes means that all paths from the same origin to the same destination, following the directions indicated by the arrows, are equivalent. In the case of this diagram it means $\pi' \circ f = g \circ \pi$.

3. Ideal observers

Let μ_X denote a measure class on $(X, \mathcal{X})$ that is "unbiased": its definition makes no reference to properties of E or π. We think of μ_X as expressing an abstract uniformity of X which exists prior to the notion of the distinguished configurations E. For example, μ_X might be a measure class invariant for some group action on X (cf. 5–1). μ_X provides an unbiased background measure class by which one can determine if an observer is an "ideal decision maker" (discussed below), and to which one can compare the actual probabilities of obtaining configuration events in some concrete universe.

By an abuse of notation, we sometimes use the same symbol, μ_X, to denote both a measure class and a representative measure in the class.

Definition 3.1. An observer satisfying the condition

$$\mu_X(\pi^{-1}(S) - E) = 0$$

is called an *ideal observer.*

This condition states that the measure of "false targets" is zero. A false target is an element of $F = \pi^{-1}(S) - E$. False targets "fool" the observer; they lead the observer to perceptual illusions. Here is why. Note that since F is a subset of $\pi^{-1}(S)$, $\pi(F)$ is a subset of S. Now suppose that some point $x \in X$ represents the property of relevance to the observer that obtains in the interaction of the observer with the object of perception. Call such a point the *true configuration.* Assume that the true configuration is in F. Then the observer receives a premise $s = \pi(x) \in S$ and arrives at the conclusion measure $\eta(s, \cdot)$. However, this measure is supported off F (and on E), and therefore gives no weight to the true configuration x in F. The conclusion measure represents, in this case, a misperception.

An ideal observer is an ideal decision maker in the following sense: *Given that the true configuration is not in E, an ideal observer almost surely recognizes this.* We emphasize the "almost surely." We claim not that observers, ideal or otherwise, are free of perceptual illusions; to the contrary, we claim that perceptual illusions, such as the cosine surface and 3-D movies, illustrate important properties of observers. But illusions are of two kinds: those that arise from a true configuration of relevance to the observer, i.e., from E itself, and those that do not. For an ideal observer the latter kind of illusion is rare, in a sense described formally by μ_X.

Also true is the following: *Given that the true configuration is in E, an observer, ideal or otherwise, always recognizes this.* True configurations in E always lead an observer to reach a conclusion measure (which measures are always supported on E), simply because $\pi(E) = S$ and η assigns a measure on E for every point in S.

Figure 3.2 summarizes these ideas in a decision diagram. The diagram displays two kinds of true configurations across the top: E, which indicates that the true configuration is in E, and -E, which indicates that the true configuration is in $X - E$. The diagram displays the two possible decisions of the observer along the left side. Inside each box in the right column is a number which is a conditional probability, namely the unbiased (μ_X) conditional probability that an ideal observer arrives at the decision indicated to the left side of the diagram given that the true configuration is in $X - E$. Inside each box in the left column is a number; in this left column the number 1 is a shorthand for "certainly" and 0 for "certainly not." The numbers in this left column hold simply by the definition of observer; if the true configuration is in E, then since $S = \pi(E)$ and the observer always decides that the true configuration is in E given a premise in S, the observer always decides correctly. Also inside each box is a label in quotes which describes the type of decision represented by that box.

As an example of how to read this diagram, consider the box labelled "false alarm." It contains a 0. This means that the conditional probability is zero that an ideal observer will decide that the true configuration is in E given that in fact it is not. (The one in the box labelled "correct reject" is the complementary conditional probability).

A sufficient condition for an observer to be ideal is the following:

$$\pi_* \mu_X(S) = 0. \tag{3.3}$$

This condition states that $\mu_X(\pi^{-1}(S)) = 0$, which implies that $\mu_X(\pi^{-1}(S) - E) = 0$, and therefore that the observer is ideal. This condition often obtains in observers whose distinguished configurations are defined by algebraic equations.

The definition of an ideal observer makes essential use of the measure μ_X, a measure defined without regard to properties of any external world. Therefore an ideal observer is ideal regardless of the relationship between the ideal observer and any external world. However, μ_X may not accurately reflect the measures of events in the appropriate world external to the observer. We discuss this in later chapters.

That aspect of the inference presented in Figure 3.2 is not the only one of interest. An observer decides not only if the true configuration is in E; it produces in addition a probability measure supported on E which is its best guess as to which events in E are likely to have occurred, together with their likelihoods. One can

True Configuration

Decision	E	-E
E	1 "Hit"	0 "False Alarm"
-E	0 "Miss"	1 "Correct Reject"

FIGURE 3.2. *Decision diagram for ideal observers.*

ask if this measure is accurate. The answer to this requires the establishment of a formal framework in which observer and observed can be discussed. This is the subject of chapter five. The issue of perceptual accuracy can then be understood in terms of stabilities of dynamics of participators on these frameworks. In particular, we can ask whether the conclusion kernel η of the observer is compatible with these stabilities; this leads to "perception=reality" equations, discussed in chapter eight.

4. Noise

Thus far we have considered only observer inferences whose premises are represented by single points $s \in S$. Such inferences are free of noise in the sense that the premise is known precisely. But if there is noise, if the premise is not known precisely but only probabilistically, what conclusions can an observer reach?

A natural way to represent a noisy premise is as a probability measure λ on Y. A precise premise $s \in S$ is then the special case of a Dirac measure supported on s. λ models noise or measurement error as follows: for $B \in \mathcal{Y}$, $\lambda(B)$ is the probability that the set of premises B contains the "true premise."

Given a probability measure λ on Y the natural conclusion for the observer to reach is the following:

$$\begin{cases} \text{with probability } \lambda(Y - S) \text{ there is no interpretation;} \\ \text{with probability } \lambda(S) \text{ the distribution of interpretations is } \nu, \end{cases}$$

where, for $\Delta \in \mathcal{E}$,

$$\nu(\Delta) = \lambda(S)^{-1} \int_S \eta(s, \Delta \cap \pi^{-1}(s))\lambda(ds). \tag{4.1}$$

Intuitively, $\lambda(S)$ is the probability of having received a "signal," i.e., a distinguished premise, and $\lambda(Y - S)$ is the probability of not having received a signal.

Thus the definition of observer provides a formalism which, by means of the interpretation kernel η, unifies perceptual inferencing "policies" in the presence of noise. Moreover the effects of various kinds of noise can be analyzed within a given inferencing system. (For example, there may be regularities of the noise worth exploiting. A common approach to noise represents the set of noisy signals as a markovian kernel K on $Y \times \mathcal{Y}$, where $K(y, \cdot)$ is computed by, say, convolving a fixed gaussian distribution with the Dirac measure $\epsilon_y(\cdot)$ located at y.) These ideas need to be studied systematically and to be compared with the ideas of signal detection theory and various decision theories.

5. Examples of observers

In this section we consider several current explanations of specific perceptual capacities and exhibit these explanations as instances of the definition of observer.

Example 5.1. *Structure from motion (Ullman 1979).* One can devise dynamic visual displays for which subjects, even when viewing monocularly, report seeing motion and structure in three dimensions. This perceptual capacity to perceive three-dimensional structure from dynamic two-dimensional images is often called "structure from motion."[3] To explain this capacity, Ullman proposes what he calls the *rigidity assumption*:

[3] Among the formal studies of structure from motion are Ullman (1979, 1981, 1984), Longuet-Higgins and Prazdny (1980), Webb and Aggarwal (1981), Hoffman and Flinchbaugh (1982), Hoffman and Bennett (1985, 1986), and Koenderink and van Doorn (1986).

> " Any set of elements undergoing a two-dimensional transformation which has a unique interpretation as a rigid body moving in space should be interpreted as such a body in motion."[4]

Moreover, he proves a theorem which allows one to determine whether a given collection of moving elements has a unique rigid interpretation. This *structure from motion theorem* states:

> " Given three distinct orthographic views of four noncoplanar points in a rigid configuration, the structure and motion compatible with the three views are uniquely determined [up to reflection]."[5]

The observer corresponding to Ullman's theorem has a configuration space consisting of all three sets of four points, where each point lies in $\mathbf{R}^3$. Since Ullman takes one of the four points to be the origin, we find that the configuration space X is $\mathbf{R}^{27}$. The premise space is the space of all triples of four points, where each point lies in $\mathbf{R}^2$ (i.e., in the image plane). We find that the premise space Y is $\mathbf{R}^{18}$. Now denoting a point in $\mathbf{R}^3$ by (x, y, z) and recalling that the map $p: \mathbf{R}^3 \to \mathbf{R}^2$ given by $(x, y, z) \mapsto (x, y)$ is an orthographic projection, we find that the perspective π of Ullman's observer is the map $\pi: X \to Y$ induced by p. E, the distinguished configurations, consists of those three sets of four points, each point in $\mathbf{R}^3$, such that the four points in each set are related to the four points in every other set of the triple by a rigid motion. One can write down a small set of simple algebraic equations to specify this (uncountable) subset of X, but this is unnecessary here. It happens that E has Lebesgue measure zero in X. S, the distinguished premises, consists simply in $\pi(E)$. Intuitively, S consists of all three *views* of four points that are compatible with a rigid interpretation. S happens to have Lebesgue measure zero in Y; therefore the Lebesgue measure of "false targets", i.e., elements of $\pi^{-1}(S) - E$, is also zero. Finally, for each $s \in S$, $\eta(s, \cdot)$ can be taken to be the measure that assigns a weight of $\frac{1}{2}$ to each of the two points of E which, according to the structure from motion theorem, project via π to s. This would correspond to an observer that saw each interpretation with equal frequency. If one interpretation was seen, e.g., 90% of the time then the appropriate measure would assign weights of .9 and .1.

Example 5.2. *Stereo (Longuet-Higgins 1982).* Because one's eyes occupy differ-

---

[4] Ullman (1979), p. 146.

[5] Ullman (1979), p. 148. The comment in brackets is ours; there are actually two solutions which are mirror images of each other, as Ullman points out elsewhere.

ent positions in space, the images they receive differ subtly. Using these differences, one's visual system can recover the three-dimensional properties of the visual environment. This capacity to infer the third dimension from disparities in the retinal images is called stereoscopic vision.[6] To explain this capacity, Longuet-Higgins assumes that the planes of the horizontal meridians of the two eyes accurately coincide. He then proves several results, of which we consider the following:

> "If the scene contains three or more nonmeridional points, not all lying in a vertical plane, then their positions in space are fully determined by the horizontal and vertical coordinates of their images on the two retinas."[7]

The observer corresponding to Longuet-Higgins' explanation has a configuration space consisting of all two sets of three points, where each point lies in $\mathbf{R}^3$. Longuet-Higgins does not take one of the three points to be the origin, so the configuration space X is $\mathbf{R}^{18}$. The premise space is the space of all two sets of three points, where each point lies in $\mathbf{R}^2$. Therefore the premise space Y is $\mathbf{R}^{12}$. The perspective of Longuet-Higgins' observer is the map $\pi: X \to Y$ induced by the map p of Example 5.1. E, the distinguished configurations, consists of all pairs of sets of three points, each point in $\mathbf{R}^3$, such that the three points in each set are related to the three points in the other set by a rigid motion whose rotation is about an axis parallel to the vertical axes of the two retinal coordinate systems. One can write down straightforward equations to specify this (uncountable) subset of X. S, the distinguished premises, is $\pi(E)$. And for each $s \in S$, $\eta(s, \cdot)$ is Dirac measure on the unique (generically, according to Longuet-Higgins' result) point of E that projects via π to s.

Example 5.3. *Velocity fields along contours in 2-D (Hildreth 1984).* Because of the ubiquity of relative motion between visual objects and the viewer's eye, retinal images of occluding contours (and other salient visual contours) almost perpetually translate and deform. For smooth portions of a contour, attempts to measure precisely the local velocity of the contour must face the so-called "aperture problem": if the velocity of the curve at a point s is $\mathbf{V}(s)$, only the component of velocity orthogonal to the tangent at s, $v^{\perp}(s)$, can be obtained directly by local measurement.

---

[6] Among the formal studies of stereoscopic vision are Koenderink and van Doorn (1976), Marr and Poggio (1979), Grimson (1980), Longuet-Higgins (1982), Mayhew (1982), and Richards (1983).

[7] Longuet-Higgins (1982).

The tangential component of the velocity field, viz., $\mathbf{V}^t(s)$, is lost by local measurement. The visual system apparently overcomes the aperture problem and can recover a unique velocity field for a moving curve. This capacity to infer a complete velocity field along a two-dimensional curve given only its orthogonal component is called the measurement of contour velocity fields.[8] To explain this capacity, Hildreth proposes that the visual system chooses the "smoothest" velocity field (precisely, one minimizing $\int |\frac{\partial \mathbf{V}}{\partial s}|^2 ds$) compatible with the given orthogonal component. She then proves the following result:

> " If $v^{\perp}(s)$ is known along a contour, and there exists at least two points at which the local orientation of the contour is different, then there exists a unique velocity field that satisfies the known velocity constraints and minimizes $\int |\frac{\partial \mathbf{V}}{\partial s}|^2 ds$."[9]

The observer corresponding to Hildreth's explanation has a configuration space X consisting of all velocity fields along all one-dimensional contours embedded in $\mathbf{R}^2$. Y, the space of premises, consists of all velocity fields along one-dimensional contours such that the velocity vector assigned to each point of the contour is orthogonal to the local tangent to the contour. The distinguished premises S are those contours-cum-orthogonal-velocity-fields where the contour is *not straight*. The perspective of Hildreth's observer is the map $\pi: X \to Y$ which takes each contour-cum-full-velocity-field in X to its corresponding contour-cum-orthogonal-velocity-field in Y by simply stripping off the tangential component of the full velocity field. For each premise $y' \in Y, \pi^{-1}(y')$ is all velocity fields which have y' as their orthogonal component. According to Hildreth's result, for each distinguished premise $s' \in S$ (i.e., each contour-cum-orthogonal-velocity field where the contour is not straight) the fibre $\pi^{-1}(s')$ contains a unique contour-cum-velocity-field e' which minimizes her measure of smoothness. E, the distinguished configurations, is the union of all such e'. For each $s' \in S, \eta(s', \cdot)$ is Dirac measure on the corresponding e'.

Example 5.4. *Visual detection of light sources (Ullman 1976).* The visual system is adept at detecting surfaces which, rather than simply reflecting incident light, are themselves luminous. This perceptual capacity is called the visual detection of light sources. To explain this capacity, Ullman proposes that it is unnecessary to con-

---

[8] Among the formal studies of optical flow are Koenderink and van Doorn (1975, 1976, 1981), Marr and Ullman (1981), Horn and Schunck (1981), Waxman and Wohn (1987).

[9] Hildreth (1984).

sider the spectral composition of the light and the dependence of surface reflectance on wavelength. He considers the case of two adjacent surfaces, A and B, with reflectances r_A and r_B. (The reflectance of a surface, under Ullman's proposal, is a real number between 0 and 1 inclusive, which is the proportion of incident light reflected by the surface.)[10] He assumes that the light incident to surface A at some distinguished point 0 has intensity I_0 and that the intensity of the incident light varies linearly with gradient K. Thus a point 1 on surface B at distance d from 0 receives an intensity $I_1 = I_0 + Kd$. (Ullman restricts attention to a one-dimensional case and stipulates that d is positive if 1 is to the right of 0.) If A is also a light source with intensity L, then the *retinal image* of the point 0 receives, on Ullman's model (which ignores foreshortening), a quantity of light $e_0 = r_A I_0 + L$. On the assumption that the light source, if any, is at A (which can be accomplished by relabelling the surfaces if necessary) the *retinal image* of point 1 receives a quantity of light $e_1 = r_B I_1$. The gradient of light in the *image* of surface A is $S_A = r_A K$, whereas in the *image* of surface B it is $S_B = r_B K$. Ullman then argues that the visual system detects a light source at A when the quantity $\hat{L} = e_0 - e_1(S_A/S_B) + S_A d$ is greater than $e_1(S_A/S_B) - S_A d$; furthermore, $\hat{L}$ is the perceived intensity of the source.

The observer corresponding to Ullman's explanation has a configuration space consisting of all six-tuples

$$(r_A, r_B, I_0, d, K, L),$$

where

$$r_A, r_B \in [0,1], \quad K, d \in \mathbf{R}, \quad I_0, L \in [0, \infty),$$

and L is the light source intensity. Thus

$$X = [0,1] \times [0,1] \times [0,\infty) \times \mathbf{R} \times \mathbf{R} \times [0,\infty).$$

The premise space consists of all five-tuples

$$(e_0, e_1, S_A, S_B, d),$$

where

$$e_0, e_1 \in [0,\infty), \quad S_A, S_B, d \in \mathbf{R}.$$

---

[10] Among the formal theories of shading are Horn (1975), Koenderink and van Doorn (1980), Ikeuchi and Horn (1981) and Pentland (1984). Among the formal theories of reflectance are Land and McCann (1971), Horn (1974), Maloney (1985), and Rubin and Richards (1987). For reviews see Horn (1985) and Ballard and Brown (1982).

Thus

$$Y = [0, \infty) \times [0, \infty) \times \mathbf{R} \times \mathbf{R} \times \mathbf{R}.$$

The perspective of Ullman's observer is the map $\pi: X \to Y$ defined by

$$(r_A, r_B, I_0, d, K, L) \mapsto (r_A I_0 + L, r_B(I_0 + Kd), r_A K, r_B K, d).$$

S, the distinguished premises, consists of that subset of Y satisfying

$$\hat{L} > e_1(S_A/S_B) - S_A d.$$

Similarly E, the distinguished configurations, consists of that subset of X satisfying

$$L > r_A(I_0 + Kd) - r_A K d.$$

For each distinguished premise $s = (e_0, e_1, S_A, S_B, d) \in S$, $\eta(s, \cdot)$ can be taken to be any probability measure supported on those distinguished configurations in $\pi^{-1}(s)$ satisfying $L = e_0 - e_1(S_A/S_B) + S_A d$ (since Ullman's explanation seeks to recover only the light source intensity, not the other aspects of the configuration).

Example 5.5. *Regularization (Poggio et al. 1985).* According to Poggio, Torre, and Koch, early vision problems such as edge detection, shape from shading, and surface reconstruction, have a common structure: they are *ill-posed* problems, a notion first defined by Hadamard (1923). A problem is well-posed if it has a solution, the solution is unique, and the solution depends continuously on the initial data. A problem is ill-posed if it fails to satisfy one or more of these conditions.

Poggio et al. denote by the term *regularization* any method that makes an ill-posed problem well-posed. Usually regularization involves bringing to bear a priori knowledge, often expressed in variational principles that constrain the possible solutions or statistical properties of the solution space. In standard regularization theory, developed by Tikhonov (1963, 1977), there are two primary methods for solution, as Poggio et al. describe:

> "The regularization of the ill-posed problem of finding z from the 'data' y
>
> $$Az = y \qquad (1)$$
>
> requires the choice of norms $\|\cdot\|$ and of a stabilizing functional $\|Pz\|$. In standard regularization theory, A is a linear operator, the norms are quadratic and P is linear. Two methods that can

be applied are: (1) among z that satisfy $||Az - y|| \leq \varepsilon$ find z that minimizes (ε depends on the estimated measurement errors and is zero if the data are noiseless)

$$||Pz||^2 \quad (2)$$

(2) find z that minimizes

$$||Az - y||^2 + \lambda||Pz||^2 \quad (3)$$

where λ is a so-called regularization parameter."[11]

Although several early visual processes have explanations fitting nicely into the methods of standard regularization theory, Poggio et al. note that others do not, primarily because no quadratric functional can express the a priori constraints. In this case there are usually many local minima in addition to the global one that is the desired solution, and stochastic regularization techniques become attractive. Simulated annealing, for instance, can be used to search for the global solution, or the search can be done using the technique of Markov random fields. In the latter case the a priori knowledge is represented in terms of probability distributions; a solution is chosen that maximizes some likelihood criterion.

The space of possible solutions for an ill-posed problem correspond to the configuration space of an observer. Those z that minimize the stabilizer correspond to its distinguished configurations. The possible data y correspond to its distinguished premises. A corresponds to its perspective map. Since by definition a regularization method gives unique solutions, the class of explanations described by regularization techniques (standard, stochastic, or otherwise) correspond to a subclass of observers satisfying the following:

$$\forall s \in S, \ \pi^{-1}(s) \cap E \text{ contains one point.}$$

For these observers, therefore, $\eta(s, \cdot)$ must be a Dirac measure (for all $s \in S$). As Poggio et al. are well aware, many visual capacities do not arrive at unique interpretations and are therefore not described by regularization methods. That is, when given some initial data y the visual system often reaches not one solution z but two or more. The multistable visual figures, such as the Necker cube, are well known examples. Another example is the visual perception of structure from motion (Example 5.1). Human observers routinely perceive at least two distinct

[11] Poggio et al. (1985).

interpretations, and in some cases many more, when presented with the appropriate motion displays. No interpretation is the global one with the rest being local; all are equally solutions and all are perceived (usually sequentially). For this reason, Poggio et al. are correct in being careful to propose regularization as a technique only for early vision problems.

However the regularization approach might be extended to cover more perceptual problems by using distinct stabilizers for the distinct perceptual interpretations. To tie these distinct regularizations together one could associate with each a probability indicating, for each initial datum y, the relative weight the perceptual system gives to the associated solutions. This is accomplished in observer theory through the interpretation kernels η.

Since a regularization technique always gives, by definition, a unique solution point z, it follows that the precision of this solution is independent of the precision of the initial data. Certainly the particular z picked out by a regularization algorithm can depend on the precision of the initial data. But a single precise point z is, by definition, picked out whether the measurement error in the initial data is zero or infinite. For example, given the initial data y_0 with error $\varepsilon_0 = 0$ the solution might be z_0 whereas given the initial data y_1 with error $\varepsilon_1 = \infty$ the solution might be the point z_1. But the solution z_1 is still a precise point even though the error is infinite. Taken seriously as a model of early human vision, then, regularization predicts that in no case should blurring or otherwise corrupting the visual stimuli lead to any loss of clarity in the resulting percept. That is, as one increases the corruption of the visual stimuli there should be no increase in the variance of subject responses to any early vision task. There may be a shift in the percept, but no increase of variance about that percept. This prediction is clearly false. Regularization theory, by its very definition, cannot have a realistic treatment of noise.

Example 5.6. *Rigid fixed-axis motion (Hoffman and Bennett 1986).* In chapter one we constructed a "biological motion" observer with a bias toward perceiving rigid planar motion in certain visual displays. We now construct an ideal observer with a bias toward perceiving rigid fixed-axis motion, a bias more general than the previous one. This observer addresses a problem of interest to vision researchers: most human subjects, when shown certain visual displays in two dimensions, report perceiving rigid fixed-axis (RFA) motion in three dimensions. Let us call such perceptions of the two-dimensional displays *RFA interpretations*. To construct this observer we make use of the following result:

(i) Assume one is given three distinct orthographic projections of three points in

$\mathbf{R}^3$, which points move rigidly about a fixed axis. Then generically these projections restrict to two the number of possible RFA interpretations. (ii) Assume one is given three distinct orthographic projections of three points in $\mathbf{R}^3$, which points move arbitrarily in three dimensions. Then generically these projections restrict to zero the number of possible RFA interpretations.[12]

Because of this result we can construct an observer that, when possible, reaches RFA interpretations when given three distinct parallel projections of three points moving in three dimensions. Without loss of generality, we assume that the observer takes one of the points, O, to be the origin of a cartesian coordinate system in three dimensions, and represents the positions of the other two points, A_1 and A_2, relative to that origin. This is illustrated in Figure 5.7.

In this case the configuration space X is the space of all triples of pairs of points, where each point lies in $\mathbf{R}^3$. That is,

$$X = \{(\mathbf{a}_{ij}) \mid \mathbf{a}_{ij} = (x_{ij}, y_{ij}, z_{ij}); i = 1,2; j = 1,2,3\} = \mathbf{R}^{18}.$$

The premise space Y is the set of all triples of pairs of points in $\mathbf{R}^2$, i.e.,

$$Y = \{(\mathbf{b}_{ij}) \mid \mathbf{b}_{ij} = (x_{ij}, y_{ij}); i = 1,2; j = 1,2,3\} = \mathbf{R}^{12}.$$

The perspective is then $\pi: \mathbf{R}^{18} \to \mathbf{R}^{12}$ induced by $(x_{ij}, y_{ij}, z_{ij}) \mapsto (x_{ij}, y_{ij})$. The σ-algebras $\mathcal{X}$ and $\mathcal{Y}$ are the appropriate Borel algebras. It is reasonable to take, as an underlying uniformity of X, the group of rigid motions on it. Thus, the unbiased measure class μ_X (required for an ideal observer) can be taken to be that of Lebesgue measure. The measure class of $\pi_* \mu_X$ is also that of Lebesgue measure on $Y = \mathbf{R}^{12}$.

To define the distinguished configurations E, we use notation as illustrated in Figure 5.7. The three points are O, A_1, and A_2. As above, let $\mathbf{a}_{ij}$ denote the vector in three dimensions between points O and A_i in view j ($j = 1, 2, 3$). E is that subset of X consisting of three pairs of points, each point of the pair lying in $\mathbf{R}^3$, such that there is a rigid translation and rigid rotation about a single axis relating each pair plus the origin point to the others. It happens in this case that E is an algebraic variety (the solution set of a collection of polynomial equations) defined by the following eight vector equations:

$$\mathbf{a}_{11} \cdot \mathbf{a}_{11} - \mathbf{a}_{12} \cdot \mathbf{a}_{12} = 0, \qquad (5.8)$$

---

[12] This is stated and proved in Hoffman and Bennett (1986). The term "generically" here refers to Lebesgue measure class in (ii) and to a natural transporting of Lebesgue measure class to an appropriate set in (i). This set will be discussed shortly.

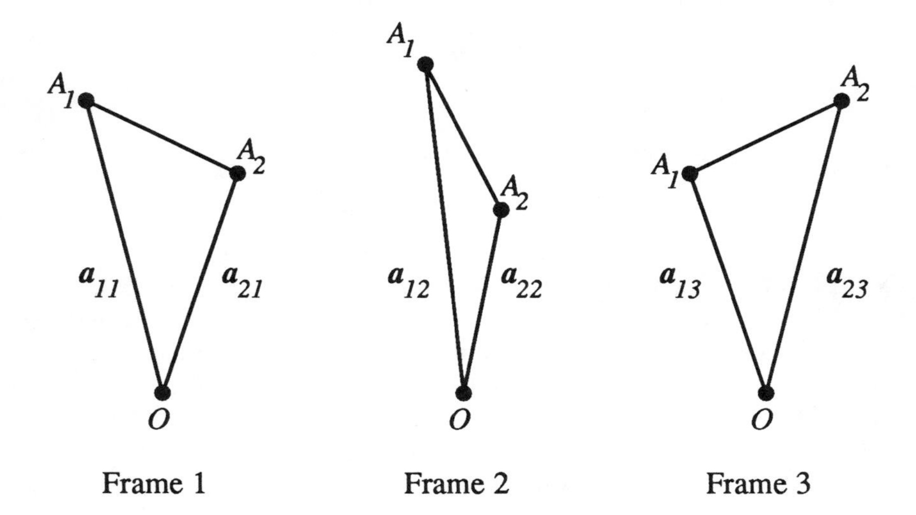

FIGURE 5.7. *Rigid fixed-axis motion: Three arrangements of three points in 3-D.*

$$\mathbf{a}_{11} \cdot \mathbf{a}_{11} - \mathbf{a}_{13} \cdot \mathbf{a}_{13} = 0, \tag{5.9}$$

$$\mathbf{a}_{21} \cdot \mathbf{a}_{21} - \mathbf{a}_{22} \cdot \mathbf{a}_{22} = 0, \tag{5.10}$$

$$\mathbf{a}_{21} \cdot \mathbf{a}_{21} - \mathbf{a}_{23} \cdot \mathbf{a}_{23} = 0, \tag{5.11}$$

$$\mathbf{a}_{11} \cdot \mathbf{a}_{21} - \mathbf{a}_{12} \cdot \mathbf{a}_{22} = 0, \tag{5.12}$$

$$\mathbf{a}_{11} \cdot \mathbf{a}_{21} - \mathbf{a}_{13} \cdot \mathbf{a}_{23} = 0, \tag{5.13}$$

$$(\mathbf{a}_{11} - \mathbf{a}_{12}) \cdot [(\mathbf{a}_{11} - \mathbf{a}_{13}) \times (\mathbf{a}_{21} - \mathbf{a}_{22})] = 0, \tag{5.14}$$

$$(\mathbf{a}_{11} - \mathbf{a}_{12}) \cdot [(\mathbf{a}_{11} - \mathbf{a}_{13}) \times (\mathbf{a}_{21} - \mathbf{a}_{23})] = 0. \tag{5.15}$$

In these equations the operation $\cdot$ indicates scalar (dot) product and $\times$ indicates vector (cross) product. The first six equations specify that the three points move rigidly. The last two specify that the points rotate about a fixed axis. E so defined has dimension less than that of X; the distinguished premises $S = \pi(E)$ have dimension less than Y. Therefore S has Lebesgue measure zero in Y. Since the measure class $\pi_*\mu_X$ on Y is that of Lebesgue measure, S has $\pi_*\mu_X$ measure zero in Y. We conclude from 3.3 that this is an ideal observer.

With effort it can be shown that, generically on S, the fibre $\pi^{-1}\{s\}$ of π over a point $s \in S$ contains two points of E. We can chose $\eta(s, \cdot)$ to be the probability distribution on E which gives weight, say, of one half to each of the two points. This ideal observer is as follows:

$$\begin{array}{ccccl} X = \mathbf{R}^{18} & \supset & E & = & \textit{rigid fixed-axis motions} \\ \downarrow \pi & & \downarrow \pi & & \\ Y = \mathbf{R}^{12} & \supset & S & & \end{array} \qquad (5.16)$$

Example 5.7 *Parsing sentences of a language (Hopcroft and Ullman 1969).* When you read or hear a sentence such as *John hit the ball* you perceive, according to current psycholinguistic theory, not just the individual words and their meanings, but also the syntactic structural relationships between the words: e.g., you perceive that *John hit the ball* has two major parts (the noun phrase *John* and the verb phrase *hit the ball*) and that the second part itself has subparts (the verb *hit* and the noun phrase *the ball*). A convenient way to display these constituents of a sentence is the "bracket" notation; in the case of our example sentence this notation yields *[[John] [[hit] [the ball]]]*, where matched brackets indicate the boundaries of constituents; e.g., the brackets about *hit the ball* indicate the verb phrase, and the brackets about *the ball* indicate a noun phrase nested within the verb phrase.

Of course sentences do not come with their brackets neatly displayed; the brackets must be inferred. And such an inference must, in general, be nondemonstrative: given a sentence of, say, English having n words there are many distinct possible ways of assigning matched brackets, of which only one, or at most a very few, are inferred by speakers of English. Clearly, such speakers employ powerful assumptions, assumptions that greatly reduce the number of bracket interpretations for each string of English words. These assumptions are known as the *rules of grammar* for English.

It is common to specify a grammar for a language L as a four-tuple $(\mathcal{T}, \mathcal{N}, \mathcal{R}, S)$, where $\mathcal{T}$ is the "terminal vocabulary" (e.g., in the case of English, words like *John, ball, the,* and *hit*), $\mathcal{N}$ is the "nonterminal vocabulary" (e.g., vocabulary like "noun phrase" (NP), "verb" (V), or "verb phrase" (VP)), $\mathcal{R}$ is a collection of "rewrite rules" (e.g., rules like VP→[V] [NP]), and S, the "start symbol" is an element of $\mathcal{N}$ always used as the first step in a sequence of rewrite rules leading to a sentence in the language L.

The corresponding "parsing observer" takes strings of symbols from $\mathcal{T}$ and infers all appropriate bracketings. Specifically, its premise space Y is $\mathcal{T}^*$, the set of all strings composed of symbols from the terminal vocabulary. Its set of distinguished premises S is the language L. For each premise y in Y the collection of compatible configurations $\pi^{-1}(y)$ is the set of all possible bracketings for y; if y is a string of n symbols then there are at least

$$\frac{\binom{2n}{n}}{n+1}$$

elements of $\pi^{-1}(y)$.[13] (For a string of 10 symbols this works out to at least 16,796 elements and for a string of 20 symbols to at least 6.5 billion.) The configuration space X is the union of all these collections of compatible configurations; i.e., $X = \cup_{y \in Y} \pi^{-1}(y)$. The distinguished configurations E are sentences in L together with brackets that properly specify, according to the grammar of L, their constituent structure. For each premise in S there may, of course, be more than one appropriate bracketing (corresponding to syntactically ambiguous sentences); the interpretation kernel η gives a probability distribution over these bracketings. π takes a configuration consisting of a string together with matched brackets, and simply strips away the brackets.

6. Transduction

In this section we apply the definition of observer to the problem of defining "transduction." We begin with some questions.

Whence come the premises for perceptual inferences? As conclusions of other inferences? Or as consequences of noninferential processes? "Both," appears to be the answer from perceptual theorists of the information processing persuasion (see, e.g., Marr 1982, Zucker 1981). Marr, for instance, proposes that vision involves, in effect, a hierarchy of inferences. In Marr's proposal, the *conclusions* of early perceptual inferences about edges and their terminations contribute to the contents of a "primal sketch." This primal sketch, in turn, provides *premises* for intermediate perceptual inferences such as stereovision and structure from motion. The *conclusions* of these inferences contribute, in their turn, to the contents of a "$2\frac{1}{2}$-D sketch." And the $2\frac{1}{2}$-D sketch provides *premises* for inferences that eventuate in "3-D models." Such a proposal has proven fruitful as a program for research on human vision.[14]

---

[13] This formula gives the number of unlabelled, ordered, rooted, trivalent trees with n leaves (Catalan, 1838). Parsing, of course, is not restricted to producing trivalent trees, but there does not seem to be a formula for the total number of trees that have n leaves. We thank Ronald Vigo for discussions on this point.

[14] Vision researchers debate the specifics of Marr's proposal; whether, for exam-

It also suggests the interesting project of constructing observers for the perceptual inferences at each level of the hierarchy, and then finding precisely how the conclusions of observers at one level contribute to the premises of those at the next.

But most computational theorists also suggest that this hierarchy of perceptual inferences must have a bottom; that while it may be typical, say in the case of vision, for premises of visual inferences to derive from conclusions of other visual inferences, there must be some inferences whose premises are detected *directly,* i.e., as the result of a noninferential process called "transduction." Transduction is typically defined as a mechanical process that converts information from one physical form to another, e.g., from an optic array to a pattern of rod and cone activity. But, as Fodor and Pylyshyn (1981) point out, this definition is far too broad for purposes of cognitive theorizing, for it is compatible with the entire visual system, indeed the entire organism, being a transducer for any stimulus to which it can selectively respond. Indeed, it has proved quite difficult to give any adequate definition of transducer. As an example of the problems that arise consider, for instance, the definition proposed by Fodor and Pylyshyn (1981, p. 161):

> Here, then, is the proposal in a nutshell. We say that the system S is a detector (transducer) for a property P only if (a) there is a state S_i of the system that is correlated with P (i.e., such that if P occurs, then S_i occurs); and (b) the generalization *if* P *then* S_i is counterfactual supporting—i.e., would hold across relevant employments of the method of differences.

Recall that to say that a generalization "if P then S_i" is counterfactual supporting is (1) to specify a collection of "possible worlds," usually chosen such that the laws of science obtain in each possible world, and (2) to claim that in each such world in which P obtains it is the case that S_i obtains. The method of differences can be used to check whether "if P then S_i" is, indeed, counterfactual supporting: one arranges worlds in which P obtains and checks if S_i obtains as well. If S_i does not obtain in some world in which P does, one concludes that "if P then S_i" is not counterfactual supporting. To say that the employment of the method of differences is "relevant"

---

ple, some perceptual capacities whose conclusions contribute to the $2\frac{1}{2}$-D sketch (say, shape from shading) might take premises not from the primal sketch but directly from an image. These debates are, for our current purposes, irrelevant. What is interesting is that these researchers agree, by and large, with Marr's general notion that the conclusions of some visual capacities serve as premises for others. A similar conclusion, and similar debates, arise in theories of language processing; among the levels of representation proposed are (in hierarchical order) the phonetic, phonological, lexical, syntactic, and so on.

is to say that the world one arranges is in the collection of "possible worlds."

Fodor and Pylyshyn use their definition to conclude, contrary to certain claims of Gibson (1966, 1979), that properties of light, but not properties of the layout (the environment), are directly detected. Here in paraphrase is their story. Suppose that you are looking at a layout (e.g., the inside of an office) and that the state of your retinal receptors is correlated with properties of the light from that layout; as the light varies, so too, in an appropriate manner, does the state of your receptors. On this assumption it follows that the state of your receptors is also correlated with properties of the layout. Now suppose that you want to find out if layout properties are directly detected. According to the counterfactual support condition (b) you must do an experiment: you present the layout without the light and then the light without the layout. In the first case you turn out the lights, and the layout disappears. In the second case you present, say, a hologram, and an illusory layout appears. You conclude that layout properties are not directly detected; if they were (1) you could not have layout illusions, and (2) removing the light would not preclude seeing the layout.

Of course Fodor and Pylyshyn want it to come out that properties of the light *are* directly detected under their definition of transduction, even though properties of the layout are not. The story would be that certain properties of light are directly detected and that these properties of the light *specify* properties of the layout for the perceiver, i.e., the perceiver uses the light to infer the layout. It is reasonable to ask, then, if *any* properties of the light are directly detected. Fodor and Pylyshyn suggest that relevant employments of the method of differences would reveal that some are, and that one should not, therefore, be able to construct light illusions. We should not, according to them, be able to dismiss the hypothesis that properties of the light are directly detected in the same manner that they dismiss the hypothesis that properties of the layout are directly detected. This is an empirical claim of some interest.

To check it, let us recall the normal etiology of receptor activity in, say, rod vision. Each rod contains a visual pigment, rhodopsin, consisting of two parts: a protein molecule called opsin and a chromophore called retinal_1. In the resting state, retinal_1 is in its 11-*cis* form and fits snugly in the opsin. When a photon wanders too close it is absorbed by the chromophore causing it to isomerize (change structurally), straightening out into the all-*trans* configuration and, in the process, releasing energy. Thereafter occurs a rapid succession of energy-releasing reactions which eventuate, if physiologic conditions are normal and sufficient numbers of rods are stimulated, in the perception of light. The only role of light in this process is to isomerize the chromophore from the 11-*cis* to the all-*trans* configuration.

So we have two kinds of properties correlated with each other and correlated with our perception of light: viz., properties of the light and properties of chromophores. This suggests a relevant employment of the method of differences for light that parallels the one given by Fodor and Pylyshyn for the layout: present the light without the isomerization and then the isomerization without the light. Presumably a physicist or biochemist could tell us how to construct the first case, perhaps by cooling the rods and cones a bit. But the second case is easy: turn out the light and rub your eyes. The resulting phosphenes, i.e., illusory perceptions of light, are commonplace and, for lucky individuals, quite entertaining. One can get similar results, though we cannot recommend doing it, by putting a small electric current across the eye. One can even get light illusions *without functioning eyes*: Brindley and Lewin (1971, 1968) and Button and Putnam (1962), for instance, have produced them in blind subjects by direct electrical stimulation of primary visual cortex.

But light illusions are, on Fodor and Pylyshyn's criteria, incompatible with properties of the light being transduced. So if something is transduced (i.e., directly detected) in visual perception it is not, on their definition, properties of the light.[15] Perhaps, then, it is chromophore isomerization? A moment's thought, however, suggests this cannot be right either. Recall that, according to Fodor and Pylyshyn's definition, a system S is a transducer for a property P only if there is a state S_i of the system that is correlated with P, i.e., such that if P occurs, then S_i occurs. But the cortical stimulation experiments indicate that the entire retina is unnecessary for the sensation of light, that even when a subject has no retina the subject can still have sensations of light. So the directly detected properties cannot be retinal properties, and *a fortiori* cannot be properties of the chromophores. And anyhow, logical considerations aside, the chromophore gambit would be a strange move, indeed: all this time we have thought we were detecting light; in fact, we were detecting not light but isomerization. Science can be surprising, but this conclusion would tax our credulity.

Science can also lead us to revise our definitions. And in view of all difficulties just considered, transduction seems a good candidate for redefinition. We suggest

[15] It might be protested that rubbing the eyes or passing current through them is not a *relevant* employment of the method of differences. But it seems hardly less relevant than constructing holograms. Until one specifies what counts as relevant the issue is moot. The real point is this: one *can* have sensations of light even in total darkness, just as one *can* perceive layouts even in their absence. Light illusions are as easy to produce as layout illusions. If one claims that layout illusions preclude the direct detection of layouts then it is unjustified to deny that light illusions preclude the direct detection of light.

the following rather old idea, but in new dress: let us relativize the notion of transduction to observers, so that what is directly detected depends on which observer is in question. Specifically, given an observer O with space of premises Y, let us say that an observer O_i is an *immediate transducer* relative to O if and only if the conclusions of O_i, or deductively valid consequences of these conclusions, are among the premises in Y. What is *directly detected,* relative to O, are its premises Y.

On this account, for example, what is directly detected relative to Hildreth's contour-velocity observer are contours with orthogonal velocity fields. The corresponding immediate transducers are observers whose nondemonstrative inferences reach conclusions about such contours. However, relative to these latter observers it is not contours with orthogonal velocity fields that are directly detected but rather, say, properties of light. (The precise answer here awaits, of course, well-confirmed accounts of the observer(s) that infer the contours-cum-velocity-fields which serve as premises for Hildreth's observer.) And, relative to an observer that infers 3-D motion from 2-D curves with smooth velocity fields, it may be that what is directly detected are the conclusions of Hildreth's observer and that Hildreth's observer therefore counts as a transducer. In short, inference permeates even direct detection. What is directly detected relative to one level is always, relative to another "lower" level, the result of an inference; the premise, the "appearance," at a given level arises as the conclusion of an inference at a previous level.

We have not yet defined a transducer, only an "immediate transducer." Let us do so. Suppose that O_1 is an immediate transducer for O_2 and O_2 is an immediate transducer for O_3; it does not follow that O_1 is an immediate transducer for O_3: the relation "immediate transducer" is not transitive. However, we can use the relation "immediate transducer" to generate a new relation that is transitive, and this new relation will be our definition of "transducer." To wit, let be given a collection, $\mathcal{O}$, of observers. Suppose that $\mathcal{O}$ contains some observers, say $O_1, O_2, \ldots, O_n$, such that O_i is an immediate transducer for O_{i+1}. Then we say that O_i is a transducer for every O_j such that $i < j$.[16] Intuitively, the relation "transducer" is to "immediate transducer" as the relation "ancestor" is to "parent." Again intuitively, O_i is a transducer for O_j if there is some path of information flow whereby the conclusions of

[16] More formally, the relation "transducer" is the minimal transitive relation that contains the relation "immediate transducer." Recall that a relation on a set $\mathcal{O}$ is a subset of $\mathcal{O} \times \mathcal{O}$. If R is a relation, we can consider the collection of all transitive relations R' such that R' contains R (as a subset of $\mathcal{O} \times \mathcal{O}$). This collection contains the full relation $\mathcal{O} \times \mathcal{O}$ itself and is therefore nonempty. The minimal transitive relation that contains R is then the intersection of all the R''s in this nonempty collection.

O_i affect the premises for O_j.

Using this account of transduction and immediate transduction, we can put in new perspective some of the disagreement between Gibson's (1966, 1979) ecological optics and Fodor and Pylyshyn's "establishment" theory. Gibson insists that higher-level visual entities, e.g., 3-D shapes, are directly detected. We agree. Relative to an observer with the appropriate premise space Y, 3-D shapes are directly detected. Fodor and Pylyshyn insist that 3-D shapes are inferred. We agree. Relative to an observer with the appropriate configuration space X, 3-D shapes are inferred. On our view where Gibson erred was in denying that inference ever took place in vision. And where Fodor and Pylyshyn erred was in asserting that there is a noninferential bottom to the hierarchy of inferences in perception, that inferential processes are *ipso facto* not transductive, and that only properties of light can be directly detected in vision. Choosing, as we propose, to relativize the definition of transduction to the observer leads, in some good measure, to a rapprochement of these theories.

It also leads to some claims about psychophysical laws: e.g., that psychophysical laws not only can, but invariably do, involve perceptual concepts whose tokenings are inferentially mediated. This is perhaps no news to a psychophysicist busy studying the lawful relationship between stereo disparity and inferred depth, or to one studying the lawful relationship between parameters of structure-from-motion displays and inferred depth, or to one studying the lawful relationship between interaural phase lags and inferred locations in space of a sound source. But it is bad news for theories that attempt to provide a naturalized (i.e., nonintentionally specified) semantics for observation terms based on the contrary assumption: viz., based on the assumption that psychophysical laws only involve perceptual concepts whose tokenings are not inferentially mediated (see, e.g., Fodor 1987, p. 112ff). Unfortunately for these theories, psychophysical "laws" simply are not counterfactual supporting—not even the laws pertaining to the most elementary of sensations in vision, audition, or somesthesis. All such sensations can be produced even when the physical properties to which they (are assumed to) normally correspond are absent.

7. Theory neutrality of observation

In this section we apply the definition of observer to the problem of defining what it means for observation to be theory neutral. We begin by discussing some current conceptions of theory neutrality from the philosophy of science.

Science progresses through the interplay of theory and observation. Precisely how, and towards what, is, to put it mildly, not yet generally agreed upon. What does seem uncontroversial, however, is that an adequate philosophy of science awaits an adequate theory of observation, and here several issues loom large. Perhaps the foremost issue is this: is observation itself theory laden or theory neutral? Or, to put it another way, can the scientific theories we hold affect the character of our perceptual experience? Inevitably, one's answer depends upon one's precise definitions of theory neutrality and theory ladenness; and here there seems little consensus. Churchland (1988), for instance, suggests that "an observation judgment is *theory neutral* just in case its truth is not contingent upon the truth of any general empirical assumptions, just in case it is free of potentially problematic presuppositions" (p. 170). Evidence that observation is inferential (i.e., requires background knowledge) would, on Churchland's definition, imply that it is theory laden. Fodor (1984) argues, on the other hand, that to conclude that observation is theory dependent "you need not only the premise that perception is problem solving, but also the premise that perceptual problem solving has access to ALL (or, anyhow, arbitrarily much) of the background information at the perceiver's disposal" (p. 35). To get the theory ladenness of observation, on Fodor's definition, one needs not only evidence that observation is inferential but also evidence that it is *cognitively penetrable*: i.e., that all of one's background knowledge and theories (e.g., one's scientific theories) can affect the appearance of what one observes—the appearance of colors, shapes, motion, textures, sounds, and the like. Fodor and Churchland agree that observation is inferential, i.e., that some background knowledge is required. But they disagree about its degree of cognitive penetration, Churchland arguing for a very high degree and Fodor for almost none. Whereas Churchland (and New Look psychology) suggests that our scientific theories can change our observational experience, Fodor suggests that our scientific theories leave our experience alone, changing only the descriptions we give to experience and, thereby, the beliefs we hold in consequence of experience.

One focus of the debate on cognitive penetrability are the multistable visual figures, such as the Necker cube, the rabbit/duck, and the face/vase. Regarding these illusions Churchland suggests that "in all of these cases one learns very quickly to make the figure flip back and forth at will between the two or more alternatives, by changing one's assumptions about the nature of the object or about the conditions of viewing" (p. 172). Fodor responds that "It may be that you can resolve an ambiguous figure by deciding what to attend to. But (a) which figures are ambiguous is *not* something you decide; (b) nor can you decide what the terms of the ambiguity are" (1988, p. 191). So they each draw a different conclusion from the same examples, Churchland impressed that there *are* alternative perceptions and Fodor that there are so *few* and that we have no choice in what they are. We can see what is at issue more clearly in the language of observers. Multistable perceptions are possible for an observer $O = (X, Y, E, S, \pi, \eta)$ only if for some points s in S (i.e., for some of O's distinguished premises) the sets $\pi^{-1}(s) \cap E$ (i.e., the distinguished interpretations compatible with s) each contain more than one interpretation. For each such premise s, O's conclusion is a probability measure giving weight to the two or more distinguished interpretations compatible with s. What Churchland is arguing, in essence, is that one can switch between the interpretations in $\pi^{-1}(s) \cap E$ for a given s, and that this is evidence for the cognitive penetration of O. Fodor, on the other hand, when he points out that you cannot decide what are the terms of the ambiguity, is arguing that multistable figures are not evidence that one can change η, and that therefore they are not evidence for the cognitive penetration of O. The question we must answer, then, is: what is a natural definition of the cognitive penetration of O? Shall we say, with Churchland, that selection among the interpretations given nonzero weight by O constitutes cognitive penetration of O? Or shall we say, with Fodor, that altering η (i.e., the "theory" used by O to interpret its premises) is necessary for the cognitive penetration of O? Of the two alternatives, the latter is by far the most invasive of O. The first definition only requires that higher cognitive processes select among the *outputs* of O, whereas the latter requires that higher cognitive processes alter the *internal structure* of O. In light of these considerations, we are inclined to adopt the latter definition (though we shall be more precise shortly) and therefore to agree with Fodor that multistable figures do not give evidence for the cognitive penetration of perception. There may or may not be evidence for the synchronic or diachronic penetration of perception, but multistable figures are not such evidence.

Well, is observation theory neutral? If we adopt Churchland's definition, viz., that inductive risk in perception implies its theory ladenness, then observer theory would agree with Churchland that observation is not theory neutral. Fodor would also agree, if he adopted Churchland's definition. But the real debate between them seems to be not about the presence of inductive risk in perception, both acknowledge the risk, but about whether cognition—especially a scientific theory one believes—can penetrate perception. If it can, then the theories we hold can change the data we get from our senses, and this seems troublesome for the objectivity of science.

Can cognition penetrate perception? To answer this we must, of course, first consider the question: what is the distinction between perception and cognition? Again, there is no general consensus. New Look theorists, e.g., Bruner (1973), suggest that both are a matter of inference and that any distinction between them is at best heuristic. Fodor (1983) suggests that both are a matter of inference, but that there is an important distinction: cognition is isotropic and relatively domain neutral whereas perceptual input systems are domain specific and informationally encapsulated. This requires some spelling out, so here is what we propose to do. First we will briefly describe Fodor's account of domain specificity, informational encapsulation, isotropy, and domain neutrality. Next we will translate these notions into the language of observer theory, both as a way to make them more precise and as a way to exercise the definition of observer. Something will get lost in the translation: we will find that these notions, like the notion of transducer, are not absolute, but make sense only when relativized to an observer. And this will dictate our definition of "cognitive." In fact, it will turn out that if observer O_1 is transductive relative to O_2 then O_2 is "cognitive" relative to O_1. Then, getting back to the cognitive penetration issue, we will define the penetration of one observer by others. And finally, with a relativized notion of "cognitive" in hand, we will be able to propose a definition of the theory neutrality of a collection of observers: a collection of observers $\mathcal{O}$ is theory neutral iff $\mathcal{O}$ is an irreflexive partially ordered set under the relation "cognitive." We will leave open the empirical question as to whether there are any theory neutral collections of observers in the human perceptual systems.

Now to begin this program. Fodor (1983) proposes a trichotomous functional taxonomy of mental processes: transducers, input systems, and central processors. In Fodor's account transducers provide, as we have discussed, a noninferential interface between mental processes and certain properties of the physical world. Thereafter information flows first through the input systems and thence to central processors. Both input systems and central processors are, according to Fodor, inferential, but with this important distinction: input systems are modular whereas central systems are not.

Definitions now commence to come fast and thick. First, modularity amounts, in essence, to input systems being *domain specific* and, more importantly, *informationally encapsulated*. An inferential system is informationally encapsulated if it is constrained "in respect of the *body of data* that can be consulted in the evaluation of any given hypothesis" (p. 122). It is domain specific if it is constrained "in respect of the *class of hypotheses*" to which it has access (p. 122). For example, your visual perception of 3-D shapes via stereovision appears to use data about the disparities of the images in your two eyes and, arguably, *nothing else*. Thus stereovision is informationally encapsulated; other knowledge you may have, e.g., that you are watching a 3-D movie and the screen is flat, simply are not among the data available to your stereovision inference. Furthermore, turning now to domain specificity, the kinds of hypotheses available for confirmation via stereovision are restricted to propositions, roughly, of the type "the 3-D position of this feature in the visual field is such and such relative to that feature," and, arguably, *no other type*. Thus stereovision is domain specific; other interesting hypotheses about the visual world, such as that an elephant is walking by and that this feature corresponds to part of its trunk, simply are not in the repertoire of the stereovision processor.

Let us translate a bit. For any observer $O = (X, Y, E, S, \pi, \eta)$ the premise space Y specifies all possible data that can be consulted by O, and, thereby, the informational encapsulation of O. Moreover the σ-algebra (i.e., collection of events) on the configuration space X, viz., $\mathcal{X}$, specifies, roughly, all possible hypotheses to which O has access, and, thereby, the domain specificity of O. More precisely, the possible hypotheses are not $\mathcal{X}$ itself, but rather the possible markovian kernels on $Y \times \mathcal{X}$.

Getting back to Fodor, a central processor, in contrast to an input system, is an inferential system that is *isotropic* and relatively *domain neutral*. An inferential system is isotropic (as opposed to informationally encapsulated) if it is not constrained in respect of the body of data that can be consulted in the evaluation of any given hypothesis. As Fodor puts it, "isotropy is the principle that *any* fact may turn out to be (ir)relevant to the confirmation of any other" (p. 109). An inferential system is relatively domain neutral (as opposed to domain specific) if it has access to a relatively large class of hypotheses. The idea here seems to be that whereas each input system is specialized to one mode of inference, say to inferences about the syntactic structures of utterances or to inferences about the 3-D structures of rigid bodies in motion, central processors are *multimodal* in the hypotheses that they can entertain and (dis)confirm. A central processor can, with equal facility, consider hypotheses about syntax, 3-D structure, politics, and so on; an input system cannot.

While Fodor allows that central processors are *relatively* domain neutral, he does not allow that they are *completely* domain neutral. An inferential system that is completely domain neutral he calls "epistemically unbounded"; such a system has "no interesting endogenous constraints on the hypotheses accessible to intelligent problem-solving" (p. 122). Epistemic boundedness holds for central processors and input systems (and, so far as we can tell, for observers); but input systems, being domain specific, are more bounded than central processors.

To translate these notions into the language of observers, consider a collection, $\mathcal{O}$, of observers which are *immediate transducers* relative to an observer $O' = (X', Y', E', S', \pi', \eta')$. Recall that this means that the conclusions of each observer $O_i = (X_i, Y_i, E_i, S_i, \pi_i, \eta_i)$ in $\mathcal{O}$, or deductively valid consequences of these conclusions, are among the premises, Y', of O'. Now note that while each O_i in $\mathcal{O}$

may have its own idiosyncratic domain of accessible hypotheses (viz., kernels on $Y_i \times \mathcal{X}_i$), and may therefore be quite domain specific, the domains of distinct such O_i need not overlap at all; e.g., O_1 might have 3-D motions as its domain whereas O_2 might have certain olfactory properties in its domain. Since the conclusions of these diverse inferential domains all figure among the premises Y' of O', it follows that *O' is isotropic relative to its immediate transducers $\mathcal{O}$.* O' is not constrained, relative to its immediate transducers, in respect of the body of data that it can consult in the evaluation of its hypotheses; whereas each immediate transducer O_i traffics in its own idiosyncratic modality, O' traffics in the modalities of all.

The isotropy of O' relative to its immediate transducers also implies that O' is domain neutral relative to these transducers. For, in the typical case, the perspective $\pi' : X' \to Y'$ is many to one and, in any case, it is surjective; therefore a richer collection of premises Y' implies a richer collection of configurations X' and this, in turn, implies a richer collection of accessible hypotheses, viz., markovian kernels on $Y' \times \mathcal{X}'$.

Since O' is isotropic and domain neutral relative to its immediate transducers $\mathcal{O}$, and since isotropy and domain neutrality are, in Fodor's story, the essence of central, or "cognitive," processors, we are led to stipulate: if $\mathcal{O}$ is a collection of observers that are immediate transducers relative to an observer O', we will say that O' is "immediately central" or "immediately cognitive" relative to $\mathcal{O}$.

Since the relation "immediate transducer" is intransitive so is the relation "immediately cognitive." However, just as we used the relation "immediate transducer" to generate the transitive relation "transducer" so we can use the relation "immediately cognitive" to generate a transitive relation "cognitive." Perhaps this is the simplest way to define "cognitive": if O is a transducer (not necessarily immediate) relative to O' then O' is cognitive relative to O. "Cognitive" includes "immediately cognitive" as a special case, just as "transducer" includes "immediate transducer" as a special case.

It is quite possible, given this definition, that O' is cognitive relative to a collection, $\mathcal{O}$, of observers, and that O' is also transductive relative to some other observer O'' that is not in $\mathcal{O}$. In this case O'' is cognitive relative to O'. Transduction and cognition are, on this story, opposite sides of the same coin, and both are defined only relative to an observer. There is no such thing as *the* transductive level or *the* cognitive level. What is cognitive and what is transductive depends on which observer you ask.

We are now in a position to define the cognitive penetration of one observer by another. The definition is simple. Let O and O' be two observers with O' cognitive relative to O. Then we will say that *O' cognitively penetrates O* if O' is also transductive relative to O.

Why? Because if O', being cognitive relative to O, is also transductive relative to O this means that the conclusions of O' are among the data used by O to (dis)confirm its hypotheses; that is, the conclusions of O' penetrate the inferences of O. Notice that, according to this definition, if O' cognitively penetrates O then O also cognitively penetrates O'.

We are, finally, in a position to propose a definition of the theory neutrality of a collection of observers. Again the definition is simple. We will say that a collection of observers is theory neutral if no observer in the collection cognitively penetrates any other in the collection. (More formally, a collection of observers is theory neutral if the collection forms an irreflexive partially ordered set under the relation "cognitive.") What theory neutrality demands, according to this definition, is that there be no cycles in the collection of observers; that if O is a transducer for O' then O' is not also a transducer for O.

What seems to be emerging here is a picture of the mind that acknowledges the role of transductive and cognitive processes without being forced to introduce a fundamental trichotomy. Given an observer O, some observers are transductive relative to O, and others are cognitive relative to O. There seems to be no need to postulate three distinct denizens of the mind: transducers, input systems, and central processors. Postulate, instead, observers in hierarchical relationships, and the properties we want, the ones that led to the postulation of a trichotomy in the first place, just fall out. We will discuss the hierarchical nature of perception more thoroughly in chapter nine, where we introduce the notion of "specialization."

CHAPTER THREE

PERCEPTION AND COMPUTATION

In this chapter we indicate how the class of observers properly contains the class of Turing machines. We discuss the simulation of observers by Turing machines.

1. Turing observers

We begin with a brief review of Turing machine terminology. The theory of automata considers several characterizations of Turing machines. All characterizations are equivalent to defining a Turing machine as a language recognizer. Let Σ be the "terminal alphabet" of a Turing machine T; Σ is the set of all elementary symbols which can be input to T. Let Σ^* be the set of all strings of finite length of elements of Σ. The *language recognized by* T is the subset $L \subset \Sigma^*$ consisting in those strings which, when input, cause T to halt in an "accept state." The property of a subset L of Σ^* which allows it to be recognized by some Turing machine is called "recursive enumerability," and sets enjoying this property are called "recursively enumerable," abbreviated *RE*.[1] More generally, given any countable set C we can define a subset $B \subset C$ to be RE in C if C can be embedded in some Σ^* in such a way that B corresponds to an RE language in Σ^*. In this sense we can speak of a Turing machine "recognizing a subset B of C." Intuitively, B is RE in C if there exists a procedure with this property: given an arbitrary element x of C, if $x \in B$ the procedure will determine this in finitely many steps. If $x \notin B$, however, the procedure may not halt. In fact, if B is RE in C, its complement $B - C$ may not be RE. If both B and

[1] There are various ways to give a mathematical characterization of the collection all RE subsets of a given Σ^*, but we will not need to do so here.

$C - B$ are RE in C, we say simply that B is a *recursive* subset of C. This means intuitively that there is a recursive procedure which will determine in finitely many steps whether or not any given element of C is in B. A function f with a countable domain D and range R is called *recursive* or *Turing computable* if the graph Γ of f is RE in $D \times R$. The Turing machine which computes f is then the one which recognizes Γ. In fact, to compute $f(d)$ for $d \in D$ the machine can enumerate the elements of Γ until it reaches the unique one whose first component is d; the second component is then $f(d)$. Thus, Turing machines can also be characterized as computers of recursive functions. It can be shown that both the support and range of a recursive function are RE sets.

All Turing machines have sufficient structure to be viewed as observers. We describe below how the class of Turing machines is a subclass of the class of observers. Simply stated, this subclass consists of observers whose inferences are deductively valid, and the deduction in question is a Turing computation. This accounts for but a small subclass of observers; observers more generally perform inferences that are not deductively valid (while they have some degree of inductive strength). Moreover, even if the inferences of an observer are deductively valid, they need not be Turing computable.

Let T be a Turing machine, with terminal alphabet Σ, that recognizes the language $L \subset \Sigma^*$. We associate to T an observer (X, Y, E, S, π, η) as follows: we will view Σ^* as a measurable space whose σ-algebra is its full power set. Let $X = Y = \Sigma^*$, $E = S = L$, π = the identity map on Σ^*. Then for $s \in S$, $\pi^{-1}\{s\}$ is just a copy of the point s, now considered as an element of E. $\eta(s, \cdot)$ must therefore be Dirac measure ϵ_s concentrated on this point. We will denote by ϵ the kernel defined by $\epsilon(s, \cdot) = \epsilon_s$. With this notation we can state how the class of Turing machines is a subclass of the class of observers.

1.1. The assignment

$$T \mapsto (\Sigma^*, \Sigma^*, L, L, \text{identity}, \epsilon)$$

embeds the class of Turing machines in the class of observers.

The observers which arise from Turing machines in this manner are called *Turing observers*. An observer (X, Y, E, S, π, η) is isomorphic to a Turing observer if and only if X is countable, E is an RE subset of X, and π is bijective.

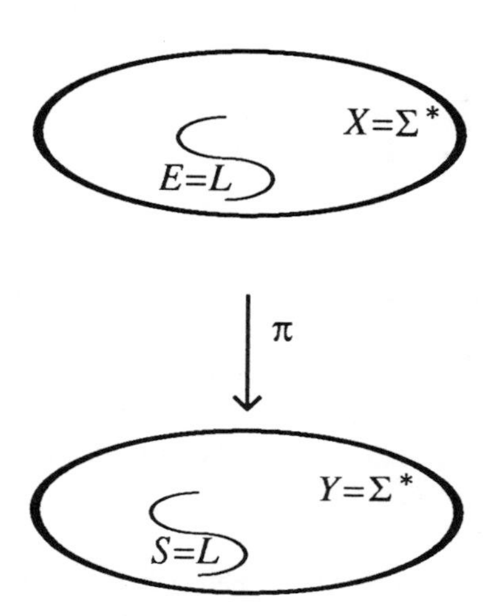

FIGURE 1.2. *A Turing observer.* $X = Y = \Sigma^*$. $E = S = L$. π *being bijective means that the Turing observer's conclusions are deductively valid.*

2. Turing simulation

Once we recognize Turing machines as a subclass of observers, we see that most observers are not Turing machines: perception is a more general concept than computation. However one can ask whether, for a given observer, there exist Turing machines which simulate that observer and, if so, how these machines are related. For an observer with uncountable X, Y, E, or S we ask whether there exist Turing machines which simulate discrete approximations of the observer. To study these questions we here define a canonical procedure for the simulation of discrete observers. In the next section we consider the issue of discretization.

Let $O = (X, Y, E, S, \pi, \eta)$ be the observer to be simulated. The objective of the simulation is the computation of $\eta(s, A)$, for all sensorial points s and $A \in \mathcal{X}$. However, such a computation is meaningful as stated only when S and $\mathcal{X}$ are countable sets. Let us assume that X is countable and that $\mathcal{X}$ is just 2^X. S is then countable (since $S \subset Y$ with $\pi: X \to Y$ surjective), but of course $\mathcal{X}$ is uncountable in general. The natural way to handle this difficulty is to restrict our attention to the recursively enumerable subsets A of X. In fact, let $\mathcal{A}$ denote the collection of these subsets. $\mathcal{A}$ itself is countable, as is well-known, so that with our restriction we can view the objective of the simulation as the computation of the function $\eta(\cdot, \bullet)$ whose domain is now the countable set $S \times \mathcal{A}$. Moreover the question of the computability of η then takes a much simpler form, as follows. Let A be any subset of X. The infinite sum

$$\sum_{x \in A} \eta(s, \{x\})$$

converges abstractly to $\eta(s, A)$, but without a procedure for enumerating the elements of A the sum has little computational meaning. If A is recursively enumerable, however, there is an effective procedure for enumerating these elements; hence there is an effective procedure for approximating the value $\eta(s, A)$ provided that for each $x \in A$, $\eta(s, \{x\})$ is computable. In this way, the restriction of our attention to sets $A \in \mathcal{A}$ leads us to consider the question of the computability of the $\eta(s, \{x\})$ for all $x \in X$. We now define canonical simulation.

Definition 2.1. Let O be an observer whose X is countable[2] and whose $\mathcal{X} = 2^X$. We will associate to O the function $f: S \times X \to \mathbf{R}$ defined by

$$f(s, x) = \eta(s, \{x\})$$

The *canonical Turing simulator* of O is the machine T which recognizes S in Y and then computes f.

It is clear that T exists if and only if O satisfies the requirements:

(i) S is recursively enumerable in Y.

(ii) f is recursive.

Generally, X and S are uncountable, so by definition there is no canonical simulator for these observers. But even when everything is countable, the conditions (i) and (ii) above will not be satisfied in general, so simply by making a discrete approximation to an observer we cannot expect that it will have a Turing simulation. However, at least in certain instances of interest to vision researchers, discrete approximations may allow Turing simulation. For these reasons and others it is essential to have a general theory of discretization of observers. We now give some indication of this.

---

[2] This can be generalized to include observers whose X is not necessarily countable, but whose measures $\eta(s, \cdot)$ on X are “atomic.” We will not develop this generalization here; but it is discussed in Bennett, Hoffman and Prakash (1987).

3. Discretization

Our purpose in this chapter is to illustrate some ideas, and not to present a complete theory. Accordingly we will restrict attention to Euclidean configuration spaces X and premise spaces Y (with their standard Borel algebras), and assume that $\pi: X \to Y$ is a projection. Let $O = (X, Y, E, S, \pi, \eta)$ be an observer with $X = \mathbf{R}^{n+m}$, $Y = \mathbf{R}^n$, and π projection, say onto the first n coordinates. In order to effect a discretization, we assume an additional datum—a finite measure λ on S. Intuitively, λ and η come from the same source, namely a probability measure ρ on E which expresses the actual probabilities of distinguished configurations in a specific universe.[3] In this case the natural choice for λ is $\pi_*(\rho)$, just as the natural choice for η is a version of the regular conditional probability distribution (rcpd) of ρ with respect to π. In our case, since λ and η are assumed given, we can simply define the measure ρ on E by $\rho = \lambda\eta$:

$$\rho(A) = \int_S \lambda(ds)\eta(s, A), \quad A \in \mathcal{E}.$$

We will describe a canonical procedure for discretization in terms of this ρ. This procedure will result in observers with countable configuration spaces.

Let δ be a simultaneous partition of X and Y by measurable subsets of nonzero Euclidean volume. Let X_δ and Y_δ denote the sets whose elements represent the distinct subsets of the respective partitions. *We will assume that for $\bar{y} \in Y_\delta$, $\pi^{-1}(\bar{y})$ is a union of elements of X_δ.* (For example, we can partition X and Y into hypercubes whose edges have length d, and whose vertices have coordinates which are integer multiples of d. The resulting sets of hypercubes are then the X_δ and Y_δ. See Figure 3.1.) Given this assumption, π induces a map $\pi_\delta: X_\delta \to Y_\delta$. Let E_δ denote the collection of those sets $\bar{x}$ in X_δ such that $\rho(E \cap \bar{x}) > 0$. Let $S_\delta = \pi_\delta(E_\delta)$. As a consequence of these definitions, if $\bar{e} \in E_\delta$ then $\rho(\bar{e}) > 0$, and if $\bar{s} \in S_\delta$, $\lambda(\bar{s}) > 0$. We will define below a kernel η_δ (depending on the original kernel η and on δ) such that $O_\delta = (X_\delta, Y_\delta, E_\delta, S_\delta, \pi_\delta, \eta_\delta)$ is an observer. We can think of this O_δ as a "δ-discretization" of O.

So that we can outline our intentions, let us assume for the moment that η_δ has already been defined. Our intention is to compare the various discretizations (for different δ) with each other and with the original observer. To this end, we give a canonical embedding of the discrete spaces E_δ and S_δ in the original X and Y. More

---

[3] Such a λ arises naturally in the discussion of noisy perceptual inferences (cf. 2–4).

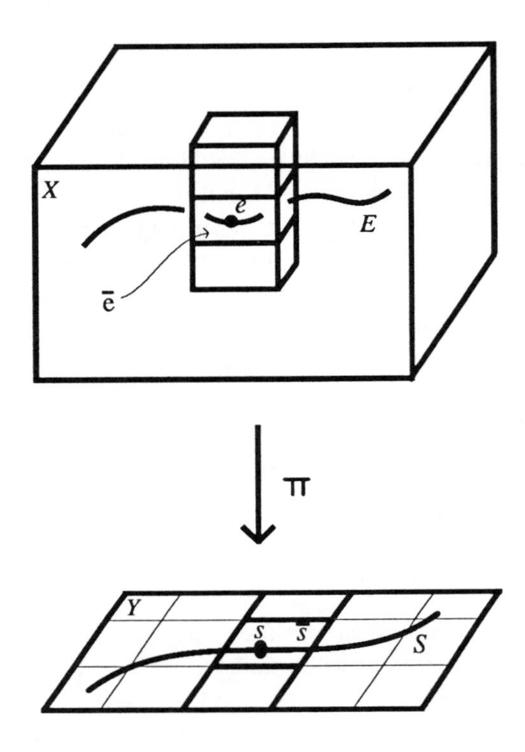

FIGURE 3.1. *A discretization of an observer.*

precisely, we associate to each $\bar{e} \in E_\delta$ a point in X and to each $\bar{s} \in S_\delta$ a point in Y by means of mappings $\alpha: E_\delta \to X$ and $\beta: S_\delta \to Y$, such that the diagram

$$\begin{array}{ccc} E_\delta & \xrightarrow{\alpha} & E'_\delta \subset X \\ \downarrow{\scriptstyle \pi_\delta} & & \downarrow{\scriptstyle \pi} \\ S_\delta & \xrightarrow{\beta} & S'_\delta \subset Y \end{array}$$

commutes. Here we have put $E'_\delta = \alpha(E_\delta)$, $S'_\delta = \beta(S_\delta)$; these are countable and hence measurable. When this is done, any kernel on E_δ relative to S_δ via π_δ can be transported, using α and β, to a kernel on E'_δ relative to S'_δ via π. In particular, η_δ may be transported in this manner to η'_δ. In this sense we can then consider an observer $O'_\delta = (X, Y, E'_\delta, S'_\delta, \pi, \eta_\delta)$. We think of O'_δ as a geometric embedding of O_δ into the original spaces X and Y, and as a discrete *approximation* of the original observer $O = (X, Y, E, S, \pi, \eta)$. E'_δ and S'_δ do not actually lie on E and S

in general, but converge to E and S as the partition δ gets arbitrarily fine.

To achieve this let us first consider how to embed S_δ in Y. Given the subset of Y represented by the element $\bar{s} \in S_\delta$, we may find its center of mass with respect to the measure λ (restricted to $\bar{s}$). This center of mass will not, in general, lie in S, but it is the natural punctual representative of $\bar{s}$ in Y. Recalling that for $\bar{s} \in S_\delta$ $\lambda(\bar{s}) > 0$, we may now define the embedding β: $S_\delta \to Y$ by

$$\beta(\bar{s}) = \int_{\bar{s}} s\, \lambda_{\bar{s}}(ds) \tag{3.2}$$

with

$$\lambda_{\bar{s}}(ds) = \frac{1}{\lambda(\bar{s})} 1_{\bar{s}}(s)\lambda(ds), \quad \bar{s} \in S_\delta.$$

That is, $\lambda_{\bar{s}}$ is the normalized restriction of λ to the hypercube $\bar{s}$.

Similarly, we wish to define a center-of-mass embedding for E_δ using appropriate measures on X. For purposes of finding the center of mass of $\bar{e}$ in E_δ, it may seem natural to use the normalization of the restriction of ρ to $\bar{e}$. However, as we shall see below, a slightly different choice of measure on $\bar{e}$ is much better suited to the task at hand. To this end, let $\rho_{\bar{e}}$ be the normalized restriction of ρ to $\bar{e}$, that is,

$$\rho_{\bar{e}}(C) = \frac{\rho(C \cap \bar{e})}{\rho(\bar{e})}.$$

By construction of E_δ, this yields a probability measure on $\bar{e}$. It is straightforward to verify that since η is the rcpd of ρ with respect to π, the measure $\rho_{\bar{e}}$ also possesses an rcpd with respect to π, a version of which is given by the formula

$$\eta_{\bar{e}}(s, de) = \frac{\eta(s, de)}{\eta(s, \bar{e})} 1_{\bar{e}}(e)$$

(which is defined up to a set of $\pi_* \rho_{\bar{e}}$-measure zero in its first argument, and which we may take to be a markovian kernel off this zero-measure set). As usual, by composing $\eta_{\bar{e}}$ with the measure $\pi_* \rho_{\bar{e}}$ we can reconstruct $\rho_{\bar{e}}$. We shall, however, compose $\eta_{\bar{e}}$ with $\lambda_{\pi(\bar{e})}$ instead, defining a new measure $\nu_{\bar{e}}$ as

$$\nu_{\bar{e}}(C) = \int_{\pi(\bar{e})} \lambda_{\pi(\bar{e})}(ds) \cdot \eta_{\bar{e}}(s, C), \quad \bar{e} \in E_\delta,$$

where C is any measurable subset of $\bar{e}$. This is, by construction, a probability measure supported on $\bar{e}$, which gives the embedding of E_δ in X by the map α as follows:

$$\alpha(\bar{e}) = \int_{\bar{e}} e\, \nu_{\bar{e}}(de), \quad \bar{e} \in E_\delta. \tag{3.3}$$

As indicated above we will denote the image $\alpha(E_\delta)$ in X by E'_δ and the image $\beta(S_\delta)$ in Y by S'_δ.

We now show that these embeddings α and β respect the original map π in the sense that for any $\bar{e} \in E_\delta$, $\pi(\alpha(\bar{e})) = \beta(\pi_\delta(\bar{e}))$. This is satisfying, as it displays a consistency of the perspective maps at all scales, and expresses a connection between the discretizations at the various scales.

To see why $\pi(\alpha(\bar{e}))$ should equal $\beta(\pi_\delta(\bar{e}))$, note that since π is linear, we may take π inside the integral defining $\alpha(\bar{e})$, so that

$$\begin{aligned}\pi(\alpha(\bar{e})) &= \int_{\bar{e}} \pi(e)\nu_{\bar{e}}(de) \\ &= \int_{\pi(\bar{e})} \lambda_{\pi(\bar{e})}(ds) \int_{\bar{e}} \eta_{\bar{e}}(s, de)\pi(e).\end{aligned}$$

But $\eta_{\bar{e}}(s, \cdot)$ is supported on the fibre where $\pi(e) = s$, so that

$$\begin{aligned}\pi(\alpha(\bar{e})) &= \int_{\pi(\bar{e})} \lambda_{\pi(\bar{e})}(ds) \quad \cdot \quad s \int_{\bar{e}} \eta_{\bar{e}}(s, de) \\ &= \beta(\pi_\delta(\bar{e})).\end{aligned}$$

If we had used the measure $\rho_{\bar{e}}$ in defining the embedding α of E_δ, we would not have obtained this result.

Finally, we come to the definition of η_δ, which appears in $O_\delta = (X_\delta, Y_\delta, E_\delta, S_\delta, \pi_\delta, \eta_\delta)$, and $O'_\delta = (X, Y, E'_\delta, S'_\delta, \pi, \eta_\delta)$. η_δ is the discretization of η

$$\eta_\delta(\bar{s}, \{\bar{e}\}) = \int_{\bar{s}} \lambda_{\bar{s}}(dt)\eta(t, \bar{e}), \quad \bar{s} \in S_\delta, \bar{e} \in E_\delta. \tag{3.4}$$

This is by construction a markovian kernel on $S_\delta \times \mathcal{E}_\delta$. Here we are merely averaging the contributions from the various original fibres of π in the given partition subset $\bar{e}$. We can view η_δ as a kernel on $S'_\delta \times \mathcal{E}'_\delta$, simply by using the identifications α and β.

In general, E_δ and S_δ need not be recursively enumerable, and a fortiori the function f, defined as in 2.1 above using η_δ, need not be recursive. Thus a discretization O_δ of a non-Turing observer O may not have a Turing simulation.

4. Effective simulation: The algebraic case

There is at least one natural class of observers for which suitable discretizations sometimes have canonical Turing simulations. These are the “algebraic observers,” such as the biological motion observer of chapter one or the structure-from-motion observer of chapter two. In the case of the structure-from-motion observer (section four of chapter two), E is the locus of points in $\mathbf{R}^{18}$ satisfying Equations **2–4.2** through **2–4.9**, and S is the image of E in $\mathbf{R}^{12}$ by the projection π. The polynomial equations defining E have integer coefficients. Thus we can apply the following general result:

4.1. Suppose $Y = \mathbf{R}^n$, $X = \mathbf{R}^{n+m}$, and $\pi: X \to Y$ is projection onto a set of n of the coordinates of X. Suppose E is the locus of zeroes in X of a finite set of polynomial equations (in the $n + m$ variables of X) with integer coefficients. Let $S = \pi(E)$, and let $X_\delta, Y_\delta, E_\delta, S_\delta, \pi_\delta$ be the discretizations resulting from the partition δ of X and Y as described in the previous section, where δ can be any partition into subsets whose boundaries are defined by any integer coefficient algebraic equations.[4] Then

(i) S_δ is a recursive subset of Y_δ;

(ii) E_δ is a recursive subset of X_δ. For all $\bar{y} \in Y_\delta$, $\pi_\delta^{-1}(\bar{y}) \cap E_\delta$ is a recursive subset of $\pi_\delta^{-1}(\bar{y})$ (and therefore of X_δ).

This result obtains by applying the Theorem of Tarski on the decidability of polynomial inequalities.[5] We omit the details here.

Condition (i) of 4.1 corresponds to the first requirement (given in section two above) for the Turing simulator of O_δ to exist. Condition (ii) is a necessary condition for the function f associated to the observer O_δ to be recursive, but it is certainly not sufficient for this purpose; this depends ultimately on the nature of η_δ.

Finally, we suggest that the real issue vis-à-vis the relationship between perception and computation is not so much the existence of a Turing simulation for a given discretization of the observer, but is rather the structure of the collection of all the Turing simulations (assuming they exist) for the discretizations of the observer at a collection of scales. Here we give only a brief sketch of these ideas.

Recall that with the introduction of the observer O'_δ we have a natural way to compare the discretizations of the original observer O for various partitions δ. Let us consider a set Δ of partitions, which we can view as partially ordered by "fineness": δ_1 is finer than δ_2 if every element of X_{δ_1} is a subset of some element of X_{δ_2}. Let us further assume that if δ_1 is finer than δ_2, and if moreover O_{δ_1} and O_{δ_2}

---

[4] This includes the cases where the partitioning subsets are hyperrectangles or hypercubes. Recall that the cylinder $\pi_\delta^{-1}(\bar{y})$ is a union of elements of X_δ.

[5] See, e.g., Jacobson 1974.

have canonical Turing simulations T_1 and T_2, then there is a natural way to compare T_2 with T_1 as Turing machines. Finally, assume that we have fixed an appropriate notion of equivalence of Turing machines. Granting all this, the following sample definition gives the flavor of what we have in mind:

Definition 4.2. O has a Δ*-effective simulation* if

1. Each O_δ for $\delta \in \Delta$ has a canonical Turing simulation.
2. The comparisons between the machines corresponding to sufficiently fine δ's is an equivalence.
3. As δ gets fine, the limit of the η_δ is η.[6]

O has a Δ-effective simulation if the family of discretized observers obtained from O using the partitions in Δ has a certain stability. Intuitively, what is significant is not the particular family of partitions Δ, but rather that there exists even one Δ for which the definition is satisfied, provided that this Δ contains arbitrarily fine partitions. The definition then asserts that the original O, although it may be given as a non-discrete object, has a Turing machine representation which is stably scale-independent. This motivates the following sequel to Definition 4.2:

Definition 4.3. With the notation and assumptions as above, suppose that there exists a family Δ which contains arbitrarily fine partitions for which O has a Δ-effective simulation. Then we will say simply that O has an *effective simulation.*

Here is a sample conjecture to accompany our sample definition:

4.4. Suppose $O = (X, Y, E, S, \pi, \eta)$ satisfies the hypotheses of 4.1. Suppose that for some integer k, exactly k points of E lie over each point s of S via π, and that $\eta(s, \cdot)$ assigns probability $1/k$ to each of these k points. Then O has an effective simulation.

We cannot give a detailed analysis of 4.4 here since the notion of Turing equivalence used in Definition 4.2 has not been precisely specified. We mention, however, that the key idea is to find a family Δ of partitions so that, for all sufficiently fine $\delta \in \Delta$, the following property holds: For each $s \in S$ and $\bar{e} \in E_\delta$, $\bar{e} \cap E$ contains at most one point from the original fibre $\pi^{-1}(s) \cap E$. For this purpose the δ's

---

[6] Here we mean that the transports of the η_δ to E'_δ converge to η as the E'_δ converge to E.

cannot, in general, be hypercube partitions; in fact the simplest δ's that work are hyperrectangle partitions, where the proportions of the rectangles depend on the "slope" of E relative to S. In particular these proportions will need to vary within the same partition δ, depending on the location of the hyperrectangle in X. In any case, once the δ's have this property, all the maps π_δ are k-to-one, and one can check (using Definition 3.4 of η_δ) that given $\bar{s} \in S_\delta$, $\eta_\delta(\bar{s}, \cdot)$ is simply the constant function $1/k$ on $\pi^{-1}(\bar{s}) \cap E_\delta$ (and is identically 0 on $X_\delta - (\pi^{-1}(\bar{s}) \cap E_\delta)$). Since the set $\pi^{-1}(\bar{s}) \cap E_\delta$ is RE by 4.1, it then follows that $\eta_\delta(\bar{s}, \cdot)$ is Turing computable.

We summarize the main ideas: For a Δ-effective simulation, as $\delta \in \Delta$ gets finer, both the combinatorial geometry of the maps π_δ and some essential computational character of the η_δ must stabilize. Moreover, the O_δ must converge to O. What we have, then, is a system of successively finer discretizations O_δ, converging to O, whose stable structural properties (i.e., properties which hold for all sufficiently small δ) reflect the perceptually relevant properties of the original O. Thus, the fundamental structure of O is accessible at finite stages of discretization, in a manner which is independent of scale, at least for sufficiently small scales. It seems clear that, in the absence of this kind of stability, the existence of Turing simulations for the individual O_δ's alone is an insufficient hypothesis to justify a "perception as computation" viewpoint. We propose, rather, that the analysis of effective simulation is an appropriate context in which to investigate the relationship between perception and computation.

CHAPTER FOUR

SEMANTICS

We have a definition of observer, but not of the observed. A theory of perception cannot be complete without some account of the objects of perception. Parsimony suggests that we not postulate a new ontological category for these objects. We therefore explore the possibility that the objects of perception are themselves observers. We develop this proposal in the context of an investigation of the meaning and truth conditions of conclusion measures. To this end, we introduce a "primitive semantics" and an "extended semantics" for the representations appearing in the definition of observer.

1. Observer/world interface: Introduction

What are true perceptions? Without addressing this central question, no theory of perception can be complete. In observer theory the perceptions of an observer are represented by its conclusion measures so that, rephrasing, we may ask the question: What are true conclusion measures? Now on a correspondence theory (as opposed to, say, a consensus or consistency theory) the truth of a conclusion measure depends primarily on two factors: (1) the meaning of the measures and (2) the states of affairs in an appropriate external environment. Recall, however, that Definition **2**–2.1 of observer nowhere refers to a real world or to an environment external to the observer. The spaces X and Y represent properties of the interaction between the observer and its environment but are not the environment itself. Therefore to study true perceptions we first propose a minimal structure for environments and for the relationship between observers and environments, thereby advancing a primitive theory of semantics for observers. We extend this theory in section four. In the next chapter we begin to build a model for the theory by the introduction of "reflexive observer frameworks."

In chapter two we describe the observer-world relationship as follows:

1.1. When the observer (X, Y, E, S, π, η) is presented with a state of affairs in the world which corresponds to a point x of X, the point $\pi(x) \in Y$ "lights up." If $\pi(x) \notin S$ then the observer outputs no conclusion measure. If $\pi(x) = s$ is in S then the observer outputs the conclusion measure $\eta(s, \cdot)$.

Our task is to explain this statement.

We distinguish two levels of semantics: primitive semantics and extended semantics. In primitive semantics a "state of affairs" is an undefined primitive (much as, in geometry, a "point" is an undefined primitive); in extended semantics it is directly defined. Primitive semantics is the "local" semantics of a single observer, a minimal semantics which interprets the observer's conclusion measure η in terms of an external environment. Structure in addition to that of the observer is necessary for this purpose since conclusion measures are representations internal to the observer and have no a priori external interpretation. (In other words, the internal representation embodied in the conclusion measure is not itself a conclusion. For a conclusion is by definition a proposition: it is an assertion about states of affairs in some environment.) The necessary additional structure consists in a formal description of an environment; in terms of this description, meaning can be assigned to the representation η, and this meaning is the conclusion in the correct sense of the term.

In primitive semantics we assume that the "states of affairs" with which an observer is presented are undefined primitives, and that "presenting an observer with a state of affairs" is a primitive relation. States of affairs are not objects of perception. We reserve the term "object of perception" to refer to "that with which an observer interacts" in an act of perception. Rather, intuitively, *states of affairs are relationships between the observer and its objects of perception.* For now these relationships are undefined primitives; the environment of states of affairs is, in the primitive semantics, an abstract formalism. The primitive semantics provides a dictionary between the internal representations of the observer and this abstract formalism.

By contrast, in extended semantics the states of affairs themselves—not only the single observer—are directly defined. At this level, the environment of the observer, as well as the states of affairs in it, have a priori meaning independent of the observer's conclusion measure.

This environment of states of affairs is not to be regarded as a theatre for all possible phenomena; it need only be rich enough in structure to provide a concrete model of the theoretical environment posited at the first-level. The environment is not accessible to the given observer; its perceptual conclusions are the most it can know in any instant. The environment may, however, be accessible to other "higher-level" observers under various conditions; this leads to the notion of "specialization" which we take up in chapter nine. The first three sections of this chapter consider primitive semantics. Section four studies extended semantics.

2. Scenarios

We begin with a fixed observer $O = (X, Y, E, S, \pi, \eta)$. As an abstract observer, O consists only of its mathematical components X, Y, E, S, π, η as set forth in Definition 2–2.1. We want to view O as embedded in some environment as a perceiver. Therefore we must provide additional structure to represent such an embedding. We call this structure a *scenario* for O. Given a definition of scenario we can then discuss the semantics of O's conclusions.

The definition of scenario involves an unusual notion of time. Just as we assume no absolute environment, so also we assume no absolute time. We assume only that there is given, as part of each scenario, an "active time"; the instants of this active time are the instants in which O receives a premise. This active time is discrete. Perception itself is fundamentally discrete; any change of percept is fundamentally discontinuous. To put it briefly: we model perception as an "atomic" act. An atomic perceptual act is one whose perceptual significance is lost in any further temporal subdivision. This view is developed in later chapters, but a few remarks are in order here.

As we have indicated, observer theory is not a fixed-frame theory in which all phenomena are objectively grounded in a single connected ambient space—an analytical framework which plays the role of an absolute "spacetime." Absolute spacetime is surely of interest both psychologically and physically, but in neither case is this due to a principled requirement that every scientific model must begin with it. In particular, this is true of absolute time. In building a theory which is centered on acts of perception there is no reason to assume, in general, that the active times of (the scenarios of) different observers bear any describable relationship to each other. Thus there may be no natural way to embed the active times of two different observers into a third time-system (in some order-preserving manner). In special cases, however, it is natural to assume that the active times may be so embedded; this occurs, for example, when the observers occupy the same "reflexive framework" (Definition 5–2.2). In other cases the active times of different observers admit comparisons of various kinds. For example, one instant of the active time of a "higher level" observer may correspond to an entire (random) subsequence of instants of the active time of a "lower level" observer.

Definition 2.1. A *scenario* for the observer $O = (X, Y, E, S, \pi, \eta)$ is a triple $(C, R, \{Z_t\}_{t \in R})$, where

(i) C is a measurable space whose elements are called *states of affairs;*
(ii) R is a countable totally ordered set called the *active time;*
(iii) $\{Z_t\}_{t \in R}$ is a sequence of measurable functions, all defined on some fixed probability space Ω and taking values in $C \times Y$.

In other words, a scenario is a stochastic process (6–1) with state space $C \times Y$ and indexed by R.

Terminology 2.2. Z_t is called the *observation* at time t or the *presentation of the observer with a state of affairs* at time t or the *channeling* at time t. If Z_t takes the value (c_t, y_t) with $c_t \in C$ and $y_t \in Y$, we say that c_t is the *state of affairs* at time t and y_t is the *premise* (or *sensation* or *sensory input*) at time t. For any sample point $\omega \in \Omega$, the sequence $\{Z_t(\omega)\}_{t \in R}$ corresponds to a sequence of points $\{(c_t, y_t)\}_{t \in R}$ in $C \times Y$. We call this an *observation trajectory.*

The "states of affairs" in Definition 2.1 are external to the observer in the sense that they are not part of its structure. This does not imply that these states of affairs are states (or parts) of a physical world.[1] In fact, physical properties are an observer's symbols for these states of affairs, or for stable distributions of these states of affairs. Any attempt to ground a theory of the observer in an a priori fixed physical world encounters great difficulties from the outset. Contemporary physics, for instance, holds that physical theory itself must include the observer. This is evident

[1] In particular, when we define the collection of states of affairs to be a measurable space C, we are not claiming that any part of a physical world is a set.

at the quantum level, where it seems impossible to escape the conclusion that acts of observation influence the evolution of physical systems. It is also seen in relativistic formulations, where the theory, by its very definition, consists in the study of statements which are invariant under certain specified changes in the perspective, or frame of reference, of observers. For such reasons it is scientifically regressive to cling to a fixed "physical world" as the ultimate repository for states of affairs. We do not deny the existence of physical worlds but suggest that, habit aside, it is more natural to ground physical theory in perceptual theory than vice versa.

To summarize: we distinguish between perceptual conclusions, states of affairs, and objects of perception. In primitive semantics the states of affairs are undefined primitives whose existence is assumed as part of a given scenario. These states of affairs are relationships between the observer and its objects of perception, which are not specified. The observer is presented randomly in discrete time with states of affairs. This presentation is a primitive, assumed as part of the scenario. The presentations consist in a stochastic sequence (in the given discrete time) of pairings of states of affairs with premises from the premise space Y of the observer. These elements of Y constitute the only information accessible to the observer about the scenario, i.e., about its "environment." The scenario provides the syntactical structure to which semantics can be attached.

However, in the scenario itself there is no semantics: there is no conclusion in the correct sense of the word. Namely, the data of the scenario alone contain no direct relationship between the states of affairs in C and the conclusion measure η or, for that matter, the observer's configuration space X. (We regard the indirect relationship, at each instant t, which exists because the conclusion measure $\eta(s,\cdot)$ is deterministically associated to s, as a purely syntactical relationship: the symbol $\eta(s,\cdot)$ is formally attached to the symbol s, which in turn is formally attached to c_t via $Z_t = (c_t, s)$.) The scenario directly relates states of affairs with points of Y—not with points of X.

The only information an observer directly receives is a premise, a sensory input, at each instant of active time. The scenario is a minimal formalism for an external world whose states of affairs are related in some unknown manner to the successive production of these premises. This world must be external to the observer, because the internal structure of the observer, by definition, consists only in X, Y, E, S, π, η; these alone say nothing about the production in a time sequence of elements of Y.

To go further, to posit a relationship between the states of affairs and X that is compatible with the scenario data, brings us to the issue of meaning.

3. Meaning and truth conditions

Let there be given an observer O and a scenario (C, R, Z_t) (Definition 2.1). We have been referring to the "conclusion of the observer" as the *meaning* of its conclusion measure. This meaning is a proposition regarding a relationship between the conclusion measure and the scenario. Now the truth or falsity of this proposition can be decided only in the presence of a concrete model of the scenario, i.e., only in the presence of an extended semantics. Prior to such a model, i.e., within a primitive semantics, we are free to assign meaning to O's conclusion measure by *postulating* a relationship between it and the scenario. In the definition to follow we state this relationship. In chapter eight we discuss truth conditions for the postulated relationship in the context of an extended semantics.

Definition 3.1. Let pr_1 and pr_2 be the projections of $C \times Y$ onto the first and second coordinates respectively. The *meaning* of the conclusion measure η is the following pair of postulates:

Postulate 1. There exists a measurable injective function $\Xi : C \to X$ such that, for all $t \in R$, if $Z_t = (c_t, y_t)$ then $y_t = \pi \circ \Xi(c_t)$.

Let $X_t = \Xi \circ \mathrm{pr}_1 Z_t$. Then X_t is a measurable function with the same base space as Z_t and taking values in X. Letting ν_t be the distribution of X_t, denote its restriction to $\pi^{-1}(S)$ by ν_t^S: for $A \in \mathcal{X}$, we have $\nu_t^S(A) = \nu_t(A \cap \pi^{-1}(S))$.

Postulate 2. ν_t^S is a nonzero measure and η is its rcpd with respect to π.

To specify a meaning for η in a given scenario, we need only specify a Ξ such that $\nu_t(\pi^{-1}(S)) > 0$; the interpretation of η is then established by Postulate 2.

Terminology 3.2. The measurable function Ξ is the *configuration map;* $\Xi(c)$ is the *configuration* of c. If Definition 3.1 holds, $(R, C, \{Z_t\}, \Xi)$, is called a *primitive semantics* (for O). A state of affairs $c \in C$ is called a *distinguished state of affairs* if $\Xi(c) \in E$.

Discussion of Postulate 1 of 3.1

The existence of the configuration map Ξ, asserted in Postulate 1 of 3.1, means that there is a time-invariant relationship between the states of affairs in C and the configurations in X; we therefore can now say what X represents. Until now X was simply part of the internal formalism of the observer, an abstract representational system. It is only by virtue of Ξ that X represents the states of affairs; indeed Ξ defines that representation. The postulate states further that the pairing in the scenario between c_t and y_t (via the channeling Z_t) is imitated within the observer by the pairing between $\Xi(c_t) = x_t$ and $\pi(x_t) = y_t$. We may say that $(x_t, \pi(x_t))$ is a picture of (c_t, y_t).

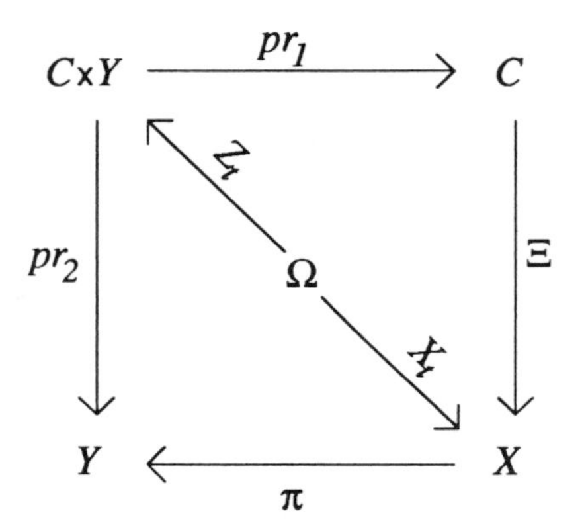

FIGURE 3.3. *Postulate 1 says there exists a Ξ for which this diagram commutes.*

Given the configuration map Ξ satisfying the properties of Postulate 1, we may effectively replace C with X, at least for the purposes of the primitive semantics. Because Ξ is one-to-one, the internal formalism of the observer, specifically X, Y and π, gives a good representation of the interaction of the observer with its environment (as provided in the scenario). Thus we can formally bypass C, and view the scenario as consisting, in essence, of a discrete-time probabilistic source of elements of X, i.e., as the sequence of measurable functions $\{X_t\}_{t \in R}$. These measurable functions take values now in X, and are related to the original measurable functions Z_t of the scenario by $X_t = \Xi \circ \text{pr}_1 Z_t$. To emphasize this simplification, we will sometimes use the word "configuration" in place of "state of affairs." Of course, this is an abuse of language; when we say, for example, "a configuration x channeled to the observer," we mean that a state of affairs c, for which $x = \Xi(c)$, channeled to the observer. Figure 3.3 illustrates Postulate 1.

The condition that the X_t's have identical conditional distributions over points $s \in S$, namely the distributions $\eta(s, \cdot)$, expresses an assumption built into the observer that its relevant environment is stationary: the distribution of states of affairs which channel to the observer, resulting in premises in S, does not vary with time. We mean neither that the observer has made a considered or learned inference to this effect, nor that it has made a scientific judgement about the stability of its environment. Rather, our viewpoint is that a de facto assumption of stationarity is fundamental to perceptual semantics; we are here modeling perception at the level where each instantaneous percept involves the output of a de facto assertion of some stationarity in the environment. The stationarity condition given above is the strongest such assertion that the observer can make without exceeding the capacity of its language.

Discussion of Postulate 2 of 3.1

The set $\pi^{-1}(S)$ consists of the configurations of those states of affairs whose channelings could result in a distinguished premise $s \in S$. Postulate 2 says, then, that there is a nonzero probability $\nu_t(\pi^{-1}(S))$ that such channelings occur. Moreover, it assigns meaning to the conclusion measures $\eta(s, \cdot)$. Since $\eta(s, \cdot)$ is deterministically associated to $s \in S$ it can be viewed as the "output" given s as "input"; in fact we have tacitly but consistently viewed it in this way up to now. Using this terminology, and given Postulate 1, the meaning assigned by Postulate 2 may be expressed as follows:

3.4. If the premise at time t is $s \in S$, then the observer outputs the conditional distribution, given s, of the configurations of states of affairs whose channeling could result in s; this conditional distribution is $\eta(s, \cdot)$. It is independent of the value of t. If the premise at time t is not in S, then the observer outputs no conclusion.

This explains statement **1.1** in the first section.

For Postulate 2 to hold at all times t, it is necessary that the distributions of the X_t have identical rcpd's over S. Now the observer itself cannot verify such a stationarity in the distributions. For the observer has no language other than that provided by η, with which to represent information about the distributions of the X_t's. In fact, it can say nothing about what happens when $y_t \notin S$; the observer is necessarily inert at such instants t. Nevertheless this stationarity in the observer's environment is fundamental to our perceptual semantics; we as modelers can verify the existence of such a stationarity.

As noted in section two, truth conditions for the conclusions of an observer amount to giving additional conditions on the scenario under which these conclusions are true propositions. Thus the truth conditions will be satisfied in some models (of the abstract scenario formalism), and not in others. We reiterate that, for this reason, the truth conditions can only be verified in the extended semantics where a concrete model of the scenario is given.

Terminology 3.5. Given an observer in a scenario and given a model of that scenario (i.e., an extended semantics for the observer) we say that *the observer's conclusion is true at time* t or that *the observer has true perception at time* t if the postulates of Definition 3.1 are true in that extended semantics. If the observer has true perception at time t for all t, and if the map Ξ is the same for each t, then we simply say that *the observer has true perception.*

Terminology 3.5 allows truth an instantaneous character.

4. Extended semantics

So far we have assigned meaning to the observer's conclusion measures, but not to the states of affairs. A "state of affairs" in C is a relationship between the observer and its objects of perception. The objects of perception do not appear explicitly in the definition of scenario, although each channeling arises from an interaction between the observer and these objects. In order to assign meaning to the states of affairs, i.e., in order to *extend* our semantics, we must construct models for the scenario in which the objects of perception are specified.

In the next section we propose one such specification of the objects of perception. Here we ask the following question: In order to be able to extend our primitive semantics, what relationship must obtain between the set of objects of perception and the primitive semantics? Let us denote the set of objects of perception by $\mathcal{B}$.

The primitive semantics, as above, is (R, C, Z_t, Ξ). In an extended semantics the set C of states of affairs plays a dual role, both as the set of referents for O's conclusions and as the set of relationships between O and $\mathcal{B}$. The answer to our question must ensure a compatibility between these roles. The elements of $\mathcal{B}$ are the source of the channelings, they can in principle be individuated by O only to the extent that they are individuated by the relationships in C. We may now state our requirement of compatibility between $\mathcal{B}$ and (R, C, Z_t, Ξ).

Assumption 4.1. Suppose that we have a primitive semantics (R, C, Z_t, Ξ); in particular, suppose Ξ exists and has the property stated in Postulate 1. Suppose that we are given a set $\mathcal{B}$ such that at the instant t of O's active time there is at most one channeling to O, and that this channeling arises from the interaction of O with a single element of $\mathcal{B}$. The class of such interactions is parametrized by C. Suppose further that the primitive semantics (R, C, Z_t, Ξ) induces an equivalence relation on $\mathcal{B}$: two elements, say B_1 and B_2 of $\mathcal{B}$, are equivalent if and only if any channeling at time t arising from the interaction of O with B_1 or B_2 results in the same value of the measurable function X_t, where X_t is defined as in 3.1. Since distinct elements of X_t correspond to distinct elements of C the equivalence classes are in one-to-one correspondence with elements of C. Let $\mathcal{B}_c$ denote the equivalence class in $\mathcal{B}$ which corresponds to the element $c \in C$ for the equivalence relation just defined.

We can now say precisely what is the meaning of the elements of C as relationships between O and $\mathcal{B}$:

Condition 4.2. To say that an observer stands in the particular relationship c of C to $\mathcal{B}$ at time t means that the observer interacts with some element of the equivalence class $\mathcal{B}_c$ at time t, and that a channeling at time t arises from this interaction; the channeling results in the value $\Xi(c)$ for the measurable function X_t.

Since the state of affairs c is specified by the corresponding equivalence class $\mathcal{B}_c$ we can think informally of the relationship corresponding to c as the "activation" of the class $\mathcal{B}_c$. As defined, the notion is instantaneous. The formal definition of extended semantics is then the following:

Definition 4.3. Given a primitive semantics $(R, \mathcal{C}, Z_t, \Xi)$ for the observer O, an *extension* of this semantics consists in a set $\mathcal{B}$ for which the hypotheses of 4.1 hold (for some notion of "interaction"). $\mathcal{B}$ is then called the set of *objects of perception*. Such extensions of primitive semantics are called *extended semantics*. In an extended semantics, the *meaning* of the states of affairs as relationships between O and $\mathcal{B}$ is described by 4.2.

Once we are in an extended semantics, it is usually convenient simply to bypass the states of affairs $\mathcal{C}$ and to speak only of the objects of perception $\mathcal{B}$ and the configuration space X of the observer. For the states of affairs map injectively to the configurations by Ξ, so no information is lost thereby. Moreover, by assumption, all channelings originate in interactions of O with elements of $\mathcal{B}$. Thus the essential information in an extended semantics for O is $R, \mathcal{B}, \Phi$, and X_t, where

$$\Phi : \mathcal{B} \to X$$

is defined by $\Phi(B) = \Xi(c)$ for that c such that $\mathcal{B}_c$ is the equivalence class (described in 4.1) which contains B. In this way, the equivalence classes now appear as the sets $\Phi^{-1}\{x\}$, for $x \in X$, so that the original information carried by the states of affairs is not lost.

Terminology 4.4. We refer to "the extended semantics defined by $(R, \mathcal{B}, \Phi, X_t)$." $(\mathcal{B}, \Phi)$ is called the *environment* of the extended semantics. We retain the terminology "configuration map" for Φ; now we can speak of the configuration $\Phi(B)$ of the object of perception B. We call B a *distinguished object of perception* if $\Phi(B)$ is in E. We say that B *channels to O at time t* if a channeling arises from the interaction of O with B at time t.

The postulates of Definition 3.1 assume a new significance in the context of extended semantics. Postulate 1 is required to hold in order that the extended semantics exist. Postulate 2 is now also a truth condition whose veracity can be tested in $(R, \mathcal{B}, \Phi, X_t)$.

5. Hierarchical analytic strategies and nondualism

In an extended semantics for an observer O, the states of affairs C are relationships between O and a set $\mathcal{B}$ of objects of perception, as stipulated in Definition 4.3. The objects of perception represent the minimal entities that can interact instantaneously with the observer: at each instant of the observer's active time a channeling occurs, and there is at most one channeling, corresponding to the interaction of the observer with exactly one element of $\mathcal{B}$. Thus a channeling indicates an interaction of O with an object of perception. The conclusion of O—expressed by the output of the conclusion measure $\eta(s, \cdot)$—is an irreducible perceptual response of O to the channeling. The interaction is an irreducible perceptual stimulus for O. The word "irreducible" here refers not to an absolute indecomposability, but to an indecomposability relative to the observer's perceptual act: In some (hypothetical) decomposition of both the observer and its object of perception, a single channeling might involve many "microchannelings" between components of the observer and its object. But these microchannelings have no direct perceptual significance for the original observer—neither a channeling nor a conclusion on the part of the original observer are associated to a single microchanneling.

Up to now we have been considering the interactions of systems without reference to their further decomposition—what one might call "direct" interactions (not to be confused with the direct *detection* of **2–6**). In this section we direct attention, briefly and informally, to the problem of analyzing the interaction between "complex systems," i.e., systems each admitting more than one distinct level of structure. Assume for the moment that the levels have already been distinguished. We suggest that an appropriate analysis of such an interaction involves matching levels of the respective systems in such a way that the total interaction appears to consist of separate direct interactions between the constituents at each of these matched levels. The constituents of any given level, or stratum, are entities which are not decomposable in that stratum, although they may be decomposable in terms of entities at lower levels of the stratification. It may be that only one level of each system interacts directly with a corresponding level of the other system, or it may be that any pair of levels, one level from each system, interacts directly. We also assume that information flows between the various levels within each system separately, so that the effects of the direct interaction at any one level can propagate to other levels. Thus it is not restrictive to require that an interaction should admit a decomposition, for purposes of analysis, into separate direct interactions between entities at certain matched levels. Nor is such a requirement to be taken as a statement about the absolute character of reality. It is rather a matter of choosing an analytical strategy.

In practice we want the freedom to choose the stratifications so as to display effectively the total interaction in terms of direct interactions at appropriate levels. (We wish to understand the total interaction, not to embed some previously distinguished elementary levels in a larger context.) This kind of freedom requires that our concept of stratification has some flexibility, that its application is not rigidly determined in every case (although each application must produce strata whose mathematical relationship to one another is of some well-defined type). The question of what principles should govern the selection and "matching" of strata rests in turn on the question of what constitutes "direct interaction," because the purpose of the matching of strata is to display direct interaction. There need not be a unique answer to this question, even in a concrete situation. Indeed, because of the internal flow of information between the levels in each system, there may be many ways to select a certain set of levels as being the sites of direct interaction. But however the definitions of stratification and direct interaction are ultimately fixed in a particular case, we would adduce at least the following general requirements:

1. **Irreducibility.** The notion of "level" is sufficiently robust so that irreducibility relative to a level makes sense: If P is an irreducible constituent of a level L in a system A (i.e., the constituent P of A is a site for direct interaction at level L), then although P may be decomposable in some way in the total system A, there is no such decomposition within L itself.
2. **Matching.** To match levels L and L', in the respective systems A and A', means that every irreducible constituent of L can in principle interact directly with every irreducible constituent of L'.
3. **Homogeneity.** There is homogeneity within any given level in the sense that the minimal syntax required to distinguish the level L from other levels is not sufficient to discriminate among the irreducible constituents of L.
4. **Transitivity.** The notion of direct interaction is transitive: Given three entities P_1, P_2, P_3, if P_1 can interact directly with P_2, and P_2 can interact directly with P_3, then P_1 can interact directly with P_3.

Terminology 5.1. An approach to the analysis of any type of interaction of complex systems, which involves a notion of "direct interaction," and a corresponding notion of stratification of the respective interacting systems into levels at which direct interaction occurs, will be called a *hierarchical analytic strategy* if the requirements 1–4 above are fulfilled.

This terminology is informal, since we have not rigorously grounded it. However it is useful as it stands for purposes of motivation and description. Here is how we apply the terminology in observer theory, in a particular perceptual context where a hierarchical analytic strategy has been adopted:

5.2. To specify the objects of perception for an observer is to specify what constitutes direct interaction for that observer.

This proposal is reasonable, for we have already characterized the objects of perception for O as "minimal entities with which O can interact instantaneously," or "irreducible perceptual stimuli of O" in a given extended semantics. If we imagine this semantics sitting at one level in a hierarchy, this characterization of O's objects of perception models "direct interaction" at that level.

Now suppose we are given a hierarchical system, say A, in which the observer O is an irreducible entity at some distinguished level L. If B is any other system, perceptual or otherwise, with which A can interact, then in virtue of 5.2 the level L' of B which is matched with L must consist of *objects of perception* for O. We claim that other entities, say P, in A at the same level L as O must also be be objects of perception for O. For by requirement 2 above, the entities in L' can interact directly with these. And by 4, O itself can in principle interact directly with such P. Thus, on the one hand the entities P at the same level L as O may be represented as objects of perception of O; they are structurally equivalent to objects of perception in the given analytical framework. On the other hand, by 3, these P are structurally indistinguishable from O, at least in terms of the syntax associated to the level L. We finally conclude that the P's also have some of the structure of observers. This suggests the

Hypothesis 5.3. The objects of perception for an observer O have the same structure as O in the following sense: the objects of perception share with O that part of O's structure which defines it as an irreducible entity at the fixed level L of the given hierarchical analysis. Stated succinctly, the objects of perception of O may themselves be represented as observers.

Hypothesis 5.3 makes sense only in the context of a hierarchical analytic strategy; since that notion is not rigorous, it is clear that the argument given above which leads to 5.3 is not intended to be rigorous. However 5.3 motivates the construction of rigorous models of extended semantics, models which are designed to be incorporated in a particular, well-defined hierarchical analytic strategy. This is the spirit of the reflexive observer frameworks, which we define in the next chapter. One particular hierarchical analytic strategy, which incorporates the extended semantics resulting from reflexive observer frameworks, is called *specialization*; we consider it in chapter nine.

Hypothesis 5.3 says that a fundamental nondualism is associated with the various levels of the hierarchy; more precisely the nondualism is a property of the syntax associated with each such level, which is the minimal syntax necessary to distinguish that level. Thus, in the presence of a hierarchical analytic strategy, the apparently "dualistic" interaction of two complex systems is decomposable into a set of "nondualistic" interactions between entities at matched levels, together with information propagation through the levels of each system. On the other hand, one could take an approach which simply begins with a suitable hypothesis of nondualism and observe that it suggests (though it certainly does not require) hierarchical strategies. For example we might begin with a meta-proposition similar to the following:

Meta-Proposition. Insofar as any two entities interact they are congruent: the part of their respective structures which is congruent delineates the nature and extent of the primary aspect of their interaction. Any aspect of the interaction which cannot be described in terms of this congruence is secondary, and arises from the propagation of the effects of the primary interaction by the internal flow of information within the separate entities.

We can then take our notion of "direct interaction" to be the "primary interaction" of this meta-proposition, so that direct interaction is automatically nondualistic. Stratification of interacting systems can then be defined in terms of levels of structure at which congruence occurs.

Hierarchical analytic strategies differ significantly from "fixed frame" analytic strategies. In the latter, there is a single unchanging framework (such as spacetime) in which all phenomena of interest are embedded.

CHAPTER FIVE

REFLEXIVE FRAMEWORKS

In this chapter we develop a framework, called a reflexive observer framework, in which the objects of perception of an observer O are themselves observers having the same X, Y, E, and S as has O. We display the relationship between reflexive observer frameworks and environments for extended semantics. We illustrate the definition of reflexive observer framework with several examples.

1. Mathematical notation and terminology

The examples of reflexive observer frameworks given in this chapter make use of several mathematical concepts from group theory. In this section we collect basic terminology and notation for the convenience of the reader.[1]

A *topological group* G is a group that is also a topological space and satisfies (i) the map $G \to G$ which sends every element to its inverse is a homeomorphism and (ii) the map $G \times G \to G$ describing the group operation is continuous. A *measurable group* G is a group that is also a measurable space, such that the maps in (i) and (ii) above are measurable. Every topological group is also a measurable group, with respect to the measurable structure associated to the topology (cf. **2**–1).

If $\mathcal{H}$ is an equivalence relation on a set G, then the set of all equivalence classes is called the *quotient set* of G by $\mathcal{H}$ and is denoted by $G/\mathcal{H}$. The map $\pi: G \to G/\mathcal{H}$ which assigns to each $g \in G$ the equivalence class to which g belongs is called the *canonical map.* If G is a topological space, then $G/\mathcal{H}$ has a canonical topology: the *quotient topology* is the finest topology on $G/\mathcal{H}$ which makes the canonical map π continuous. If G is a measurable space, then $G/\mathcal{H}$ has a canonical measurable structure: the *quotient measurable structure* is the largest σ-algebra on $G/\mathcal{H}$ which makes π measurable.

Let $(G, \cdot)$ be a group with subgroup $(H, \cdot)$, and a an arbitrary element of G.

[1] For more background we suggest Gilbert (1976).

The set $Ha = \{ha \mid h \in H\}$ is a *right coset* of H in G. The set $aH = \{ah \mid h \in H\}$ is a *left coset* of H in G. The relation of belonging to the same left coset is an equivalence relation on G; similarly for right cosets. A subgroup $(H, \cdot)$ of a group $(G, \cdot)$ is called a *normal subgroup* of $(G, \cdot)$ if $g^{-1}hg \in H$ for all $g \in G$ and $h \in H$. If $(H, \cdot)$ is a normal subgroup of $(G, \cdot)$, the left cosets of H in G are the same as the right cosets of H in G. In this case the set of cosets $G/H = \{Hg \mid g \in G\}$ has a natural group structure induced by that of G, i.e., $(Hg_1) \cdot (Hg_2) = H(g_1 \cdot g_2)$.

If $(G, \cdot)$ and $(H, *)$ are two groups, the function $f: G \to H$ is called a *group morphism* or a *group homomorphism* if $f(a \cdot b) = f(a) * f(b)$ for all $a, b \in G$. A bijective group morphism is called a *group isomorphism*. If $f: G \to H$ is a group morphism, then the *kernel* of f, denoted by $\mathrm{Ker} f$, is the set of elements of G that are mapped by f to the identity of H; $\mathrm{Ker} f$ is a normal subgroup of G.

A group $(G, \cdot)$ *acts on the left* on the set M if (1) there is a function $\psi: G \times M \to M$ such that, letting $gm = \psi(g, m)$, we have $(g_1 g_2)m = g_1(g_2 m)$ for all $g_1, g_2 \in G, m \in M$, and (2) $\imath m = m$ if $\imath$ is the identity of G and $m \in M$. (G *acts on the right* if condition (1) is replaced by $\psi(g_1 g_2, m) = \psi(g_2, \psi(g_1, m))$; in this case we write $\psi(g, m) = mg$. All actions here are left actions unless otherwise stated.) If G acts on M, we say that M is a G-set. If M is a topological (respectively measurable) space, the action is said to be *continuous* (respectively *measurable*) if for all $g \in G$ the map $m \mapsto gm$ is a continuous (respectively measurable) map from M to M. The set of elements of G that fix $m \in M$, i.e., $\{g \in G \mid gm = m\}$, is called the *stabilizer* of m and is denoted Σ_m; each stabilizer is a subgroup of G. If each $m \in M$ is stabilized only by the identity $\imath$ of G, we say that G acts *faithfully* on M. G *acts transitively on* M if for every $m_1, m_2 \in M$ there exists $g \in G$ such that $gm_1 = m_2$. M is a *principal homogeneous space* for G if G acts both transitively and faithfully on M. The set of all images of an element $m \in M$ under the action of a group G is called the *orbit* of m under G, and is denoted by Gm; $Gm = \{gm \mid g \in G\}$. The orbits are the equivalence classes for an equivalence relation on M; two elements of M are in this relation precisely when they are in the same orbit. The quotient set for this relation is therefore the set of distinct orbits; it is denoted M/G.

Let G act measurably on M. A measure μ on M is called G-invariant if, for every measurable set A of M, $\mu(A) = \mu(gA)$ for any $g \in G$. If G acts on X, and $E \subset X$, then E is an *invariant subset* for the action if $GE = E$.

2. Definition of reflexive observer framework

We now begin to study "participator dynamics" or, more properly, "participator dynamical systems on reflexive observer frameworks." The phrase *reflexive observer framework* refers to a structure for the set $\mathcal{B}$ of objects of perception and for the configuration map $\Phi: \mathcal{B} \to X$ of an environment (4–4.4). In this chapter we introduce reflexive observer frameworks and the subclass of *symmetric observer frameworks*; we study this subclass because it is natural and mathematically tractable. Dynamics enters the picture in the next chapter. We will find that, in the context of this dynamics, the question of true perception can be treated in a principled manner; we discuss this in chapter eight. The dynamics underlies a general-purpose theory of interaction which is nondualistic and which employs a hierarchical analytic strategy (cf. 4–5). X_t will appear as one aspect of this dynamics.

We begin with an observer $O = (X, Y, E, S, \pi, \eta)$. We want to construct a model of an environment $(\mathcal{B}, \Phi)$ for O, as per 4–4. The nondualism of the model results, as stated before, from the assumption that *the objects of perception are observers*. We take $\mathcal{B}$ to be some set of observers whose X, Y, E and S are the same as that of O. Then Φ assigns to every such observer an element of X. A reflexive observer framework furnishes the relationship between an observer $B \in \mathcal{B}$ and the element $\Phi(B)$ as follows. There is given a map Π which assigns to each $e \in E$ a map from X to Y; thus for $e \in E$ we have

$$\Pi(e): X \to Y.$$

If $\Phi(B) = e \in E$, then we require that the perspective map of the observer B is $\Pi(e)$, so that in this case $B = (X, Y, E, S, \Pi(e), \eta)$ for some η. But if $\Phi(B) = x \notin E$, we require nothing. The word "reflexive" indicates that each $e \in E$ represents both a distinguished configuration and a set of observers which perceive the distinguished configurations of E—namely the set of those observers $B \in \mathcal{B}$ whose perspective is $\Pi(e)$. This set of observers is represented by the preobserver $(X, Y, E, S, \Pi(e))$.

Once this structure is in place, we notice that the original observer O plays no role other than to specify the X, Y, E and S. And for this purpose, any of the observers in $\mathcal{B}$ serve equally well. In fact, we think of a reflexive observer framework as providing an environment simultaneously for all the observers in $\mathcal{B}$; each of these observers has the same set of objects of perception, namely $\mathcal{B}$ itself. We now present these ideas formally.

Notation 2.1. Given two measurable spaces $(X, \mathcal{X})$ and $(Y, \mathcal{Y})$, we denote the measurable maps from X to Y by $\text{Hom}(X, Y)$.

Definition 2.2. Let $(X, \mathcal{X})$ and $(Y, \mathcal{Y})$ be fixed measurable spaces. Let $E \subset X$ and $S \subset Y$ be measurable subsets. A *reflexive observer framework on* X, Y, E, S is an injective map $\Pi : E \to \text{Hom}(X, Y)$ such that for each $e \in E$, $\Pi(e)$ is surjective, and $\Pi(e)(E) = S$.

Terminology 2.3. We denote a reflexive observer framework by

$$(X, Y, E, S, \Pi).$$

If Π has been fixed, we write $\pi_e = \Pi(e)$, so that we can use the notation

$$(X, Y, E, S, \pi_{\bullet})$$

to represent the framework in this case; the subscript "$\bullet$" represents a variable on E. In this way the reflexive family is displayed as a family of preobservers parametrized by E. X is called the *configuration space of the framework.* Y is called the *premise space of the framework.* E is called the *distinguished configurations of the framework.* S is called the *distinguished premises of the framework.* Sometimes we drop the word "observer" and use the expression *reflexive framework.*

Π will have, in general, some additional structure. If, for example, X and Y are topological spaces and all the maps π_e are continuous, then Π might be continuous for some suitable topology on the set of continuous maps from X to Y. However such restrictions do not belong in the general definition.

We give a concrete example of a reflexive framework at the end of this section (and in the next section we present classes of formal examples). We first make more explicit the connection between reflexive frameworks and environments.

As we have seen, a reflexive framework identifies each distinguished configuration $e \in E$ with a perspective. The notation $(X, Y, E, S, \pi_{\bullet})$ of 2.3 suggests another way to interpret reflexive frameworks. Suppose we begin with a set $\mathcal{B}$ of observers all of which have the same X, Y, E, S. $\mathcal{B}$ might be, for example, the set of *all* observers with these X, Y, E, and S (and with arbitrary perspective maps and conclusion kernels). Then if $e \in E$ is given, we can interpret the notation

(X, Y, E, S, π_e) to mean the subset of $\mathcal{B}$ consisting of all those observers whose perspective map is π_e for that particular e. If we want to identify $\mathcal{B}$ explicitly in this notation we write $(\mathcal{B}; X, Y, E, S, \pi_e)$ or just $\mathcal{B}_e$. The elements, if any, of this set $\mathcal{B}_e$ are individuated only by their conclusion kernels. Let $\mathcal{B}_E$ denote the subset of $\mathcal{B}$ consisting of those observers whose perspective map is one of the π_e's, so that

$$\mathcal{B}_E = \bigcup_{e \in E} \mathcal{B}_e. \tag{2.4}$$

Then $(X, Y, E, S, \pi_\bullet)$ denotes the partition of $\mathcal{B}_E$ into the sets $\mathcal{B}_e = (X, Y, E, S, \pi_e)$ for $e \in E$. If we must make $\mathcal{B}$ explicit we write $(\mathcal{B}; X, Y, E, S, \pi_\bullet)$ or just $\mathcal{B}_\bullet$. We summarize:

2.5. Let (X, Y, E, S, Π) be a reflexive framework. An alternate notation for the framework is $(X, Y, E, S, \pi_\bullet)$. Let also be given a set of observers $\mathcal{B}$, all having the same X, Y, E, and S. Then we can interpret the notation $\mathcal{B}_\bullet = (X, Y, E, S, \pi_\bullet)$ to mean the partition of the subset $\mathcal{B}_E$ of $\mathcal{B}$ into the sets $\mathcal{B}_e = (X, Y, E, S, \pi_e)$, $e \in E$. This context fixes a meaning for the preobserver (X, Y, E, S, π_e): it is a particular set of observers—namely $\mathcal{B}_e$.

We can now state formally the basic connection between reflexive frameworks and environments.

Definition 2.6. Let $(\mathcal{B}, \Phi)$ be the environment of an extended semantics for an observer $O = (X, Y, E, S, \pi, \eta)$, where $\mathcal{B}$ is a set of observers all having the same X, Y, E, and S as O, and where Φ is the configuration map of the extended semantics,

$$\Phi : \mathcal{B} \rightarrow X.$$

Let $(X, Y, E, S, \pi_\bullet)$ be a reflexive framework on X, Y, E, and S. Suppose that if $\Phi(B) = e \in E$ (i.e., if $B \in \mathcal{B}_e$) then π_e is the perspective of B. We then say that *the reflexive framework supports the environment of the extended semantics.*

In this case, each observer $B \in \mathcal{B}_E$ has its perspective determined by its configuration $\Phi(B)$. 2.4 becomes

$$\mathcal{B}_E = \Phi^{-1}(E), \tag{2.7}$$

indicating that $\mathcal{B}_E$ is the set of distinguished objects of perception (cf. 4–4.4). By contrast, there need be no relation between the perspective of an observer in $\mathcal{B} - \mathcal{B}_E$ and its configuration in $X - E$.

If a reflexive framework supports an environment $(\mathcal{B}, \Phi)$ then, with notation as above, we assume that the map

$$\Xi : \mathcal{C} \to X$$

is bijective, where $\mathcal{C}$ is the set of states of affairs for the semantics. Then the subsets $\mathcal{B}_e$ of $\mathcal{B}$ defined above play the role of the equivalence classes $\mathcal{B}_c$ of $\mathcal{B}$ associated, as in 4–4, to the distinguished states of affairs $c \in \mathcal{C}$; in fact $\mathcal{B}_c = \mathcal{B}_e$ when $\Xi(c) = e$.

Suppose that $O = (X, Y, E, S, \pi, \eta)$ is an observer, and $(R, \mathcal{B}, \Phi, X_t)$ is an extended semantics for O, where $\mathcal{B}$ is a set of observers with the same X, Y, E, S as O. Suppose that no reflexive framework is given at the outset, but that the map Φ has the following property: for each $e \in E$, all observers in $\Phi^{-1}(e)$ have the same perspective. Then we can construct a reflexive framework which supports the environment $(\mathcal{B}, \Phi)$: we simply construct the map Π which defines the framework by letting $\Pi(e)$ be the perspective of any observer $B \in \Phi^{-1}(e)$.

Terminology 2.8. If a reflexive framework supports an environment $(\mathcal{B}, \Phi)$, we call the elements of $\mathcal{B}$ the *observers in the framework*. We view $\mathcal{B}$ as the set of objects of perception for each observer in $\mathcal{B}$, and we take the given map $\Phi : \mathcal{B} \to X$ to be the configuration map for each observer in $\mathcal{B}$. If we are given a reflexive framework $(X, Y, E, S, \pi_\bullet)$ without specifying a particular environment which the framework supports, we still use the expression "observer in the framework" to refer to any observer having the same X, Y, E, S and having one of the π_e's for its perspective. In other words, an observer in the framework is any observer which completes a preobserver (X, Y, E, S, π_e) for some $e \in E$. We will sometimes use the expression "perspective in the framework" to refer to a point of E, i.e., we abuse language by identifying e with π_e.

This terminology emphasizes that a reflexive framework represents a family of observers that observe each other. This family can be taken to be the set $\mathcal{B}$ of any environment which is supported by the framework.

We illustrate the concept of reflexive framework with an example depicted in Figure 2.9. Here the configuration space X of the framework is the plane $\mathbf{R}^2$, a

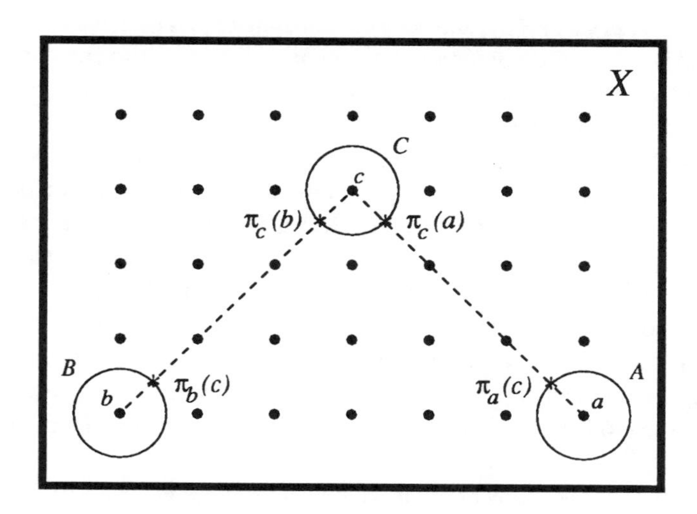

FIGURE 2.9. *A reflexive observer framework.*

portion of which is represented by the rectangle in the figure. The distinguished configuration set is the set E of points in the plane that have integer coordinates. A few such points are represented by dots inside the rectangle. The premise space Y is the unit circle, plus one point at the center of the circle (call it s_0). We view X and Y with the measurable structures associated to their topologies (c.f. **2**–1). The distinguished premise set S is s_0 together with the set of points on the unit circle in Y which correspond to angles having rational tangents. We view Y as a measurable space where $\mathcal{Y}$ is the σ-algebra generated by the standard Borel algebra on the unit circle, along with $\{s_0\}$.

Now to describe the framework, we must assign to each $e \in E$ a measurable function $\pi_e\colon X \to Y$ such that $\pi_e(E) = S$. We do this as follows. To each point e of E associate a unit circle centered at e. We think of these circles as translated, but not rotated, copies of the unit circle of Y. Let $x \in X, x \neq e$. Then $\pi_e(x)$ is the point where the line determined by e and x intersects the unit circle centered at e; since this circle is a copy of Y, we view $\pi_e(x)$ as a point of Y. We define $\pi_e(e) = s_0$ in Y. If $e \neq e'$, since both have integer coordinates the line joining them has rational slope, so that the point $\pi_e(e')$ on the circle represents an angle with rational tangent. It follows that $\pi_e(E) = S$ as desired.

Figure 2.9 shows this procedure for three points of E: a, b, and c. In particular it shows $\pi_a(c)$, $\pi_b(c)$, $\pi_c(a)$, and $\pi_c(b)$ on separate copies of Y which are depicted as centered at a, b, c. Each observer in the framework has its own copy of Y, at most one point of which "lights up" at any given instant. (However, when viewing Figure 2.9 the reader should realize that the circles representing these copies are drawn *inside* X only for convenience in visualizing the maps π_a, π_b, π_c.) For example, suppose that A, B, C are three observers in the framework whose perspectives are π_a, π_b, π_c respectively. Suppose, moreover, that at a particular instant t, B and C channel with each other. Then, as shown in Figure 2.9, at that instant the point $\pi_b(c)$ lights up on B's copy of Y and $\pi_c(b)$ on C's copy. The point $\pi_c(a)$ in the figure does not light up at time t in this case. The point $\pi_a(c)$ *may* light up at time t, but if so it is not due to a channeling between A and C, for an observer interacts with at most one object of perception at any instant. It would be due to a channeling of A with some other observer whose perspective corresponds to a point of X on the same line through a as c.

We will need one further definition, which provides the syntax for the discussion of interpretation kernels in the context of reflexive frameworks.

Definition 2.10. A family of kernels $\{\eta_e\}_{e \in E}$ is called a *family of interpretation kernels* for the reflexive framework $(X, Y, E, S, \pi_\bullet)$ if, for each $e \in E$, $(X, Y, E, S, \pi_e, \eta_e)$ is an observer.

A family of interpretation kernels is a way to associate a single observer to each perspective in the framework, i.e., the observer $(X, Y, E, S, \pi_e, \eta_e)$ is associated to the perspective π_e. Equivalently, it is a way to complete each preobserver (X, Y, E, S, π_e) (for $e \in E$) to an observer.

3. Channeling on reflexive frameworks

We now make precise the term "channeling" on a reflexive framework. Recall that, in the primitive semantics, channeling denotes the presentation of an observer with a premise from an undefined probabilistic source (4–2.2). In the extended semantics, we speak of an object of perception "channeling" to an observer (4–4.4); this means that a given channeling arises from an interaction of the observer with that object of perception. Let us consider an environment $(\mathcal{B}, \Phi)$ supported by a reflexive framework. We have a set $\mathcal{B}$ of observers—the observers in the framework—which is the set of objects of perception for each of its members. Now, according to the assumptions of extended semantics for an observer O (4–4.1), at each instant of time O participates in at most one channeling, implying that O interacts with but one of its objects of perception. For a given instant t, let $L \subset \mathcal{B}$ denote those observers in $\mathcal{B}$ which channel at time t. For any $B \in L$, let $\tilde{\chi}(B) \in L$ be the observer with which B channels; in view of the assumption just recalled, $\tilde{\chi}: L \to L$ is a well-defined function. B may channel to itself: $B = \tilde{\chi}(B)$ is permissible.

We make one further, and independent, assumption about channeling in this reflexive framework. This assumption supports a strategy which seeks to use direct interactions between observers as the foundation for an analysis of dynamics.

Assumption 3.1. Let $(\mathcal{B}, \Phi)$ be the environment of an extended semantics supported by a reflexive framework. With notation as above, let $A, B \in \mathcal{B}$. Suppose at time t that B channels to A, i.e., that B is the object of perception for A at that time. Then A also channels to B at time t, i.e., A is the object of perception for B.

This means that $\tilde{\chi}$, viewed as a map $\tilde{\chi}: L \to L$, has the property that $\tilde{\chi}^2 = \mathrm{Id}_L$ (the identity map on L); a map with this property is called an *involution* of L. We arrive at the following definition:

Definition 3.2. Let $(X, Y, E, S, \pi_{\bullet})$ be a reflexive framework that supports the environment $(\mathcal{B}, \Phi)$ (4–4.4).

(i) A $(\mathcal{B}, \Phi)$*-channeling on the framework* is a pair $(L, \tilde{\chi})$ consisting of a nonempty subset $L \subset \mathcal{B}$ and an involution $\tilde{\chi}: L \to L$. (When there is no danger of confusion about $\mathcal{B}$ and Φ we simply say "channeling on the framework.")

(ii) Such a channeling is *elementary* if there are at most two elements in L.

With the hypotheses and notation of Definition 3.2, let $A, B \in \mathcal{B}$ and suppose that at time t, A and B channel to each other, so that $A = \tilde{\chi}(B)$. Then $\pi_{\Phi(A)}$ and $\pi_{\Phi(B)}$ denote the perspectives of A and B respectively. Thus the premise for A's perceptual inference resulting from this channeling is

$$\pi_{\Phi(A)}(\Phi(B)),$$

and similarly the premise for B's perceptual inference is $\pi_{\Phi(B)}(\Phi(A))$. More generally, we can use the $\tilde{\chi}$-notation, and summarize as follows:

3.3. With the hypotheses and notation of 3.2, let $(L, \tilde{\chi})$ be a channeling, and let $A \in L$. Then A's premise resulting from this channeling is

$$\pi_{\Phi(A)}(\Phi(\tilde{\chi}(A))).$$

Terminology 3.4. Given a channeling $(L, \tilde{\chi})$, we denote

$$D = \bigcup_{A \in L \cap \mathcal{B}_B} \{A, \tilde{\chi}(A)\}, \qquad \chi = \tilde{\chi}|_D.$$

(χ is the restriction of $\tilde{\chi}$ to D.) We call the channeling (D, χ) the *distinguished part* of $(L, \tilde{\chi})$.

4. Formal examples of reflexive frameworks

This section presents formal examples of reflexive frameworks. The examples do not represent a broad spectrum of types of frameworks, nor do they display an obvious relevance to everyday perception. Rather, they have been chosen to direct the exposition toward the particular subclass of *symmetric frameworks.* These we develop in the next section; they are the frameworks of primary interest in this book. In section six we develop in detail a perceptual example.

Example 4.1. Let G be a measurable group (see 5–1), and E and H measurable subgroups of G. Denote by $Y = G/H$ the set of left H-cosets with its quotient measurable structure; H need not be normal. Let $\pi: G \to G/H$ be the canonical map, and let $S = \pi(E) = EH/H$. (EH denotes the set $\{eh \mid h \in H \text{ and } e \in E\}$, so that EH/H is the set of left cosets of H by elements of E.) Define $\Pi: E \to \mathrm{Hom}(G, G/H)$ as follows: for each $e \in E$, $\Pi(e)$ is the map $\pi_e: G \to G/H$ given by $\pi_e(g) = \pi(ge^{-1})$. We then have $\pi_e(E) = \pi(Ee^{-1}) = \pi(E) = S$ for all e (since E is a group), as required by the definition of a reflexive framework. For each $e \in E$, $\pi_e^{-1}(S) = \pi^{-1}(S) = EH$.

$$\begin{array}{ccccc} & E & \subset & G & = X \\ & \downarrow{\scriptstyle \pi_e|_E} & & \downarrow{\scriptstyle \pi_e} & \\ S = & HE/H & \subset & G/H & = Y \end{array}$$

In this particular reflexive framework the set of fibres $\{\pi_e^{-1}(y) \mid y \in Y\}$ is independent of e (as a set of subsets of X); in fact for each e the fibres are the left H-cosets in X. To change e is simply to permute the fibres.

Example 4.2. This example generalizes the previous one. Again let G be a measurable group. But now let H be an arbitrary group which acts measurably on G on the right. (Thus the elements of H correspond to bijective, bimeasurable maps from G to itself, maps which are not necessarily group homomorphisms.)

Let G/H denote the orbits in G for the action of H, and $\pi: G \to G/H$ the canonical map. Let E be a measurable subgroup of G, and let EH/H denote the subset of G/H consisting of those orbits which contain an element of E. For $e \in E$, define $\pi_e(g)$ to be $\pi(ge^{-1}) = H(ge^{-1})$, i.e., the H-orbit on G containing ge^{-1}. Let $X = G$, $Y = G/H$, E the given subgroup of G, $S = EH/H$, and π_e as defined above.

$$\begin{array}{ccccc} & E & \subset & X & = G \\ & \downarrow{\scriptstyle \pi|_E} & & \downarrow{\scriptstyle \pi} & \\ EH/H = & S & \subset & Y & = G/H \end{array}$$

In the case where the H in this example is a subgroup of G, acting on G by left translation, we simply recover the previous Example 4.1. However this case accounts for only a very small class of "natural" measurable actions of one group on another. In fact, the example illustrated in Figure 2.9 is of the type of 4.2, but not 4.1. In the next example we present the n-dimensional generalization of the one in Figure 2.9. In the general situation of Example 4.2 it is not true (as it was in Example 4.1) that all the maps π_e for $e \in E$ have the same set of fibres over S. This is evident from the next example.

Example 4.3. With the notation of 4.1, let $X = G = (\mathbf{R}^n, +)$ be the n-dimensional vector group; "+" denotes vector addition. Let $H = (\mathbf{R}_+, \text{multiplication})$, i.e., H is the multiplicative group of positive real numbers acting by dilation (scalar multiplication) on $\mathbf{R}^n$. Then $Y = G/H$ is the set of half-rays emanating from the origin, together with one point s_0 which is the orbit consisting of the origin itself. Since the set of half-rays is naturally identified with the $(n-1)$-dimensional unit sphere $\mathbf{S}^{n-1}$ centered at the origin in $\mathbf{R}^n$, we have $Y = G/H = \mathbf{S}^{n-1} \cup \{s_0\}$.

Now let $E = (\mathbf{Z}^n, +)$, the subgroup of points with integer coordinates, or let $E = (\mathbf{Q}^n, +)$, the subgroup of points with rational coordinates. In either case the image by π of E in Y is the same: it is the set consisting of the point s_0 together with all points on $\mathbf{S}^{n-1}$ with the property that the ratio of any pair of coordinates is rational. This set is denoted $\mathbf{S}_r^{n-1}$ in the following diagram.

$$\begin{array}{ccccccc} \mathbf{Q}^n \text{ or } \mathbf{Z}^n = & E & \subset & X & = \mathbf{R}^n \\ & \downarrow{\scriptstyle \pi_e|_E} & & \downarrow{\scriptstyle \pi_e} & \\ \mathbf{S}_r^{n-1} = & S & \subset & Y & = \mathbf{S}^{n-1} \cup \{s_0\} \end{array}$$

For $e \in \mathbf{R}^n = X$ we may conceptualize π_e as follows: translate the unit sphere $\mathbf{S}^{n-1}$ (originally centered at the origin) to e. For any $v \in \mathbf{R}^n$, if $v \neq e$ take the ray from e to v, and intersect it with this translated $\mathbf{S}^{n-1}$ to obtain $\pi_e(v)$. Define $\pi_e(e) = s_0$.

Example 4.4. Here is a further generalization of Example 4.2 in which the constructions can be described without substantial change in the syntax. In its generality this example contains all the others of this section. Again, let G be a measurable group. We suppose that G has a partition in measurable subsets; denote this partition as well as the corresponding equivalence relation by $\mathcal{H}$. Let $Y = G/\mathcal{H}$ and let $\pi: G \to Y$ be the canonical map. We take for the σ-algebra $\mathcal{Y}$ the quotient measurable structure. Let J be a measurable subgroup of G with the property that $\pi(J) \subset Y$ is measurable. We set $S = \pi(J)$.

Moreover, let us assume that we have a measurable space X on which G acts measurably (on the left). Let x_0 be a distinguished point of X, and let $E = Jx_0 \subset X$. We also assume the following:

(i) G acts transitively on X.

(ii) Let $e \in E$, and $g, g' \in G$. If $ge = g'e$ then g, g' are in the same H-class in G.

From this we now describe a reflexive framework on X, Y, E, S. (i) and (ii) insure that we can define π_e in a manner consistent with the previous examples. In fact, for $e \in E$ and $x \in X$, let xe^{-1} denote any element $g \in G$ such that $ge = x$. Such a

g exists because of (i). Then define $\pi_e(x) = \pi(xe^{-1})$. Assumption (ii) means that this definition of $\pi_e(x)$ is independent of the choice of xe^{-1}, i.e., π_e is well defined. To see that $\pi_e(E) = S$ for all e, let $e_1 \in E$, and suppose that $e = jx_0$, $e_1 = kx_0$, where $j, k \in J$. kj^{-1} is then one choice for e_1e^{-1}, so

$$\pi_e(e_1) = \pi(e_1e^{-1}) = \pi(kj^{-1}) \in \pi(J) = S.$$

Moreover it is clear that as e_1 runs over E, kj^{-1} runs over J, so that all elements of S are represented.

$$\begin{array}{ccccc} E = & Jx_0 & \subset & X & \\ & \downarrow \pi_e|_E & & \downarrow \pi_e & \\ S = & \pi(J) & \subset & G/H & = Y \end{array}$$

Let Σ_e denote the *stabilizer* of e (i.e., the subgroup of G which leaves e fixed). In view of (i) above we may identify X with G/Σ_e; under this identification $x \in X$ corresponds to the coset $g\Sigma_e$ where $g \in G$ is any element such that $ge = x$. For $g, g' \in G$, $ge = g'e$ if and only if g and g' are in the same left coset of Σ_e. Thus (ii) above is equivalent to the assertion that every coset of Σ_e is contained in one H-class, or equivalently that each H-class is a union of cosets of Σ_e. We can then associate to each $e \in E$ a natural map

$$X = G/\Sigma_e \to G/H = Y$$

as follows. If $x \in X$ with $x = ge$, x is identified as above with $g\Sigma_e$ in G/Σ_e which is then mapped to the element of G/H which represents the H-class containing $g\Sigma_e$. But, since g here is one choice for xe^{-1}, this map from X to G/H is just our π_e defined above.

Example 4.4 generalizes 4.2 in two respects. First, the equivalence relation H on G which gives the canonical map π need not arise from the orbits of a group action. Secondly, the action of G on X need not be faithful: for example, whereas in 4.2 $X = G$, here we can have $X = G/\Sigma$ where Σ is a non-normal subgroup of G. However the action of G on X still must be transitive.

Example 4.5. We show how to get a class of generalizations of Example 4.1, where H is still a subgroup of G acting by translation, but now X is a measurable, transitive G-set for which the action is not faithful. This means that X may be identified with G/Σ, the left cosets of the stabilizer Σ of some fixed $x_0 \in X$ (as we saw in Example

4.4). We assume that the measurable structure of X is given by the quotient structure of G/Σ.

As in 4.1, let $Y = G/H$. We assume

1. $\Sigma \subset H$

and by so doing get a canonical surjective (and measurable) map $\pi: X \to Y$ given by $\pi(g\Sigma) = gH$.

Let J be a measurable subgroup of G and set $E = Jx_0$. We think of E as $J\Sigma/\Sigma$: the left cosets of Σ by J. Then the map π restricts to $\pi|_E: J\Sigma/\Sigma \to JH/H$. We set $S = \pi(E) = JH/H$.

Example 4.4 tells us that we can define the map Π of a reflexive framework if its assumption (ii) is satisfied: $g\Sigma_e \subset gH$ for all $e \in E$ and $g \in G$. If $e \in E$, then $e = jx_0$ for some $j \in J$ and $\Sigma_e = j\Sigma j^{-1}$. We therefore impose another condition.

2. For all $j \in J, j\Sigma j^{-1} \subset H$.

(For example, J may be contained in the normalizer of Σ, i.e., $j\Sigma j^{-1} = \Sigma$, or j may be contained in the normalizer of H.) We have

$$\begin{array}{ccccc} E = Jx_0 = & J\Sigma/\Sigma & \subset & G/\Sigma & = X \\ & \downarrow{\scriptstyle \pi|_E} & & \downarrow{\scriptstyle \pi} & \\ S = & JH/H & \subset & G/H & = Y \end{array}$$

The maps π_e are well-defined as follows: if $e = j\Sigma$ and $x = g\Sigma$ (i.e., $e = jx_0$, $x = gx_0$), then

$$\pi_e(x) = (gj^{-1})H.$$

If $\Sigma = \{\imath\}$ this example reduces to 4.1, and in any case it shares with 4.1 the property that all the maps π_e, $e \in E$, have the same set of fibres, namely the cosets of H (mod Σ). In order that we get a nontrivial situation, we must assume

3. $J \neq \Sigma$ (otherwise E is a singleton),
   $J \neq G$ (otherwise $E = X$ and $S = Y$),
   $J \not\subset H$ (otherwise S is a singleton).

5. Symmetric observer frameworks

All of our examples of reflexive frameworks have involved groups, although this is certainly not required by Definition 2.2. In every example in section three, X is a G-set for some group G in such a way that E is a J-set for a subgroup J of G;

the actions are transitive. Moreover, in each case the maps π_e in the framework are deduced "by translation" from some fixed measurable map $\pi: G \to Y = G/\mathcal{H}, \mathcal{H}$ being an equivalence relation on G. In fact $\pi_e(x) = \pi(xe^{-1})$, where xe^{-1} denotes any element of G such that $(xe^{-1})e = x$. In other words xe^{-1} is the difference between x and e measured in terms of G. This means (using the terminology of 2.8) that the observations by an observer O with perspective e in the framework depend only on the structure of X *relative to* e (in the sense of the action of G.)

Consider Example 4.4. It is not misleading to think of each $e \in E$ as the center of a "frame for observation" which consists of the structure (G, Y, J, S, π) "translated" to e, where translation here refers to the action of G. This frame provides the syntax for the perceptual representations of any observer in the framework *relative to* O; the notion "relative" is grounded in the G-space structure of X. This is the basis for a symmetric theory of observer interaction; the symmetry in question is that of the group G. When we present the dynamics in the subsequent chapters we focus on this symmetric setting. One can certainly construct examples of reflexive observer frameworks which are not of this type and then study interaction dynamics on them in depth, but we will not do so explicitly in this book.

Definition 5.1. A *symmetric observer framework* is a reflexive observer framework $(X, Y, E, S, \pi_\bullet)$ for which there exists a measurable group G, a measurable subgroup $J \subset G$, and a measurable surjective map $\pi: G \to Y$ satisfying two requirements:

(i) G acts transitively and measurably on X, inducing a transitive action of J on E (which is automatically measurable).

(ii) For all $e \in E$ and $x \in X$, $\pi_e(x) = \pi(g)$, where g is *any* element in G such that $ge = x$ (i.e., $g =$ "xe^{-1}.")

The requirements on the maps $\pi_e: X \to Y$ in a reflexive framework, namely that π_e is surjective and $\pi_e(E) = S$, impose nontrivial conditions on the map π. However, the best way to understand the whole definition is to realize the following:

Proposition 5.2. The definition of symmetric observer framework is equivalent to the Example 4.4 of the previous section.

Proof. The fibres of the map π of 5.1 form a partition of G. The relation of joint membership in a fibre is an equivalence relation: call it $\mathcal{H}$. Then Y is identified with $G/\mathcal{H}$. Since the action of J on E is transitive, E is identified with Je_0 for any $e_0 \in E$. It remains to verify (ii) of 4.4, but this is implicit in (ii) of 5.1. ∎

Terminology 5.3. We will use the notation (X, Y, E, S, G, J, π) for a symmetric observer framework; the notation π_e will refer to the maps from X to Y defined in terms of π as in (ii) of the definition. The structure (G, Y, J, S, π) is called the *fundamental frame* of the framework. π is the *fundamental map*, G and J are the *configuration group* and the *distinguished subgroup* respectively; we retain our original terminology for X, Y, E, S, namely *configuration space, premise space, distinguished configurations, distinguished premises.* We will frequently use the informal terminology "symmetric framework" rather than "symmetric observer framework."

In Definition 5.1 it is necessary only for group actions to exist at the level of X and E, not Y and S. Furthermore, the fundamental map $\pi: G \to Y$ need not arise in any particular group-theoretic way. Y can be $G/\mathcal{H}$ for *any* equivalence relation $\mathcal{H}$ on G for which the notation "$\pi(xe^{-1})$" makes sense (so that the π_e's are well-defined by (ii) of 5.1). As we have seen in 4.4, this is tantamount to saying that for all $e \in E$ and $g \in G$, $g\Sigma_e$ is contained in a single $\mathcal{H}$ equivalence class. (The equivalence relation $\mathcal{H}$ here is just the set of fibres of π.)

An important special case is when X is a *principal homogeneous space* for G. This means that G acts faithfully as well as transitively on X; in other words, all the stabilizers Σ_x are trivial. In this case, given any $x \in X$ we can identify X with a copy of G "centered at x," i.e., the element $g \in G$ is identified with $gx \in X$. Moreover when $x = e \in E$, this identification of X with G also identifies E with J. When X is a principal homogeneous G space, then for any x and e in X the element xe^{-1} is uniquely determined. In this case the condition (ii) in Definition 5.1 does not impose any requirements on π. We therefore have

5.4. Let G be a measurable group and $J \subset G$ a measurable subgroup. Let X be a principal homogeneous space for G on which the action of G is measurable. Suppose $E \subset X$ is a measurable J-invariant subset (so that the G-principal homogeneous structure of X induces a J-principal homogeneous structure for E). Let Y be a measurable space and $\pi: G \to Y$ be *any* measurable, surjective function; this is equivalent to saying that $Y = G/\mathcal{H}$ where $\mathcal{H}$ is an equivalence relation on G for which the equivalence classes are measurable subsets of G. Let $S = \pi(J)$. Then (X, Y, E, S, G, J, π) is a symmetric observer framework. For each $e \in E$ we define $\pi_e: X \to Y$ by $\pi_e(x) = \pi(xe^{-1})$, where xe^{-1} denotes the *unique* element $g \in G$ such that $ge = x$. We call these "principal homogeneous symmetric frameworks," or “principal frameworks” for short.

Example 5.5. This is the same as Example 4.3, where we now make explicit its structure as a principal framework: Let $G = (\mathbf{R}^n, +)$, $J = (\mathbf{Z}^n, +) \subset G$. Let $X = \mathbf{R}^n$ and $E = \mathbf{Z}^n$. We think of G acting on X by translation; it is obvious that X is principal homogenous for this action and that E is J-invariant. (In 4.3 we identified G with X at the outset, so that E is itself a subgroup of G and there is no need to introduce J. However here we are making the distinction in principle between G and X; the point is that while one can always identify a group G with a principal homogeneous G-space X, the identification is not canonical.) Let $Y = \mathbf{S}^{n-1} \cup \{s_0\}$, where $\mathbf{S}^{n-1}$ denotes the $n-1$-dimensional sphere and s_0 is a point (which we can visualize at the center of the sphere). We now define the map π. To do this, let $e_0 \in E$ denote the the origin in G. Identify the $\mathbf{S}^{n-1}$ in Y with the unit sphere centered at e_0. With this identification, for any $x \in X, x \neq e_0$, let $\pi(x)$ be the point of Y which is the intersection of $\mathbf{S}^{n-1}$ with the line joining e_0 and x. Let $\pi(e_0) = s_0$. It is evident that the maps π_e in 4.3 can be defined in terms of this π by the formula $\pi_e(x) = \pi(x - e)$ (where we use the additive notation “$x - e$” instead of xe^{-1}).

Finally, we elaborate the notion of a family of interpretation kernels (2.10) in the special case of symmetric frameworks.

Definition 5.6. A family $\{\eta_e\}_{e \in E}$ of interpretation kernels for the symmetric observer framework (X, Y, E, S, G, J, π) is said to be *symmetric* if there exists a markovian kernel $\eta: S \times \mathcal{J} \to [0, 1]$ such that for all $e \in E$, $s \in S$ and $\gamma \in \mathcal{E}$,

$$\eta(s, \pi^{-1}\{s\} \cap J) = 1,$$

and $$\eta_e(s, \Gamma) = \eta(s, \Gamma e^{-1}).$$

η is then called the *fundamental kernel* of the family η_e.

One way a family can be symmetric is as follows. Suppose we are given a symmetric observer framework (X, Y, E, S, G, J, π) and a measure ν on J. Since J acts transitively on E, given any $e \in E$ we get a surjective map $c_e: J \to E$ by sending $\imath$ to e. ($\imath$ denotes the identity element of J.) c_e identifies E with the quotient space $J/\Sigma_e \cap J$, where Σ_e is the stabilizer of e in G. Let $\nu_e = (c_e)_*(\nu)$; this is the measure ν transported to E by "centering a copy of J at e."

Terminology 5.7. With the hypotheses and notation of the previous paragraph, if ν is a measure on J, the family of measures ν_e on E is called the *symmetric family of measures associated to* ν; ν is called the *fundamental measure of the family.* Concretely, if $\Gamma \in \mathcal{E}$, then $\nu_e(\Gamma) = \nu(c_e^{-1}(\Gamma)) = \nu\{j \in J \mid je \in \Gamma\}$.

Now given a probability measure ν, and its associated symmetric family $\{\nu_e\}$, we can define a family of kernels $\eta_e\colon S \times \mathcal{E} \to [0, 1]$ which are the rcpd's of the ν_e, i.e., we can let

$$\eta_e(s, \Gamma) = m_{\pi_e}^{\nu_e}(s, \Gamma)$$

(notation as in **2–1**). Another way to describe this family of kernels is as follows: Let $\eta = m_{\pi|_J}^{\nu}$, where $\pi|_J$ is the fundamental map of our symmetric framework restricted to the subgroup J of G.

$$\begin{array}{ccc} \nu & J & m_{\pi|_J}^{\nu}\colon S \times \mathcal{J} \to \mathbf{R} \\ & \big\downarrow \pi|_J & \mathcal{J} = \text{ the Borel sets of } J. \\ & S & \end{array}$$

We have the diagram

$$\begin{array}{ccccc} \nu,\ \eta & J & \xrightarrow{c_e} & E & \nu_e,\ \eta_e \\ & \pi|_J \searrow & & \swarrow \pi_e|_E & \\ & & S & & \end{array}$$

which commutes (i.e., $\pi|_J = \pi_e|_E \circ c_e$) by definition of the π_e. From this and the fact that $\nu_e = (c_e)_*(\nu)$, it follows from the meaning of rcpd that for $\Gamma \in \mathcal{E}$ and $s \in S$, $\eta_e(s, \Gamma) = \eta(s, c_e^{-1}(\Gamma))$. Note that $c_e^{-1}(\Gamma) = \{j \in J \mid je \in \Gamma\}$; so it is consistent with our previous notation to write $c_e^{-1}(\Gamma) = \Gamma e^{-1}$.

Notation 5.8. Given a symmetric family of kernels $\{\eta_e\}$ (respectively, measures $\{\nu_e\}$), then η (respectively, ν) will always denote the fundamental kernel (respectively, measure).

Note that the measure ν never appears in the Definition 5.6; intuitively only its rcpd appears, in the form of the fundamental kernel η. Thus in order to determine ν we would need to know the measure $\pi_*\nu$ on S. The precise statement is

5.9. A symmetric family η_e of interpretation kernels, together with a measure λ on S, uniquely determine a symmetric family of measures ν_e on E (and conversely) via the relation:

$$\eta = m^{\nu}_{\pi|_J}, \qquad \lambda = (\pi|_J)_*(\nu).$$

The definition of symmetric framework expresses the role of groups in creating a theory of observer interactions which permits "relativization." The reflexive frameworks we study in this book are primarily principal frameworks. These include the framework of instantaneous rotation observers presented in the next section, the frameworks for which we develop the theory of true perception in chapter eight, those employed in the investigation of hierarchical perceptual organization in chapter nine, and the frameworks which arise in our discussion of the applications of observer theory to physics in chapter ten. However, the general theory of participator dynamics developed in chapter seven is not restricted to the principal homogeneous case.

6. Example: Instantaneous rotation

We now study one example of the visual perception of structure in three dimensions given image motion in two dimensions, namely the perception of rigid, fixed-axis motion from a premise consisting of two views of $n+1$ points. For this purpose n can be any integer ≥ 3. We think of these views as occurring in successive instants of some underlying discrete time.

Given $n+1$ points moving arbitrarily in $\mathbf{R}^3$, let $(P_0, P_1, \ldots, P_n)$ and $(Q_0, Q_1, \ldots, Q_n)$ be their positions at two successive instants of time. Let us assume that the viewer is using a moving coordinate system in which $P_0 = Q_0 = (0,0,0)$. Then this data (viz., the P_i's and Q_i's) is equivalent to the array $\mathbf{a} = (\mathbf{a}_{11}, \mathbf{a}_{21}, \ldots, \mathbf{a}_{n1}; \mathbf{a}_{12}, \mathbf{a}_{22}, \ldots, \mathbf{a}_{n2})$ of $2n$ vectors in $\mathbf{R}^3$, where $\mathbf{a}_{i1} = P_i - P_0$, $\mathbf{a}_{i2} = Q_i - Q_0$, $i = 1, \ldots, n$. To say that $Q_0, Q_1, \ldots, Q_n$ are obtained from $P_0, P_1, \ldots, P_n$ by a rigid motion of $\mathbf{R}^3$ is equivalent to saying that $\mathbf{a}_{12} \ldots \mathbf{a}_{n2}$ are obtained from $\mathbf{a}_{11} \ldots \mathbf{a}_{n1}$ by a rotation about an axis through the origin. We call this an *instantaneous rotation* since two successive positions of an object in discrete time corresponds to instantaneous motion. Thus to infer an arbitrary rigid motion of $n+1$ points from two views is the same thing as inferring an instantaneous rotation of n vectors from two views.

We will define a symmetric framework $\boldsymbol{\Theta} = (X, Y, E, S, G, J, \pi)$ in which the observers are instantaneous rotation observers. It turns out that in order to get the group structure here, the observer must utilize configurations which are *pairs* $(\mathcal{A}, \mathbf{a})$, where $\mathbf{a}$ is a $2n$-tuple of vectors in $\mathbf{R}^3$ as above, and $\mathcal{A}$ is a "reference axis":

Terminology 6.1. An *axis* in $\mathbf{R}^3$ is an oriented line through the origin, i.e., a line with its positive direction specified. We will denote the set of such axes by $\mathbf{A}$.

The set $\mathbf{A}$ of axes corresponds to the set of points on the unit sphere $\mathbf{S}^2$ centered at the origin: each such point determines a line through the origin, whose positive direction is taken to be the direction from the origin to the point.

The axis-body configuration $(\mathcal{A}, \mathbf{a})$ represents the motion

$$\mathbf{a}_{11} \ldots \mathbf{a}_{n1} \longrightarrow \mathbf{a}_{12} \ldots \mathbf{a}_{n2}$$

"referred" to the axis $\mathcal{A}$. Since we do not detect rotational motion of points on the axis itself, we consider only those axis-body configurations $(\mathcal{A}, \mathbf{a})$ such that none of the the vectors $\mathbf{a}_{11}, \ldots, \mathbf{a}_{n2}$ lie on the line through $\mathcal{A}$. By an abuse of notation, we express this assumption simply by $\mathbf{a} \notin \mathcal{A}$. Let

$$X = \{(\mathcal{A}, \mathbf{a}) \mid \mathcal{A} \in \mathbf{A}, \mathbf{a} \in (\mathbf{R}^3)^{2n}, \mathbf{a} \notin \mathcal{A}\}. \tag{6.2}$$

X is the configuration space of our framework $\boldsymbol{\Theta}$. Explicitly,

$$X = \left\{(\mathcal{A}; \mathbf{a}_{11}, \ldots, \mathbf{a}_{n1}; \mathbf{a}_{12}, \ldots, \mathbf{a}_{n2}) \mid \mathcal{A} \in \mathbf{A}, \mathbf{a}_{ij} \in \mathbf{R}^3, \mathbf{a}_{ij} \notin \mathcal{A}\right\}. \tag{6.3}$$

Let Y be the set of ordered pairs of n-tuples of vectors in $\mathbf{R}^2$, so that

$$Y = (\mathbf{R}^2)^{2n}.$$

We denote the elements of Y explicitly by

$$Y = \left\{(\mathbf{b}_{11}, \ldots, \mathbf{b}_{n1}; \mathbf{b}_{12}, \ldots, \mathbf{b}_{n2}) \mid \mathbf{b}_{ij} \in \mathbf{R}^2\right\}. \tag{6.4}$$

Let us fix a coordinate system, say (x, y, z) on $\mathbf{R}^3$. Let

$$p: X \to Y$$

be the map which forgets the axis $\mathcal{A}$, and which associates to each of the vectors $\mathbf{a}_{ij} \in \mathbf{R}^3$ its projection onto the (x, y)-plane viewed as a copy of $\mathbf{R}^2$. Thus

$$p(\mathcal{A}; \mathbf{a}_{11}, \ldots, \mathbf{a}_{n1}; \mathbf{a}_{12}, \ldots, \mathbf{a}_{n2}) = (\mathbf{b}_{11}, \ldots, \mathbf{b}_{n1}; \mathbf{b}_{12}, \ldots, \mathbf{b}_{n2}),$$

where

$$\mathbf{a}_{ij} = (x_{ij}, y_{ij}, z_{ij}), \quad \mathbf{b}_{ij} = (x_{ij}, y_{ij}). \tag{6.5}$$

We will see below how to define the fundamental map π of our framework in terms of this p.

Let E be the set of those elements of X in which the two n-tuples of vectors $(\mathbf{a}_{11}, \ldots, \mathbf{a}_{n1})$ and $(\mathbf{a}_{12}, \ldots, \mathbf{a}_{n2})$ of $\mathbf{R}^3$ are related by a rotation of $\mathbf{R}^3$ about the given axis $\mathcal{A}$. Thus

$$E = \{(\mathcal{A}; \mathbf{a}_{11}, \ldots, \mathbf{a}_{n1}; \mathbf{a}_{12}, \ldots, \mathbf{a}_{n2}) \in X \,|\, \sigma(\mathbf{a}_{i1}) = \mathbf{a}_{i2}; 1 \leq i \leq n; \text{ where } \sigma \in \mathrm{SO}(3, \mathbf{R}) \text{ is a rotation about } \mathcal{A}\}. \tag{6.6}$$

Remark 6.7. For $n \geq 3$, (Lebesgue) almost all n-tuples $(\mathbf{a}_{11}, \ldots, \mathbf{a}_{n1})$ of points of $\mathbf{R}^3$ do not lie in any proper linear subspace of $\mathbf{R}^3$. Since the rotation σ in 6.6 is a linear map it is therefore uniquely determined by where it sends these $\mathbf{a}_{ij}$. Moreover, the axis of the rotation σ is uniquely determined up to orientation. We conclude: For almost all points of E the σ in 6.6 is uniquely determined. Moreover, for almost all points $e = (\mathcal{A}, \mathbf{a}) \in E$ (where $\mathcal{A} \in \mathbf{A}$ and $\mathbf{a} \in (\mathbf{R}^3)^{2n}$) there is exactly one other point $e' = (\mathcal{A}', \mathbf{a}') \in E$ such that $\mathbf{a} = \mathbf{a}'$. In that case $\mathcal{A}$ and $\mathcal{A}'$ differ only in their orientation.

To recapitulate, we can think of X as the set of configurations which correspond to two successive positions of n vectors moving arbitrarily in $\mathbf{R}^3$, together with a choice of reference axis $\mathcal{A}$; "successive" refers to some particular discrete time scale. We will call such a configuration an "axis-referenced instantaneous motion of n vectors in $\mathbf{R}^3$," or just an "instantaneous motion" for short. Then E consists of those instantaneous motions which are in fact (rigid) rotations about their respective reference axes. Finally, we let

$$S = p(E) \subset Y. \tag{6.8}$$

We now have a preobserver (X, Y, E, S, p). For this preobserver, the two n-tuples of vectors in $\mathbf{R}^2$, which comprise a premise $y \in Y$, are interpreted as two successive two-dimensional projections via p of $n+1$ fixed feature points on an object moving in three dimensions. Each projection is a "view" of the object; the two n-tuples in a premise y represent the images on the observer's "retina" resulting from the two views. In other words, the interpretation of the preobserver is that the premise $y \in Y$ arises from some instantaneous motion $x \in X$ such that $p(x) = y$. (Strictly speaking there is no interpretation unless the premise y is in S. Furthermore it is observers—not preobservers—that make interpretations.)

Each point x of X includes a reference axis $\mathcal{A}$ as part of the motion it represents, even though for general points of X this motion is not a fixed-axis motion, much less a rigid fixed-axis motion about $\mathcal{A}$. Only when $p(x) = y$ is in S is it possible to infer that the instantaneous motion being viewed is a rigid rotation about its reference axis; the interpretations consistent with this inference correspond to configurations x in $p^{-1}(y) \cap E$. Is it necessary to include the reference axis as part of the configuration? Not if we simply want to describe a single instantaneous rotation observer. However it is necessary in order define the group actions of a symmetric framework. Moreover it seems clear that one's perception, when one is presented with the appropriate displays, includes a direction of rotation; this is equivalent mathematically to choosing an orientation for the axis.

For the sake of intuition, we state without proof some facts about the geometry of (X, Y, E, S, π). Details may be found in Bennett et al. (1989).

6.9. S is contained in the solution set in $Y = (\mathbf{R}^2)^{2n}$ of a family of polynomial equations (in $4n$ variables). The dimension of S is $3n+2$. Thus if μ_Y denotes Lebesgue measure on Y, $\mu_Y(S) = 0$. (This implies by **2**–3.3 that the preobserver (X, Y, E, S, p) is ideal.) The dimension of E is $3n+3$. For almost all $s \in S$, $p^{-1}(s) \cap E$ is a 1-dimensional manifold. This manifold has four connected components, corresponding to the two types of "reflections" which act on the fibre: the first is the reversal of orientation of the reference axis $\mathcal{A}$ (but leaving the points in the configuration fixed) and the second is a reflection of the entire structure about the image plane.

Thus, up to choice of orientation of the reference axis and reflection in the image plane, every distinguished premise s is compatible with a one-parameter family of instantaneous-rotation interpretations. Two such interpretations for a given premise are illustrated in Figure 6.9.1. In the figure, each interpretation is represented by a system of n ellipses with the same eccentricity; the ith ellipse contains the image vectors $\mathbf{b}_{1i}$ and $\mathbf{b}_{2i}$, $i = 1, \ldots, n$. The minor axes of the ellipses in each system lie on the same line through the origin, namely the projection into the image plane of the actual axis of rotation of the corresponding interpretation. In the figure the system of ellipses for one interpretation is drawn with solid lines, and for the other interpretation with dotted lines. Note that the projected axis of rotation is the same (M) for the two interpretations. This holds true in general: For any $s \in S$, the axes of all of the distinguished configurations compatible with s project to the same line in the image plane.

Since we have defined X, Y, E and S, in order to describe the symmetric framework Θ we need to define the groups G and J and to define their actions on X and E. We also need to define the fundamental map π. For these purposes we give an alternate description of X and E in terms of which the group actions can be clearly expressed. We represent each element $x \in X$ in the form

$$x = \begin{pmatrix} \mathcal{A} & \mathbf{v}, c_{21}, \ldots, c_{n1} & h_{11}, \ldots, h_{n1} & l_{11}, \ldots, l_{n1} \\ & c_{12}, c_{22}, \ldots, c_{n2} & h_{12}, \ldots, h_{n2} & l_{12}, \ldots, l_{n2} \end{pmatrix} \tag{6.10}$$

where we have fixed a coordinate system in $\mathbf{R}^3$, and where

$\mathcal{A}$ is an oriented line through the origin in this coordinate system, i.e., an axis;
$\mathbf{v}$ is a unit vector at the origin, perpendicular to $\mathcal{A}$;
c_{ji} are angles with $0 \leq c_{ji} < 2\pi$;
h_{ji} are arbitrary real numbers; and
l_{ji} are strictly positive real numbers.

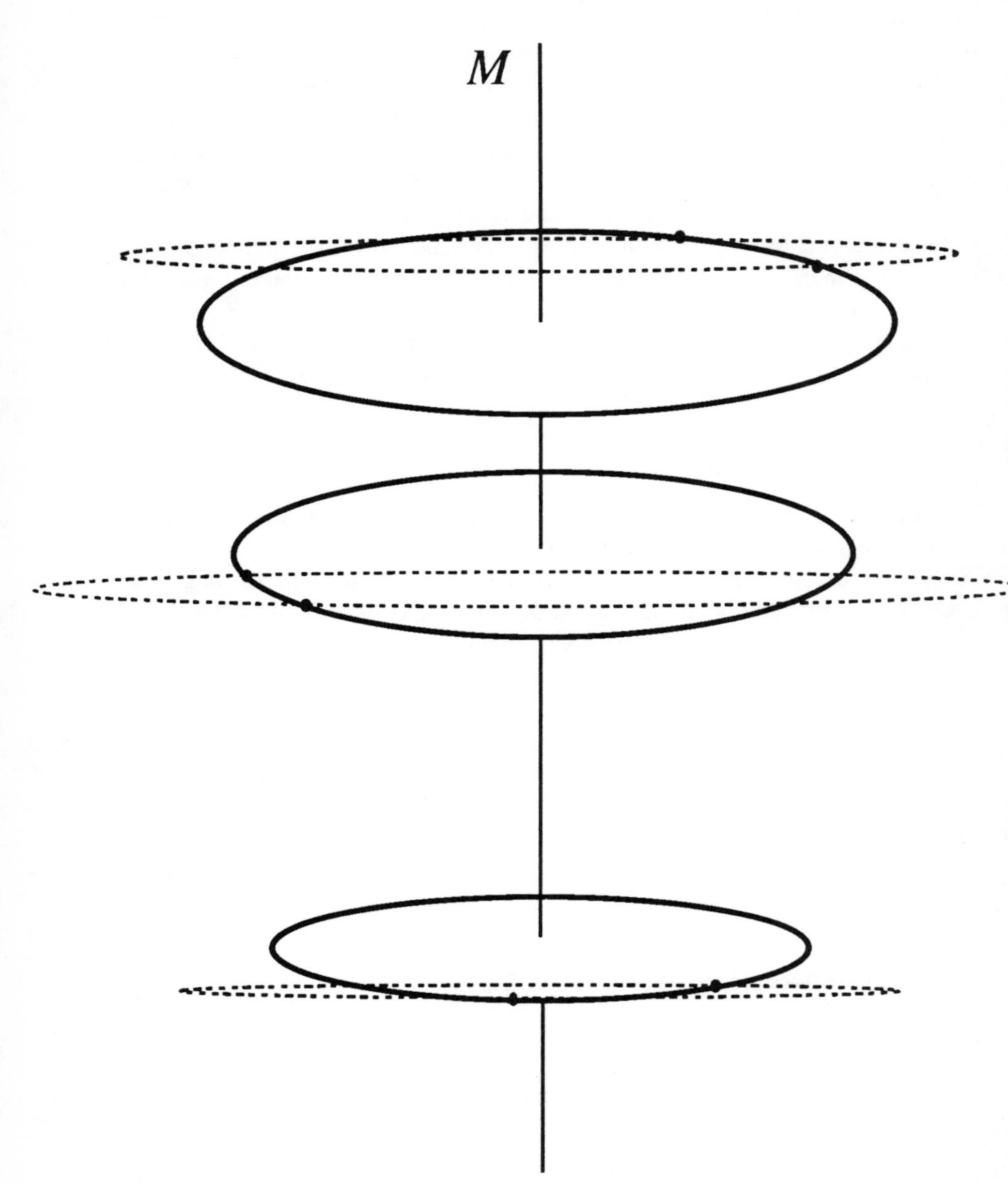

FIGURE 6.9.1. *Two rigid interpretations from the one-parameter family.*

6.10 is essentially a "cylindrical coordinate" representation of the original configuration

$$x = (\mathcal{A}; \mathbf{a}_{11}, \ldots, \mathbf{a}_{n1}; \mathbf{a}_{12}, \ldots, \mathbf{a}_{n2})$$

as follows. Let P_{ji} denote the point at the tip of vector $\mathbf{a}_{ji}$. Given $\mathcal{A}$, imagine the point P_{ji} as being connected to $\mathcal{A}$ by a vector $\mathbf{r}_{ji}$ which is perpendicular to $\mathcal{A}$ (see Figure 6.11). l_{ji} is the length of $\mathbf{r}_{ji}$; h_{ji} is the coordinate on $\mathcal{A}$ at the point where $\mathcal{A}$ meets $\mathbf{r}_{ji}$; and $\mathbf{v}$ is the direction of the projection of $\mathbf{r}_{11}$ in the plane L through the origin and perpendicular to $\mathcal{A}$. Then $c_{ji}((i,j) \neq (1,1))$ describes the angular displacement of $\mathbf{r}_{ji}$ relative to $\mathbf{r}_{11}$; it is the counterclockwise angle between $\mathbf{v}$ and the projection of P_{ji} in L. Here the notion of "counterclockwise" is determined using the right-hand rule by the orientation of $\mathcal{A}$.

By the requirement that $\mathbf{a} \notin \mathcal{A}$ in 6.2, the vectors $\mathbf{r}_{ji}$ are all non-zero, so that the unit vector $\mathbf{v}$ and the angles c_{ji} are well-defined.

We can think of (c_{ji}, h_{ji}, l_{ji}) as cylindrical coordinates of P_{ji} with respect to the axis $\mathcal{A}$ and the vector $\mathbf{v}$.

The representation of X given in (6.10) and illustrated in Figure 6.11 shows that X is a "good" configuration space in the sense that it is coordinatized by a set of geometric descriptors, namely c_{ji}, h_{ji}, l_{ji}, which are directly adapted to the perception of the geometry of arrays of points relative to a fixed axis. In particular, the instantaneous rotations may be described within X in a very natural way as the solution set of equations which are *linear* in these coordinates.

Proposition 6.12. E is the subset of X consisting of those elements x whose representation in the form (6.10) has the following properties:

(i) $c_{12} = c_{22} - c_{21} = \ldots = c_{n2} - c_{n1}$.

(ii) $h_{j1} = h_{j2}$ for each $j = 1, \ldots, n$.

(iii) $l_{j1} = l_{j2}$ for each $j = 1, \ldots, n$.

Proof. Let e denote an element of X for which these conditions are satisfied. Let us denote by θ the common value of $c_{22} - c_{21}, \ldots, c_{n2} - c_{n1}$. For each $j = 1, \ldots, n$ denote by h_j and l_j the common values of $h_{j1} = h_{j2}$ and $l_{j1} = l_{j2}$. If also we drop the superscripts on the $c_{21}, \ldots, c_{n1}$ then we can write e in the form

$$e = (\mathcal{A}, \mathbf{v}, c_2, \ldots, c_n, \theta, h_1, \ldots, h_n, l_1, \ldots, l_n). \tag{6.13}$$

As before, let P_{j1} be the point of $\mathbf{R}^3$ whose cylindrical coordinates relative to $\mathcal{A}$ are (c_j, h_j, l_j), where the angle c_1 is measured with respect to $\mathbf{v}$ (so that $c_1 = 0$). Let σ denote the rotation about the axis $\mathcal{A}$ through the angle θ. Then

$$e = (\mathcal{A}, P_{11}, \ldots, P_{n1}; P_{12}, \ldots, P_{n2}) \in E. \quad \blacksquare \tag{6.14}$$

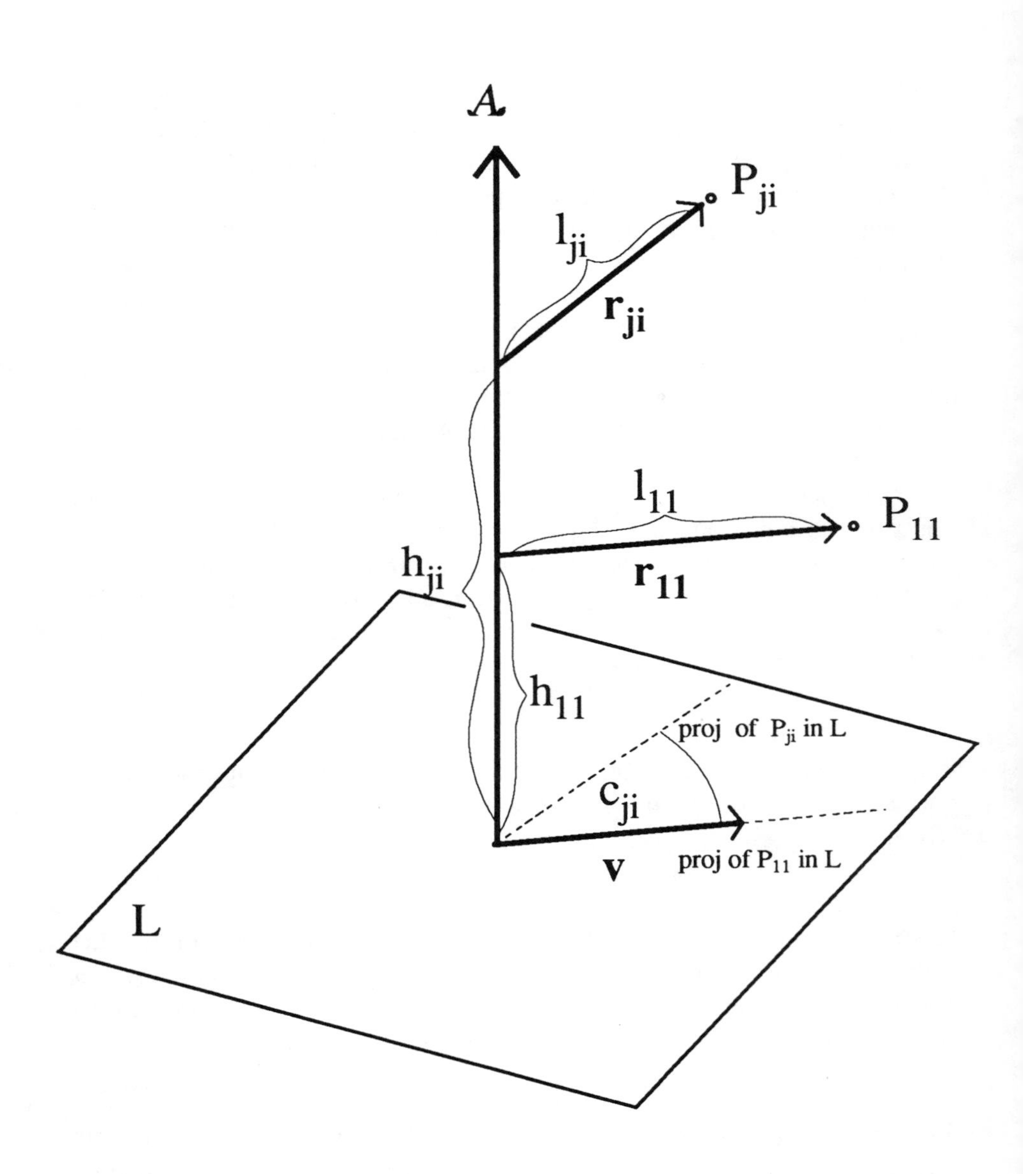

FIGURE 6.11. *Cylindrical coordinate representation of a configuration* ($\mathcal{A}$, $\mathbf{a}_{11}, \ldots, \mathbf{a}_{n1}$; $\mathbf{a}_{12}, \ldots, \mathbf{a}_{n2}$). P_{ji} *is the tip of the vector* $\mathbf{a}_{ji}$.

We now introduce the groups G and J.

$$\begin{aligned} G &= SO(3,\mathbf{R}) \times (\mathbf{S}^1)^{n-1} \times (\mathbf{S}^1)^n \times \mathbf{R}^n \times \mathbf{R}^n \times (\mathbf{R}^*)^n \times (\mathbf{R}^*)^n. \\ J &= SO(3,\mathbf{R}) \times (\mathbf{S}^1)^{n-1} \times \mathbf{S}^1 \times \mathbf{R}^n \times (\mathbf{R}^*)^n. \end{aligned} \tag{6.15}$$

$\mathbf{S}^1$ is the circle group, namely the additive group $\mathbf{R}/2\pi\mathbf{Z}$, and $\mathbf{R}$ and $\mathbf{R}^*$ are the additive and multiplicative real number groups respectively. Let us denote elements g of G in the form

$$g = \begin{pmatrix} \beta & & \gamma_{21},\ldots,\gamma_{n1} & \zeta_{11},\ldots,\zeta_{n1}\, n & \lambda_{11},\ldots,\lambda_{n1} \\ & \gamma_{12} & \gamma_{22},\ldots,\gamma_{n2} & \zeta_{12},\ldots,\zeta_{n2} & \lambda_{12},\ldots,\lambda_{n2} \end{pmatrix} \tag{6.16}$$

with $\beta \in SO(3,\mathbf{R})$, the γ's in $\mathbf{S}^1$, the ζ's in $\mathbf{R}$, and the λ's in $\mathbf{R}^*$. We will write elements $\jmath$ of J in the form

$$\jmath = (\beta, \gamma_2, \ldots, \gamma_n, \delta, \zeta_1, \ldots, \zeta_n, \lambda_1, \ldots, \lambda_n) \tag{6.17}$$

We view J as a subgroup of G by identifying $\jmath$ in (6.17) with the element g of G given by

$$g = \begin{pmatrix} \beta & & \gamma_2,\ldots,\gamma_n & \zeta_1,\ldots,\zeta_n & \lambda_1,\ldots,\lambda_n \\ & \delta & \gamma_2+\delta,\ldots,\gamma_n+\delta & \zeta_1,\ldots,\zeta_n & \lambda_1,\ldots,\lambda_n \end{pmatrix}.$$

We now describe the action of G on X. Let $x \in X$ be as in (6.10) and $g \in G$ as in (6.16). Then

$gx =$

$$\begin{pmatrix} \beta A & \beta\mathbf{v} & (c_{21}+\gamma_{21}),\ldots,(c_{n1}+\gamma_{n1}) \\ & c_{12}+\gamma_{12} & (c_{22}+\gamma_{22}),\ldots,(c_{n2}+\gamma_{n2}) \end{pmatrix}$$

$$\begin{matrix} (h_{11}+\zeta_{11}),\ldots,(h_{n1}+\zeta_{n1}) & \lambda_{11}l_{11},\ldots,\lambda_{n1}l_{n1} \\ (h_{12}+\zeta_{12}),\ldots,(h_{n2}+\zeta_{n2}) & \lambda_{12}l_{12},\ldots,\lambda_{n2}l_{n2} \end{matrix}\Bigg). \tag{6.18}$$

Here $\beta\mathcal{A}$ and $\beta\mathbf{v}$ denote the axis and vector in $\mathbf{R}^3$ which are the images of $\mathcal{A}$ and $\mathbf{v}$ under the rotation β. This induces an action of J on E which may then be described as follows: If e is as in (6.13) and $\jmath$ is as in (6.17), then

$$\begin{aligned}\jmath e = (\beta\mathcal{A}, \beta\mathbf{v}, (c_2 + \gamma_2), \ldots, (c_n + \gamma_n), \\ \theta + \delta, (h_1 + \zeta_1), \ldots, (h_n + \zeta_n), \lambda_1 l_1, \ldots, \lambda_n l_n).\end{aligned} \tag{6.19}$$

We can now see that, given any pair $(x, \bar{x})$ of elements of X, there is a unique $g \in G$ such that $\bar{x} = gx$. For suppose x is as in 6.10 and $\bar{x}$ has components $\bar{\mathcal{A}}$, $\bar{\mathbf{v}}$, $\bar{c}_{21}$ etc. Given any two pairs $(\mathcal{A}, \mathbf{v})$ and $(\bar{\mathcal{A}}, \bar{\mathbf{v}})$, each consisting of an oriented axis and a unit vector orthogonal to it, there is a unique β such that $(\bar{\mathcal{A}}, \bar{\mathbf{v}}) = (\beta(\mathcal{A}), \beta(\mathbf{v}))$. This gives us the coordinate β of the required $g \in G$. Referring to Figure 6.11 and Equation 6.18, it is clear that the remaining coordinates are fixed by the requirements that

$$\begin{aligned}\gamma_{ji} &= \bar{c}_{ji} - c_{ji} \quad (\mathrm{mod}\ 2\pi), \\ \zeta_{ji} &= \bar{h}_{ji} - h_{ji}, \\ \lambda_{ji} &= \bar{l}_{ji}/l_{ji}.\end{aligned}$$

Therefore, X is a principal homogeneous space for G, and E is a principal homogeneous space for J. (It follows from this that the dimension of E is the same as the dimension of J which is $3 + 3n$, as is easily seen from 6.15.)

To complete the description of our symmetric framework $\Theta = (X, Y, E, S, G, J, \pi)$ we need to define the fundamental map $\pi: G \to Y$; the definition uses the map $p: X \to Y$ of (6.5). Actually, there is no single canonical choice of π here, but rather a canonical set of π's, and the relations between them can be stated precisely.

For each $x_0 \in X$, we have a bijective map $f_{x_0}: G \to X$ defined by $f_{x_0}(g) = g(x_0)$. That is, we identify X with G by displaying it as the orbit, under the action of G, of a distinguished element $x_0 \in X$. Then, for $x_0 \in E$, we let

$$\pi^{x_0} = p \circ f_{x_0}: G \to Y. \tag{6.20}$$

Thus,

$$G \xrightarrow{\pi^{x_0}} Y$$

is the composition

$$G \xrightarrow{f_{x_0}} X \xrightarrow{p} Y.$$

Since $x_0 \in E$, then $f_{x_0}(J) = Jx_0 = E$ so that $\pi^{x_0}(J) = p(E) = S$ by definition of S (6.8). We summarize:

6.21. With notation as above, for each choice of $x_0 \in E$,

$$\Theta = (X, Y, E, S, G, J, \pi^{x_0})$$

is a symmetric observer framework with fundamental map π^{x_0}.

We then get a reflexive framework

$$\{(X, Y, E, S, \pi_e^{x_0}) \mid e \in E\}.$$

Recall that the perspective maps $\pi_e^{x_0}: X \to Y$ are defined from the fundamental map π^{x_0} by the formula

$$\pi_e^{x_0}(x) = \pi^{x_0}(xe^{-1})$$

where xe^{-1} denotes the unique element of G sending e to x. Suppose, for example, that $x = ke$, i.e., $xe^{-1} = k$. Then, by definition of π^{x_0} this formula may be written

$$\pi_e^{x_0}(ke) = p(kx_0). \tag{6.22}$$

This may be interpreted as saying that the use of π^{x_0} as the fundamental map of the framework means that each observer in the framework "thinks of itself" as having configuration x_0 and perspective p. To understand this, view group elements in G as indicating "displacement." Then 6.22 says the following: the premise acquired by an observer with configuration e (in the framework whose fundamental map is π^{x_0}) when interacting with an observer displaced from it by k, is the same as the premise acquired by an observer with fixed perspective $p: X \to Y$, when interacting with an observer displaced from it by k.

Finally, we note that a straightforward calculation shows that the dependency of this structure on the noncanonical choice of x_0 can then be stated as follows:

6.23. For $e, x_0, x_0' \in E$

$$\pi_e^{x_0} = \pi_{(x_0' x_0^{-1})e}^{x_0'}.$$

In chapter nine we use this framework to give a participator-dynamical interpretation of "incremental rigidity schemes" for the human visual perception of rigid motion.

CHAPTER SIX

INTRODUCTION TO DYNAMICS

We begin to develop "participator dynamical systems" on environments supported by reflexive frameworks. We introduce the notions of action kernel and participator. For the cases of one and two participator systems, we give a description of the participator dynamics in the language of Markov chains. This chapter is motivational; it deals intuitively with very restricted cases. In the next chapter we consider a more general case.

1. Mathematical notation and terminology

The dynamics developed in this chapter makes use of several mathematical concepts from the theory of Markov chains. In this section we collect basic terminology and notation for the convenience of the reader.[1] We assume a familiarity with the notions of conditional probability and expectation.

Let $(E, \mathcal{E})$ be a measurable space. The set of measurable functions $f: E \to \mathbf{R}$ that are bounded is denoted by $b\mathcal{E}$, and the set of measurable nonnegative functions by $\mathcal{E}_+$.

Recall from chapter two that a kernel P on E is said to be *positive* if its range is in $[0, \infty]$. It is called a *transition probability* or a *submarkovian kernel* if $P(e, E) \leq 1$ for all $e \in E$. It is called *markovian* if $P(e, E) = 1$ for all $e \in E$. The abbreviation T.P. is sometimes used for transition probability. If P is a positive kernel and $f \in \mathcal{E}_+$, for example, then P can be viewed as an *operator*

---

[1] For more background, beginning readers might refer to Breiman (1969) or Narayan Bhat (1984). For advanced readers we suggest Revuz (1984).

taking f to the function Pf defined by $Pf(e) = \int_E P(e, dh) f(h)$. Similarly, if ν is a positive measure on $\mathcal{E}$, then P can be viewed as the operator on measures $\nu P(A) = \int_E \nu(dh) P(h, A)$ for $A \in \mathcal{E}$. The *composition* or *product* of two positive kernels P and Q is the kernel $PQ(e, A) = \int_E P(e, dh) Q(h, A)$. The n-fold product of a kernel P with itself is denoted P_n.

Let $(\Omega, \mathcal{F}, P_0)$ be a probability space and $Z = \{Z_n\}_{n \geq 0}$ a sequence of random variables $Z_n : \Omega \to E$. Such a structure is called a *stochastic process* with *base space* $(\Omega, \mathcal{F}, P_0)$ and *state space* E. A sequence $\{\mathcal{G}_n\}_{n \geq 0}$ of subσ-algebras of $\mathcal{F}$, such that $\mathcal{G}_n \subset \mathcal{G}_{n+1}$ $\forall n$, is called a *filtration* on $(\Omega, \mathcal{F})$. Let $\mathcal{F}_n = \sigma(Z_m, m \leq n)$ and $\mathcal{G}_n$ be a filtration such that $\mathcal{G}_n \supset \mathcal{F}_n$ for every n. The sequence $Z = \{Z_n\}_{n \geq 0}$ is called a *Markov chain with respect to the filtration* $\{\mathcal{G}_n\}_{n \geq 0}$ if, for every n, the σ-algebras $\mathcal{G}_n$ and $\sigma(Z_m, m \geq n)$ are conditionally independent with respect to Z_n; i.e., if for every $A \in \mathcal{G}_n$ and $B \in \sigma(Z_m, m \geq n)$, $P_0[A \cap B | Z_n] = P_0[A | Z_n] P_0[B | Z_n]$ a.s. The σ-algebras $\mathcal{F}_n$ are referred to as "past" σ-algebras. When we say simply that Z *is a Markov chain (with base space* $(\Omega, \mathcal{F}, P_0)$*)* we mean that it is so with respect to the past algebras $\mathcal{F}_n$. Intuitively, a sequence of random variables is a Markov chain if the probabilities for passing into the next state are completely determined by the current state of the system.

A sequence $Z = \{Z_n\}_{n \geq 0}$ of random variables is called a *homogeneous Markov chain with respect to the filtration* $\{\mathcal{G}_n\}$ *with transition probability* P if, for any integers m, n with $m < n$ and any function $f \in b\mathcal{E}$, we have $E_0[f(Z_n) | \mathcal{G}_m] = P_{n-m} f(Z_m)$, P_0 a.s., where E_0 denotes the mathematical expectation operator with respect to P_0. The probability measure ν defined by $\nu(A) = P_0[Z_0^{-1}(A)] \equiv P_0[Z_0 \in A]$, for $A \in \mathcal{E}$, is called the *starting measure.*

Let P be a T.P. on E. It is customary to extend the state space $(E, \mathcal{E})$ to the space $(E_\Delta, \mathcal{E}_\Delta)$, where Δ is a point not in E called the *cemetery*, $E_\Delta = E \cup \{\Delta\}$, and $\mathcal{E}_\Delta = \sigma(\mathcal{E}, \{\Delta\})$. P extends to a markovian kernel on $(E_\Delta, \mathcal{E}_\Delta)$ by setting $P(e, \{\Delta\}) = 1 - P(e, E)$ if $e \neq \Delta$, and $P(\Delta, \{\Delta\}) = 1$. A *canonical probability space* is the space $(\Omega, \mathcal{F}, P_0)$ where $\Omega = \prod_{n=0}^{\infty} E_\Delta^{(n)}$, and $E_\Delta^{(n)}$ is a copy of E_Δ; where the σ-algebra $\mathcal{F}$ is generated by the semi-algebra of *measurable cylinders* of Ω (namely sets of the form $\prod_{n=0}^{\infty} A_n$, where $A_n \in \mathcal{E}_\Delta^{(n)}$, and A_n differs from $E_\Delta^{(n)}$ for only finitely many n); and where P_0 is a *probability* measure. A point $\omega = \{\omega_n, n \geq 0\}$ of Ω is called a *trajectory* or *path*. The mapping $Z_n : \Omega \to E_\Delta^{(n)}$ taking $\omega = (\omega_0, \omega_1, \omega_2, \ldots) \in \Omega$ to its nth entry ω_n is called the *nth coordinate mapping*. If the sequence $Z = \{Z_n\}$ of coordinate mappings on the canonical probability space forms a homogeneous Markov chain with T.P. P, we call it the *canonical Markov chain with T.P. P*.

The *shift operator* θ is the point transformation on Ω defined by $\theta(\omega_0, \omega_1,$

$\ldots, \omega_n, \ldots) = (\omega_1, \omega_2, \ldots, \omega_{n+1}, \ldots)$. We write θ_n for the n-fold iteration of θ: $\theta(\omega_0, \omega_1, \ldots) = (\omega_n, \omega_{n+1}, \ldots)$. A *stopping time* T of the canonical Markov chain Z is a random variable defined on $(\Omega, \mathcal{F})$ with range in $\mathbf{N} \cup \{\infty\}$ and such that for every integer n the event $\{T = n\}$ is in $\mathcal{F}_n$. ($\mathbf{N}$ is the set of natural numbers including 0.) The *σ-algebra associated with* T is the family $\mathcal{F}_T$ of events $A \in \mathcal{F}$ such that for every n, $\{T = n\} \cap A \in \mathcal{F}_n$. Notice that then the random variable $Z_{T(\omega)}(\omega)$ is $\mathcal{F}_T$-measurable.

Let G be a group that is locally compact with countable basis (LCCB), and let $\mathcal{G}$ denote the σ-algebra of its Borel sets. Given probability measures μ_1, μ_2 on $\mathcal{G}$, their *convolution* $\mu_1 * \mu_2$ is defined to be the probability measure which assigns to $K \in \mathcal{G}$ the measure $(\mu_1 * \mu_2)(K) = \int\int 1_K(x + y)\mu_1(dx)\mu_2(dy)$. A *right (left) random walk on* G is a Markov chain with state space $(G, \mathcal{G})$ and transition probability $\epsilon_g * \mu$ ($\mu * \epsilon_g$), where μ is a probability measure on $(G, \mathcal{G})$ which is called the *law* of the random walk, and ϵ_g is Dirac measure supported at the point $g \in G$. On an abelian group there is only one random walk of law μ, and it is invariant under translations.

2. Fundamentals of dynamics

The conclusion of an observer O's perceptual inference is represented, as we have discussed, by a probability measure $\eta(s, \cdot)$. This conclusion is true in a given semantics, according to Definition 4–3.5, if $\eta(s, \cdot)$ is the actual regular conditional distribution, given s, of the measurable functions X_t (defined in 4–3.1). $\{X_t\}$ is a sequence of random variables indexed by a discrete time t, taking values in configuration space X, and whose domain is some unspecified probability space Ω. In extended semantics (4–4) there is a set $\mathcal{B}$ of objects of perception; for each t, a value of X_t is associated with an interaction of O with an element of $\mathcal{B}$. These interactions are called channelings. In the case of an environment supported by a reflexive framework (5–2.6) we have a set of observers $\mathcal{B}$ which is also the set of objects of perception for each of its members. At each instant of "reference" time (which, as we shall see, is not the time t of the random variables X_t) the totality of channeling interactions at that instant is described by a subset L of $\mathcal{B}$ and a relation $\tilde{\chi}$ on L as in 5–3.

We now begin to construct a class of models for environments supported by reflexive frameworks; these models are called "participator dynamical systems." We do this using entities called "participators"; a participator manifests as an observer in $\mathcal{B}_E$ at each instant of reference time. The subset D of $\mathcal{B}$ at reference time n always contains the set of participator manifestations at time n. The determination of D and χ can be discussed in terms of participators (we discuss this in 7–2). In the process of this development, an analytical viewpoint emerges in which the participators themselves are the center of attention.

This chapter is informal; for clarity we present many of the ideas in special cases. In the next chapter we provide a formal development.

The motivation for dynamics

Consider two observers, A and B, in a reflexive framework $(X, Y, E, S, \pi_\bullet)$ of the type shown in Figure 5–2.9. Recall (from 5–2.8) that this means there exist points $a, b \in E$ such that $A = (X, Y, E, S, \pi_a, \eta_A)$ and $B = (X, Y, E, S, \pi_b, \eta_B)$, where η_A, η_B are some conclusion kernels. We depict this in Figure 2.1, where the observers A and B channel to each other. Each makes an inference about the perspective map of the other, i.e., about the point of E that represents the perspective of the other. Figure 2.1 shows the premise $s = \pi_a(b)$ of A's perceptual inference, and the ray of configuration points x such that $\pi_a(x) = s$ (labelled in the figure as $\pi_a^{-1}\{s\}$). A's conclusion measure η_A is supported on the set $\xi = \pi_a^{-1}\{s\} \cap E$, which includes b. But ξ includes infinitely many perspectives other than B's as well, some of which are indicated by the smaller dashed circles with numbers above. Thus A is faced with perceptual uncertainty: What was the perspective of the observer that channeled? Was it $1, 2, b, 3, \ldots$? In general, A cannot pick just one perspective as the answer to this question. Instead A concludes that it is perspective 1 with probability P_1, perspective 2 with probability P_2, perspective b with probability P_b, and so on. This is the content of A's conclusion measure $\eta_A(s, \cdot)$.

How is A's conclusion measure $\eta_A(s, \cdot)$ to be chosen? On what basis can A conclude that the other observer's perspective was 1 with probability P_1, 2 with probability P_2, etc? The answer we give is roughly as follows. A markovian dynamics of perspectives naturally arises in the context of reflexive frameworks. That observers in the framework perceive truly means that their η's should be related to the asymptotic behavior of this dynamics. Intuitively, the probability assigned by $\eta(s, \cdot)$ to a point $e \in E$ should be a conditional probability derived from the frequency with which the perspective corresponding to that e is adopted by participators in the given dynamical context. In this sense, the given dynamics plays the role of the "environment" in which these observers are embedded. To make these ideas more precise, we begin by discussing how a dynamics of perspectives arises

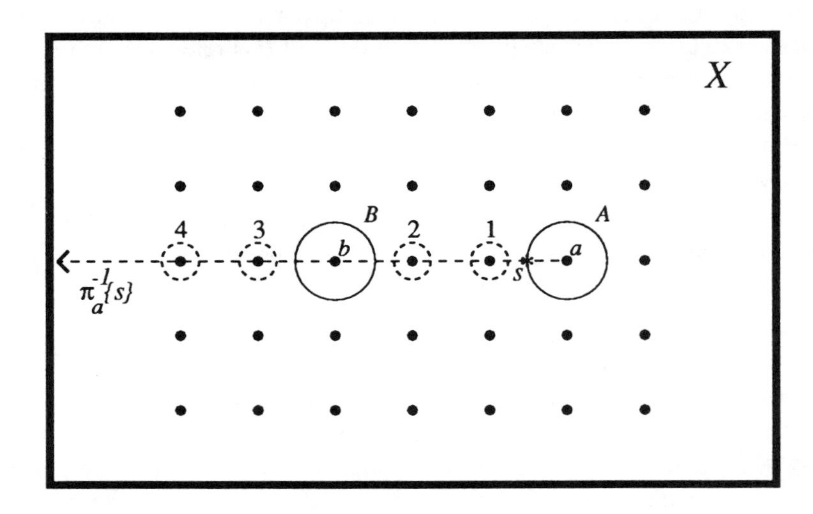

FIGURE 2.1. *Perceptual uncertainty in a reflexive framework.*

on reflexive frameworks.

When A and B channel, the premise s of A's perceptual inference greatly restricts what A can conclude about B's perspective. Yet A has, in general, infinitely many choices remaining, for B's perspective could be any in $\pi_a^{-1}\{s\} \cap E$. Suppose A and B retain their perspectives after channeling. Then if they channel again A has precisely the same set of choices—and the same ambiguity—regarding B's perspective as before. In other words, if the observers do not alter their perspectives after an observation then there is no point to further observations. A can channel with B as many times as you like, but the same premise s will result every time, and with it the same ambiguity of interpretation. Moreover, should A and B never change perspectives the whole question of how η_A is chosen would be trivial: the ideal $\eta_A(s, \cdot)$ would be Dirac measure supported on b, and $\eta_A(s', \cdot)$ for $s' \neq s$ would need not be defined. Indeed, the construction of reflexive frameworks would be pointless.

Let us, then, allow observers in a reflexive framework to change perspective following a channeling. That is, let us allow some kind of dynamics of perspectives on reflexive frameworks. Several questions immediately arise. How shall observers change perspective? Since the perspective of an observer in a reflexive framework (together with its conclusion measure) is its only means of individuation, does not a change in perspective actually mean a change in observer? If so, then what is it that is manifesting itself as a different observer at each step of the dynamics? Furthermore, dynamics requires sequence. What is the formal structure of this sequence? What is the formal structure of the dynamics? How, precisely, shall η be related to the resulting dynamics? We consider these questions in turn here, and in succeeding chapters.

Action kernels

How should we allow observers to change perspective in reflexive frameworks? There are two basic issues. First, what information should be used to select the new perspective of an observer after a channeling? Second, should the new perspective be chosen deterministically or probabilistically? We discuss these issues in the context of Figure 2.2. This figure shows observers A and B channeling to each other. In consequence of the channeling, A's premise is s_A, and B's premise is s_B. The figure shows A changing its perspective from π_a to $\pi_{a'}$, and B changing from π_b to $\pi_{b'}$. Of course, after these changes A and B are no longer the same observers since they no longer have the same perspectives. We denote the new observers A' and B'. As can be seen in the figure, the only information available to choose A's new perspective is its current perspective and the premise s_A. Similarly, mutatis mutandis, for B. Therefore, for maximum generality, we assume that an observer's next perspective is some function of its current perspective and current premise. Shall this function be deterministic or probabilistic? Again, for maximum generality, we assume that the next perspective is chosen probabilistically, according to some measure. (The deterministic case is the special case that the measure governing the choice of next perspective is a Dirac measure.) Further, we assume this measure to be a probability measure; after we introduce the notion of *participator,* we will interpret this assumption.

In light of these considerations, we could propose that the change in perspective of an observer A should be governed by a probability measure that is selected based on A's current perspective and current premise. However, a sense of symmetry suggests that A's probability measure should depend not on its absolute perspective, but on the "difference" between its perspective and that of B. Symmetry also suggests that the probability that A moves to A' should depend only on the "difference" in perspective between A and A'. Now to talk about differences of perspective in E requires some structure on E. For instance, E might be a principal homogeneous space for some group of "translations." More generally, the minimum structure necessary here is a symmetric framework (Definition 5–5.1). However, since the purpose of

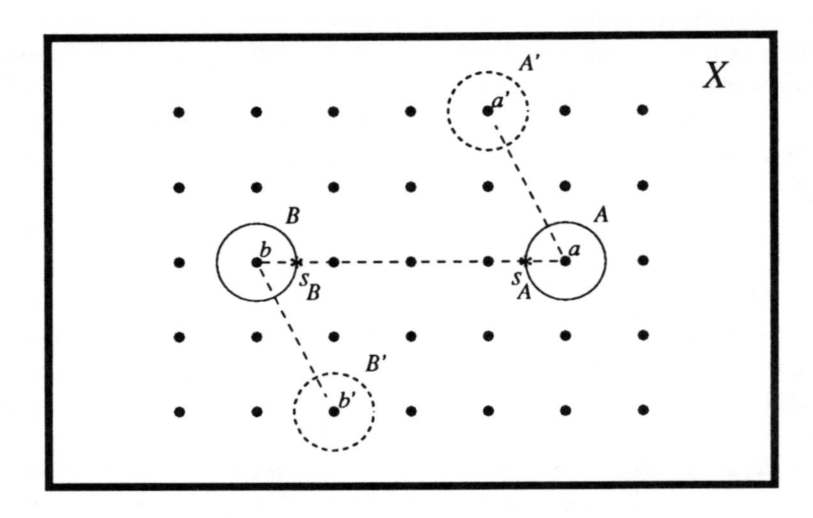

FIGURE 2.2. *Changing perspective on a reflexive framework.*

this chapter is to introduce basic ideas of observer dynamics, we defer (until chapter seven) a systematic presentation at this level of generality. Throughout this chapter we assume, for simplicity,

Assumption 2.3. We are working in a symmetric framework (X, Y, E, S, G, J, π) in which $G = X$ is an abelian group written additively and $J = E$ is a subgroup. Equivalently, we can say that $(X, Y, E, S, \pi_\bullet)$ is a reflexive framework in which X is an abelian group, $E \subset X$ is a subgroup, and there exists a map $\pi: X \to Y$ such that for each $e \in E$, $\pi_e(x) = \pi(x - e)$.

Thus we can speak of "differences in perspective" without thinking twice. The reader may rely for intuition on examples like Example 5–4.3: one can think of X as $\mathbf{R}^n$ (with vector addition as the group operation) and E as a measure zero subgroup thereof.

We return now to the question of the probability measure governing changes in perspective. In light of our assumptions, this is a measure on a group E, telling how probable are various translations from the current perspective. We can capture the dependence of the measure on the observer's current premise by associating to each premise s of the observer a measure on the group of translations that acts on E. The appropriate mathematical device to do this is a kernel Q that we call an *action kernel*. For each premise s, the measure $Q(s, \cdot)$ is a probability measure on the group of translations that acts on E, (the group being, in this chapter, E itself).

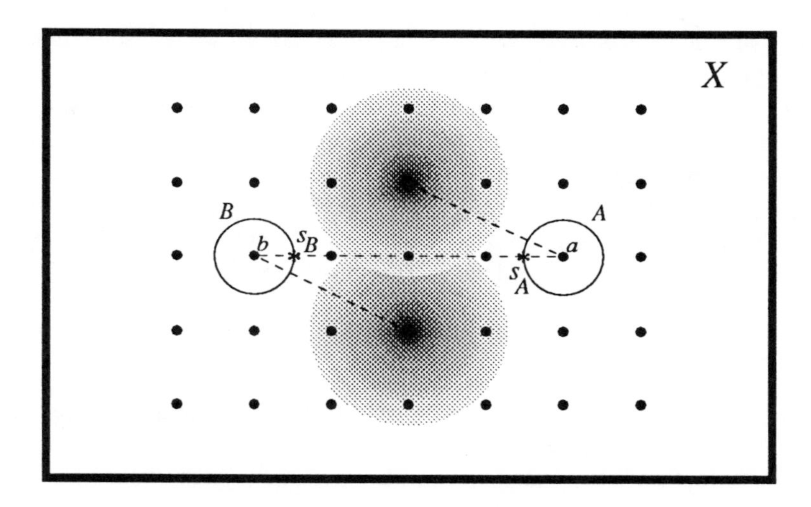

FIGURE 2.4. *Action kernels. The shading of the upper circular region represents the density of the probability distribution* $Q_A(s_A, \cdot)$. *Similarly, the shading of the lower circular region represents the density of the probability distribution* $Q_B(s_B, \cdot)$.

These notions are illustrated in Figure 2.4. Once again, two observers A and B channel with each other. A's premise is s_A. The measure $Q_A(s_A, \cdot)$, derived from A's action kernel Q_A, is depicted by a shaded disk with a dashed line drawn from A to the center of the disk. The darkness of a region within this disk encodes the probability that A will adopt a perspective in that region as its next perspective. Darker regions are more probable than lighter ones. A's expected new perspective happens, in the case illustrated, to be the perspective represented by the center of the disk. In general there will be some probability that an observer does not change its perspective after a channeling. (However for pictorial clarity the disk is not drawn large enough to include A's own perspective.)

Definition 2.5. Under Assumption 2.3, an *action kernel* is a markovian kernel $Q: E \times \mathcal{E} \to [0, 1]$ such that $Q(e, \cdot) = Q(e', \cdot)$ if $\pi(e) = \pi(e')$. Given Q, to each $e_1 \in E$ we can associate a kernel $Q_{e_1}: E \times \mathcal{E} \to [0, 1]$ by $Q_{e_1}(e, \Gamma) = Q(e - e_1, \Gamma)$.

Suppose Q is an action kernel. Since $Q(e, \cdot)$ depends only on $\pi(e)$ we could equally well define it as a kernel $S \times \mathcal{E} \to [0, 1]$. In fact we will sometimes write $Q(s, \cdot)$; this will mean $Q(e, \cdot)$ for any e such that $\pi(e) = s$. Similarly $Q_{e_1}(e, \cdot)$ depends only on $\pi_{e_1}(e)$. The interpretation of the action kernel is as follows: $Q(e, \Gamma)$ is the probability that the observer will change perspective by an increment in the set Γ, given that it channeled with an observer whose perspective differed from its perspective by e. If the first observer is at e_1, then $Q_{e_1}(e_1 + e, \Gamma)$ is an equivalent way to write this. The terminology "action kernel," when used for a given kernel $Q: E \times \mathcal{E} \to [0, 1]$, signals our intention to consider the family of kernels $\{Q_e\}_{e \in E}$.

Participators

In our discussion of action kernels we have spoken as though an observer in a reflexive framework could change its perspective map π. We said, for instance, that an action kernel gives the probabilities with which an observer might adopt various new perspectives. Now this way of speaking, though convenient, cannot be correct; the definition of observer does not permit a given observer to change its perspective. On the contrary, the definition requires an observer to have a fixed perspective map $\pi: X \to Y$. Therefore, the formal entity that changes perspective according to the dictates of an action kernel is not itself an observer. Instead this entity manifests itself at each instant as an observer in the context of a reflexive framework. This new formal entity we call a "participator."

Definition 2.6. A *participator* on a reflexive framework $(X, Y, E, S, \pi_\bullet)$ (under Assumption 2.3) is a triple, $(\xi, \{Q(n)\}_n, \{\eta(n)\}_n)$, where n varies over the nonnegative integers, ξ is a probability measure on E, each $Q(n)$ is an action kernel, and each $\eta(n)$ is a family of interpretation kernels for the reflexive framework. (That is, $\eta(n) = \{\eta_e(n)\}_{e \in E}$, where, for each $e \in E$, $(X, Y, E, S, \pi_e, \eta_e(n))$ is an observer.) If all the $Q(n)$ are equal to a fixed action kernel Q, we denote the participator simply by $(\xi, Q, \eta(n))$, and call it a *kinematical participator with action kernel* Q. If, for some n, a participator $A = (\xi, \{Q(n)\}_n, \{\eta(n)\}_n)$ on a reflexive framework $(X, Y, E, S, \pi_\bullet)$ has perspective π_n, then we call the observer $A_n = (X, Y, E, S, \pi_n, \eta(n))$ the *manifestation of A at time n*. We also say that A *manifests* as A_n. A *preparticipator* is a pair $(\xi, \{Q(n)\}_n)$ with ξ and $Q(n)$ as in a participator.

The formal definition of participator is based upon the following intuitions. A participator must have a first perspective; this is the purpose of ξ. The probability measure ξ on E, called the *initial measure* of the participator, governs the choice of the first perspective of the participator. When we say that a participator is initially "at e" or "has perspective e" we mean a participator for which ξ is Dirac measure at e; formally, we write $\xi = \epsilon_e$. A participator must also have a means of changing perspective; this is the purpose of the action kernels $Q(n)$. The changes in perspective are discrete and sequential, with respect to a notion of time that we discuss shortly. The notation means that the nth change of perspective in this sequence is governed by the action kernel $Q(n)$. Since the action kernels give probabilities for change of perspective conditioned by premises arising from channelings, the perspective changes of participators are probabilistic and are driven by channelings. The terminology "kinematical participator," for the special case when all the $Q(n)$ are identical, indicates that this case gives rise to systems with a property analogous to constant velocity. This does not mean that the motion of the participators is "linear" in the usual geometric sense of the word. Rather, it means that the instantaneous state-change data (in this case, given by the action kernel) is time invariant.

We discuss shortly a dynamics of perspectives that arises from the mutual observations of an ensemble of participators in a common reflexive framework. This dynamics is a Markov chain whose state space is a product of copies of E, one for each participator in the ensemble. In this chapter we consider a simplified version of the dynamics which is determined entirely by the action kernels and initial measures of the participators. To specify a (canonical) Markov chain on some space one need only give its initial measure and transition probability. The initial measure of the markovian dynamics of perspectives is simply the product of the initial measures of the participators; we study the transition probability in chapter seven. In the special case of kinematical participators the resulting Markov chains are *homogeneous*. In this case we will sometimes use the word *kinematics* rather than *dynamics*.

A participator dynamics on a reflexive framework incorporates a nondualistic model of extended semantics. There is some set $\mathcal{B}$ of observers in the framework; $\mathcal{B}$ serves as the objects of perception for each observer in the framework. In participator dynamics the set $\mathcal{B}$ has a special property; this property consists in a precise condition on the subset $\mathcal{B}_E$. Let us begin with a fixed set K of participators; say it is this set of participators whose dynamical interaction constitutes the given participator dynamical system. *$\mathcal{B}_E$ is then the set of all possible instantaneous manifestations for the participators in K.* To be precise, suppose each $j \in K$ is represented $(\xi_j, \{Q_j(n)\}_n, \{\eta_j(n)\}_n)$. Then

$$\mathcal{B}_E = \bigcup_n \{(X, Y, E, S, \pi_e, \eta_j(n)) \mid e \in E, j \in K\}. \tag{2.7}$$

Taking a union over the various instants of time n implies that we do not distinguish the observers $(X, Y, E, S, \pi_e, \eta_j(n))$ and $(X, Y, E, S, \pi_e, \eta_j(n'))$ (for e and j fixed) if it happens that the kernels $\eta_j(n)$ and $\eta_j(n')$ are equal for distinct times n, n'. By contrast, for $j \neq j' \in K$ and for a given $e \in E$, the observers $(X, Y, E, S, \pi_e, \eta_j(n))$ and $(X, Y, E, S, \pi_e, \eta_{j'}(n))$ are counted as distinct elements of $\mathcal{B}$, even if the kernels $\eta_j(n)$ and $\eta_{j'}(n)$ are the same.

Definitions of $\mathcal{B}_E$ other than 2.7 are possible. For example we could have taken a *disjoint* union over n rather than ordinary union as we did in 2.7. This means that the manifestations of a given participator at distinct moments n, n' would always be viewed as distinct elements of $\mathcal{B}$, even if the perspectives and conclusion kernels of the two observers were identical. This would allow the present manifestation of a participator to interact with a previous manifestation of the same participator—let us call this a "memory interaction"—in a manner which permits keeping track of the distinct times. However, using 2.7 it is still possible for a present and a past manifestation of a single participator to interact. The difference is that now, if these two manifestations happen to be identical as observers, then they are also considered identical as objects of perception; they are represented by the same element $b \in \mathcal{B}$. Thus the interaction in question is characterized by b channeling with itself. (According to **5**–3.2 and **5**–3.4 this means that at the given instant there is a distinguished subset $D \subset \mathcal{B}$ containing b, and an involution χ of D such that $\chi(b) = b$.) In other words, in the context of 2.7, a memory interaction may be analytically indistinguishable from a self-channeling, whereas in the alternate (disjoint union) approach memory interaction and self-channeling are always distinct. Whether this difference is theoretically significant is an open question.

We can now interpret the requirement that action kernels are markovian (2.5), i.e., that if Q is an action kernel then for each $e \in E$ the measure $Q(e, \cdot)$ is a probability measure on E. This means that the set of participators which manifest themselves as observers is the same set at each instant of time: participators do not appear or disappear while a scenario is running. To see this, recall that if Q is the action kernel of a participator A, the measure $Q(e, \cdot)$ assigns probabilities to A's perspective at time $n+1$ (given that, at time n, A channeled with some participator whose perspective is e). And if Q is not markovian, i.e., if $Q(e, E) < 1$, then there is positive probability that A has no perspective at time $n+1$, so that it is not manifested as an observer in the framework at that time. However, though A must manifest as an observer at each time n, A's manifestation need not channel at each time n. In other words, the subset L of $\mathcal{B}$ which is the domain of the channeling relation at time n may be a proper subset of the set of all participator manifestations at time n. We see, then, that the markovian requirement on action kernels is a matter of convention, not a restrictive assumption: since we do not require the participators to channel at every instant, and since the dynamics is driven by channeling, the net effect on the dynamics is the same whether a participator does not manifest at time n, or manifests but does not channel at time n.

Reference and proper times

Dynamics requires some notion of time or sequence. Our notion of time in the context of participator dynamics is guided in part by the ideas of Einstein:

> "The experiences of an individual appear to us arranged in a series of events; in this series the single events which we remember appear to be ordered according to the criterion of 'earlier' and 'later,' which cannot be analyzed further. There exists, therefore, for the individual, an I-time, or subjective time. This in itself is not measurable. I can, indeed, associate numbers with the events, in such a way that a greater number is associated with the later event than with an earlier one; but the nature of this association may be quite arbitrary."[2]

The only events in a reflexive framework with which to associate numbers are the discrete acts of observation and the consequent changes in perspective. To each participator, then, we assign a number, called the "proper time" of that participator, such that the number increases only when the participator makes an observation. Every channeling that involves that participator increases its proper time. Thus discrete acts of observation constitute the units of subjective time in this framework. We will give a more formal treatment of proper time in chapter seven; the examples

[2] Einstein (1956), p. 1.

we present in this chapter are simplified (artificially) so that the proper time of each participator coincides with "reference time" (defined below).

The setting of the dynamics described here is different from the spacetime setting assumed in physics. In place of physical space we have the space of possible observer perspectives, and in place of physical time we have the sequence of discrete observations of participators.

A particular channeling may not include the perspectives of some participators in the dynamics. In this case the proper times of the excluded participators are not increased, but the proper times of the others are increased. Therefore, even if the proper times of all participators begin with the same value, say zero, their proper times will eventually differ due to channelings that exclude some participators. We cannot then, in general, take the proper time of any particular participator to be the time parameter of the markovian dynamics of the ensemble. For this we need a time parameter that increases for every channeling whether or not that channeling includes a particular participator. This time parameter we call "reference time." In a given dynamical setting in which we have a fixed set K of participators, we may take the reference time to be a copy of the nonnegative integers, called "R," which is the domain of the time index "n" of Definition 2.6 for all the participators in K. Thus in speaking of reference time we are making the assumption that these indices have a common domain.

The reference time in a given dynamical context (corresponding to a set K of participators) is not the same as the *active time* in the sense of 4–2.1 for the observers in the set $\mathcal{B}_E$ of 2.7. In fact, reference time is associated to a set of participators, not to a set of observers. And the reference time need not include those instants when the participators channel only to non-distinguished objects of perception. It need only include those instants when participator observations occur, and by the term 'observation' we always mean a channeling which results in a distinguished premise (which causes the output of a conclusion, etc.). Now a channeling with a non-distinguished object of perception may result in a distinguished premise ("false targets"), and an instant of time in which this occurs (for the manifestation of a participator) would have to be included in reference time. But if no distinguished premises occurred at the given instant for any of the participators, then that instant would be excluded from reference time.

Recall, by contrast, that since the active time of an observer indexes the X_t's, it consists by definition precisely of those instants when the observer receives *any* channeling, from a distinguished object of perception or not.

Definition 2.8. With the terminology of 5–3, (i) a *participator channeling sequence* is a function, ζ, from the natural numbers to the space of channelings, $\zeta: \mathbf{N} \to \mathcal{I}$, with the following property. Let $\zeta(n) = (L_n, \tilde{\chi}_n)$, where $L_n \subset \mathcal{B}$ and $\tilde{\chi}_n$ is an involution of L_n. Let $K_n = (D_n, \chi_n)$ denote the distinguished part (5–3.4) of $\zeta(n)$. *Then for each $n \in \mathbf{N}$, D_n is not empty.* $\mathbf{N}$ is called the *reference time* for the sequence.[3] (ii) As in 2.6, let $A_n \in \mathcal{B}_E$ denote the manifestation of participator A at reference time n. To each participator A in the dynamics is associated its *proper time*, $\mathcal{T}_A: \mathbf{N} \to \mathbf{N}$, defined inductively as follows:

$$\mathcal{T}_A(n) = \begin{cases} 0 & \text{if } n = 0 \\ \mathcal{T}_A(n-1) + 1 & \text{if } A_n \in D_n \text{ and } \pi_{\Phi(A_n)}(\Phi(\chi_n(A_n))) \in S \\ \mathcal{T}_A(n-1) & \text{otherwise.} \end{cases}$$

At every instant of reference time, the proper time of at least one participator is increased. Definition 2.8 says that the unit of subjective time for a participator is a single act of channeling, i.e., the performance of a single perceptual inference. Since at any step of reference time some participator manifestations may not channel, it follows that the proper times for different participators vary: proper time is relative to the participator. In fact it will be seen in chapter eight that, given any ensemble of participators, each participator's proper time is a *stopping time* for the associated dynamical Markov chain.

According to Definition 2.8, the proper time of a participator A increases not only if its manifestation channels with a distinguished object of perception, but also if it channels with a false object. A false object is an object of perception $B_n \in \mathcal{B} - \mathcal{B}_E$ such that $\pi_{\Phi(A_n)}(\Phi(B_n)) \in S$. If B_n is a false object then, using the terminology of 2–3, $\Phi(B_n)$ is a false target. Channelings with false objects affect participator dynamics since participators, unable to distinguish false objects from true, change perspective according to their action kernels upon channeling with false objects. In this book we attempt no serious investigation of the role of such channelings in participator dynamics. In fact we ignore false objects and assume that, at each instant of reference time, participator manifestations channel only with

[3] Thus a participator channeling sequence assigns a nonempty channeling to each instant of reference time. At every instant of reference time the manifestation of at least one participator channels. In this book we consider only those sequences such that the sets D_n have some fixed maximum size.

other participator manifestations. (As an informal justification for this one might assume that the statistical properties of the action kernels somehow take into account these extraneous channelings.) This is the content of the following "closed system" assumption:

Assumption 2.9. *Closed system.* For each reference time n, D_n is contained in the set of participator manifestations at time n.

One further assumption should be noted. We conceive of the change of perspectives of participators on a reflexive framework as probabilistic. However, we have not given explicit details of the underlying probability spaces on which the dynamical mechanism depends. Our proposal for the underlying framework will be made in the next chapter. Here we note only the following characteristic:

Assumption 2.10. *Independent action.* At any instant of reference time, and given the current perspectives of all participators and the current channeling involution, the perspectives of the participators at the next instant of reference time are independent random variables.

For example, suppose we have three participators A, B and C with action kernels Q_A, Q_B and Q_C respectively, and with channeling involution $\chi = \{(A, B)\}$ (so that C is not channeled to). Then the probability that, at the next instant, $A \in \Gamma_A$, $B \in \Gamma_B$, and $C \in \Gamma_C$ is

$$Q_{A,e_A}(e_B, \Gamma_A) Q_{B,e_B}(e_A, \Gamma_B) 1_{\Gamma_C}(e_C).$$

That is, we need simply take a product of the appropriate probabilities for the individual participators.

3. Kinematics of a single participator

In this section we consider the kinematics of perspectives that arises in a system consisting of a single kinematical participator. We find that this kinematics is a random walk. In the next section we consider a kinematics of two participators. We consider the general case in the next chapter.

Consider a single participator on a symmetric framework (X, Y, E, S, G, J, π) satisfying Assumption 2.3. Let $\xi = \epsilon_e$, $e \in E$. The first manifestation of this participator then has perspective map π_e, defined by $\pi_e(g) = \pi(g - e), g \in X$. The only channeling possible, since there is but one participator, is a "self channeling," viz., a channeling in which $\chi(e) = e$. The participator's premise is then $\pi_e(e)$, i.e., $\pi(0)$, where 0 denotes the identity element of our additive abelian group E. This applies to each instant of the participator's proper time and, since there are no other participators, the system is inert at all other instants. It follows from this that the same perceptual premise $s_0 = \pi(0) \in S$ obtains at each step of the kinematics. And, denoting by Q the action kernel of the participator, this implies that the same probability measure $Q(s_0, \cdot)$ for the next perspective obtains at each step of the kinematics. This implies that the kinematics is a random walk of law $Q(s_0, \cdot)$ with respect to the discrete time which is the participator's proper time and, in this special case, the reference time.

4. Kinematics of pairs

We now consider a system involving two kinematical participators. In such a system each participator might channel with itself, with the other participator, or not at all, at each step of reference time. In this section we assume for simplicity that each participator channels with the other at each step of the kinematics. In the next chapter we consider the general case.

Again we are in the situation of Assumption 2.3. When two participators, A and B, observe each other, each changes its perspective according to its action kernel. This leads to a new *difference* in their perspectives. This change in the relationship between their perspectives is governed by a kernel P which we can define as follows: for each $e \in E$ and $\Gamma \in \mathcal{E}$, $P(e, \Gamma)$ is the probability that, as the result of a change in their perspectives, the new perspective of B relative to A (i.e., the difference of their new perspectives) will lie in the set Γ, given that the present difference in their perspectives is e. We can compute P from the action kernels of the individual participators as illustrated in Figure 4.1. The figure shows two participators with initial perspectives a and b. The perspective of B relative to A is e (that of A relative to B is $-e$). After observing, A changes perspective by an amount dk and B changes perspective by an amount dh. This leads to a new difference in perspective $e - dk + dh$ (or $-(e - dk + dh)$).

Let Q and R denote the action kernels of the participators whose current perspectives are a and b respectively. Then the probability that A changes perspective by an amount dk given that B's perspective differs from A's by an amount e is $Q(e, dk)$. Similarly, the probability that B changes perspective by an amount dh given that A's perspective differs from B's by an amount $-e$ is $R(-e, dh)$. The probability of the joint event that A changes by dk and B by dh is, by Assumption 2.10, $Q(e, dk)R(-e, dh)$. That is, the probability that the new difference in perspective is $e - dk + dh$, given that the old difference in perspective was e, is given by $Q(e, dk)R(-e, dh)$. Thus, to determine what is the probability that the new difference in perspective lies within a region $\Gamma \in \mathcal{E}$, we simply find the measure of the region $\{(k, h) \in E \times E | e - k + h \in \Gamma\}$ with respect to the product measure $Q(e, dk) \otimes R(-e, dh)$ on $E \times E$. This is the same as the integral

$$\int_{E\times E} 1_\Gamma(e - k + h)Q(e, dk)R(-e, dh);$$

we conclude that $P(e, \Gamma)$ is this integral.

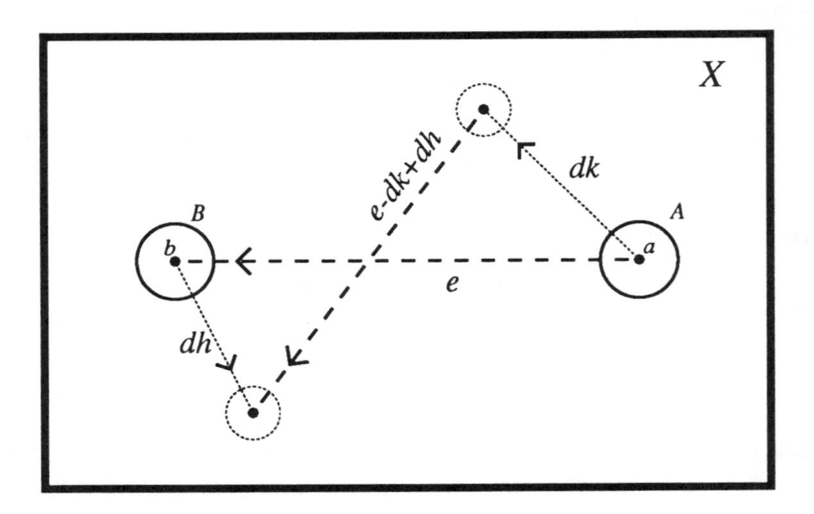

FIGURE 4.1. *Two participators change perspective.*

Note that P is time independent (assuming, as we do, that Q and R are) and is also independent of the absolute perspective. Thus we can summarize:

4.2. Suppose A and B are participators with action kernels Q and R respectively. Assume a channeling sequence where A channels only to B and vice versa. Then the proper times of A and B are the same. With respect to this proper time the successive perspectives of B relative to A (i.e., the successive differences in their perspectives) form a homogeneous Markov chain with state space E and transition probability P given by $P(e, \Gamma) = \int_{E\times E} 1_\Gamma(e - k + h) Q(e, dk) R(-e, dh)$.

The dependence of P on the action kernels Q and R can be conveniently and suggestively expressed in terms of a natural "bracket operation" which is derived from convolution of measures.

First, recall that if α, β are measures on the group $(E, \mathcal{E})$, then *the convolution of α with β*, denoted $\alpha * \beta$, is the measure on $(E, \mathcal{E})$ defined by

$$\alpha * \beta(\Gamma) = \int_{E\times E} 1_\Gamma(k + h)\alpha(dk)\beta(dh) \qquad (\Gamma \in \mathcal{E}).$$

Notation 4.3. If N is a kernel on $(E, \mathcal{E})$,

(i) $N^\dagger$ denotes the kernel $N^\dagger(e, \Gamma) = N(-e, -\Gamma)$, $(e \in E, \Gamma \in \mathcal{E})$;

(ii) $N_e(\cdot)$ denotes the measure $N(e, \cdot)$.

Definition 4.4. If Q and R are kernels on $(E, \mathcal{E})$, $[Q, R]$ is the kernel on $(E, \mathcal{E})$ given by

$$[Q, R](e, \Gamma) = (Q_e * R_e^\dagger)(e - \Gamma).$$

Proposition 4.5. With notation as above, $P = [Q, R]$.

Proof.

$$P(e, \Gamma) = \int_{E\times E} 1_\Gamma(e - k + h) Q(e, dk) R(-e, dh)$$

$$= \int_{E\times E} 1_{e-\Gamma}(k-h)Q(e, dk)R(-e, dh);$$

change variables so that h is replaced by $-h$:

$$= \int_{E\times E} 1_{e-\Gamma}(k+h)Q(e, dk)R(-e, -dh)$$

$$= \int_{E\times E} 1_{e-\Gamma}(k+h)Q(e, dk)R^{\dagger}(e, dh)$$

$$= (Q_e * R_e^{\dagger})(e-\Gamma) = [Q, R](e, \Gamma).$$

For the moment, let P' denote the kernel for the Markov chain of perspectives of A relative to B. On the one hand, it is geometrically evident that $P'(e, \Gamma) = P(-e, -\Gamma)$ (where, as above, P denotes the kernel for the perspectives of B relative to A). On the other hand, from Proposition 4.5 we find that $P' = [Q, R]$. We conclude

Proposition 4.6. For any kernels Q, R,

$$[Q, R] = [R, Q]^{\dagger}.$$

This may also be verified directly from Notation 4.3 and Definition 4.4.

We close this section with several remarks. First, nothing prevents A and B from occupying the same perspective in E at a given instant. Second, the situation considered in this section, where each participator channels only to the other (and not to itself) is the opposite extreme of that treated in the previous section, where a participator channels only to itself. To make the comparison appropriate, imagine two kinematical participators A and B, each channeling only to itself. In this case we would get a Markov chain on $E \times E$; in each factor we would have a random walk, (one for A and one for B) as in the previous section. These random walks would be completely "uncoupled." In the situation treated in this section the perspectives of A and B are completely coupled: it is very unlikely that we would get anything resembling a random walk by looking at their sequences of states separately (or jointly). In the general setting, the question of the relative frequencies of cross-channelings and self-channelings in, say, a two participator dynamical system is described by an additional datum, called a τ-distribution, which we think of as describing the "informational conductivity" of E. Depending on the τ-distribution, the dynamical chain generated by an ensemble of participators with given action kernels will express some degree of coupling of the random walks each participator would undergo were there no cross-channelings. We will study this in more detail in the next chapter. The main idea here is that, given an ensemble of participators and a τ-distribution, a dynamical Markov chain is generated.

5. True perception among pairs

We have seen that a dynamics of perspectives arises naturally on reflexive frameworks. Intuitively, the purpose of the dynamics is to allow the participators to "perceive truly," i.e., to choose conclusion measures $\eta(s, \cdot)$ which in fact reflect the probabilities of events on the reflexive framework. Specifically, if participator A channels with B, leading to a premise s_A, then A should arrive at a conclusion measure $\eta_A(s_A, \cdot)$ which correctly describes with what probability the perspective of B, relative to A, lies in various subsets of $\pi_a^{-1}(s_A) \cap E$. In this section we specify conditions in which each participator, in a system of two mutually observing participators, can perceive truly the perspective of the other. Chapter eight addresses the issue of true perception formally and in greater generality.

We assume, as in the previous section, that there are no self-channelings; all channelings are cross-channelings. In chapter seven we consider more general dynamics, but several ideas are revealed by considering the simpler case.

We found in the last section that the kinematics of relative perspectives for two participators is markovian with transition probability P. The theory of Markov chains describes some interesting properties of this kinematics that are relevant to the problem of true perception. We describe these properties informally now, and formally in the next chapters.

Depending on the details of the transition probability P, one finds that the state space E of the markovian dynamics contains different "pockets" which act like traps; if the state of the chain happens to enter one of these pockets, then the chain will forever stay within that pocket almost surely. For this reason these pockets are called "absorbing sets." The complement in the state space of all the absorbing sets is a pool of states called the "transient states." This is depicted in Figure 5.1, where the white disks represent absorbing sets and the states outside the disks are the transient

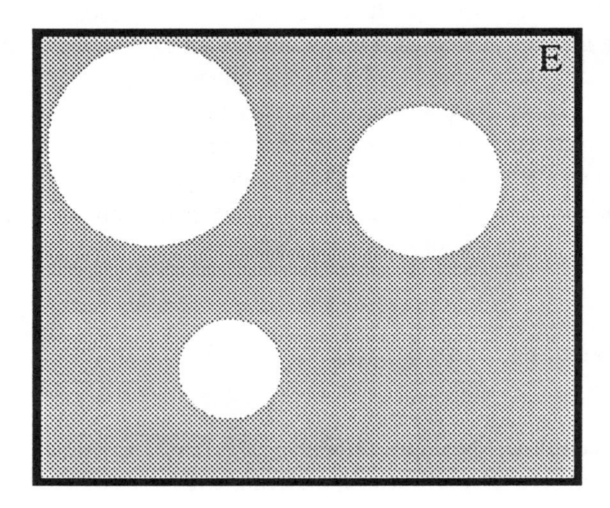

FIGURE 5.1. *Absorbing sets on the state space of a markovian dynamics. White disks represent absorbing sets. Stippled regions represent transient states.*

states. An absorbing set may contain infinitely many states. If a chain enters an absorbing set, the chain then marches probabilistically from state to state within the absorbing set, and almost surely never enters a state outside of the absorbing set.

One finds that, for each absorbing set C, there is a unique probability measure supported on C which describes the long term behavior of the chain, once it is trapped in C. This measure, say m, gives for each subset D of the absorbing set a probability, $m(D)$; $m(D)$ can be interpreted as the relative frequency that the trapped chain is found within D over a very long time. The measure m is called a "stationary" measure; an example of such a measure for a dynamics of two participators is shown in Figure 5.2. Darker regions indicate higher frequency states. The little circles drawn over the stationary measure indicate the perspectives each participator happens to adopt at some instant of the dynamics.[4]

Now if a two participator dynamical chain enters an absorbing set with stationary measure m, then each participator can reach true perceptual conclusions if its

[4] Figure 5.2 does not represent the stationary measure on the original state space of the Markov chain. The original state space is a product space, E^2, where there are two participators in the chain. Figure 5.2 represents the stationary measure on a single copy of E, which describes the perspective of B *relative* to A.

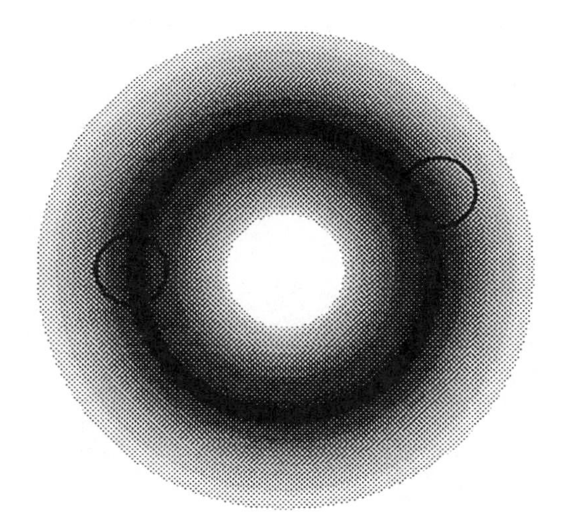

FIGURE 5.2. *A stationary measure. Darker regions indicate higher probability states.*

conclusions η are related appropriately to m. That is, a participator perceives truly if its perceptual conclusions η are matched to the dynamical reality observed, namely m. The way to match η to m is to make the measures $\eta(s, \cdot)$ the appropriate conditional probability measures of m, as depicted in Figure 5.4. This figure shows the stationary measure m of the dynamics of one participator relative to another, where the latter's perspective is always taken to be the origin at each step. At the instant shown, the two participators are channeling, leading the participator at the origin to have premise s. It can be seen that the appropriate conclusion η for this premise is the conditional probability of m when m is restricted to the line between the participators, viz., the line $\pi^{-1}(s)$. By choosing $\eta(s, \cdot)$ to be this probability measure, the participator at the origin has its perceptual conclusions matched to reality. Thus, in the case of a two participator dynamics involving only cross-channelings, the equation that specifies when perception matches reality simply asserts that the conclusion kernel η is the rcpd with respect to π of a stationary measure m. A measure m is stationary under the action of the transition probability P if $m = mP$, i.e., if

$$m(I - P) = 0, \qquad (5.3)$$

where I is the identity operator. In the dynamics considered here, this equation, together with the stipulation that η is the rcpd of m, is the "perception = reality" equation. Note that there are in general many absorbing sets, each with its own stationary measure, so that the measure m is not uniquely determined even when P is fixed. Therefore, to determine if perception matches reality, we must be careful to use the appropriate stationary measure.

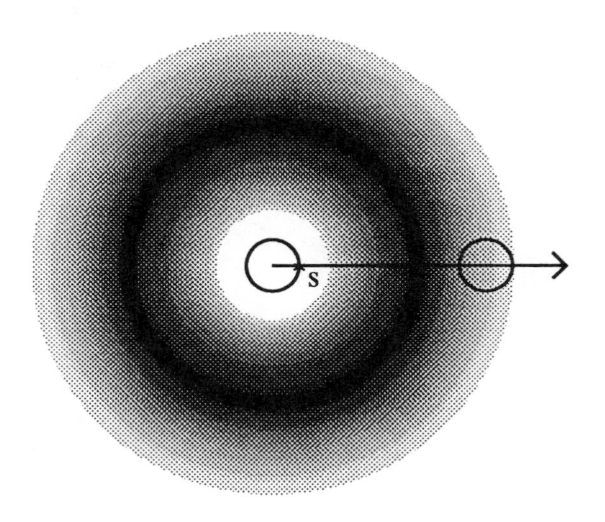

FIGURE 5.4. *A participator's conclusion measure should be derived as the rcpd of the appropriate stationary measure.*

Now if the chain never enters an absorbing set, i.e., if the dynamics is not stable, then there is no stationary probability measure to use to compute η. True perception is not possible. There are no probability measures $\eta(s, \cdot)$ that are matched to the dynamical reality. We see that a *stable* dynamics of perspectives is necessary for true perception.

In chapter ten we discuss how, to each absorbing set, there are associated in a natural manner complex-valued eigenfunctions of the transition probability P. We show that the squared amplitude of these eigenfunctions yields a probability measure which is stationary or *asymptotic* (a property, to be discussed later, which is slightly weaker than stationarity).

6. An example

We close this chapter with an illustration of participator dynamics by means of a specific and elementary example, including a computation of its stationary measures. Consider the symmetric framework (X, Y, E, S, G, J, π), where

$$\begin{aligned} X &= \mathbf{R}, \qquad E = \mathbf{Z} \text{ (the integers)}, \\ Y &= S = \{1, 0, -1\},\ G = \langle \mathbf{R}, + \rangle,\ J = \langle \mathbf{Z}, + \rangle, \\ \pi(x) &= \text{sgn}(x) \end{aligned} \tag{6.1}$$

and where the signum function "sgn" is given by

$$\text{sgn}(x) \quad = \quad \begin{cases} 1, & \text{if } x > 0; \\ 0, & \text{if } x = 0; \\ -1, & \text{if } x < 0. \end{cases} \tag{6.2}$$

Suppose we have two participators labelled "1" and "2" respectively, which channel with each other at each instant of reference time. As before, we do not allow self-channeling. Both participators are assumed to have the same action kernel Q, defined as follows:

$$Q(0, \cdot) \quad = \quad \epsilon_0(\cdot)$$

(where $\epsilon_0(\cdot)$ is Dirac measure at 0); if $r \neq 0$,

$$Q(r, x) \quad = \quad \begin{cases} \rho, & \text{if} \quad x = \text{sgn}(r); \\ 1 - \rho, & \text{if} \quad x = \text{sgn}(-r); \\ 0, & \text{otherwise.} \end{cases} \tag{6.3}$$

(Here r is the relative position before channeling and x is the the participator's change in position after channeling; we assume that the quantity ρ lies between 0 and 1). In words: if a channeling came from the participator's current position, there is no movement. Otherwise, the participator moves one step in the direction from which the channeling came, with a probability of ρ, or one step away from that direction, with the complementary probability of $1 - \rho$.

Imagine that the two participators are initially separated by a nonzero distance. After they channel, their relative distance will either remain unchanged, or will have changed by two units. These are the only possibilities. (If they were initially at the same position in E, nothing will change.) This is expressed in the following derivation of the dynamical kernel P of the joint markovian dynamics (as introduced in section four above). Note that the dynamics is *relativized*; it is a dynamics on the group $\mathbf{Z}$ of the relative displacements of participator 2 with respect to participator 1.

$1 - \rho \leftarrow \bullet \rightarrow \rho$ $\qquad\qquad$ $\rho \leftarrow \bullet \rightarrow 1 - \rho$

$* * *| * * * *| * * * * \bigcirc * * * * | * * * *| * * * *| * * * *| * * * * \bigcirc * * * * | * * * *| * * *$

Participator 2 $\qquad\qquad$ Participator 1

FIGURE 6.4. *A markovian two-participator dynamics with* $E = \mathbf{Z}$. *The current relative separation is* $r = -5$. *After a channeling each participator will jump in the indicated directions with the given probabilities.*

Proposition 6.5. Let r denote the current relative separation and q the relative separation after channeling. Then the kernel P of the dynamics is given by
If $r = 0$,

$$P(0, q) = \epsilon_0(q). \tag{6.6}$$

If $q = r$, $r \neq 0$,

$$P(r, q) = 2\rho(1 - \rho). \tag{6.7}$$

If $q = r - 2\,\mathrm{sgn}(r)$, $r \neq 0$,

$$P(r, q) = \rho^2. \tag{6.8}$$

If $q = r + 2\,\mathrm{sgn}(r)$, $r \neq 0$,

$$P(r, q) = (1 - \rho)^2. \tag{6.9}$$

If $q \neq r$, and $q \neq r \pm 2$

$$P(r, q) = 0. \tag{6.10}$$

Proof. The result is a consequence of the assumption of independence between the jumps of the individual participators, as expressed in Proposition 4.5. By that Proposition we see that

$$\begin{aligned} P(r,q) &= [Q,Q](r,q) \\ &= \sum_{z,w} Q(r,z)Q(-r,w)\,1_q(r-z+w) \\ &= \sum_{w} Q(r,(r-q)+w)Q(-r,w). \end{aligned} \tag{6.11}$$

The result then follows from the definition 6.3 of Q, after analyzing the possibilities into the indicated cases. ▮

Notice that $\sum_q P(r,q) = 1$, for all $r \in \mathbf{Z}$.

Up to an arbitrary initial probability measure ξ on the group **Z**, we have described the Markov chain which is the (relative) dynamics. We may now inquire into the long-term behavior of the dynamics, as introduced in section five.

Suppose that ν is a probability measure on **Z**. Recall that ν is said to be *stationary* for the chain with T.P. P if

$$\nu P = \nu,$$

i.e., if for all $q \in \mathbf{Z}$,

$$\sum_r \nu(r)P(r,q) = \nu(q).$$

This is just equation 5.3 transcribed to our situation. For convenience we extract the $r = 0$ term in the sum on the left, to get

$$\sum_{r \neq 0} \nu(r)P(r,q) + \nu(0)\epsilon_0(q) = \nu(q). \tag{6.12}$$

If $\rho = 1$, the participators simply move towards each other after any channeling. Imagine that the participators are initially an even distance apart. Then they will move towards each other until they are at the same point, thenceforth to remain there. If they were to start an odd distance apart, they would eventually find themselves one unit apart. From then on they would oscillate, with relative positions of ± 1.

Thus when $\rho = 1$ there are two stationary measures: Dirac measure $\epsilon_0(\cdot)$ at the origin and a measure μ given by $\mu(+1) = \mu(-1) = 1/2, \mu(q) = 0$ if $q \neq \pm 1$.

In general, the set of measures stationary with respect to a given T.P. is always a convex set. That is, if λ and σ are stationary, so is $a\lambda + b\sigma$ whenever $0 \leq a, b \leq 1$ and $a + b = 1$. In particular, in our situation when $\rho = 1$ the set of stationary measures consists of all convex combinations $a\epsilon_0(\cdot) + b\mu(\cdot)$.

Note that, regardless of the value of ρ, $\nu(\cdot) = \epsilon_0(\cdot)$ is always a stationary measure for P. It is interesting that the only set of values of ρ for which the dynamics has a stationary measure other than $\epsilon_0(\cdot)$ is the interval $(\frac{1}{2}, 1]$. In the rest of this section we will demonstrate this fact and explicitly determine the stationary measures.

If $\rho = 0$ it is intuitively clear from 6.3 that the chain wanders off to infinity, if it is not already at the origin. Thus, if $\rho = 0$, the Dirac measure at zero is in fact the only stationary measure. Henceforth we assume $\rho \neq 0$.

Now applying Proposition 6.5 to equation 6.12, we identify the following cases:

(i) If $q = 0$,

$$\nu(0) = \rho^2(\nu(2) + \nu(-2)) + \nu(0). \tag{6.13}$$

(ii) If $q = \pm 1$,

$$\nu(\pm 1) = 2\rho(1-\rho)\nu(\pm 1) + \rho^2\nu(\mp 1) + \rho^2\nu(\pm 3). \tag{6.14}$$

(iii) If $q = \pm 2$,

$$\nu(\pm 2) = 2\rho(1-\rho)\nu(\pm 2) + \rho^2\nu(\pm 4). \tag{6.15}$$

These cases are special; for the general case $|q| \geq 3$, we have

$$\nu(q) = 2\rho(1-\rho)\nu(q) + \rho^2\nu(q + 2\,\mathrm{sgn}(q)) + (1-\rho)^2\nu(q - 2\,\mathrm{sgn}(q)),$$

which, with a little algebra, may be re-expressed as follows:

(iv) If $|q| \geq 3$,

$$\nu(q) = c^2\nu(q + 2\,\mathrm{sgn}(q)) + s^2\nu(q - 2\,\mathrm{sgn}(q)). \tag{6.16}$$

where

$$c^2 = \frac{\rho^2}{\rho^2 + (1-\rho)^2}, \qquad s^2 = \frac{(1-\rho)^2}{\rho^2 + (1-\rho)^2}; \tag{6.17}$$

note that $c^2 + s^2 = 1$.

Equation 6.16 is a linear difference equation with constant coefficients. It's solutions may be obtained by substituting the trial solution $\nu(q) = x^q, x \neq 0$.

Doing so, we get

$$x^q = c^2 x^{q+2\,\mathrm{sgn}(q)} + s^2 x^{q-2\,\mathrm{sgn}(q)}, \qquad |q| \geq 3 \tag{6.18}$$

Now the substitution $x \to x^{-1}$ into 6.18 converts any solution for $q \geq 3$ into one for $q \leq -3$, as may easily be checked. This allows us to concentrate on 6.18 for positive q only. So doing, and dividing out by x^{q-2}, we arrive at the characteristic equation

$$c^2 x^4 - x^2 + s^2 = 0. \tag{6.19}$$

Solving this for x^2, we get $x^2 = 1$ or $(s/c)^2$. (A quick way to see this is to set $c = \cos\theta$ and $s = \sin\theta$ and to use elementary trigonometric formulas.)

If $s = c$, these two solutions to 6.19 are the same. This happens when $\rho = 1/2$. For the moment, assume $s \neq c$. Put

$$t = \left(\frac{s}{c}\right)^2 = \left(\frac{1-\rho}{\rho}\right)^2. \tag{6.20}$$

We may immediately solve 6.16 for ν at the even integers. If $\rho \neq 1/2$ (i.e., $t \neq 1$), every solution to (6.16) is, at even values of q, of the form

$$\nu(2k) = \begin{cases} a_+ + b_+ t^k, & \text{if } k \geq 2 \\ a_- + b_- t^{|k|}, & \text{if } k \leq -2 \end{cases} \qquad (t \neq 1) \tag{6.21}$$

for some constants $a_\pm, b_\pm$.

Consider now $t = 1$. Then $s^2 = c^2 = 1/2$ and, by 6.16, $\nu(q)$ is an average of $\nu(q+2)$ and $\nu(q-2)$:

$$\nu(q) = \tfrac{1}{2}\nu(q+2) + \tfrac{1}{2}\nu(q-2).$$

The characteristic equation of this difference equation is

$$x^4 - 2x^2 + 1 = 0,$$

so that x^2 can only be unity. In this case, we have

$$\nu(2k) = \begin{cases} a_+ + b_+ k, & \text{if } k \geq 2 \\ a_- + b_- |k|, & \text{if } k \leq -2 \end{cases} \qquad (t = 1), \tag{6.22}$$

for some constants $a_\pm$ and $b_\pm$, as the general solution of (6.16).

Lemma 6.23. If ν is a stationary measure with respect to the T.P. P of Proposition 6.5, then

$$\nu(2k) = 0 \quad \text{for all } k \in \mathbf{Z},\, k \neq 0.$$

Proof: Since ν is a probability measure, $\{\nu(2k)\}_{k=0}^{\infty}$ is a summable sequence of non-negative terms. Hence $a_+ = a_- = 0$. If $\rho = 1$ (i.e., $t = 0$ by 6.20), by 6.21 we are done.

Next assume that $0 < t \neq 1$. By 6.13 we have $\rho^2(\nu(2) + \nu(-2)) = 0$. But, since $\rho \neq 0$, the non-negative quantities $\nu(2)$ and $\nu(-2)$ are both null. By (6.14), the same holds for $\nu(4)$ and $\nu(-4)$. When $k = 2$, (6.21) says

$$0 = \nu(4) = 0 + b_+ t^2$$

$$0 = \nu(-4) = 0 + b_- t^2,$$

that is, $b_+ = b_- = 0$. Thus the result obtains if $t \neq 1$.

If $t = 1$, the same requirement of summability shows, using 6.22, that only $\nu(0)$ could possibly be nonzero. ∎

We turn now to the computation of ν at odd integral points. Assume that $\rho \neq \frac{1}{2}$ (i.e., $t \neq 1$). We solve the formal difference equation in 6.16 for ν at the odd integers. The general solution has the form

$$\begin{aligned} \nu(2k+1) &= c_+ + d_+ t^{|k|}, &\quad \text{if } k \geq 0; \\ \nu(2k-1) &= c_- + d_- t^{|k|}, &\quad \text{if } k \leq 0, \end{aligned} \tag{6.24}$$

for some constants c_+, d_+, c_-, and d_-. As in the even case, summability requires that $c_+ = c_- = 0$ and that $t < 1$. Thus, in terms of $q = 2k + 1$ (for $k \geq 0$) or $q = 2k - 1$ (for $k \leq 0$), our general solution is,

$$\text{for } \rho \neq \frac{1}{2} \qquad \nu(q) = \begin{cases} d_+ t^{|q-1|/2}, & \text{for odd } q \geq 0; \\ d_- t^{|q+1|/2}, & \text{for odd } q \leq 0. \end{cases} \tag{6.25}$$

In particular,

$$\nu(1) = d_+, \qquad \nu(-1) = d_-. \tag{6.26}$$

Since $\sum_q \nu(q) = 1$, we have that $\sum_{q\text{odd}} \nu(q) \leq 1$. Thus

$$\sum_{k \leq 0} d_- t^{|k|} + \sum_{k \geq 0} d_+ t^{|k|} = \frac{d_+ + d_-}{1 - t} \leq 1. \tag{6.27}$$

In terms of ρ (using the definition 6.20 of t), this says that

$$1 \geq \rho \geq \frac{1}{1 + \sqrt{1 - (d_+ + d_-)}} \tag{6.28}$$

(which restricts ρ to the interval $(\frac{1}{2}, 1]$). We know that $\nu(2k) = 0$ if $k \neq 0$ (Proposition (6.23)). Thus, by 6.27,

$$\nu(0) + \frac{d_+ + d_-}{1 - t} = 1$$

or

$$\nu(0) = \frac{2\rho - 1 - \rho^2(d_+ + d_-)}{2\rho - 1}, \qquad \frac{1}{2} < \rho \leq 1. \tag{6.29}$$

We are now in a position to delineate all possible stationarities of this chain. This is significant, for once we know the stationary measures it is possible to describe the "true perception" of the dynamical situation by a given participator, as discussed in the previous section of this chapter. We shall not delve into such detail here; our purpose is to give a feel for how the dynamics is analyzed. We end this chapter with the following theorem.

Theorem 6.30.

(i) If $\frac{1}{2} < \rho \leq 1$, there is a one-parameter family of probability measures stationary with respect to the T.P. P (given in 6.5) of the dynamical chain of our example. With parameter denoted by d, this family may be described as:

$$\nu(q) = \begin{cases} d\left(\dfrac{1-\rho}{\rho}\right)^{|q-1|}, & \text{if } q \text{ is odd and } q > 0; \\ d\left(\dfrac{1-\rho}{\rho}\right)^{|q+1|}, & \text{if } q \text{ is odd and } q < 0; \\ 0, & \text{if } q \text{ is even and } q \neq 0; \\ \dfrac{2\rho - 1 - 2\rho^2 d}{2\rho - 1}, & \text{if } q = 0. \end{cases}$$

The range of allowed values of the parameter d is contained in the closed interval $[0, 1]$. For fixed $\rho \in (\frac{1}{2}, 1]$ the range is $[0, (2\rho - 1)/2\rho^2]$.

(ii) If $0 \leq \rho \leq \frac{1}{2}$, the only stationary measure is $\epsilon_0(\cdot)$.

Proof. Consider (i). For q odd we have equation 6.25. Recalling from 6.20 that $t^{1/2} = (1 - \rho)/\rho$, we obtain the first two formulas below.

$$\nu(q) = \begin{cases} d_+ \left(\dfrac{1-\rho}{\rho}\right)^{|q-1|}, & \text{if } q \text{ is odd and } q > 0; \\ d_- \left(\dfrac{1-\rho}{\rho}\right)^{|q+1|}, & \text{if } q \text{ is odd and } q < 0; \\ 0, & \text{if } q \text{ is even and } q \neq 0; \\ \dfrac{2\rho - 1 - \rho^2(d_+ + d_-)}{2\rho - 1}, & \text{if } q = 0. \end{cases}$$

The third formula above is Lemma 6.23 and the fourth is equation 6.29.

Substituting the formula for odd q into 6.14 we get

$$d_\pm = 2\rho(1-\rho)d_\pm + \rho^2 d_\mp + \rho^2 d_\pm \left(\frac{1-\rho}{\rho}\right)^{|\pm 2|},$$

which reduces to $d_+ = d_-$. Set $d = d_+ = d_-$; the range of allowed values of the parameter d as given in the statement is computed by requiring that

$$0 \leq \nu(0) = \frac{2\rho - 1 - 2\rho^2 d}{2\rho - 1} \leq 1.$$

This concludes (i).

It remains to verify (ii). We have already done so for $0 < \rho < 1/2$, since 6.28 shows us that the fact that ν is a probability measure requires that $\rho \geq 1/2$. Moreover, the instance $\rho = 1/2$ requires, in the same way as in 6.22 above, that

$$\nu(2k+1) = \begin{cases} a_+ + b_+ k, & \text{if } k \geq 1 \\ a_- + b_-|k|, & \text{if } k \leq -1 \end{cases}$$

which is only summable if it is in fact zero. ▮

CHAPTER SEVEN

FORMAL DYNAMICS

We develop in greater generality the participator dynamics introduced in special cases in chapter six.

1. Some fundamentals

In this chapter we develop the basic formalism for participator dynamics. Properly speaking, this is a dynamical system on a set of observers, namely the set $\mathcal{B}$ of objects of perception for an environment supported by a reflexive framework (X, Y, E, S, $\pi_{\bullet}$) (5–2.6). However, given certain special assumptions which we review below, we can view the dynamics as taking place on E rather than $\mathcal{B}$. We are interested in the case where the reflexive framework is a symmetric framework (X, Y, E, S, G, J, π) (5–5.1); when appropriate we will indicate the special form that our emerging results and definitions take in this case. For simplicity, when we consider a symmetric framework *we assume throughout this chapter that E is a principal homogeneous J-space,* although J need not be abelian.

We first define the concept of *action kernel* at this level of generality. Intuitively, as discussed in 6–2, an action kernel describes how a participator, at a given moment of reference time, changes perspective in response to a channeling. This change depends, in part, on the perspective of the participator, so that an action kernel is actually a family of kernels, one for each point of E. In the case of a symmetric framework we use the group action to define the notion of a *symmetric action kernel.* Such a kernel is generated from a single kernel on J, giving a symmetric description of the perspective-change law. In chapter six we studied a simplified version of this symmetric case.

Definition 1.1. (i) An *action kernel* on the reflexive framework $(X, Y, E, S, \pi_\bullet)$ is a family $\{Q_e\}_{e \in E}$ of kernels on E such that, for each e, Q_e is a markovian kernel, $Q_e: E \times \mathcal{E} \to [0, 1]$, and satisfies $Q_e(e_1, \cdot) = Q_e(e_2, \cdot)$ if $\pi_e(e_1) = \pi_e(e_2)$.

(ii) A *symmetric action kernel* on the symmetric observer framework (X, Y, E, S, G, J, π) is an action kernel $\{Q_e\}_{e \in E}$ with the following property: there exists a markovian kernel $Q: J \times \mathcal{J} \to [0, 1]$ such that $Q(j, \cdot) = Q(j', \cdot)$ if $\pi(j) = \pi(j')$, and each Q_e is deduced from Q by the formula $Q_e(e_1, \Delta) = Q(e_1 e^{-1}, \Delta e^{-1})$. We say that *the symmetric action kernel is generated by* Q.

Here, as usual, $e_1 e^{-1}$ denotes the element of J which sends e to e_1; it is unique since we assume E is principal homogeneous for J. Similarly, for $\Delta \in \mathcal{E}$, Δe^{-1} is the set of all elements of J which send e into Δ.

In general we simply use the notation Q for the entire action kernel, so that Q stands for the whole family $\{Q_e\}_{e \in E}$. In the special case of symmetric action kernels the symbol Q denotes both the action kernel itself (i.e., the family of kernels $\{Q_e\}_{e \in E}$) and the kernel which generates it. However these notions contain the same information, so this abuse of language will not cause any problem. In the general case, i.e., part (i) of Definition 1.1, there are no compatibility requirements within the family $\{Q_e\}_{e \in E}$. In practice, however, the families that we consider have various kinds of internal consistency, but it is inappropriate to incorporate these in the basic definition.

We can now use the notion of *participator* as in Definition 6–2.6. A participator is a triple $(\xi, \{Q(n)\}_n, \{\eta(n)\}_n)$, where ξ is a probability measure on E, $\{Q(n)\}_n$ is a sequence of action kernels, and $\{\eta(n)\}_n$ is a sequence of families of interpretation kernels for the reflexive framework. In this chapter we suppress mention of $\eta(n)$; in particular we do not consider the crucial question of the role played by the $\eta(n)$ in some generalized notion of action kernel. (Thus the dynamics we develop here is actually a preparticipator dynamics (6–2.6).) However, our present formalism does permit a participator's action kernel to vary in time, and intuitively $\eta(n)$ may be responsible in part for this evolution.

A participator manifests at each instant of reference time as an observer in the framework. The manifestation is probabilistic, so that we can think of the participator as a time sequence of random variables taking values in the set of observers in the framework. Since we suppress the interpretation kernels $\eta(n)$, only the perspectives of the observers vary. Therefore we can think of a participator A as a sequence of random variables, say $W_1, W_2, \ldots$ taking values in E. ξ is then the distribution of W_0. $Q_e(n)(e_1, \cdot)$ is the distribution of W_{n+1} given that the value of W_n was e and given that the participator's manifestion at time n channeled with an observer in the framework whose perspective is represented by $e_1 \in E$ (via the map Π defining the framework as in 5–2.2). Therefore, the process $W_1, W_2, \ldots$ is not a Markov chain: the distribution of W_{n+1} depends not just on the value e of W_n, but also on $\pi(e_1)$.

However, if we consider collectively a "closed system" of participators (6–2.9) and if we assume some regularity to the distribution of channelings, then we can canonically associate certain Markov chains to the system. These Markov chains contain complete information about the extended semantics for each potential manifestation of the participators. These potential manifestations together constitute the set of distinguished objects of perception $\mathcal{B}_E$ for the environment (4–4.4, 6–2.7).

In this chapter we introduce and study certain Markov chains canonically associated to discrete-time, participator dynamical systems. We make the following restrictive assumptions:

1. The interpretation kernels $\eta(n)$ of the various participators have no explicit role in the dynamical formalism, so that we can view the participators as being individuated only by their perspectives.
2. The participator dynamical systems are *closed* (6–2.9).
3. The *independent action* postulate holds (6–2.10).
4. The choice of channeling at each instant of reference time may be described by a "τ-distribution" (defined in section two of this chapter).

To begin, we choose an integer $k \geq 1$, and consider k participators

$$A_i = \{(\xi_i, \{Q_i(n)\}_n)\},\ i = 1, \ldots, k$$

on our framework. We assume that there is a discrete time, at each instant of which each participator manifests as some observer in the framework, and at each instant of which there is a channeling; this is the same as the *reference time* of 6–2. In effect we are studying an extended semantics in which these observer manifestations of the participators are the distinguished objects of perception. We make the *closed system assumption* (6–2.9) that at each instant the distinguished part of the channeling involves only observers which are participator manifestations at that instant. In other words, at any time n the only channelings involving participator manifestations are channelings between the participator manifestations themselves. Thus we assume that at any instant n of a participator channeling sequence (6–2.8), the domain D_n of the distinguished part of the channeling at that instant is a subset of the set of participator manifestations at time n; hence, D_n contains at most k observers. We need a consistent way to refer to the possible channelings among these observers:

Notation 1.2. Denote by $\mathcal{I}(k)$ the set of all involutions on subsets of $\{1, \ldots, k\}$. Thus an element of $\mathcal{I}(k)$ is a pair consisting of a subset $D \subset \{1, \ldots, k\}$ and a function $\chi: D \to D$ such that $\chi^2 \equiv \chi \circ \chi = \mathrm{id}_D$. More generally, if V is any set we denote by $\mathcal{I}(V)$ the set of all involutions of subsets of V. If V' and V'' are disjoint subsets of V with $\chi' \in \mathcal{I}(V')$ and $\chi'' \in \mathcal{I}(V'')$, we denote by $\chi' \cup \chi''$ the element of $\mathcal{I}(V' \cup V'')$ described by χ' on V' and by χ'' on V''. For $\chi \in \mathcal{I}(k)$, $D(\chi)$ denotes, as indicated above, the domain of χ.

Once we have fixed the integer k and the participators $A_1, \ldots, A_k$, the element χ of $\mathcal{I}(k)$ refers to the channeling in which, for each $i \in D(\chi)$, the manifestations of A_i and $A_{\chi(i)}$ channel to each other and in which, for $j \notin D(\chi)$, the manifestation of A_j does not channel. Henceforth, for simplicity, we will say "A_i and $A_{\chi(i)}$ channel to each other at time n" rather than the correct but cumbersome "the manifestations of A_i and $A_{\chi(i)}$ at time n channel to each other." Similarly, we will simply say "A_i has perspective (or 'position') e_i at time n" rather than "the manifestation of A_i at time n has perspective which is $\Pi(e_i)$." Thus, to say "$\chi \in \mathcal{I}(k)$ is the channeling at time n" means that, for $i \in D(\chi)$, A_i and $A_{\chi(i)}$ channel at time n, and for $j \notin D(\chi)$, A_j does not channel at time n. This is the same as saying that in the participator channeling sequence $(D_n, \chi_n) = (D(\chi), \chi)$. Thus, the $\mathcal{I}(k)$ notation permits us to consider channelings in which some participators are inactive, some channel to themselves, and so on.

As a result of a channeling at a given time t_0, each active participator changes its perspective, i.e., its position in E, in a manner dictated by its action kernel at time t_0. According to our participator notation the action kernel of A_i at time t_0 is $Q_i(t_0)$. Suppose the channeling is represented by $\chi \in \mathcal{I}(k)$. Then if $i \in D(\chi)$, the position of A_i at $t_0 + 1$, i.e., at the next instant of reference time, is a random variable with distribution $Q_{ie_i}(t_0)(e_{\chi(i)}, \cdot)$. As in part (i) of Definition 1.1 above, $Q_{ie_i}(t_0)$ denotes the markovian kernel that governs the perspective change of A_i from time t_0 to $t_0 + 1$ given that A_i has perspective e_i at t_0. In action kernel notation this means the following: for $\Delta_i \in \mathcal{E}$, the probability that the perspective of A_i will be in Δ_i at time $t_0 + 1$ is $Q_{ie_i}(t_0)(e_{\chi(i)}, \Delta_i)$. According to the independent action postulate, given the perspectives of the participators at time t_0 and given the channeling χ, the k E-valued random variables describing the next perspectives of the k participators are *independent*. As a result we have the following proposition:

Proposition 1.3. Suppose we are given, at time t_0, k participators $A_1, \ldots, A_k$ with action kernels $Q_1, \ldots, Q_k$. Moreover suppose that, at time t_0, A_i is at e_i, for $i = 1, \ldots, k$. Let $\chi \in \mathcal{I}(k)$ be the channeling at t_0, so that A_i and $A_{\chi(i)}$ channel to each other for each $i \in D(\chi)$ and so that A_j is inert if $j \notin D(\chi)$. Let $\Delta_1, \ldots, \Delta_k \in \mathcal{E}$, and let $N_{t_0,\chi}(e_1, \ldots, e_k; \Delta_1 \times \ldots \times \Delta_k)$ denote the probability that, at time $t_0 + 1$, A_i will have perspective in Δ_i, for $i = 1, \ldots, k$. Then

$$N_{t_0,\chi}(e_1, \ldots, e_k; \Delta_1 \times \ldots \times \Delta_k) = \prod_{i \in D(\chi)} Q_{ie_i}(t_0)(e_{\chi(i)}, \Delta_i) \prod_{j \notin D(\chi)} 1_{\Delta_j}(e_j).$$

In the case of symmetric action kernels the formula is

$$\prod_{i \in D(\chi)} Q_i(t_0)(e_{\chi(i)} e_i^{-1}, \Delta_i e_i^{-1}) \prod_{j \notin D(\chi)} 1_{\Delta_j}(e_j).$$

Proof. Straightforward. The independent action postulate justifies the products in the formulas above. ∎

We frequently express the formulae of 1.3 in *infinitesimal form,* replacing each Δ_i with dy_i and each $1_{\Delta_j}(e_j)$ with $\epsilon_{e_j}(dy_j)$. (Recall that $\epsilon_e(dy)$ is Dirac measure concentrated at e.) The first formula becomes

$$N_{t_0,\chi}(e_1, \ldots, e_k; dy_1, \ldots, dy_k) = \prod_{i \in D(\chi)} Q_{ie_i}(t_0)(e_{\chi(i)}, dy_i) \prod_{j \notin D(\chi)} \epsilon_{e_j}(dy_j).$$

In the symmetric case this is

$$\prod_{i \in D(\chi)} Q_i(t_0)(e_{\chi(i)} e_i^{-1}, dy_i e_i^{-1}) \prod_{j \notin D(\chi)} \epsilon_{e_j}(dy_j).$$

2. The τ-distribution

k participators, interacting via channeling, change their manifestations probabilistically in a manner governed by their action kernels; intuitively the result is a stochastic process indexed by reference time, with state space $\mathcal{B}^k$ (or more precisely $\mathcal{B}^k_E \subset \mathcal{B}^k$). Since we focus only on the *perspectives* of the manifestations, we can view this process as having state space E^k. We take our k participators to be $A_1, \ldots, A_k$ as above. Suppose we assume, artificially, that the same channeling pattern, say $\chi \in \mathcal{I}(k)$, occurs at each instant of reference time. In other words, suppose we assume that the only participator channeling sequence in the dynamics is the constant sequence with value χ: A_i always channels with $A_{\chi(i)}$. Then Proposition 1.3 says, in effect, that our stochastic process is a Markov chain whose transition probability from time t_0 to $t_0 + 1$ is the kernel $N_{t_0,\chi}(\cdot,\cdot)$. Recall that in **6–4** we treat a simple case of this artificial situation for $k = 2$. We there assume that the system consists of two participators which channel to each other at each instant of reference time. Thus, of the five elements of $\mathcal{I}(2)$, we assume, artificially, that the only relevant one is χ, where $\chi(1) = 2$.[1]

Although we consider in this book only systems where the number k of participators is fixed, we believe it is unreasonable to build a general theory on the further assumption that the channeling arrangement χ is also fixed. But then on what does χ depend? One might suppose, for example, that each participator comes equipped with a set of channeling affinities, one for each participator in the ensemble. But this, too, seems artificial. For participators are individuated instantaneously by their perspectives, and it is natural to suppose that the channeling affinities depend, at least in part, on these perspectives. This idea suggests that channeling affinity is attached somehow to E, wherein it describes "mutual perceptual accessibility" or "informational conductivity" between pairs of perspectives. In symmetric frameworks the affinity might depend only on the *difference* of perspectives, i.e., on the group J.

What form should information on channeling affinities take in order that we may use it to compute the transition probabilities for the markovian dynamics in our participator ensemble? If we want to base our computations on formulae like those in Proposition 1.3, we need to know the probabilities, denoted $\tau(e_1, \ldots, e_k; \chi)$, of

[1] We do not use the kernel $N_{t_0,\chi}$ form for the transition probability of the dynamics in **6–4** although we could have done so. Instead, we there represent the dynamics in a form which is "relativized with respect to the first participator." This means that we are looking at a chain whose states are the displacements (in the group J) of the second participator with respect to the first.

the various possible χ at time t_0, conditioned by the perspectives of the A_i at t_0, i.e., conditioned by $(e_1, \ldots e_k)$. If we know these $\tau(e_1, \ldots, e_k; \chi)$ we can take the weighted sum

$$N_{t_0}(e_1,\ldots,e_k;\, \Delta_1 \times \ldots \times \Delta_k) = \sum_{\chi \in \mathcal{I}(k)} \tau(e_1, \ldots, e_k;\, \chi) N_{t_0,\chi}(e_1,\ldots,e_k;\, \Delta_1 \times \ldots \times \Delta_k). \tag{2.2}$$

$N_{t_0}(e_1,\ldots,e_k;\, \Delta_1 \times \ldots \times \Delta_k)$ is the probability of a perspective change from $(e_1, \ldots, e_k)$ to $\Delta_1 \times \ldots \times \Delta_k$ from time t_0 to $t_0 + 1$, regardless of the channeling pattern: it is the desired transition probability for the chain in E^k generated by the participator ensemble $A_1, \ldots, A_k$.

One natural way to define the probabilities τ might be to utilize a *metric* on E. Intuitively one could define the "elementary" probability that two observers will channel to each other in terms of the distance in this metric between the points of E representing their perspectives. $\tau(e_1,\ldots,e_k;\, \chi)$ could then be computed in some canonical way using these elementary probabilities. However, since the study of the Markov chains is our primary interest, we simply assume the existence of a τ satisfying certain formal properties. Thus we do not consider the interesting question of the possible relation of τ to other intrinsic data such as metrics on E.

We assume that the τ-distribution is attached to the reflexive framework itself, and not to any particular set of participators. Therefore, τ should be defined for any k, and its expression for various values of k should be consistent. The following definition is a minimal one with these properties:

Definition 2.3. A *τ-distribution* is a family $\tau = \{\tau_k\}_{k=1}^{\infty}$ where each τ_k is a markovian kernel on $E^k \times 2^{\mathcal{I}(k)}$,[2] i.e., a map

$$\tau_k\colon E^k \times 2^{\mathcal{I}(k)} \to [0,\, 1]$$

satisfying the following conditions:

1. $\tau_k(\cdot\,;\chi) \in \mathcal{E}^k$ for all $\chi \subset \mathcal{I}(k)$, and $\tau_k(y_1, \ldots, y_k;\, \cdot)$ is a probability distribution on $\mathcal{I}(k)$ for all $(y_1, \ldots, y_k) \in E^k$.
2. *Consistency condition.* Given $k' < k$, let $S' = \{1, \ldots, k'\}$, $S = \{1, \ldots, k\}$. Then, (with the notation of 1.2 above) for any

[2] This notation means that we are viewing $\mathcal{I}(k)$ as a measurable space with σ-algebra $2^{\mathcal{I}(k)}$.

$$(y_1, \ldots, y_{k'}, z_{k'+1}, \ldots, z_k) \in E^k, \chi \in \mathcal{I}(k'),$$

we have

$$\tau_{k'}(y_1, \ldots, y_{k'}; \chi) = \frac{\sum_{\chi'' \in \mathcal{I}(S-S')} \tau_k(y_1, \ldots, y_{k'}, z_{k'+1}, \ldots, z_k; \chi \cup \chi'')}{\sum_{\substack{\chi' \in \mathcal{I}(S') \\ \chi'' \in \mathcal{I}(S-S')}} \tau_k(y_1, \ldots, y_{k'}, z_{k'+1}, \ldots, z_k; \chi' \cup \chi'')}.$$

3. *Symmetry conditions.* If our reflexive framework is a symmetric framework, we consider two symmetry conditions on τ corresponding to two notions of equivalence on E^k. First, we define two k-tuples, $y = (y_1, \ldots, y_k)$ and $x = (x_1, \ldots, x_k) \in E^k$, to be *configuration equivalent* if for every i and l satisfying $1 \leq i, l \leq k$ we have $x_i x_l^{-1} = y_i y_l^{-1}$ (notation as in 1.1). We define them to be *translation equivalent* if there exists a $j \in J$ with $x_i = j y_i$, for all $1 \leq i \leq k$. Then
   (i) τ is *configuration symmetric* if $\tau(x; \cdot) = \tau(y; \cdot)$ whenever x and y are configuration equivalent;
   (ii) τ is *translation symmetric* if $\tau(x; \cdot) = \tau(y; \cdot)$ whenever x and y are translation equivalent.

Intuitively, condition 2 states that the probability of any particular channeling among a system S' of observers is not affected by the addition of extra observers to the system as long as there is no "cross-channeling," i.e., as long as one conditions the probability of channeling by those channelings which pair no member of S' with one of the added observers. It is this condition which unites the separate τ_k's for various k.

In condition 3, if J were commutative then configuration equivalence and translation equivalence would be identical. In this case configuration symmetry and translation symmetry would be identical conditions on τ. When J is noncommutative, however, the two conditions are different. In fact the two notions of equivalence on E^k may not even be comparable (in the sense that an equivalence class from one relation is not necessarily a union of equivalence classes from the other).

Except when we wish to emphasize a particular k, we omit the subscript k of the τ; we simply write $\tau(y_1, \ldots, y_k; \chi)$.

We do not require $\tau(y_1, \ldots, y_k; \cdot)$ to be invariant under permutations of $y_1, \ldots, y_k$. Thus, the formalism permits the encoding of channeling affinities between specific participators even though such affinities seem naturally attached to the framework itself and not to specific participator ensembles.

Remark 2.4. For each k, consider the product space $E^k \times \mathcal{I}(k)$; denote it $\hat{E}^k$. Let $\hat{\mathcal{E}}^k$ denote the σ-algebra on $\hat{E}^k$ which is generated by $\mathcal{E}^k = \mathcal{E} \otimes \ldots \otimes \mathcal{E}$ and the algebra of all subsets of $\mathcal{I}(k)$. Let $p = \mathrm{pr}_1$ denote projection on the first factor of $\hat{E}^k$, i.e., $p: \hat{E}^k \to E^k$. p is measurable, and each fibre of p is a copy of $\mathcal{I}(k)$. As defined in 2.3, the τ-distribution is a kernel on $E^k \times 2^{\mathcal{I}(k)}$. We may also view it as a kernel on $E^k \times \hat{\mathcal{E}}^k$ as follows. Let $A \in \hat{\mathcal{E}}^k$ be a measurable set in $\hat{E}^k$ and let $(e_1, \ldots, e_k) \in E^k$. Define

$$\bar{\tau}(e_1, \ldots, e_k; A) = \tau(e_1, \ldots, e_k; \mathrm{pr}_2[A \cap p^{-1}\{(e_1, \ldots, e_k)\}]),$$

where $\mathrm{pr}_2 : \hat{E}^k \to \mathcal{I}(k)$ is projection onto the second factor of $\hat{E}^k$. $\mathrm{pr}_2[A \cap p^{-1}\{(e_1, \ldots, e_k)\}]$ consists of just those channelings χ such that $(e_1, \ldots, e_k; \chi)$ is in A.

It is clear from Definition 2.3 that $\bar{\tau}$ is a markovian kernel on $E^k \times \hat{\mathcal{E}}^k$ such that $\bar{\tau}(e_1, \ldots, e_k; \cdot)$ is concentrated on $p^{-1}\{(e_1, \ldots, e_k)\}$. In the sequel, we think of τ as this $\bar{\tau}$, using the same symbol τ for both.

3. Augmented dynamics

In this section we discuss the underlying probabilistic framework for the participator dynamics. In section two the τ distribution was motivated by the need to compute the transition probability for the Markov chain whose states are the positions in E of the k participators in a given ensemble. Thus the state space of this chain is E^k, and it is called the (absolute) *position chain* of the dynamics. (The word "absolute" here is sometimes used, in the context of a symmetric framework, to distinguish this chain from other chains which express the positions relative to some fixed observer or to one of the participators; these latter chains have state space J^k or J^{k-1}, respectively.)

Now a knowledge only of the positions of the participators in perspective space is insufficient for many purposes; we need information not only about positions, but also about channelings. The situation at any moment of reference time is most completely described, in our development, by a vector in $\hat{E}^k$ (defined in 2.4 as $E^k \times \mathcal{I}(k)$). We may refer to the elements of $\hat{E}^k$ as being "augmented" by the inclusion of the channeling involution in the description. The stochastic process with state space $\hat{E}^k$ is then the underlying probabilistic framework for all other processes discussed in this chapter and the next one. We refer to the process in $\hat{E}^k$ as the *augmented position chain*.

Before describing the augmented dynamics, we note that there are yet other chains relevant to participator dynamics. For example, the symmetrized perspective space is E^k/S_k (S_k being the symmetric group of permutations of k objects). In this state space we are unconcerned with the identities of the k participators and note only the set of perspectives assumed by them. The corresponding stochastic process is called the "symmetrized position chain." On a different tack, we may to our dynamical situation associate "stopped chains," i.e., chains descended from the reference time chains via *stopping times*. For example, we might stop the reference time chains when a given participator A is channeled to, and note the positions of all participators only at such times. Such a chain is clearly derived from the augmented position chain, to the study of which we now turn.

3.1. Let Θ denote the reflexive observer framework $(X, Y, E, S, \pi_\bullet)$. Suppose we are given a τ-distribution on Θ as in Definition 2.3 above. We will describe the *augmented dynamics of an ensemble of k participators* $(\xi_1, Q_1(n)), \ldots, (\xi_k, Q_k(n))$ *on* Θ. This is a Markov chain indexed by reference time t, with state space $\hat{E}^k = E^k \times \mathcal{I}(k)$; a state of this chain encodes the location in E of each of the participators at a given reference time, as well as specifying the channeling relation among them at that time.

To describe a Markov chain it suffices to give a starting measure on the state space, and a one-step transition probability for each time t. In our present situation this transition probability will be a markovian kernel

$$\hat{N}_t \colon \hat{E}^k \times \hat{\mathcal{E}}^k \to [0, 1].$$

Here $\hat{\mathcal{E}}^k$ denotes the σ-algebra (defined in Remark 2.4) on $\hat{E}^k = E^k \times \mathcal{I}(k)$ generated by all sets of the form $\Delta \times \{\chi\}$ where $\Delta \in \mathcal{E}^k$ and $\chi \in \mathcal{I}(k)$. Thus $\hat{N}_t$ is completely determined once we express

$$\hat{N}_t(e_1, \ldots, e_k, \chi_0; \Delta \times \{\chi_1\})$$

in terms of our given participators. This notation means the following: $\hat{N}_t$ is the probability that at time $t + 1$ our k-tuple of participators will have perspectives represented by a point in $\Delta \subset E^k$ and will channel to each other as dictated by an involution χ_1 in $\mathcal{I}(k)$, given that at time t they had perspectives $(e_1, \ldots, e_k)$ and channeled to each other according to $\chi_0 \in \mathcal{I}(k)$.

These considerations suggest the following definition:

Definition 3.2. Let $(e, \chi_0) \in E^k \times \mathcal{I}(k)$, with $e = (e_1, \ldots, e_k)$. Let $\Delta \times \{\chi_1\} \in \hat{\mathcal{E}}^k$. Define

$$\hat{N}_t(e, \chi_0;\, \Delta \times \{\chi_1\}) = \int_\Delta N_{t,\chi_0}(e_1, \ldots, e_k;\, dy_1 \ldots dy_k)\tau(y_1, \ldots, y_k;\, \chi_1),$$

where N_{t,χ_0} is as in Proposition 1.3. In other words

$$\begin{aligned} &\hat{N}_t(e, \chi_0;\, \Delta \times \{\chi_1\}) \\ &= \int_\Delta [\prod_{i \in D(\chi_0)} Q_{ie_i}(t)\, (e_{\chi_0(i)}; dy_i) \prod_{j \notin D(\chi_0)} \epsilon_{e_j}(dy_j)]\tau(y_1, \ldots, y_k; \chi_1). \end{aligned}$$

If our participators are kinematical, i.e., time independent, then $\hat{N}_t$ is independent of t, and we call it simply $\hat{N}$. In this case the augmented dynamical chain is a *homogeneous* Markov chain with transition probability $\hat{N}$.

Notation 3.3. To stress the dependence of $\hat{N}_t$ on the $Q_i(t)$ and τ, and for other reasons to be discussed later, we sometimes use the notation $\widehat{\langle Q_1(t), \ldots, Q_k(t)\rangle}_\tau$ instead of $\hat{N}_t$. Similarly, if the participators are kinematical we may use the notation $\widehat{\langle Q_1, \ldots, Q_k\rangle}_\tau$ instead of $\hat{N}$.

The action kernels of our k participators together with τ give rise to the transition probabilities of the augmented dynamical chain. Similarly, the initial measures ξ_i of these participators together with τ determine the starting measure of this chain on $E^k \times \mathcal{I}(k)$ as we now describe.

Notation 3.4. Let ξ be a measure on E^k. We denote by ξ_τ the measure on $E^k \times \mathcal{I}(k)$ given by

$$\xi_\tau(\Delta_1 \times \ldots \times \Delta_k \times \{\chi\}) = \int_{\Delta_1 \times \ldots \times \Delta_k} \xi(dy_1 \ldots dy_k)\,\tau(y_1, \ldots, y_k;\, \chi).$$

If ξ is a probability measure, so is ξ_τ.

Proposition 3.5. Let p: $\hat{E}^k = E^k \times \mathcal{I}(k) \to E^k$ be projection on the first factor, i.e., $p = \mathrm{pr}_1$. Then $p_*(\xi_\tau) = \xi$, and $m_p^{\xi_\tau} = \tau$ (using the notation of **2–1**).
Proof. The proof is an exercise in the definition of the τ-distribution (see Remark 2.4) and of a regular conditional probability distribution. The situation is especially simple since the fibres of p are copies of the discrete space $\mathcal{I}(k)$. ∎

Definition 3.6. The starting measure of the augmented dynamical chain of the ensemble of participators $(\xi_1, Q_1(t)), \ldots, (\xi_k, Q_k(t))$ is $(\xi_1 \otimes \ldots \otimes \xi_k)_\tau$.

The interpretation of this measure is straightforward: we assume that the initial positions of the participators are distributed independently, so that

$$(\xi_1 \otimes \ldots \otimes \xi_k)_\tau(\Delta_1 \times \ldots \times \Delta_k \times \{\chi\})$$

is the probability that, at starting time $t = 0$, the k-tuple of perspectives of our participators lie in $\Delta_1 \times \ldots \times \Delta_k \subset E^k$ and channel according to χ in $\mathcal{I}(k)$.

We summarize. On the reflexive framework $\Theta = (X, Y, E, S, \pi_\bullet)$ with given τ-distribution, suppose we have an ensemble of participators $(\xi_1, Q_1(t))$, ..., $(\xi_k, Q_k(t))$. Associated to this situation is a canonical Markov chain with state space $\hat{E}^k = E^k \times \mathcal{I}(k)$, called the augmented dynamical chain of the participator ensemble.

The state of this chain at time t is given by random variables $y_1(t)$, ..., $y_k(t)$ (with values in E) and $\chi(t)$ (with values in $\mathcal{I}(k)$). $y_i(t)$ is the perspective of the ith participator, and $\chi(t)$ is the channeling relation among the k participators, at time t. For fixed t these variables are not independent: the dependence of $\chi(t)$ on the $y_i(t)$ is expressed by the τ-distribution. Moreover, since the dynamics is markovian, the dependence of the distribution of the $y_i(t+1)$ and $\chi(t+1)$ on previous values can be expressed entirely in terms of the $y_i(t)$ and $\chi(t)$. This expression is contained in the one-step transition probability at time t, denoted $\widehat{\langle Q_1(t), \ldots, Q_k(t)\rangle}_\tau$ or $\hat{N}_t$ (the precise definition is given in 3.2). The starting measure of the chain is $(\xi_1 \otimes \ldots \otimes \xi_k)_\tau$ (using Notation 3.4).

Notation 3.7. The "base space" of the augmented position chain is the probability space $(\hat{\Omega}, \hat{\mathcal{F}}, \hat{P})$ on which the random variables $y_i(t), \chi(t)$ (for all i, t) are defined. Thus the "sample" space $\hat{\Omega}$ is the domain of these random variables; we take it as the space $(\hat{E}^k)^\infty$ of all trajectories $t \to (y_1(t), \ldots, y_k(t); \chi(t))$. If we want to emphasize the number k of participators generating the chain, we write $(\hat{\Omega}^k, \hat{\mathcal{F}}^k, \hat{P}^k)$ instead of just $(\hat{\Omega}, \hat{\mathcal{F}}, \hat{P})$. We write

$$\hat{y}(t) = (\hat{y}_1(t), \ldots, \hat{y}_k(t), \chi(t)),$$

so that for each t, $\hat{y}(t): \hat{\Omega} \to E^k \times \mathcal{I}(k)$. (We follow the usual probabilistic convention of suppressing explicit mention of the sample points $\hat{\omega} \in \hat{\Omega}$ unless necessary.) By our choice of $\hat{\Omega}$ then, $\hat{y}(t)$ is the "t"th coordinate vector of the trajectory. The σ-algebra $\hat{\mathcal{F}}$ is taken to be that generated in $\hat{\Omega}$ by the sequence of random variables $\{\hat{y}(t)\}$. The probability measure $\hat{P}$ on the sample space is developed from the initial measure $(\xi_1 \otimes \ldots \otimes \xi_k)_\tau$ and the transition probabilities $\hat{N}_t$ in canonical fashion. In this sense the augmented position chain is presented as a "canonical" Markov chain[3], with filtration $\{\hat{\mathcal{F}}_n\}$ where $\hat{\mathcal{F}}_n = \sigma(\hat{y}(0), \ldots, \hat{y}(n))$.

4. Augmented dynamics and standard dynamics

Suppose that we are in a reflexive framework Θ with given τ-distribution and that we have an ensemble of participators $(\xi_1, Q_1(t)), \ldots, (\xi_k, Q_k(t))$ as in the previous section. Suppose further that for all χ in $\mathcal{I}(k)$ we know $N_{t,\chi}$, as in Proposition 1.3. (Recall that $N_{t,\chi}$ is the transition probability for the k-tuple of perspectives from time t to time $t+1$ assuming that the particular channeling relation χ occurred at time t.) Then, as in Equation 2.2, we can define the kernel N_t on E^k.

Definition 4.1. For $(e_1, \ldots, e_k) \in E^k, \Delta_1 \times \ldots \times \Delta_k \in \mathcal{E}^k$,

$$\begin{aligned} &N_t(e_1, \ldots, e_k; \Delta_1 \times \ldots \times \Delta_k) \\ &\quad = \sum_{\chi \in \mathcal{I}(k)} \tau(e_1, \ldots, e_k; \chi) N_{t,\chi}(e_1, \ldots, e_k; \Delta_1 \times \ldots \times \Delta_k) \\ &\quad = \sum_{\chi \in \mathcal{I}(k)} \tau(e_1, \ldots, e_k; \chi) \prod_{i \in D(\chi)} Q_i(t)(e_{\chi(i)} e_i^{-1}; \Delta_i e_i^{-1}) \prod_{j \notin D(\chi)} 1_{\Delta_j}(e_j). \end{aligned}$$

[3] See Remark 5.9 of this chapter.

If all our participators are kinematical with fixed action kernels Q_i, then we can omit mention of t.

Notation 4.2. We sometimes use the notation $\langle Q_1(t), \ldots, Q_k(t)\rangle_\tau$ in place of N_t, or $\langle Q_1, \ldots, Q_k\rangle_\tau$ in place of N in the kinematical case.

With notation and hypotheses as above, the following definition is natural:

Definition 4.3. *The standard dynamical chain generated by an ensemble of participators* is the canonical Markov chain with state space E^k, one step transition probabilities $N_t = \langle Q_1(t), \ldots, Q_k(t)\rangle_\tau$, and starting measure $\xi_1 \otimes \ldots \otimes \xi_k$.

Notation 4.4. We denote the base sample space of this standard dynamical chain by Ω, or Ω^k if we want to emphasize the particular value of k. Thus Ω $(= \Omega^k)$ $= (E^k)^\infty$. The chain, then, consists formally of the sequence of random variables $y(t): \Omega \to E^k$ $(t = 0, 1, \ldots)$, where $y(t) = (y_1(t), \ldots, y_k(t))$.

In this section we study certain aspects of the relationship between the augmented dynamical chain and the standard dynamical chain for a given ensemble of participators. The following diagram summarizes the basic setup:

$$\begin{array}{ccccc} & & \text{augmented chain} & \hat{E}^k & \hat{N}_t \\ \hat{\Omega} = & (E^k \times \mathcal{I}(k))^\infty & \xrightarrow{\hat{y}(t)=(y_1(t),\ldots,y_k(t),\chi(t))} & E^k \times \mathcal{I}(k) & \\ & \downarrow p' & & \downarrow p=\mathrm{pr}_1 & \\ \Omega & (E^k)^\infty & \xrightarrow{y(t)=(y_1(t),\ldots,y_k(t))} & E^k & N_t \\ & & \text{standard chain} & & \end{array} \tag{4.5}$$

p' is induced by p. To exercise the notation, let $\hat{\omega}$ be an element of $\hat{\Omega}$. We can view $\hat{\omega}$ as a sequence of elements of $E^k \times \mathcal{I}(k)$ indexed by t, i.e.,

$$\hat{\omega} = \{(e_1(t), \ldots, e_k(t), \chi(t))\}_{t=1}^{\infty}.$$

Then

$$\begin{aligned}\hat{y}(t)(\hat{\omega}) &= (e_1(t), \ldots, e_k(t), \chi(t)) \\ &= (y_1(t)(\hat{\omega}), \ldots, y_k(t)(\hat{\omega}), \chi(t)(\hat{\omega})). \\ p'(\hat{\omega}) &= \{(e_1(t), \ldots, e_k(t))\}_{t=1}^{\infty}, \\ y(t)p'(\hat{\omega}) &= (e_1(t), \ldots, e_k(t)), \quad \text{etc.}\end{aligned}$$

The top and bottom rows of diagram 4.5 represent the augmented and standard dynamical chains respectively, for which the one step transition probabilities are, respectively, $\hat{N}_t = \widehat{\langle Q_1(t), \ldots, Q_k(t) \rangle}_T$ and $N_t = \langle Q_1(t), \ldots, Q_k(t) \rangle_T$.

Now there is an abstract characterization of the structural relationship between $\hat{N}_t$ and N_t, which does not follow merely from the simple relationship between the state spaces of the two chains. It can be understood in terms of general operations on kernels which we now introduce.

The first part of the following definition merely recalls the notion of "push-down" of a measure, introduced in **2–1**. The second part then generalizes this notion to kernels.

Definition 4.6. Let $(U, \mathcal{U})$ and $(V, \mathcal{V})$ be measurable spaces and let $h: U \to V$ be a measurable function.

(i) If μ is a measure on U, the *pushdown of* μ *by* h is the measure $h_*\mu$ on V, given by

$$h_*\mu(A) = \mu(h^{-1}(A)), \quad A \in \mathcal{V}.$$

Alternatively, for any measurable $g: V \to \mathbf{R}$,

$$\int_V (h_*\mu)(dv) g(v) = \int_U \mu(du)(g \circ h)(u).$$

(ii) If M is a kernel on U, the *pushdown of* M *by* h is the kernel h_*M on $U \times \mathcal{V}$, given by

$$(h_*M)(u, A) = M(u, h^{-1}(A)), \quad A \in \mathcal{V}.$$

Again, we may restate this in terms of operations on functions:

$$(h_*Mg)(u) = \int_U M(u, du')\; g \circ h(u'), \quad g \in \mathcal{V}.$$

If μ is a probability measure, so is $h_*\mu$; if M is markovian, so is h_*M. The notion of composition of a measure and a kernel, or of two kernels, was introduced in **6**–1. We generalize it here.

Definition 4.7. Let $(U,\mathcal{U})$, $(V,\mathcal{V})$ and $(W,\mathcal{W})$ be measurable spaces. Let K be a kernel on $U \times \mathcal{V}$.

(i) If μ is a measure on U, the measure μK on V is defined by

$$\mu K(A) = \int_U \mu(du)\, K(u,A), \quad A \in \mathcal{V}.$$

(ii) If L is a kernel on $W \times \mathcal{U}$, the composition LK is the kernel on $W \times \mathcal{V}$ defined by

$$LK(w,A) = \int_U L(w,du)\, K(u,A), \quad A \in \mathcal{V}.$$

As in 4.7, we may easily write down the effect of these compositions on functions $g: V \to \mathbf{R}$. Also, if μ is a probability measure and K and L are markovian kernels, then μK is a probability measure and KL is markovian.

Combining these definitions we have the following:

Definition 4.8. Let $(U,\mathcal{U})$ and $(V,\mathcal{V})$ be measurable spaces with $h: U \to V$ measurable. Let M be a kernel on U and L a kernel on $V \times \mathcal{U}$. The *L-pushdown of M by h* is then the kernel $h_*^L M$ on V, defined by

$$\begin{aligned}(h_*^L M)(v,A) &= (L(h_*M))(v,A) \\ &= \int_U L(v,du)\, M(u,h^{-1}(A)), \quad u \in U, A \in \mathcal{V}.\end{aligned}$$

We wish to use this construction to relate the kernel $\hat{N}_t$ on $\hat{E}^k$ (in place of M on U) to the kernel N_t on E^k (where E^k replaces V). The role of h is played by $p = \mathrm{pr}_1$ on $\hat{E}^k$, while that of L is played by $\bar{\tau}$ as in 2.4. As mentioned in 2.4 we will, however, write just τ in place of $\bar{\tau}$, viewing the τ-distribution as a kernel on $E^k \times \hat{\mathcal{E}}^k$. Pictorially,

$$\begin{array}{lll} E^k \times \mathcal{I}(k) = & \hat{E}^k & \hat{N}_t\colon \hat{E}^k \times \hat{\mathcal{E}}^k \to [0,\ 1] \\ & & \tau\colon E^k \times \hat{\mathcal{E}}^k \to [0,\ 1] \\ & \big\downarrow \mathrm{pr}_1 = p & \\ & E^k & p_*^\tau \hat{N}_t\colon E^k \times \mathcal{E}^k \to [0,\ 1] \end{array}$$

Using Definition 4.8 we get the kernel $p_*^\tau \hat{N}_t$ on E^k:

$$p_*^\tau \hat{N}_t(e, A) = \int_{\hat{E}^k} \tau(e, d\hat{e}) p_* \hat{N}_t(\hat{e}, A).$$

Intuitively, the above pushdown consists in averaging the values $\hat{N}_t(\cdot, p^{-1}(A))$ with respect to the measure $\tau(e, \cdot)$. Now the measure $\tau(e, \cdot)$ is concentrated on the fibre $p^{-1}\{e\}$; recall that this fibre may be viewed as a copy of $\mathcal{I}(k)$. Thus $p_*^\tau \hat{N}_t(e, A)$ is an expectation of the values $p_* \hat{N}_t(e, \chi_0; A)$ with respective weights $\tau(e, \chi_0)$. These values can, in turn, be related to the objects N_{t,χ_0} (Proposition 1.3) as follows. We claim that, for any $A \in \mathcal{E}^k$,

$$p_* \hat{N}_t(e, \chi_0; A) = N_{t,\chi_0}(e; A). \tag{4.9}$$

For (suppressing the subscript t)

$$\begin{aligned} p_* \hat{N}(e, \chi_0; A) &= \hat{N}(e, \chi_0; p^{-1}(A)) \\ &= \hat{N}(e, \chi_0; \bigcup_{\chi \in \mathcal{I}(k)} A \times \{\chi\}) \\ &= \sum_{\chi \in \mathcal{I}(k)} \hat{N}(e, \chi_0; A \times \{\chi\}) \\ &= \sum_{\chi \in \mathcal{I}(k)} \int_A N_{\chi_0}(e; de') \tau(e'; \chi) \\ &= \int_A N_{\chi_0}(e; de') \tau(e'; \mathcal{I}(k)) \\ &= \int_A N_{\chi_0}(e; de') = N_{\chi_0}(e; A). \end{aligned}$$

Taking the expectation of this over all $\chi_0 \in \mathcal{I}(k)$ with respect to the measure $\tau(e; \cdot)$, we recover the transition probability N_t:

Proposition 4.10. $p_*^\tau \hat{N}_t = N_t$.

Proof. $\tau(e,\cdot)$ is concentrated on $p^{-1}\{e\}$, which is a copy of $\mathcal{I}(k)$, so that the τ-pushdown of $\hat{N}_t$ via p is a sum:

$$\begin{aligned} p_*^\tau(\hat{N})(e;A) & \\ &= \sum_{\chi_0 \in \mathcal{I}(k)} \tau(e;\chi_0) N_{\chi_0}(e;A) \quad \text{by (4.9)} \\ &= N(e;A) \quad \text{by Definition 4.1.} \quad \blacksquare \end{aligned}$$

The previous proposition describes the "algebraic" relationship between the kernels $\hat{N}$ and N. However, this by itself does not completely clarify the *probabilistic* relationship between the augmented and the standard chains. To achieve this further understanding, we first recall from chapter two the notion of regular conditional probability distribution, expressed in terms of the algebra of pushdowns and compositions. Using the notation of 4.7, we may state the criteria for a kernel K on $V \times \mathcal{U}$ to be a version of the rcpd of a measure μ on U with respect to h:

(i) For $h_*\mu$-almost all v, $K(v,\cdot)$ is a probability measure concentrated on $h^{-1}\{v\}$.

(ii)

$$\mu = (h_*\mu)\cdot K. \tag{4.11}$$

In this case we write $K = m_h^\mu$ and

$$\mu = (h_*\mu)\cdot m_h^\mu. \tag{4.12}$$

Now consider the *measures* $\hat{N}_t(y,\chi_0;\cdot)$ on $\hat{E}^k$ for fixed y and χ_0. Their rcpd decomposition is, if it exists,

$$\begin{aligned} \hat{N}_t(y,\chi_0;\cdot) &= [p_*\hat{N}_t(y,\chi_0;\cdot)][m_p^{\hat{N}_t(y,\chi_0;\cdot)}] \\ &= [N_{t,\chi_0}(y;\cdot)][m_p^{\hat{N}_t(y,\chi_0;\cdot)}] \end{aligned} \tag{4.13}$$

by 4.9. The measures $N_{t,\chi_0}(y;\cdot)$ in general differ for different values of y and χ_0. However, the "orthogonal" parts of the decomposition do not depend on y and χ_0.

Proposition 4.14. For any $\hat{y} \in \hat{E}^k$, $m_p^{\hat{N}(\hat{y};\cdot)} = \tau$. (As in Proposition 4.8, for simplicity of notation we have suppressed the subscript t in $\hat{N}_t$; and we continue to view τ as a kernel on $E^k \times \hat{\mathcal{E}}^k \to [0,1]$ as in 2.4.)

Proof. In view of 4.11 and 4.13, we must show that, for $\hat{y} = (y, \chi_0) \in \hat{E}^k$,

$$\begin{aligned}\hat{N}(\hat{y}; \cdot) &= \hat{N}(y, \chi_0; \cdot) \\ &= \int_{E^k} N_{\chi_0}(y; dw) \int_{p^{-1}\{w\}} \tau(w, \cdot)\end{aligned}$$

by 4.8. It is enough to verify this formula applied to sets of the form $A \times \{\chi_1\}$, with $A \in \mathcal{E}^k$ and $\chi_1 \in \mathcal{I}(k)$, since any measurable set in $\hat{\mathcal{E}}$ is a finite union of such sets. Thus, we are to show

$$\hat{N}(\hat{y}; A \times \{\chi_1\}) = \int_{E^k} N_{\chi_0}(y; dw) \int_{p^{-1}\{w\}} \tau(w; d\hat{z}) 1_{A \times \{\chi_1\}}(\hat{z}).$$

Recall now that $\tau(w; d\hat{z}) = \tau(w; \chi) d\chi$ where $d\chi$ denotes counting measure on $p^{-1}\{w\} = \{w\} \times \mathcal{I}(k)$. Thus the right hand side of the last equation may be written as

$$\begin{aligned}&\int_{E^k} N_{\chi_0}(y; dw) \sum_{\chi \in \mathcal{I}(k)} \tau(w; \chi) 1_{A \times \{\chi_1\}}(w, \chi) \\ &= \int_A N_{\chi_0}(y; dw) \tau(w; \chi_1).\end{aligned}$$

Thus our original equation is seen to be

$$\hat{N}(\hat{y}; A \times \{\chi_1\}) = \int_A N_{\chi_0}(y; dw) \tau(w; \chi_1)$$

which is the same as Definition 3.2. ∎

In the next section we consider the general setting in which the probabilistic significance of 4.9 and 4.14 is clarified.

5. Descent of Markov chains

We now consider the concept of *descent* of a Markov chain. Suppose we have a Markov chain whose base space is the probability space $(B, \mathcal{B}, \rho)$, whose filtration is $\{\mathcal{G}_t\}$, and whose state space is $(U,\mathcal{U})$. The random variables of the chain are denoted by $u_t\colon B \to U, t = 0, 1, 2, \ldots$. Now let $h\colon (U,\mathcal{U}) \to (V,\mathcal{V})$ be a measurable function, and let $v_t = h \circ u_t$.

$$\begin{array}{ccc} B & \xrightarrow{u_t} & U \\ & {\scriptstyle v_t} \searrow & \downarrow {\scriptstyle h} \\ & & V \end{array}$$

The sequence $\{v_t\}$, along with $(B, \mathcal{B}, \rho)$ and the natural filtrations $\{\sigma(v_0, \ldots, v_t)\}$, forms a stochastic process.

Terminology 5.1. The Markov chain $\{u_t\}$ *descends via* h if the stochastic process $\{v_t\}$ is also a Markov chain.

The distribution of v_t is induced by h from the distribution of u_t: If $A \in \mathcal{V}$ then $\rho(v_t \in A) = \rho(u_t \in h^{-1}(A))$. In particular, if the starting measure of the chain $\{u_t\}$ is ν, that of $\{v_t\}$ is $h_*\nu$. A well-known condition for the descent of a chain is expressed in the following definition and theorem:

Definition 5.2. Given a bimeasurable $h\colon U \to V$ and a kernel M on U, we will say that M is *h-respectful* if, for any $A \in \mathcal{V}$, $M(u_1, h^{-1}(A)) = M(u_2, h^{-1}(A))$ whenever $h(u_1) = h(u_2)$. Associated to such an M is a kernel on V, denoted $R_h M$ and defined by

$$R_h M(v, A) = M(u, h^{-1}(A)) = h_* M(u, A)$$

for any $u \in h^{-1}\{v\}$.

Remark 5.3. The bimeasurability of h ensures that $R_h M$ is indeed a kernel on V. The h-respectfulness of M is equivalent to the condition that $h_* M(\cdot, A)$, defined in 4.6, is constant on fibres of h: we have

$$h_* M(u, A) = R_h M(h(u), A).$$

Example 5.4. Suppose $f: U \to [0, \infty]$ is measurable. This gives us a kernel I_f on U defined as follows:

$$I_f(u, du') = f(u)\epsilon_u(du').$$

These are the simplest kernels; in particular, f could be 1_C for a measurable subset C of U (in which case we write I_C for I_{1_C}). The kernel I_f, then, is h-respectful if and only if f is measurable with respect to the σ-algebra $h^*\mathcal{V}$ of h, i.e., if and only if there is some measurable function g on V such that $f = g \circ h$.[4] For then, if $A \in \mathcal{V}$,

$$\begin{aligned} I_f(u, h^{-1}(A)) &= f(u)\, 1_{h^{-1}(A)}(u) \\ &= g(h(u))\, 1_A(h(u)) \end{aligned}$$

so that respectfulness holds. Furthermore,

$$R_h I_f \equiv R_h I_{g \circ h} = I_g,$$

where I_g is thought of as a kernel on V. In the special case where $f = 1_C$, the condition for respectfulness amounts to saying that $C = h^{-1}(C')$ for some subset C' of V; the measurability of C' being a consequence of the bimeasurability of h. In this instance

$$R_h I_C \equiv R_h I_{h^{-1}(C')} = I_{C'}.$$

Respectfulness allows us to prune the state space from U to V, a space which more efficiently carries the essential information of the kernel.

Theorem 5.5. With notation as above, suppose that $\{u_t\}$ is a Markov chain with respect to the family $\{\mathcal{G}_t\}$ of subσ-algebras of $\mathcal{B}$ on B. Suppose that the one step transition probabilities M_t of the chain are h-respectful. Then the chain $\{u_t\}$ descends via h; the one-step transition probabilities $R_h M_t$ of the chain $\{v_t\}$ are given, for $v \in V$ and $A \in \mathcal{V}$, by

$$R_h M_t(v, A) = M_t(u, h^{-1}(A)),$$

[4] See Parthasarathy (1977, Proposition 44.1) for a proof of this statement.

where u is *any* element in $h^{-1}\{v\}$. Moreover, $\{v_t\}$ is a Markov chain with respect to the same sequence $\{\mathcal{G}_t\}$ of σ-algebras on B (and not just the sequence $\{\sigma(v_0,\ldots,v_t)\}$).

The condition of the h-respectfulness of the $\{M_t\}$ is sufficient for the chain $\{u_t\}$ to descend via h, but it is far from necessary. In fact, we now state a different sufficient condition. In this case the chain descends in a slightly weaker sense: The $\{v_t\}$ is now a Markov chain only with respect to the subσ-algebras $\{\sigma(v_0,\ldots,v_t)\}$ of $\mathcal{B}$, and only when the measure on B is of a special type. It is worth mentioning that the two conditions on the $\{M_t\}$ appear to be completely independent, having in common only that they are both sufficient for the descent of the chain.

As before, let $(U,\mathcal{U})$ and $(V,\mathcal{V})$ be measurable spaces and let $h\colon U \to V$ be a measurable function. Suppose we are given a family $\{M_t\}_{t=0,1,2,\ldots}$ of kernels on U. In particular, for each t and each $u \in U$, $M_t(u,\cdot)$ is a measure for $\mathcal{U}$. In principle we may then consider the rcpd's of these various measures with respect to h, i.e., we may consider the kernels

$$m_h^{M_t(u,\cdot)}\colon V \times \mathcal{U} \to [0,1].$$

These rcpd's may not exist in the most general situation, but they will exist, for example, if $(U,\mathcal{U})$ and $(V,\mathcal{V})$ are standard Borel spaces.

Definition 5.6. The family of kernels $M = \{M_t\}$ is *h-decomposable* if there exists a single kernel m on $V \times \mathcal{U}$ which is, for each $u \in U$ and $t \geq 0$, a version of the rcpd of $M_t(u,\cdot)$ with respect to h. We will speak of m as a "common rcpd" of M.

We also speak of the h-decomposability of a *single* kernel, with the obvious meaning.

In case of h-decomposability, the kernels $h_*^m M_t$ on V defined in Definition 4.8 are naturally associated to M_t; we will denote them also as $D_h M_t$ when there is no confusion regarding the version of common rcpd being used. Then

$$D_h M_t(v,A) = h_*^m M_t(v,A) = \int_U m(v,du)\, M_t(u,h^{-1}(A)).$$

Example 5.7. The family of kernels $\{\hat{N}_t\}$, which are the one-step transition probabilities of an augmented dynamical chain, is p-decomposable, where as usual

$$p: \hat{E}^k \to E^k$$

is projection. Indeed, by Proposition 4.14 all of the rcpd's of the measures $\hat{N}_t(\hat{y}, \cdot)$ are equal to τ.

One might ask under what conditions the kernels I_f, defined in 5.4, are h-decomposable. A calculation shows that this happens only in a somewhat trivial case. Namely, the support of f must lie within the set of those $u \in U$ through which the fibre of h is the singleton $\{u\}$ itself. In this case a common rcpd m of I_f may be described as follows. Suppose $\bar{h}: V \to U$ is a "measurable section of the fibre bundle defined by $h: U \to V$." That is, $\bar{h}(v) \in h^{-1}\{v\}$ for all $v \in V$. Then a version of the common rcpd of the measures $I_f(u, \cdot)$ is given by

$$m(v, du') = \epsilon_{\bar{h}(v)}(du').$$

The function f, supported as it is only within the singleton fibres of h, is an h-measurable function. As such, there is some measurable function g on V such that $f = g \circ h$. A computation then shows that in fact

$$D_h I_f = R_h I_f = I_g.$$

However, we will see in Proposition 8–4.15 that the h-decomposability of a kernel K implies the h-decomposability of the product $I_f K$ for any $f \geq 0$.

In general, suppose we have a family $\{M_t\}$ of markovian kernels which we are interpreting as the one-step transition probabilities of a Markov chain $\{u_t\}$ with state space U. Thus $u_t: B \to U$, for $t = 0, 1, 2, \ldots$, is a random variable defined on the base probability sample space B. In this case $M_t(u_t, \cdot)$ is the conditional distribution of u_{t+1} given u_t, and so the h-decomposability of $\{M_t\}$ has the following interpretation: for all t, the conditional expectation of u_{t+1} given $h(u_{t+1})$ is independent of u_t. In statistical terminology, we can say that for each t the statistic h of the random variable u_{t+1} is *sufficient* for the "parameter" u_t.

From this point of view the p-decomposability of the $\{\hat{N}_t\}$, and, indeed, the conclusion of Proposition 4.14 itself, becomes intuitively clear given the definition of the τ-distribution. Namely, the fibres of $p: \hat{E}^k \to E^k$ are all copies of $\mathcal{I}(k)$. At any time t the measure on $\mathcal{I}(k)$ which describes the conditional distribution of the augmented state $\hat{e}_{t+1} = (e_{t+1}, \chi_{t+1})$, given $p(\hat{e}_t) = e_t$, is $\tau(p(\hat{e}_t), \cdot) = \tau(e_t, \cdot)$. And this depends only on the value e_t in E^k, and not on χ_t per se.

Theorem 5.8.[5] Let $(B, \mathcal{B}, \rho)$ be a probability space and let $(U, \mathcal{U})$ and $(V, \mathcal{V})$ be measure spaces. Let $\{u_t\}$, $t = 0, 1, 2, \ldots$ be a Markov chain in U with base B, and with one-step transition probabilities given by the family of kernels $\{M_t\}$. Let $h: U \to V$ be measurable and let $v_t = h \circ u_t$. Suppose that the family $\{M_t\}$ is h-decomposable; let ψ denote their common rcpd with respect to h. Let ν denote the starting measure of the chain, i.e., $\nu = u_{0*}(\rho)$, the distribution of u_0. Suppose that ψ is also the rcpd of ν with respect to h. Then $\{v_t\}$ is a Markov chain in V with base $(B, \mathcal{B}, \rho)$, transition probabilities $h_*^{\psi}(M_t)$, and initial measure $h_* \nu$.

Remark 5.9. The terminology means that $\{u_t\}$ is a Markov chain with respect to the increasing family $\{\sigma(u_0, \ldots, u_t)\}$ of subσ-algebras of $\mathcal{B}$, while $\{v_t\}$ is a Markov chain with respect to $\{\sigma(v_0, \ldots, v_t)\}$.

Before turning to the proof of Theorem 5.8 we will first recall some basic facts about the *canonical chain.*

Let $\Omega = U \times U \times \ldots$; a typical element of Ω will be denoted $\omega = (x_0, x_1, \ldots)$. Let $\mathcal{F}$ denote the σ-algebra of Ω generated by "measurable rectangles," i.e., by sets of the form $A_0 \times A_1 \times \ldots$, where the A_i are in $\mathcal{U}$ and only finitely many of them are different from U. Given the kernels $\{M_t\}$ and the starting measure ν on U, we construct a measure M_ν on $(\Omega, \mathcal{F})$ as follows:

$$M_\nu(A_0 \times A_1 \times \ldots) = \int_{A_0} \nu(dx_0) \int_{A_1} M_0(x_0, dx_1) \ldots \int_{A_n} M_{n-1}(x_{n-1}, dx_n) \ldots . \tag{5.10}$$

Let $X_t: \Omega \to U$ denote projection onto the tth factor, $t = 0, 1, \ldots$. Let $\mathcal{F}_t = \sigma(X_0, \ldots, X_t)$ be the smallest σ-algebra on Ω with respect to which the $X_0, \ldots, X_t$ are measurable. $\mathcal{F}_t$ is then the subσ-algebra of $\mathcal{F}$ generated by those measurable rectangles of the form $A_1 \times \ldots \times A_t \times U \times U \times \ldots$. Then we have

Proposition 5.11. With these hypotheses and notation:

1. The distribution of X_0 is ν.
2. $\{X_t\}$ is a Markov chain with base $(\Omega, \mathcal{F}, M_\nu)$ (with respect to the subσ-algebras $\mathcal{F}_t$) with one-step transition probabilities $\{M_t\}$. It is called the *canonical chain* for those M_t with the given starting measure ν.

[5] We are indebted to D. Revuz for informing us that a related result for continuous time may be found in Pitman and Rogers (1981).

3. Suppose $(B, \mathcal{B}, \rho)$ is a probability space and $\{u_t\}: B \to U$ is a Markov chain with the same transition probabilities $\{M_t\}$ and starting measure $u_{0*}(\rho) = \nu$. Then there is a unique (ρ-a.s.) measurable function $\phi: B \to \Omega$ such that $X_t \circ \phi = u_t$ (ρ-a.s.) and $\phi_*(\rho) = M_\nu$. This is called *the universal property of the canonical chain.*

Proof of Theorem 5.8. In view of the universal property of the canonical chain, we may assume that $(B, \mathcal{B}, \rho) = (\Omega, \mathcal{F}, M_\nu)$. We will still use the notation $\{u_t\}$ to denote the random variables defining the chain; $u_t: \Omega \to U$ is now projection on the tth factor. We still denote $v_t = h \circ u_t$. Let $\mathcal{G}_t$ now denote the subσ-algebra $\sigma(v_0, \ldots, v_t)$ of $\mathcal{F}$. Concretely, $\mathcal{G}_t$ is generated by all measurable rectangles of the form $h^{-1}(A_0) \times \ldots \times h^{-1}(A_t) \times U \times U \times \ldots$, $A_i \in \mathcal{V}$. We will temporarily denote $h_*^\psi M_t$ by K_t. Pictorially,

$$\begin{array}{ccccc} M_\nu & \Omega & \xrightarrow{u_t} & U & \nu,\ M_t \\ & v_t & \searrow & \downarrow h & \\ & & & V & K_t = h_*^\psi M_t = D_h M_t \end{array}$$

Under the assumption that all the rcpd's of the $M_t(u, \cdot)$, as well as that of ν, are equal to ψ, we are going to show that $\{v_t\}$ is a Markov chain with one step transition probabilities $\{K_t\}$. Thus we must show that for any $t \geq 1$ and any $\mathcal{V}$-measurable function f on V,

$$(K_{t-1} f)(v_{t-1}) = E[f(v_t) | \mathcal{G}_{t-1}] \quad M_\nu - a.s. \tag{5.12}$$

where $E = E_{M_\nu}$ denotes expectation with respect to the measure M_ν on Ω. To prove this, since $(K_{t-1} f)(v_{t-1})$ is clearly $\mathcal{G}_{t-1}$-measurable, it is enough to show that for any $A \in \mathcal{G}_{t-1}$ of the form $A = h^{-1}(A_0) \times \ldots \times h^{-1}(A_{t-1}) \times U \times U \times \ldots$,

$$\int_A M_\nu(d\omega)\,(K_{t-1} f)\,(v_{t-1}(\omega)) = \int_A M_\nu(d\omega) f\,(v_t(\omega))\,. \tag{5.13}$$

Now $f(v_t(\omega)) = (f \circ h)(u_t(\omega))$. Since $A \in \mathcal{G}_{t-1} \subset \mathcal{F}_{t-1}$, the right side of 5.13 may be written

$$\int_A M_\nu(d\omega)(f \circ h)(u_t(\omega)) = \int_A M_\nu(d\omega) E[(f \circ h)(u_t) | \mathcal{F}_{t-1}](\omega)\,.$$

But since the Markov chain $\{u_t\}$ has transition probabilities $\{M_t\}$, 5.13 becomes

$$\int_A M_\nu(d\omega)\,(K_{t-1}f)\,(h\circ u_{t-1}(\omega)) = \int_A M_\nu(d\omega)\,M_{t-1}\,(f\circ h)\,(u_{t-1}(\omega))\,. \tag{5.14}$$

In view of the definition of the measure M_ν (as in (5.10)) and the set A, the integrals in (5.14) can be written as iterated integrals in the variables $u_0,\ldots,u_{t-1}$ successively. Since the integrands involve only u_{t-1}, to show the integrals are equal it suffices to consider only the last iteration on each side, i.e., it suffices to show

$$\begin{aligned}\int_{h^{-1}(A_{t-1})} & M_{t-2}(u_{t-2}, du_{t-1})\,(K_{t-1}f)\,(h(u_{t-1}))\\ &= \int_{h^{-1}(A_{t-1})} M_{t-2}(u_{t-2}, du_{t-1})(M_{t-1}f\circ h)(u_{t-1})\end{aligned}$$

where $A_{t-1}\in\mathcal{V}$ and $u_{t-1}, u_{t-2}\in U$ are arbitrary. Note that if $t-1=0$ we must be careful to interpret the symbol $M_{t-2}(u_{t-2},\cdot)$ (which is then, a priori, meaningless) to be the measure $\nu(\cdot)$. In other words, we must prove

$$\int_{h^{-1}(C)} M_{t-2}(u, dx)\,(K_{t-1}f)\,(h(x)) = \int_{h^{-1}(C)} M_{t-2}(u, dx)\,M_{t-1}\,(f\circ h)\,(x), \tag{5.15}$$

where $C\in\mathcal{V}$, $u\in U$, x is a variable on U, and $M_{t-2}(u,\cdot)$ is defined to be $\nu(\cdot)$ if $t-1=0$.

We now evaluate the left side of 5.15. Recalling Definition 4.6(ii), we see that

$$\begin{aligned}\int_{h^{-1}(C)} & M_{t-2}(u, dx)\,(K_{t-1}f)\,(h(x))\\ &= \int M_{t-2}(u, dx)\,1_C(h(x))(K_{t-1}f)(h(x))\\ &= \int h_* M_{t-2}(u, dv)\,(K_{t-1}f)\,(v)\,1_C(v)\\ &= \int h_* M_{t-2}(u, dv)\,\left(h_*^\psi M_{t-1}f\right)(v)\,1_C(v)\end{aligned}$$

by definition of K_{t-1}. By Definition 4.8, this is the same as

$$\int_C h_* M_{t-2}(u, dv)\int_{1_C(v)}\psi(v, dx)\,M_{t-1}(f\circ h)(x).$$

Now we use the fact that, for any u, ψ is the rcpd of $M_{t-2}(u, \cdot)$ with respect to h. Since $\psi(v, \cdot)$ is supported on $h^{-1}\{v\}$, $1_C(v)\,\psi(v, dx)$ is the same as

$$\psi(v, dx)\, 1_{h^{-1}(C)}(x).$$

Thus the above integral is

$$\int_{h^{-1}(C)} M_{t-2}(u, dx)\, M_{t-1}(f \circ h)(x).$$

But this is just the right hand side of (5.15) above. ∎

The conditions of h-respectfulness and h-decomposability thus allow us to compute the transition probabilities of the descended chain. In case of descent via h, the distribution of $v_t = h(u_t)$ is given by $h_*(\nu M_0 M_1 \ldots M_t)$; if the descent is respectful or decomposable we may explicitly express this as $h_*\nu \cdot R_h M_0 \cdot R_h M_1 \ldots R_h M_t$ or $h_*\nu \cdot D_h M_0 \cdot D_h M_1 \ldots D_h M_t$ respectively. Further discussion of the descent conditions may be found in 8–3.

6. Summary of formulae

A. *Pushdowns*

$$h_*\mu(A) = \mu(h^{-1}(A)) \qquad (4.6(i))$$

$$h_*M(u, A) = M(u, h^{-1}(A)) \qquad (4.6(ii))$$

$$h_*^L M(v, A) = (L \cdot h_*M)(v, A) \qquad (4.8)$$

B. *Descents*

(1) Respectful

$$R_h M(v, A) = h_*M(u, A), \quad u \in h^{-1}\{v\} \qquad (5.2)$$

(2) Decomposable

$$D_h M(v, A) = m \cdot h_*M, \quad m = m_h^{M(u,\cdot)},\ \forall u \qquad (5.6)$$

C. *Initial measures*

(1) Standard

$$\begin{aligned}\xi(A) &= (\xi_1 \otimes \ldots \otimes \xi_k)(A) \\ &= \int \xi_1(dy_1)\ldots\xi_k(dy_k)\,1_A(y_1,\ldots,y_k), \quad A \in \mathcal{E}^k\end{aligned} \tag{4.3}$$

(2) Augmented

$$\xi_\tau(A \times \{\chi\}) = \int_{E^k} \xi(dy)\,1_A(y)\,\tau(y;\chi), \quad A \in \mathcal{E}^k,\ \chi \in \mathcal{I}(k) \tag{3.4}$$

D. *Transition probabilities*

(1) Fixed channeling

$$N_{t,\chi}(e,A) = \int_A \prod_{i\in D(\chi)} Q_{i,e_i}(t)(e_{\chi(i)};dy_i) \prod_{j\notin D(\chi)} \epsilon_{e_j}(dy_j) \tag{1.3}$$

(2) Augmented

$$\hat{N}_t(e,\chi_0;A\times\{\chi_1\}) = \int_{E^k} N_{t,\chi_0}(e;dy)\,1_A(y)\,\tau(y;\chi_1), \quad e \in E^k;\ A \in \mathcal{E}^k;\ \chi_0,\chi_1 \in \mathcal{I}(k) \tag{3.2}$$

(3) Standard

$$N_t(e;A) = \sum_{\chi\in\mathcal{I}(k)} \tau(e;\chi)\,N_{t,\chi}(e;A), \quad e \in E^k,\ A \in \mathcal{E}^k \tag{4.1}$$

$$N_t = p_*^\tau \hat{N}_t = D_p \hat{N}_t \tag{4.14}$$

CHAPTER EIGHT

PERCEPTIONS AND REALITIES

In this chapter we discuss the dynamics of perspectives relative to a given participator. Accordingly, we shall imagine this participator to be the first of a fixed number, say k, of participators on a symmetric framework. We then discuss general conditions in which this given participator perceives the dynamical situation truly.

1. Introduction

The study of true perception by a single participator involves a new stochastic process, one which may be arrived at from the augmented dynamics in three stages. First, our participator, call it "A_1," is ignorant of the channeling involutions: we must *standardize.* Furthermore, as discussed in earlier chapters, A_1 does not know its absolute perspective: we must *relativize* with respect to its perspective. And finally, A_1 only "looks" when it is channelled to: the relevant time parameter of our stochastic process must be the *proper time* of A_1. As we shall see, this (random) proper time is a stopping time for the augmented or standard chains we have hitherto studied.

In summary, the primary stochastic process, from which all others studied here derive, is the augmented absolute position chain. To give conditions for which perception matches reality, we are interested in the stochastic process which is obtained from the augmented chain (i) by a *standardization,* i.e., in ignorance of the full channeling involutions, (ii) by a *relativization,* i.e., in ignorance of absolute perspectives, and (iii) by a *"trace-operation,"* i.e., in ignorance of the instants when A_1 is *not* channeled to. The first question we wish to address is this: Does this triple succession of information losses yield a Markov chain? We demonstrate in section five that it does, and show there how to compute the transition probabilities of the resulting chain. We then address the implications of this result for true perception in terms of stationary measures for the Markov chains involved.

2. Relativization

Given k participators on a symmetric framework with τ-distribution, we have the associated augmented and standard dynamical chains, which we introduced in chapter seven. We will now consider *relative dynamics,* which is intuitively the (standard or augmented) dynamics seen from the viewpoint of one of the participators. Thus, the relative dynamics with respect to, say, the first participator is the standard dynamics in which the positions of the participators are now described in terms of a moving frame which is always centered at the location of the first participator. In **6–4** we considered a special case of the relative dynamics, namely for two-participator systems in a framework where E is itself an abelian group, and in which there are no self-channelings. ("No self-channelings" is a statement about the τ-distribution.) We were then able to express the relative positions of the participators as a chain in J (which in that chapter equaled E). The transition probability P was found to be obtainable from the action kernels Q, R of the separate participators in terms of a "bracket operation," i.e., $P = [Q, R]$. In this section we will consider a more general case. We consider *augmented relative dynamics* which is augmented dynamics represented from one participator's viewpoint. The procedure of passing from either the standard or augmented chains to the corresponding relative dynamics is called *relativization.* The motivation for the introduction of symmetric frameworks is that they provide the minimum structure necessary for the relativization of dynamics.

Hypothesis 2.0. As usual we assume that we are in a symmetric framework $\{X, Y, E, S, G, J, \pi\}$ with given configuration symmetric τ-distribution (**7**–2.3) and that we have k participators with symmetric action kernels $Q_1(t), \ldots, Q_k(t)$. Throughout this chapter we assume that E is a principal homogeneous space for J. Define the maps $q: E^k \to J^{k-1}$ and $\hat{q}: E^k \times \mathcal{I}(k) \to J^{k-1} \times \mathcal{I}(k)$ as follows

$$q(e) = (e_2 e_1^{-1}, \ldots, e_i e_1^{-1}, \ldots, e_k e_1^{-1});$$
$$\hat{q}(e,\chi) = (q(e),\chi); \quad e = (e_1, \ldots, e_k) \in E^k, \ \chi \in \mathcal{I}(k).$$

We denote the space $J^{k-1} \times \mathcal{I}(k)$ by $\hat{J}^{k-1}$. We have the standard dynamical chain in E^k with one-step transition probabilities given by kernels $N_t = \langle Q_1(t), \ldots, Q_k(t)\rangle_\tau$ (Definition 7–4.1) and the augmented chain in $\hat{E}^k = E^k \times \mathcal{I}(k)$ with kernels $\hat{N}_t = \widehat{\langle Q_1(t), \ldots, Q_k(t)\rangle}_\tau$ (Definition 7–3.2).

We may express the condition that the τ distribution is configuration symmetric (7–2.3) as follows: τ is symmetric iff $\tau(\cdot;\chi)$ is constant on fibres of q, i.e.,

$$q(e) = q(e') \Rightarrow \tau(e;\chi) = \tau(e';\chi).$$

We shall now see that the relativization procedure results in a markovian dynamics.

Theorem 2.1. $\hat{N}_t$ is $\hat{q}$-respectful. N_t is q-respectful.

Proof. (We drop the subscript t in the sequel.) Let us consider the kernel $\hat{N}$; the proof for N is similar. We are to show that for any $e, e' \in E^k$ such that $q(e) = q(e')$, for all $A \in \mathcal{J}^{k-1}$, and for all $\chi_0, \chi_1 \in \mathcal{I}(k)$ the following equality holds:

$$\hat{N}(e,\chi_0; q^{-1}(A) \times \{\chi_1\}) = \hat{N}(e',\chi_0; q^{-1}(A) \times \{\chi_1\}).$$

Recalling Definition 7–3.2, we have

$$\hat{N}(e,\chi_0; q^{-1}(A) \times \{\chi_1\}) = \int_{q^{-1}(A)} \prod_{i\in D(\chi_0)} Q_{ie_i}(e_{\chi_0(i)}, dy_i) \prod_{j\notin D(\chi_0)} \epsilon_{e_j}(dy_j)\,\tau(y_1, \ldots, y_k; \chi_1).$$

Here $y = (y_1, \ldots, y_k)$ is a variable on E^k.

Let $\kappa_i = y_i e_i^{-1}$; we will view this as a change of variable $\kappa = \alpha_e(y)$ and use it to express the integral as an integral on J^k:

$$\hat{N}(e,\chi_0; q^{-1}(A) \times \{\chi_1\}) = \int_{\alpha_e(q^{-1}(A))} \Big[\prod_{i\in D(\chi_0)} Q_i(e_{\chi_0(i)} e_i^{-1}, d\kappa_i) \prod_{j\notin D(\chi_0)} \epsilon_1(d\kappa_j)\Big] \cdot \tau(\kappa_1 e_1, \ldots, \kappa_k e_k; \chi_1). \tag{2.2}$$

(Recall that $\imath$ is the identity element of J). We need to show that this integral remains the same if e is replaced by e'. Suppose

$$q(e) = q(e') = (\lambda_2, \ldots, \lambda_k); \ \lambda_1 = \imath. \tag{2.3}$$

First, consider the τ term in the integral in Equation 2.2. If $1 \leq i, l \leq k$, then

$$\begin{aligned}(\kappa_i e_i)(\kappa_l e_l)^{-1} &= (\kappa_i \lambda_i e_1)(\kappa_l \lambda_l e_1)^{-1} \\ &= \kappa_i \lambda_i \lambda_l^{-1} \kappa_l^{-1} \\ &= (\kappa_i e_i')(\kappa_l e_l')^{-1}\end{aligned}$$

so that, by the symmetry of the τ-distribution on symmetric frameworks (7–2.3),

$$\tau(\kappa_1 e_1, \ldots, \kappa_k e_k; \chi_1) = \tau(\kappa_1 e_1', \ldots, \kappa_k e_k'; \chi_1). \tag{2.4}$$

Secondly, since by 2.3 $e_{\chi_0(i)} e_i^{-1} = \lambda_{\chi_0(i)} \lambda_i^{-1} = e'_{\chi_0(i)} e_i'^{-1}$, we have

$$Q_i(e_{\chi_0(i)} e_i^{-1}, d\kappa_i) = Q_i(e'_{\chi_0(i)} e_i'^{-1}, d\kappa_i). \tag{2.5}$$

Finally, consider $\alpha_e(q^{-1}(A))$. By definition of the change of variables,

$$\begin{aligned}\alpha_e(q^{-1}(A)) &= \{(j_1, \ldots, j_k) \in J^k \mid (j_1 e_1, \ldots, j_k e_k) \in q^{-1}(A)\} \\ &= \{(j_1, \ldots, j_k) \in J^k \mid q(j_1 e_1, \ldots, j_k e_k) \in A\}.\end{aligned}$$

But by Equation 2.3, $(j_i e_i)(j_1 e_1)^{-1} = j_i \lambda_i j_1^{-1}$, so that

$$q(j_1 e_1, \ldots, j_k e_k) = (j_2 \lambda_2 j_1^{-1}, \ldots, j_k \lambda_k j_1^{-1}) = q(j_1 e_1', \ldots, j_k e_k'),$$

and we get

$$\alpha_e(q^{-1}(A)) = \alpha_{e'}(q^{-1}(A)). \tag{2.6}$$

Putting 2.4, 2.5, and 2.6 together, we see that 2.2 is indeed unchanged upon replacing e with e'. ∎

As a consequence of this theorem and the theorem on respectful descent of chains (Theorem 7–5.5), we know now that the relativized augmented chain on $J^{k-1} \times \mathcal{I}(k)$ and the relativized standard chain on J^{k-1} are both markovian. Can one expect that the second chain is a descent of the first? In section five we shall see that it is.

3. Diagrammatic representation of descent conditions

In this section we reformulate the notions of respectfulness and decomposability (introduced in chapter seven) in a picturesque manner. We then discuss trace chains and their behavior under descent.

Suppose $(U, \mathcal{U})$ and $(V, \mathcal{V})$ are measurable spaces and $h: U \to V$ is a measurable function. As usual, we use the symbol $\mathcal{U}$ (respectively, $\mathcal{V}$) also for the real-valued measurable functions on U (respectively , V).

Recall that if μ is any measure on U, the function h can be used to "push down" μ to a measure on V, called $h_*\mu$:

$$h_*\mu(A) = \mu(h^{-1}(A)), \quad A \in \mathcal{V}. \tag{3.1}$$

If g is any function in $\mathcal{V}$, h can be used to "pull back" g to a function in $\mathcal{U}$, called h^*g:

$$h^*g = g \circ h. \tag{3.2}$$

h^*g is h-measurable (measurable with respect to the subσ-algebra $\{h^{-1}(A) \mid A \in \mathcal{V}\}$ of $\mathcal{U}$); indeed, every h-measurable function arises in this way, i.e., $\mathcal{U} \supset \sigma(h) = h^*\mathcal{V}$.

Now let M be a (positive) kernel on U. In what follows we will find it convenient to think of our kernels in terms of *operators*. Specifically, M is an operator on the function space $\mathcal{U}$: for any $f \in \mathcal{U}$, Mf is the function in $\mathcal{U}$ given by

$$Mf(u) = \int_U M(u, dw) f(w), \quad u \in U. \tag{3.3}$$

Now, if $g \in \mathcal{V}$ then $h^*g \in \mathcal{U}$. Acting on the latter by M we get, as in 7–4.6, an operator h_*M taking $\mathcal{V}$ into $\mathcal{U}$:

$$[h_*M]g \equiv M(h^*g). \tag{3.4}$$

To see what h_*M looks like as a kernel, choose $g = 1_A$ for $A \in \mathcal{V}$. Then

$$[h_*M](u, A) = M(u, h^{-1}(A)), \quad A \in \mathcal{V}, u \in \mathcal{U}. \tag{3.5}$$

This equation vindicates our use of h_* preceding the M: the symbol h_* acts on the second argument of M just as it does in the usual case of measures on $\mathcal{U}$ as in Equation 3.2.

The above situation is most clearly displayed by means of a commutative diagram:

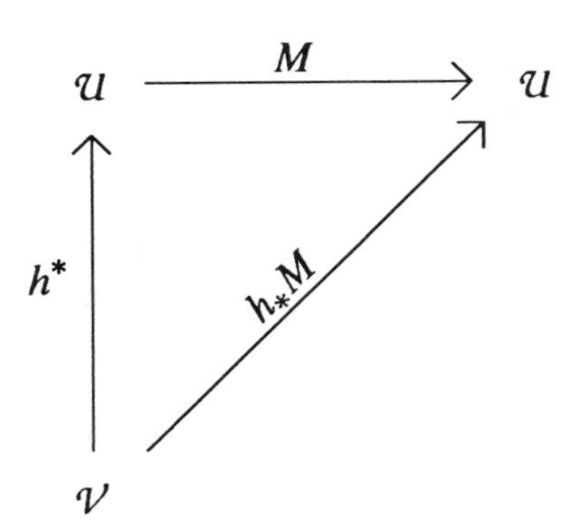

DIAGRAM 3.6. *Commutative diagram.*

In general, the vertices of a diagram signify objects and the arrows between vertices signify morphisms. A (directed) *path* between two objects in a diagram is a sequence of connected arrows from the first object to the second. A diagram *commutes* if, for any pair of objects, the composition of morphisms (in order) along any of the paths connecting the objects is the same morphism. The definition of $h_* M$ embodied in Equation 3.4 is the statement that Diagram 3.6 commutes.

We can now display diagrammatically the definition of h-respectfulness of M. Assume that h is bimeasurable and surjective. In Remark 7–5.3 we pointed out that M is h-respectful iff $h_* M(\cdot, A)$ is constant on fibres of h. But because of the bimeasurability of h, this means that $h_* M(\cdot, A)$ is in $h^* \mathcal{V}$ so that, in fact, M is h-respectful iff $h_* M: \mathcal{V} \to h^* \mathcal{V}$. An equivalent way to say this is that M restricts to an operator on $h^* \mathcal{V}$: M, viewed as an operator on the space of $\mathcal{U}$-measurable functions, leaves invariant the subspace $h^* \mathcal{V}$ of h-measurable functions. Now, since $h: U \to V$ is surjective, the pullback $h^*: \mathcal{V} \to \mathcal{U}$ is injective. Thus, if M restricts to an operator on $h^* \mathcal{V}$, there must be a unique operator, call it $R_h M$, on $\mathcal{V}$, such that Diagram 3.7 commutes:

In other words, stating the existence of an $R_h M$ (7–5.2) that makes Diagram 3.7 commute is equivalent to stating the h-respectfulness of M.

We now turn our attention to h-decomposability (7–5.6). Assume M is h-

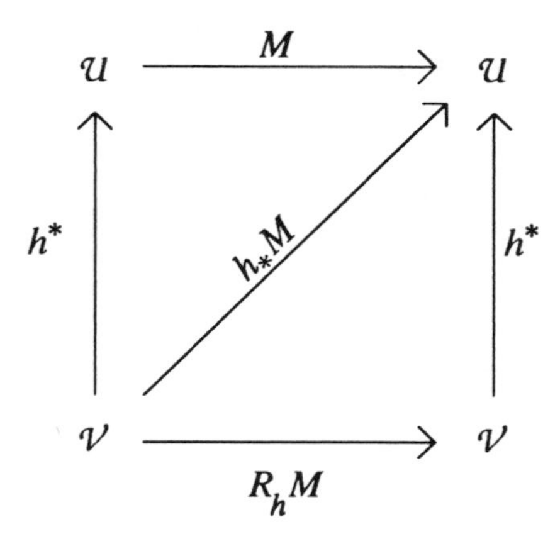

DIAGRAM 3.7. *h-respectfulness commutative diagram. h is bimeasurable.*

decomposable and call m the common version of $m_h^{M(u,\cdot)}$. That m is a kernel says that m is an operator from $\mathcal{U}$ to $\mathcal{V}$. The facts that (i) m is a markovian kernel and (ii) $m(v,\cdot)$ is a measure concentrated on $h^{-1}\{v\}$, for all $v \in V$, are both expressed in saying that (iii) $m \circ h^* = \mathrm{id}_{\mathcal{V}}$ (the identity operator on $\mathcal{V}$). To prove this, note that (i) and (ii) together imply (iii). To get (i) from (iii), apply the latter to the function $1_{V-\{v\}}$. To get (ii) from (iii), apply the latter to the function 1_V. Moreover, to say that m is the rcpd of $M(u,\cdot)$ means that

$$M(u,dw) = \int_V M(u,h^{-1}(dv))\,m(v,dw).$$

The operator formulation of this is

$$M = h_* M \cdot m \tag{3.8}$$

(where $h_* M$ is as in Equation 3.5). Thus, h-decomposability of M allows us to actually decompose M into a product of kernels (or operators). (Such an operator decomposition is not posited for general M.) Indeed we may state conversely that if there exists a *markovian* kernel m on U relative to V such that Equation 3.8 holds and such that $m \circ h^*$ is the identity on $\mathcal{V}$, then m *must* be the common rcpd of $M(u,\cdot)$ relative to h; a fortiori, M is h-decomposable. We thus have Diagram 3.9:

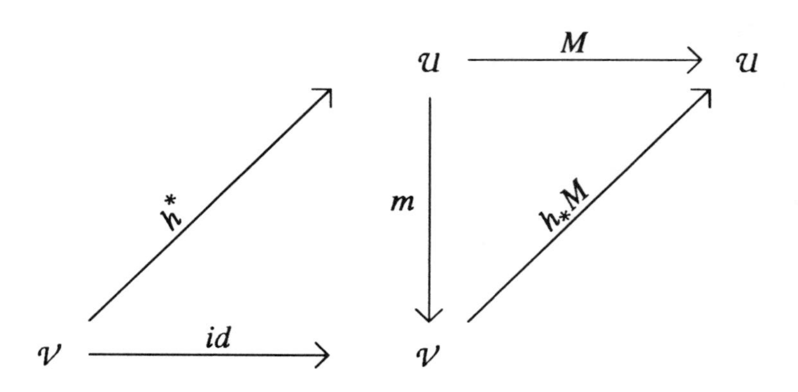

DIAGRAM 3.9. *h-decomposability commutative diagram. The left-hand triangle says that m is a markovian kernel with $m(v, \cdot)$ supported on $h^{-1}\{v\}$.*

Now we may also display the kernel $D_h M$ introduced in Definition 7–5.6. Recall that, as operators,

$$D_h M = m(h_* M). \tag{3.10}$$

This is displayed in Diagram 3.11. The rest of the diagram commutes.

Remark 3.12. The operator $h^*: \mathcal{V} \to \mathcal{U}$ is itself a kernel; explicitly,

$$h^*(u, dv) = \epsilon_{h(u)}(dv).$$

4. Trace chains and their descent

We now turn to the question of trace chains; we will use the terminology of 5–1.

Assumption 4.1. $\{X_n\}$ is a canonical Markov chain with state space $(U, \mathcal{U})$, base

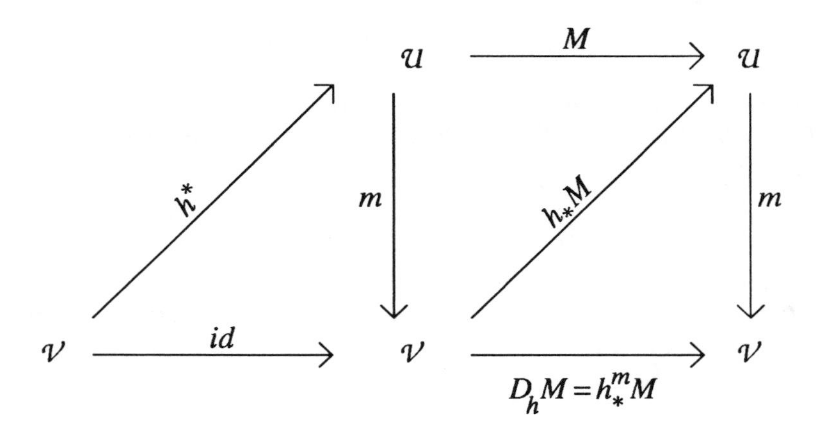

DIAGRAM 3.11. *h-decomposability commutative diagram. m is markovian.*

space $(\Omega, \mathcal{G}, M_\nu)$ where $\Omega = U^\infty$, and the "past" σ-algebras are $\mathcal{G}_n = \sigma(X_1, \ldots, X_n)$. The one-step transition probabilities of the chain are given by the sequence of kernels $M = \{M_n\}_{n\geq 0}$ on U. ν is a measure on U which is the initial measure of the chain. M_ν is the measure on Ω associated to ν via the sequence of kernels M (in the manner described in 7–5.9).

Suppose T is some stopping time. Then it may be checked that $T + 1$ is also a stopping time. For each $n \geq 0$, the nth occurrence of T is a stopping time which may be defined in terms of T by the following device: for any stopping time S, let $\theta_S : \Omega \to \Omega$ be the random variable given by

$$\theta_S(\omega) = \begin{cases} \theta_n(\omega) & \text{if } S(\omega) = n \\ (\Delta, \Delta, \ldots) & \text{if } S(\omega) = \infty \end{cases}$$

(where Δ is the cemetery). The successive occurrences of T are then the stopping times $\{T_n\}_{n\geq 0}$, defined inductively by

$$\begin{aligned} &T_0 = T, \quad T_n = T_{n-1} + T \circ \theta_{T_{n-1}+1}, \\ &\mathcal{G}_{T_n} = \{A \in \mathcal{G} \mid A \cap \{T_n = k\} \in \mathcal{G}_k, \forall k \in \mathbf{N}\}, \end{aligned} \tag{4.2}$$

where $\mathcal{G}_{T_n}$ is called the *σ-algebra associated to T_n*. The basic fact here is given by the next theorem:

Theorem 4.3. Define the sequence of random variables $\{Y_n\}_{n\geq 0}$ by $Y_n(\omega) = X_{T_n(\omega)}(\omega)$. *Then Y_n is $\mathcal{G}_{T_n}$-measurable, and the sequence $\{Y_n\}$ is a Markov chain on the base space $(\Omega, \mathcal{G}, M_\nu)$ with respect to the σ-algebras $\mathcal{G}_{T_n}$.*

We are interested here in the following case: Let C be a measurable subset of U, and define T_C, *the first hitting time of* C, and S_C, *the first return time of* C, as follows:

$$\begin{aligned} T_C(\omega) &= inf\,\{n \geq 0 \,|\, X_n(\omega) \in C\}, \\ S_C(\omega) &= inf\,\{n \geq 1 \,|\, X_n(\omega) \in C\}. \end{aligned} \tag{4.4}$$

T_C and S_C are stopping times. Recalling that I_C is the operator given by $(I_C f)(u) = 1_C(u) f(u)$ for any random variable f on U, the following result is standard in the theory of Markov chains:

Theorem 4.5. Let $C \in \mathcal{U}$ with $\nu(C) > 0$. Let $T = T_C$ and let T_n be as in Equation 4.2. Then the Markov chain $\{Y_n = X_{T_n}\}$ has transition probabilities given by

$$\begin{aligned} &\Pi_n^C(M) \\ &= I_C M_n I_C + I_C \sum_{k\geq 1} (M_n I_{C^c} M_{n+1} I_{C^c} \ldots M_{n+k-1} I_{C^c}) M_{n+k} I_C \end{aligned} \tag{4.6}$$

and initial distribution ν^C given by

$$\begin{aligned} \nu^C(A) &= M_\nu[X_{T_C(\cdot)}(\cdot) \in A] \\ &= (\nu I_C)(A) + \sum_{k\geq 1} (\nu M_0 I_{C^c} M_1 I_{C^c} \ldots M_k I_C)(A), \end{aligned} \tag{4.7}$$

where $A \in \mathcal{G}$.

Definition 4.8. The chain $\{Y_n\}$ in Theorem 4.5 is called the *trace chain on* C, or *the chain induced on* C.

If the original chain $\{X_n\}$ descends via some measurable map $h\colon U \to V$, does the trace chain $\{Y_n\}$ also descend? We first consider respectful descent. We collect some useful facts about products of kernels:

Proposition 4.9. Suppose K, L are kernels on U, and $h: U \to V$ is measurable. Then

(i) $h_*(KL) = K(h_*L)$;

(ii) If h is also bimeasurable and if L is h-respectful, $h_*(KL) = (h_*K)(R_hL)$;

(iii) If h is bimeasurable and both K and L are h-respectful, then KL is also h-respectful, and

$$R_h(KL) = R_hK \cdot R_hL.$$

Proof. Consider Diagram 4.10, where the dotted lines constitute the assumptions of parts (ii) and (iii).

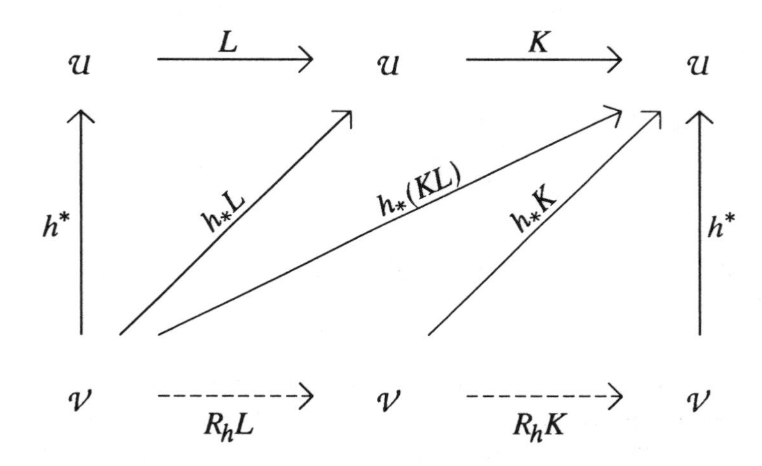

DIAGRAM 4.10. *Respectful descent.*

The proposition follows from this diagram, in view of the respectfulness criterion of Diagram 3.7. ∎

Theorem 4.11. Suppose $h: U \to V$ is bimeasurable. Let $C = h^{-1}(C')$ with $C' \in \mathcal{V}$. Suppose the chain $\{X_n\}$ descends *respectfully* via h to the chain $\{X'_n\}$ on V. Then the trace chain $\{Y_n\}$ of $\{X_n\}$ on C descends respectfully via h to the trace chain $\{Y'_n\}$ of $\{X'_n\}$ on C'.

Moreover, if the transition probabilities of $\{X'_n\}$ are denoted $R_h M = \{R_h M_n\}$, the transition probabilities of $\{Y'_n\}$ are given by

$$\Pi_n^{C'}(R_h M) = R_h(\Pi_n^{C}(M)).$$

Proof. We need to show that the $\Pi_n^C(M)$ as given in Equation 4.6 are h-respectful, and the equation above holds.

In 4.6, $\Pi_n^C(M)$ is expressed as a sum of terms. To show that it is h-respectful it suffices to show that each summand is h-respectful. Now each of these terms is a product, so that we can use Proposition 4.9. Indeed, the kernels M_n are respectful by hypothesis. The kernels I_C and I_{C^c} are respectful as we observed in 7–5.4; the formulae presented there show moreover that $R_h(I_C) = I_{h(C)} = I_{C'}$, and similarly $R_h(I_{C^c}) = I_{(C')^c}$. It then follows directly from 4.9, part (iii), that $\Pi_n^C(M)$ is h-respectful, with

$$\begin{aligned} R_h(\Pi_n^C(M)) =& I_{C'}(R_h M_n) I_{C'} \\ &+ I_{C'} \sum_{k \geq 1} (R_h M_n) I_{(C')^c} \ldots (R_h M_{n+k-1}) I_{(C')^c} (R_h M_{n+k}) I_{C'}. \end{aligned}$$

But this is evidently the same as $\Pi_n^{C'}(R_h M)$. This concludes the proof. ∎

We are going to apply Theorem 4.11 so that the role of h is played by the relativization map $\hat{q}$ of section two. We have seen (Theorem 2.1) that $\hat{N}$ is $\hat{q}$-respectful. Thus the augmented position chain $\{\hat{X}_n\}$ on $\hat{E}^k = E^k \times \mathcal{I}(k)$ descends respectfully via $\hat{q}$ to a chain $\{Z_n\}$ on $\hat{J}^{k-1} = J^{k-1} \times \mathcal{I}(k)$, which is called the *augmented relative position chain;* it represents the dynamics from the perspective of, say, the first participator. However, to make the representation relevant to a study of that participator's perception, we must consider the chain only at the participator's proper time. This amounts to taking the trace of $\{Z_n\}$ on the subset $C' = J^{k-1} \times C_1$ of $\hat{J}^{k-1}$, where $C_1 = \{\chi \in \mathcal{I}(k) \mid 1 \in D(\chi)\} = \{$those channelings which involve the first participator$\}$. In this section and the next one, however, all of our results are true for an arbitrary subset $\tilde{C}$ of $\mathcal{I}(k)$, not just for C_1. Thus, in general we will let C' denote $J^{k-1} \times \tilde{C}$, and we will write $C = E^k \times \tilde{C}$.

We will need to make explicit the relationship between the trace of $\{Z_n\}$ on C', and the trace of $\{\hat{X}_n\}$ on C. This is done in the next theorem and is depicted in the diagram below.

			trace on C		augmented chain
			$\Leftarrow$		
$\{\hat{X}_n^C\}, \Pi^C(\hat{N})$	C	$= E^k \times \tilde{C} \subset$		$\hat{E}^k$	$\{\hat{X}_n\}, \hat{N}$
$\Downarrow$	$\downarrow \hat{q}$			$\downarrow \hat{q}$	$\Downarrow$
$\{Z_n^{C'}\}, R_{\hat{q}}(\Pi^C(\hat{N}))$	C'	$= J^{k-1} \times \tilde{C} \subset$		$\hat{J}^{k-1}$	$\{Z_n\}, R_{\hat{q}}(\hat{N})$
			$\Leftarrow$		
			trace on C'		augmented relative

DIAGRAM 4.12. *Relationship between trace and relativization.*

Theorem 4.13. Let $\tilde{C}$ be any subset of $\mathcal{I}(k)$. Let $C = E^k \times \tilde{C}$ and $C' = J^{k-1} \times \tilde{C}$. Let $\{\hat{X}_n^C\}$ denote the trace on C of the augmented position chain $\{\hat{X}_n\}$, and let $\{Z_n^{C'}\}$ denote the trace on C' of the augmented relative position chain $\{Z_n\}$. Then $\{\hat{X}_n^C\}$ descends respectfully to $\{Z_n^{C'}\}$ via $\hat{q}$, and the transition probability of $\{Z_n^{C'}\}$ is

$$R_{\hat{q}}(\Pi_n^C(\hat{N})) = \Pi_n^{C'} R_{\hat{q}}(\hat{N}).$$

Proof. This is an immediate corollary of 4.11, noting that $C = \hat{q}^{-1}(C')$. ∎

Let us now turn to decomposable descents.

Proposition 4.14. Let $h: U \to V$ be measurable. Let C be a measurable subset of U, and ρ a finite positive measure on U. Let ρ_C denote the restriction of ρ to C. Let m be a version of the rcpd of ρ with respect to h. Then

(i) $h_*\rho_C\{v \in V \mid m(v, C) = 0\} = 0$, and

(ii) a version of the rcpd of ρ_C with respect to h is given by

$$m_C(v, du) = \frac{1}{m(v, C)} m(v, du)\, 1_C(u).$$

Proof. First we establish that

$$h_*\rho_C(dv) = m(v, C)\, h_*\rho(dv). \qquad (*)$$

For, if $D \in \mathcal{V}$,

$$h_*\rho_C(D) = \rho(C \cap h^{-1}(D))$$
$$= \int h_*\rho(dv) \int m(v, du)\, 1_C(u)\, 1_D(h(u)),$$

by the assumed rcpd decomposition (7–4.12). $m(v,\cdot)$ is concentrated on $h^{-1}\{v\}$. Thus the integral above is zero if $v \notin D$; otherwise it equals $m(v, C)$. Hence

$$h_*\rho_C(D) = \int h_*\rho(dv)\, m(v, C)\, 1_D(v),$$

giving (*).

The conclusion (i) immediately follows upon (*). Because of (i), the kernel m_C in (ii) is well-defined. Furthermore, it is markovian, and $m(v,\cdot)$ is supported on $h^{-1}\{v\}$. That the decomposition

$$\rho_C(A) = \int h_*\rho_C(dv)\, m_C(v, A), \quad A \in \mathcal{U},$$

holds is now easily checked using (*). ∎

Proposition 4.15. Let K and L be kernels on U, $h: U \to V$ be measurable, and L be h-decomposable with common rcpd m_L. Then KL is h-decomposable, and m_L is also a common rcpd for KL, so that

$$D_h(KL) = m_L K(h_* L).$$

Proof. Consider Diagram 4.16:

The right-hand triangle commutes since $h_*(KL) = K h_* L$ by part (i) of 4.9. The left and middle triangles commute since L is h-decomposable by the diagrammatic criterion 3.9. In view of this, the result follows by applying 3.11 to KL. ∎

Theorem 4.17. Let $\{X_n\}$ be a Markov chain on U with transition probabilities $\{M_n\}$ and initial distribution ν. Let $C \in \mathcal{U}$. Let $h: U \to V$ be measurable, and suppose that $\{X_n\}$ descends decomposably via h to $\{X_n'\}$ on V. Let $\{Y_n\}$ denote the trace chain of $\{X_n\}$ on C with transition probabilities $\Pi_n^C(M)$ and initial distribution ν^C as in 4.6 and 4.7.

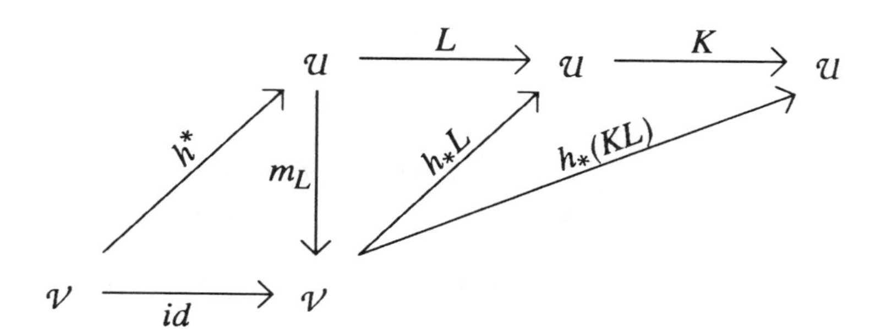

DIAGRAM 4.16. *Commutative diagram.*

Let m denote a common rcpd of M and ν. Put

$$m_C(v, du) = \frac{1}{m(v, C)} m(v, du)\, 1_C(du).$$

Then the $\Pi_n^C(M)$ and ν^C have common rcpd m_C. It follows from Theorem 7–5.8 that $\{Y_n\}$ descends decomposably via h to a Markov chain $\{Y_n' = h(Y_n)\}$ on V, with initial distribution $h_*\nu^C$ and transition probabilities

$$D_h(\Pi_n^C(M)) = m_C h_*(\Pi_n^C(M)).$$

Proof. We first consider the kernel $\Pi_n^C(M)$. By 4.6 this is a sum of terms. For simplicity we will temporarily denote the kth summand by P_k, so that $\Pi_n^C(M) = \sum_{k\geq 0} P_k$. Each P_k is itself a product which ends with $M_{n+k} I_C$. By hypothesis these M_{n+k} have the same (common) rcpd m. Now the product $M_{n+k} I_C$ means that the measures $M_{n+k}(u, \cdot)$ are restricted to C. Therefore we can apply 4.14 to deduce that these $M_{n+k} I_C$ have common rcpd m_C. Then by 4.15 it follows that each P_k has the same common rcpd m_C. Thus we can write

$$\begin{aligned}
\Pi_n^C(M) &= \sum_k P_k \\
&= \sum_k (h_* P_k) m_C \\
&= (h_* \sum_k P_k) m_C \\
&= h_*(\Pi_n^C(M)) m_C.
\end{aligned}$$

This means that the $\Pi_n^C(M)$ have common rcpd m_C as claimed.

It remains to prove the assertions about ν^C. The proof that its rcpd is m_C is almost identical to the proof for $\Pi_n^C(m)$ above: We use the expression 4.7, where ν^C is also written as a sum of products, each ending with $M_{n+k} I_C$. The previous terms of the product must now be viewed as measures starting with ν; however, measures are the special case of those kernels constant in the first argument, so we can again use 4.15 as above. ▮

In contrast to Theorem 4.13 we are not concerned here with the question of whether the descended chain $\{Y_n\}$ is itself a trace chain. In particular we do not assume here that $C = h^{-1}(C')$ for some $C' \in \mathcal{V}$.

We now apply 4.17 to the situation where the map h is $p: \hat{E}^k \to E^k$ (7–4), and the chain $\{\hat{X}_n\}$ on $\hat{E}^k$ is the augmented position chain. We have seen that the kernels $\hat{N}$ are p-decomposable with rcpd τ, so that $\{\hat{X}_n\}$ descends decomposably via p to the standard chain $\{X_n\}$ on E^k (7–4.10 and 7–5.8). As in Theorem 4.13, we let $C = E^k \times \tilde{C}$, and we take the trace of $\{\hat{X}_n\}$ on C; we will here denote this trace chain by $\{\hat{X}_n^C\}$. $\{\hat{X}_n^C\}$ has transition probabilities given by the kernels $\Pi_n^C(\hat{N})$, and initial distribution μ^C (assuming an initial distribution μ of $\hat{X}_n$). With this notation, we arrive at the next theorem:

Theorem 4.18. Let $\tilde{C}$ be a subset of $\mathcal{I}(k)$, and let $C = E^k \times \tilde{C}$. Let

$$\tau_C(x, d\hat{z}) = \frac{1}{\tau(x, C)} \tau(x, d\hat{z}) 1_C(\hat{z}).$$

Then $\Pi_n^C(\hat{N})$ and μ^C have common rcpd τ_C with respect to p. Consequently, the trace chain $\{\hat{X}_n^C\}$ descends decomposably via p to a chain $\{X_n^C\}$ on E^k. This latter chain has initial distribution $p_*(\mu^C)$ and transition probabilities

$$D_p(\Pi_n^C(\hat{N})) = \tau_C p_*(\Pi_n^C(\hat{N})).$$

Proof. This is an immediate corollary of 4.17. ∎

The situation is summarized in the diagram below.

$$\begin{array}{ccccccc}
 & & & \text{trace on } C & & \text{augmented chain} \\
 & & & \Leftarrow & & \\
\{\hat{X}_n^C\}, \Pi_n^C(\hat{N}) & E^k \times \tilde{C} = & C & \subset & \hat{E}^k & \{\hat{X}_n\}, \hat{N} \\
\Downarrow & & \downarrow p & & \downarrow p & \Downarrow \\
\{X_n^C\}, D_p(\Pi^C(\hat{N})) & & E^k & = & E^k & \{X_n\}, D_p(\hat{N})
\end{array}$$

DIAGRAM 4.19. *Relationship between standardization and trace on C.*

Remark 4.20. What is the relationship between the chains $\{X_n\}$ and $\{X_n^C\}$ in the diagram? Here $p(C) = E^k$, so C is not the inverse image by p of *any* subset of E^k. Therefore we cannot expect that $\{X_n^C\}$ is itself a trace chain. However, we can describe the situation as follows: As before, let T denote the hitting time of the subset C of $\hat{E}^k$ for the chain $\{\hat{X}_n\}$, so that $\hat{X}_n^C = \hat{X}_{T_n}$. T is not the hitting time, in general, of any subset of E^k for the chain $\{X_n\}$. Nevertheless, *T is a stopping time for $\{X_n\}$*. This happens because, in our case, p is bimeasurable, so that if $p^\infty\colon (\hat{E}^k)^\infty \to (E^k)^\infty$ is the map induced by p, for any $A \in \sigma(\hat{X}_0, \ldots, \hat{X}_n)$ we will have $p^\infty(A) \in \sigma(X_0, \ldots, X_n)$. Applying this to the sets $A_n = T^{-1}\{n\}$ gives the result. It follows that $X_n^C = X_{T_n}$ is the Markov chain of Theorem 4.3. Notice that this gives another proof that $\hat{X}_n^C$ descends; however, it fails to make explicit the *type* of descent.

5. Compatibility of multiple descents

Theorem 5.1. Let $(\hat{U},\hat{\mathcal{U}})$, $(U,\mathcal{U})$, $(\hat{V},\hat{\mathcal{V}})$, and $(V,\mathcal{V})$ be measurable spaces. Let $\hat{K}$ be a kernel on $\hat{U}$. Let $p\colon \hat{U} \to U$, $r\colon \hat{V} \to V$ be measurable, and let $\hat{q}\colon \hat{U} \to \hat{V}$,

$q: U \to V$ be bimeasurable and surjective. Suppose $r \circ \hat{q} = q \circ p$, so that the following diagram commutes.

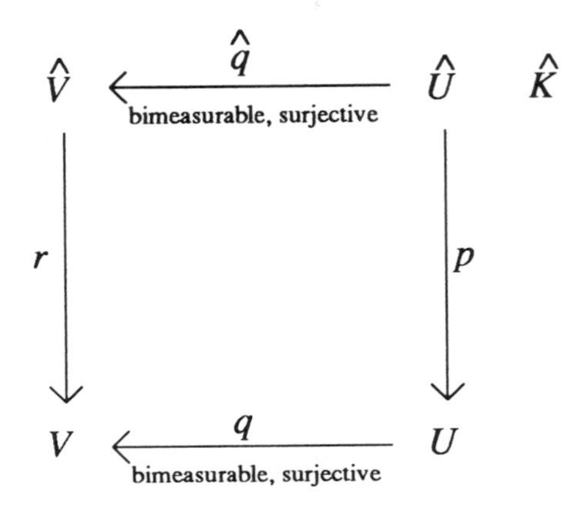

DIAGRAM 5.2. *Hypotheses of Theorem 5.1.*

Suppose that (1) $\hat{K}$ is $\hat{q}$-respectful, (2) $\hat{K}$ is p-decomposable, and (3) there is a version m of the common rcpd of $\hat{K}$ with respect to p such that, when we view m as an operator $m: \hat{\mathcal{U}} \to \mathcal{U}$, the image of $m \circ \hat{q}^*$ is contained in the image of q^* in $\mathcal{U}$. Then

(i) $R_{\hat{q}}(\hat{K})$ is r-decomposable, with common rcpd n determined uniquely by $m \circ \hat{q}^* = q^* \circ n$;

(ii) $D_p(\hat{K})$ is q-respectful; and

(iii) $R_q D_p(\hat{K}) = D_r R_{\hat{q}}(\hat{K})$.

Proof. For simplicity, we denote $\hat{M} = R_{\hat{q}}\hat{K}$, $K = D_p(\hat{K})$, and $M = D_r\hat{M}$. (We need to prove M exists.) We refer to Diagram 5.3. q^* is injective since q is surjective.

In accordance with the premises of the theorem, the solid arrows in 5.3 already constitute a commutative diagram. The *top face* displays the $\hat{q}^*$-respectfulness of $\hat{K}$. The *right-hand face* displays the p-decomposability of $\hat{K}$. The *rearmost slanted face* is induced by Diagram 5.2. The solid arrow part of the left-hand face is the definition of $r_*\hat{M}$. The commutativity of the *middle slanted face* follows from the commutativity of these faces.

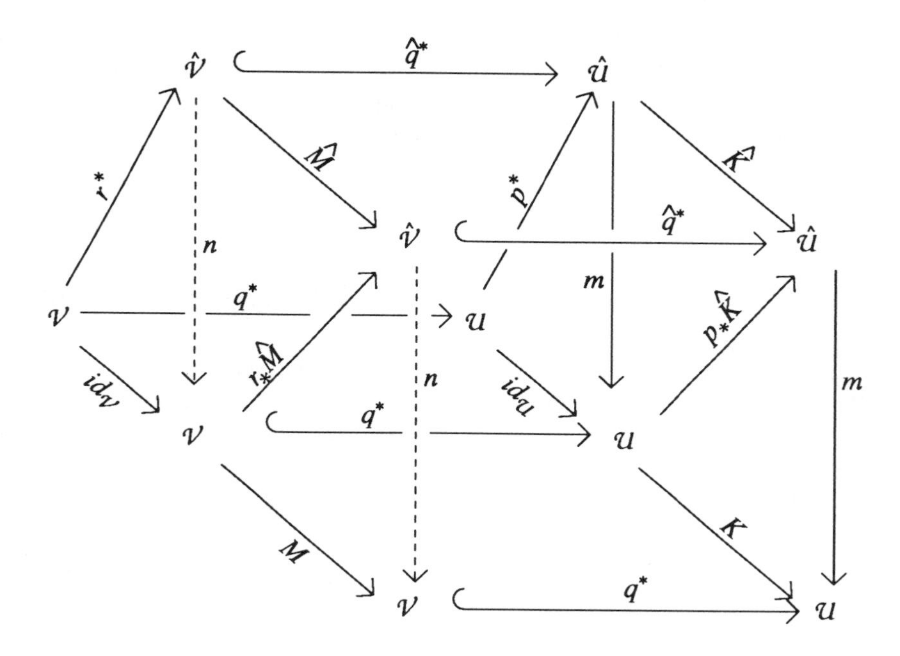

DIAGRAM 5.3. *Commutative diagram. m and n are markovian.*

The theorem will be proved when we establish the commutativity of the full diagram, including the dotted arrows. For then (i) $\hat{M}$ is r-decomposable by the left-hand face in view of the criterion 3.9 and (ii) K is q-respectful by the bottom face in view of 3.7, whence (iii) $M = D_r\hat{M}$ is then also equal to $R_q K$.

First, we define n. By hypothesis (3), for $f \in \hat{\mathcal{V}}$ we have $m \circ \hat{q}^*(f) = q^*(g)$ for $g \in \mathcal{V}$; g is unique since q^* is injective. Thus we can define $n(f) = g$. The *inner vertical face* then commutes by construction of n. This defines n as an operator, but we need n to correspond to a markovian kernel. Now it is well known that an operator comes from a kernel if and only if it is positive (i.e., preserves positivity of functions) and preserves increasing limits. Thus m, $\hat{q}^*$ and q^* have these properties (recall Remark 3.12); but then so does n, in view of the commutativity relation

$$m \circ \hat{q}^* = q^* \circ n \tag{5.4}$$

together with the injectivity of $\hat{q}^*$ and q^*. To show that n is markovian, we want $n(1_{\hat{V}}) = 1_V$. Now $r^* 1_V = 1_{\hat{V}}$, so what we want is $n \circ r^*(1_V) = 1_V$. For this, it suffices to show that $n \circ r^* = \mathrm{id}_{\mathcal{V}}$; therefore the markovian property for n will follow from the commutativity of the left-hand face of 5.3.

For the commutativity of this face, we first show that

$$n \circ r^* = \mathrm{id}_{\mathcal{V}}$$

and

$$\hat{M} = r_* \hat{M} \circ n.$$

Since q^*, $\hat{q}^*$ are injective, it is equivalent to show that (a) $q^* \circ n \circ r^* = q^*$ and (b) $\hat{q}^* \circ \hat{M} = \hat{q}^* \circ r_* \hat{M} \circ n$. By 5.4, the left-hand side of (a) is $m \circ \hat{q}^* \circ r^* = m \circ p^* \circ q^* = \mathrm{id}_{\mathcal{U}} \circ q^*$ (where the equalities depend respectively on the commutativity of the rear slanted face and the rear triangle of the right face). Thus (a) is verified. For (b), by the top face we have $\hat{q}^* \circ \hat{M} = \hat{K} \circ \hat{q}^*$. By the right face $\hat{K} \circ \hat{q}^* = p_* \hat{K} \circ m \circ \hat{q}^*$. By 5.4 this is $p_* \hat{K} \circ q^* \circ n$. Finally by the middle slanted face this is $\hat{q}^* \circ r^* \hat{M} \circ n$.

The current status of the left face is shown in the next unlabeled diagram.

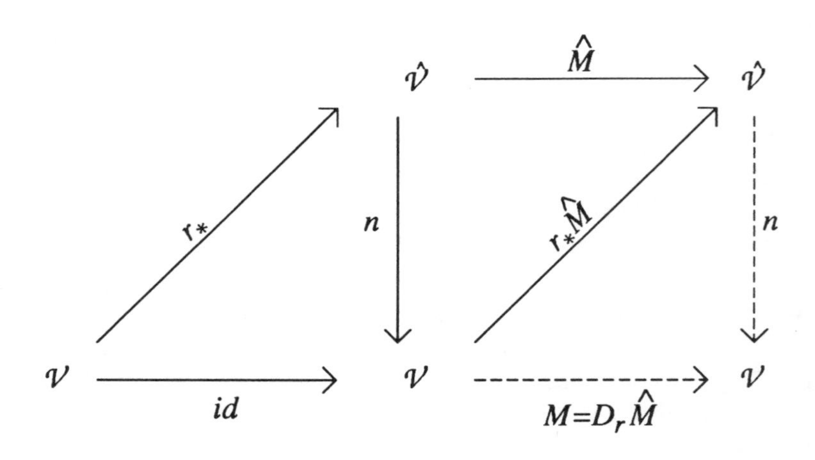

The solid arrow portion of the diagram is now known to commute. But this portion is the decomposability criterion 3.9. It follows from 3.11 that then there exists M so that the whole diagram, including the dotted arrows, commutes.

Thus, the entire left side of 5.3 commutes. The front face commutes since it is a replica of the inner vertical face. Thus the whole diagram is known to commute except the bottom face; but this follows straightforwardly from the commutativity of the other faces. ∎

In applying Theorem 5.1 to the descent of chains, we must be concerned with properties of their initial measures, as well as with properties of their kernels. In particular, for decomposable descent the initial measure must have the same rcpd as the kernel. With the notation as above, suppose then that we have a chain in $\hat{U}$ with initial measure ρ, which descends respectfully via q and decomposably via p. The descent via $\hat{q}$ yields a chain in $\hat{V}$ with initial measure $\hat{q}_*\rho$. To fully exploit 5.1 we will need to know that this measure has the correct rcpd for further decomposable descent via r. The relevant result here is itself a corollary of 5.1.

Corollary 5.5. With the same spaces and functions as in Theorem 5.1, suppose $\hat{\rho}$ is a finite positive measure on $\hat{U}$. Suppose that $\hat{\rho}$ has an rcpd m with respect to p, such that $\mathrm{Im}(m \circ \hat{q}^*) \subset \mathrm{Im} q^*$.

Let $\hat{\sigma} = \hat{q}_*\hat{\rho}$, a measure on $\hat{V}$. Then $\hat{\sigma}$ has an rcpd n with respect to r, uniquely determined by

$$m \circ \hat{q}^* = q^* \circ n. \tag{5.6}$$

Proof. Any positive measure $\hat{\rho}$ may be viewed as a kernel $\hat{K}$ on $\hat{U}$ given by $\hat{K}(\hat{u}, \cdot) = \hat{\rho}(\cdot)$. Since $\hat{K}$ is independent of $\hat{u}$, so is its rcpd m. Thus $\hat{K}$ is automatically p-decomposable. The image of $\hat{K}$ as an operator consists of constant functions: If $f \in \hat{\mathcal{U}}$ then $\hat{K}f(\hat{u}) = \hat{\rho}(f) \equiv \int_{\hat{U}} \hat{\rho}(d\hat{u}) f(\hat{u})$. Moreover, if $A \in \hat{\mathcal{V}}$ then

$$\hat{q}_*\hat{K}(\hat{u}, A) = \hat{q}_*\hat{\rho}(A) = \hat{\sigma}(A).$$

Since this is a constant function in $\hat{\mathcal{U}}$, it is, a fortiori, constant on fibres of $\hat{q}$. Therefore $\hat{K}$ is $\hat{q}$-respectful, and $R_{\hat{q}}(\hat{K}) = \hat{\sigma}$.

Thus conditions (1) and (2) of Theorem 5.1 are satisfied for $\hat{K}$. Condition (3) is also satisfied by hypothesis. We conclude from the theorem that n is uniquely determined by 5.6 and is the rcpd of $R_{\hat{q}}(\hat{K})$, i.e., of $\hat{\sigma}$. ∎

We now apply our results to observer chains in the setting of Hypothesis 2.0. As in section four, we let $\tilde{C}$ be an arbitrary subset of $\mathcal{I}(k)$, $C = E^k \times \tilde{C} \subset \hat{E}^k$, and $C' = J^{k-1} \times \tilde{C} \subset \hat{J}^{k-1}$. We then make the following identifications in Theorem 5.1 and Corollary 5.5:

$$\begin{aligned} &\hat{U} = C, \quad U = E^k, \quad \hat{V} = C', \quad V = J^{k-1}, \\ &p = \text{ restriction to } C \text{ of } \mathrm{pr}_1 : \hat{E}^k \to E^k, \\ &r = \text{ restriction to } C' \text{ of } \mathrm{pr}_1 : \hat{J}^{k-1} \to J^k, \\ &q = \text{ the relativization map as in §2}, \\ &\hat{q} = \text{ the restriction to } C \text{ of the } \hat{q} \text{ in §2}, \\ &\hat{K} = \Pi_j^C(\hat{N}) \text{ for any } j, \text{ and} \\ &\hat{\rho} = \hat{\mu}^C. \end{aligned} \qquad (**)$$

As usual, $\hat{N}$ denotes the sequence of kernels of the augmented position chain, and the $\Pi_j^C(\hat{N})$ is as defined in 4.6. $\hat{\mu}$ is the initial measure of the augmented chain, and $\hat{\mu}^C$ is as defined in 4.7. This includes the case where $\tilde{C} = \mathcal{I}(k)$, so that $C = \hat{E}^k$, $C' = \hat{J}^{k-1}$, $\hat{K} = \hat{N}$, etc.

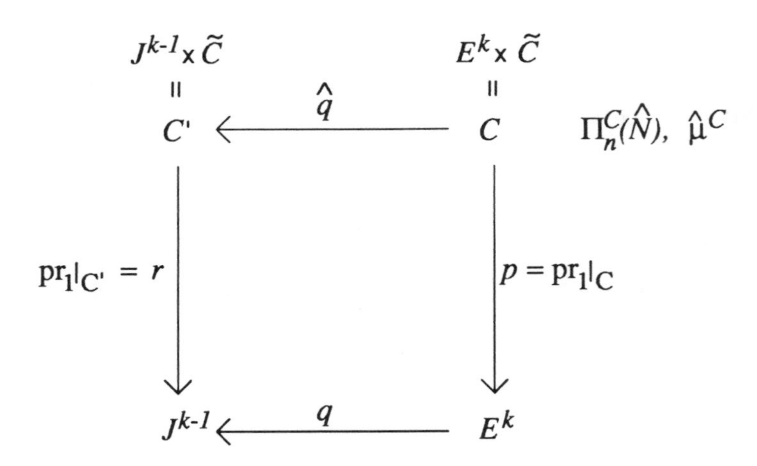

DIAGRAM 5.7. *Commutative diagram.*

We now observe that with the identifications (**), the hypotheses of Theorem 5.1 (and Corollary 5.5 for $\hat{\rho}$) are satisfied. In fact, Diagram 5.2 becomes Diagram

5.7 which is commutative, q and $\hat{q}$ are bimeasurable and surjective, $\hat{K}$ is $\hat{q}$-respectful (Theorem 4.13) and p-decomposable (Theorem 4.18). For the common rcpd m of $\hat{K}$ we may take τ_C, as given in 4.18.

It remains to check the hypothesis (3) of 5.1: $\mathrm{Im}(\tau_C \circ \hat{q}^*) \subset \mathrm{Im}(q^*)$. This is true by virtue of the configuration symmetry of the τ-distribution (part (3) of Definition 7–2.3). To see this explicitly, take f to be a measurable function on C'. Then for $e \in E^k$,

$$(\tau_C \circ \hat{q}^* f)(e) = \frac{1}{\tau(e, \tilde{C})} \sum_{\chi \in \tilde{C}} \tau(e; \chi) f(\hat{q}(e, \chi)). \tag{5.8}$$

Now the configuration symmetry of τ means exactly that for any fixed χ the mapping $e \mapsto \tau(e; \chi)$ is constant on the fibres of q; we have already noted this after 2.0. Recalling that $\hat{q}(e, \chi) = (q(e), \chi)$, this implies that the right side of 5.8, viewed as a function of e, is constant on the fibres of q, i.e., it is in the image of q. By Theorem 4.18 the measure μ^C also has rcpd τ_C; therefore, the hypotheses of Corollary 5.5 are also satisfied for $\hat{p} = \mu^C$.

Thus, we can apply Theorem 5.1 and Corollary 5.5 to the situation in Diagram 5.7, i.e., to the trace chain on C of the augmented position chain. We get the following theorem, which also summarizes Theorems 4.13 and 4.18:

Theorem 5.9. Let $\{X, Y, E, S, G, J, \pi\}$ be a symmetric framework, with E principal homogeneous for J. Let a configuration symmetric τ be given. Assume we have k participators with symmetric action kernels $Q_1, \ldots, Q_k$ and initial measures $\xi_1, \ldots, \xi_k$. Let $\hat{\mu} = (\xi_1 \otimes \ldots \otimes \xi_k)_\tau$ and $\hat{N}_n = \{\langle Q_1(n), \ldots, Q_k(n) \rangle_\tau\}$ be the initial measure and one-step transition probabilities for the corresponding augmented dynamical chain $\{\hat{X}_n\}$. Let $\{X_n\}$ denote the standard chain, and let $\{\hat{Z}_n\}$ and $\{Z_n\}$ denote the augmented relative chain and standard relative chain respectively. Let $\tilde{C} \subset \mathcal{I}(k)$ be any subset, let $C = E^k \times \tilde{C}$ and $C' = J^{k-1} \times \tilde{C}$. Let $\hat{q}$ and q be the relativization maps of section two, and let p: $\hat{E}^k \to E^k$ and r: $\hat{J}^{k-1} \to J^{k-1}$ be projections on the first factor.

Consider the Diagram 5.10, in which each double arrow indicates the chain-construction procedure as labelled. The chains in the front face of the diagram with superscript C and C' notation are defined to be the result of the appropriate arrow.

The conclusion: *Diagram 5.10 exists and is commutative.* The commutativity here means that any two sequences of procedures which have the same beginning and the same ending yield the same result. The "stopped chain" terminology means that $X_n^C = X_{T_n}$ where $T = T_C$, and $Z_n^{C'} = Z_{T_n}$ where $T = T_{C'}$. Here the use of T_C and $T_{C'}$ as stopping times is as discussed in Remark 4.20.

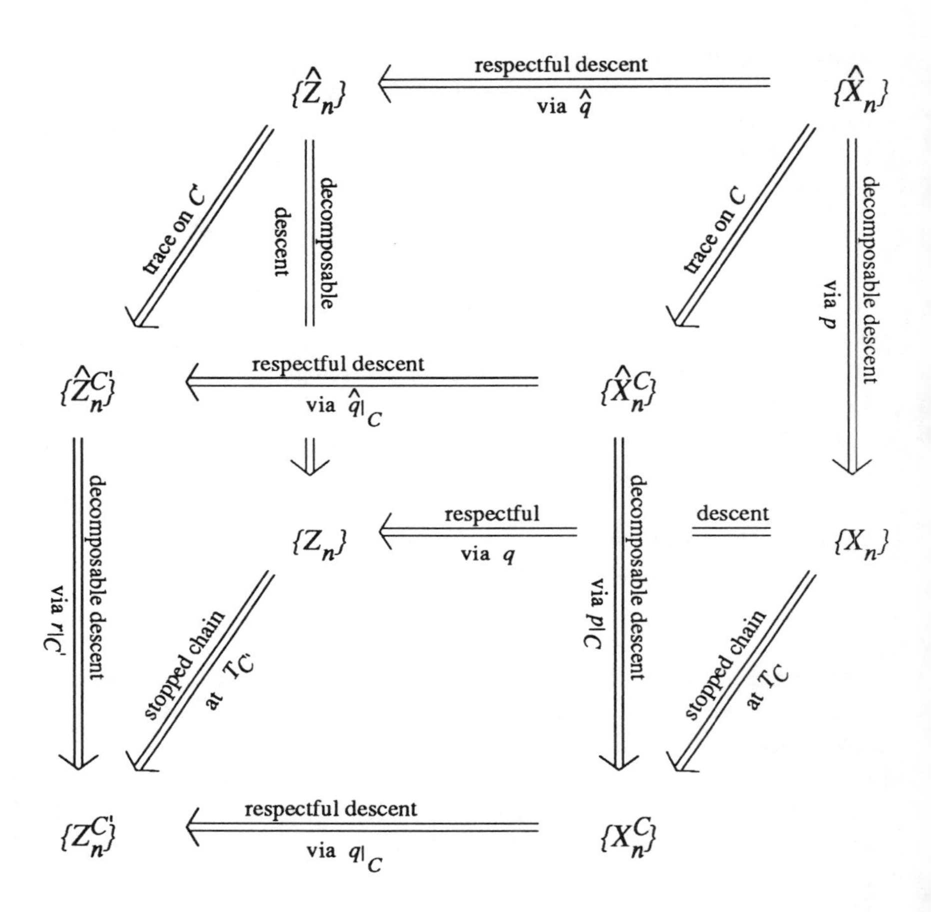

DIAGRAM 5.10. *Commutative diagram, relating the various dynamical chains.*

Remark 5.11. The commutativity of 5.10 contains the appropriate assertions about the initial distributions of the chains in question. For example, the rcpd with respect to $r|_C$ of $(\hat{q}_*(\hat{\mu}))^{C'}$ is the same as that of $\hat{q}_*(\hat{\mu}^C)$.

6. Matching perception to reality

We assume that we are in a symmetric framework with E principal homogeneous for J, and with a symmetric τ-distribution. In this setting suppose that we have k participators with symmetric action kernels. Thus we will continue to use the notation of 2.0.

It is reasonable to consider the augmented position chain $\{\hat{X}_t\}$ on $\hat{E}^k$ to be the "ultimate source" of phenomena—meaning those phenomena which arise in, or are associated to, the participator dynamics. This point of view is justified by Theorem 5.9: The theorem tells us firstly that the "derived" stochastic processes $\{X_t\}$, $\{\hat{Z}_t\}$, $\{Z_t\}$, $\{\hat{X}_t^C\}$, $\{X_t^C\}$, $\{\hat{Z}_t^{C'}\}$, $\{Z_t^{C'}\}$ are Markov chains on the same base space, which we may take to be the canonical space $\hat{\Omega}$ of the chain $\{\hat{X}_t\}$. Moreover, the theorem affirms that the character of any one of these chains is not an artifact of the particular sequence of descents used to derive it; this character depends only on the way that the given chain is probabilistically grounded in $\hat{\Omega}$. It is in this sense that the probability space $\hat{\Omega}$—which is informationally equivalent to the chain $\{\hat{X}_t\}$—is seen as the common source.

The dictionary[1] defines *phenomenon* as "anything directly apprehended by the senses or one of them: an event that may be observed: the appearance which anything makes to our consciousness: ...." One might paraphrase this (with apologies) by saying that *phenomena are the constituents of a subjective reality.* With this definition, while $\{\hat{X}_t\}$ may be viewed as the source of phenomena as above, it is not itself *phenomenal.* In fact, the derived chains $\{X_t\}$, $\{\hat{Z}_t\}$, $\{Z_t^{C'}\}$, ... (other than $\{\hat{X}_t\}$) are more appropriately called the *phenomenal chains.*

For example, we will speak of the *subjective reality chain* of, say, the first participator. As we noted in section one, the participator is ignorant of the full channeling involution: it is aware only of being channeled to, and the successive instances of this awareness define its proper time. This means that the subjective or phenomenal reality of this participator is already contained in the chain $\{X_t^C\}$ where $C = E^k \times C_1, C_1 = \{\chi \in \mathcal{I}(k) \mid 1 \in D(\chi)\}$. Moreover, if we suppose that the participator's interpretation kernel is symmetric (as in 5–5.6), then its conclusions are actually conclusions about the chain $\{Z_t^{C'}\}$ (where the relativization is, of course, with respect to the same first participator): the participator's subjective reality is contained in $\{Z_t^{C'}\}$. As we will see, the relativization procedure imposes a strong form of "unknowability" on the unrelativized chains: the existence of a stationary

[1] Kirkpatrick, E.M. (editor), *Chambers 20th Century Dictionary,* Press Syndicate of the University of Cambridge, New York, 1983.

probability measure (i.e., a stable phenomenology) on a relativized chain does not imply the existence of such a measure for the corresponding absolute chain.

In the study of specialization one considers phenomenal chains defined by subsets $\tilde{C}$ of $\mathcal{I}(k)$ more general than C_1. They correspond to subsystems of our k-participator system which function as a single ("higher level") observer. In any case, we conceptualize the various derived chains as phenomenal or subjective reality chains for suitable participators or specialized subsystems of participators. All of these chains partake of a common probabilistic source which is itself unknowable by the participators: the augmented absolute chain $\{\hat{X}_t\}$. Traditionally, the word *noumenon* denotes "an unknown and unknowable substance or thing as it is in itself."[2] Thus we might also call the chain $\{\hat{X}_t\}$ *the noumenal chain,* the inaccessible unity underlying the separate possible subjective realities.

We now study in more detail a single participator's view of the dynamical situation. We will assume that the participator's interpretation kernel is symmetric, i.e., that its perception (as well as its action) is relativized. This means that the "view" in question is appropriately expressed by the *relativized* chain $Z^{C'} = \{Z_t^{C'}\}$ of 5.9. This chain may be obtained, for example, as the relativization of X^C, or as the chain Z stopped at the time $T_{C'}$, or even as the standardization of $\hat{Z}^{C'}$. Here we use the terminology (and results) of 5.9, and we put

$$\begin{aligned} C_1 &= \{\chi \in \mathcal{I}(k) \mid 1 \in D(\chi)\}, \\ C &= E^k \times C_1, \\ C' &= J^{k-1} \times C_1 . \end{aligned} \tag{6.1}$$

We have taken the first participator as the distinguished one. The stopping time $T_{C'}$ or T_C is the proper time of the first participator. The relativization $X \Longrightarrow Z$ is taken with respect to the first participator as usual, i.e., it is the respectful descent via q or $\hat{q}$ as in section two.

Terminology 6.2. We will call our distinguished participator *participator A*. The chain $Z^{C'}$ will be called *A's (subjective) reality chain.* η will denote A's *fundamental interpretation kernel* (5–5.6). (This notation is for simplicity: a priori, η is not time invariant, and when we wish to note this we will write $\eta(t)$.)

What does it mean to say that A's perception is matched to its reality? At each

---

[2] ibid.

moment of its proper time, a point s lights up in S, and A's interpretation of this is the probability measure $\eta(s, \cdot)$ on J. *This is A's interpretation of the position of the source of the channeling relative to its current position.* Knowledge of A's absolute perspective e would enable the output $\eta_e(s, \cdot)$, which is a probability measure on E, but we are here concerned only with the relativized situation $Z^{C'}$. Thus it is reasonable to make the following preliminary definition.

Definition 6.3. A's perception, as embodied in its interpretation kernel η, matches A's reality at time t if, for any measurable subset K in J, $\eta(t)(s, K)$ is the actual probability (in the chain $Z^{C'}$) that the manifestation of at least one participator has a perspective differing from that of A by an element of the set K, given that the channeling to A at time t results in s.

This definition takes into account the fact that A's subjective reality cannot include the details of the channeling involution, i.e., we are in $Z^{C'}$ and not, say, $\hat{Z}^{C'}$. It follows that the criterion given above is not sensitive to which participator truly channeled to A. Instead, the definition asserts that $\eta(t)(s, K)$ (which is in any case the same as $\eta(t)(s, \pi^{-1}(s) \cap K)$) is the actual probability that the manifestation of a participator, having a perspective differing from that of A by an element of the set K, could have channeled to A at time t, resulting in s, i.e., that $\pi^{-1}(s) \cap K$ was occupied at this time. We now obtain an a priori expression for this probability.[3] This will enable us to express Definition 6.3 in the form of an equation.

Suppose that the distribution of the $(k - 1)$-dimensional random vector $Z_t^{C'}$ is ν_t; this is a distribution on J^{k-1}. Then the inclusion-exclusion principle allows us to compute the probability that at least one of the k-participators lies in K. The procedure is formalized in the following definition:

Definition 6.4. To each measure ζ on J^{k-1} we associate a measure on J, denoted

[3] Since we condition on a *value* of s, we should be using the expression "regular conditional probability distribution" rather than just "probability." This will be taken as understood in what follows.

$\mathcal{D}\zeta$, as follows: Let $K \in \mathcal{J}$. For $1 \leq i \leq k-1$, let

$$K_i = \left(\prod_{l=1}^{i-1} J\right) \times K \times \left(\prod_{l=i+1}^{k-1} J\right)$$

(i.e., K_i is the cartesian product of $k-2$ copies of J with one copy of K in the ith place). Then let

$$K_{i_1,i_2,\ldots,i_l} = \left(\bigcap_{j=1}^{l} K_{i_j}\right)$$

for $1 \leq i_1 < i_2 < \ldots < i_l \leq k-1$. Then put

$$\mathcal{D}\zeta(K) = \sum_{l=1}^{k-1}(-1)^{l+1} \sum_{1 \leq i_1 < \ldots < i_l \leq k-1} \zeta(K_{i_1,\ldots,i_l}).$$

The assignment $\zeta \mapsto \mathcal{D}\zeta$ is linear, and $\mathcal{D}\zeta$ is a probability measure if ζ is one.

In consequence of this definition we have the following proposition.

Proposition 6.5. Let ζ be a probability measure on J^{k-1}. Then

$$\begin{aligned}\zeta\{(v_1,\ldots,v_{k-1}) \in J^{k-1} \mid &\text{ at least one of the } v_1,\ldots,v_k \text{ lies in } K\} \\ &= \mathcal{D}\zeta(K).\end{aligned}$$

Proof. The set in question is just $\bigcup_{i=1}^{k-1} K_i$, so the result is a direct application of the inclusion-exclusion principle and the definition of $\mathcal{D}\zeta$. ∎

In particular, if ν_t is the distribution of $Z_t^{\mathcal{C}}$, $(\mathcal{D}\nu_t)(K)$ is the probability that at least one component lies in K. It follows:

Proposition 6.6. Let ν_t denote the distribution of $Z_t^{\mathcal{C}'}$. Then the conditional probability that the manifestation of at least one participator has a perspective differing from that of A by an element of the set $K \subset J$ at time t, given that the channeling to A results in s, is

$$m_\pi^{\mathcal{D}\nu_t}(s, K)$$

(rcpd notation as in 7–4.12).

We can now make our preliminary definition precise.

Definition 6.7. We will say that "A's perception matches its reality at time t," or that "A has true perception at time t" if

$$\eta(t) \text{ is a version of the rcpd } m_{\pi}^{\mathcal{D}\nu_t}.$$

If this holds *for all* t, we will simply say that "A's perception matches its reality," or "A has true perception."

The words "true" and "perception," like the word "reality," are technical terms in the above definition. "Reality" is the subjective reality chain $Z^{C'}$. In keeping with our probabilistic semantics, reality at time t is the *distribution* ν_t of the state $Z_t^{C'}$, and not the discrete states themselves. The word "perception" denotes that which is representable by the interpretation kernel η; in particular A's perceptual representations are made in the framework J (and not J^{k-1}). Thus $\mathcal{D}\nu_t$ is that aspect of the reality ν_t which is perceptually representable. Perception is "true" if the representation $\eta(t)$ agrees with this representable aspect of reality modulo the observer structure embodied by the map π. Perceptual truth is therefore several semantic levels removed even from the "subjective reality" $Z^{C'}$. This in turn is several levels removed from the "source" or "noumenal" reality $\hat{X}$. (And from the standpoint of the whole lattice of observer families, $\hat{X}$ itself is a localization.)

The time-dependent, or instantaneous character of the definition of true perception given in Definition 6.7 is required for semantic completeness: The interpretation kernel η is, a priori, time-dependent. The action kernels of the participators are time-dependent; in every respect the participator is a dynamical entity. Even if all the action kernels were time-independent, so that the chain $Z^{C'}$ is homogeneous, the distribution ν_t will in general depend on t, and hence so will $\mathcal{D}\nu_t$. However, from both the intuitive and analytic viewpoints and for purposes of both application and theoretical development, the fundamental situation occurs when $Z^{C'}$ has a stationary measure. This "stable reality" context gives rise to an important modification of Definition 6.7.

Recall that a measure ν is *stationary* for a Markov chain $\{\xi_t\}$ if $\nu P_t = \nu$ for each one-step transition probability P_t of the chain; νP denotes the operation of the kernel P on ν defined in **6–1**. It is equivalent to say that if the distribution of ξ_0 is ν, then for all $t \geq 0$ the distribution of ξ_t is also ν. Stationary measures do not always exist; when they do, they are not necessarily unique. In general, if ν_t denotes the distribution of ξ_t, the ν_t, though not stationary themselves, may converge to a stationary measure as $t \to \infty$.

Definition 6.8. We say that A has *stably true perception* if $\eta(t)$ is independent of t, and is a version of $m_\pi^{\mathcal{D}\nu}$ for a fixed stationary measure ν of $Z^{C'}$. More generally, we say that A has *stably true perception in the limit* or that A *tends* (or *converges*) *to stably true perception* if $lim_{t\to\infty}\, \eta(t)$ is a version of $m_\pi^{\mathcal{D}\nu}$ for a stationary ν.

In order to maintain flexibility, no hypothesis is made in the definition about the relationship between the actual distribution ν_t of the chain and the stationary measure ν. (The presumption, however, is that either $\nu_t = \nu$ for all t or $\nu_t \to \nu$ as $t \to \infty$.) Nor has any particular form of convergence been specified.

How good is stably true perception? Let us assume that for each t, $\nu_t = \nu$, a stationary measure. Then *the participator A with stably true perception instantiates, at each instant of its proper time, an observer whose inferences are inductively strong*. Indeed, this is the observer (G, Y, J, S, π, η) whose event set is J, whose perspective map π is the same as the fundamental map π of our original symmetric framework (X, Y, E, S, G, J, π), and whose conclusion kernel is A's fundamental interpretation kernel—the one which satisfies Definition 6.8. In fact, by hypothesis the measure $\mathcal{D}\nu$ correctly (and time-invariantly) describes the distribution in J of the population of A's "universe." This is the universe consisting of participators in the original dynamical ensemble, but only insofar as they channel with A. The conclusion kernel η then correctly describes this population distribution, conditioned by the element $s \in S$ resulting from channeling; this is the very meaning of inductive strength of an observer inference. Note further that if we imagine A to have some kind of "access" to the distribution $\pi_*(\mathcal{D}\nu)$ on S, then A knows the actual distribution $\mathcal{D}\nu$, not just its π-rcpd.

Can A make any inductively strong inference beyond that of inferring the location of anonymous channelers to A? In the first place, A has no means of identifying the other participators as individuals or even of inferring the number of participators in the ensemble. Thus, there is no basis for inferring ν itself even if $\mathcal{D}\nu$ is known. Of course, we can imagine that A builds a representation consisting of one other participator whose relative position has time-invariant distribution $\mathcal{D}\nu$, and then we might argue that this is a strong inference. However, it is really just a canonical form for the same inference as before. For example, there is no inference here of the actual number of participators. In attempting to infer from relative to absolute position, an even more fundamental obstruction arises. For here it is possible that relative positions have a stationary (probability) distribution while the absolute positions do not. We can get an example of this by considering a two participator system involving A and B; assume that the position of B relative to A has a stationary distribution while A itself executes, say, a transient random walk. These considerations and others suggest that stably true perception per se does not lead *canonically* to inductively strong inferences at a higher level than that of the subjective reality of the observer (G, Y, J, S, π, η).

CHAPTER NINE

TOWARDS SPECIALIZATION

A goal of our theory is to understand how "higher" levels of perception might emerge from "lower" ones, i.e., to understand "perceptual hierarchy." In this chapter we discuss this notion and describe a possible model of it called *framework specialization*. We illustrate framework specialization with two examples: the incremental rigidity scheme of Ullman (1983) and "specialized chain bundles." Our presentation is neither complete nor rigorous, but is an extended speculation guided by work in progress.

1. Introduction to specialization

Our approach to the study of perceptual hierarchy is illustrated by a question: Under what conditions does an ensemble of participators in a fixed reflexive framework Θ give rise to a "higher" level observer or class of observers? We believe it is misguided to restrict attention to answers which implicitly postulate a deterministic or reductionistic relationship between the ensemble and the new observers, e.g., to answers postulating that the new observers are unions or products of the participators in the ensemble. Instead, we seek an answer which exploits the fundamental character of observers: observers perform inferences which are not, in general, logically determined by the premises. In our search for a nonreductionistic answer, we have been guided by four key ideas.

Idea 1. The premises of the new observer should be deducible in some manner from the conclusions of the participators in the ensemble.

The appeal of this idea is that it connects the ensemble and the new observer nontrivially, but it also connects them nonreductionistically. For in this case the ensemble determines only the premises of the observer it gives rise to, not its conclusions. Many different observers can be constructed having the same space of premises Y.

The ensemble which gives rise to a new single observer in this way we call an *instantiation* of that observer. We do not call it *the* instantiation, for it is likely that a given observer can have many different instantiations. The resulting observer we call a *specialization* of the ensemble. Again, we do not call it *the* specialization, for a given ensemble is likely to have many different specializations. More generally, we will say that a class of inferences A is an *ascendant* of a class of inferences B if all premises for inferences in A are deductive consequences of the conclusions of the inferences in B.

Idea 2. If the premises of the specialized observer arise from the conclusions of the instantiating ensemble, then these conclusions should be reliable.

If we want to build higher levels of perception from lower levels then we want the lower levels to be secure before we start building. In chapter eight we discuss precise conditions in which the perceptual conclusions of a dynamical ensemble of participators are matched to the reality observed. The strongest such conditions we call "stably true perception" and "stably true perception in the limit" (8–6.8). For the conclusions of the participators to be reliable in these strong senses the dynamics in which they participate must have a stationary measure ν. The conclusions of the participators are then derived from this stationary measure ν via the rcpd construction $m_\pi^{\mathcal{D}\nu}$ (8–6.4, 8–6.6). The stationary measure can be viewed as describing stabilities of the asymptotic behavior of the participator dynamics. Thus the conclusions of the participators, to be reliable in a strong sense, are derived from stabilities of the asymptotic behavior of their dynamics.

In keeping with Idea 1, a channeling to a specialized observer should occur as a result of channelings in Θ to the participators of its instantiating ensemble. Furthermore, to maintain consistency with our nondualistic semantics, the objects of perception of a specialized observer should be other specialized observers. This leads to:

Idea 3. The channeling between two specialized observers is expressed by an interaction between the observers' instantiating participator ensembles, assuming these ensembles to be in the same framework Θ.

One implication of this is that a single channeling, i.e., a single instant of time, at a specialized level may involve infinitely many channelings at the instantiating level, i.e., at the level of Θ. Such an interaction perturbs the asymptotic behavior of each instantiating system. The asymptotic behavior of each system in isolation must be stable in order to make any sense of the perturbation. Granting this stability, if the perturbed asymptotics has sufficient regularity, each system can encode information about the other system which caused the perturbation.

This brings us to the fourth main idea:

Idea 4. The premise of a specialized observer's inference is a stable perturbation of the asymptotics of the observer's instantiation, a perturbation which results from an interaction with another participator system.

Up to this point we have not given a formal definition of "perceptual hierarchy", i.e., of what it means for one inferencing system to be at a higher level than another. One notion of hierarchy would be a set together with a partial order on it. However, there is no reason to suppose that the intuitive idea of specialization outlined above can be so expressed. If A is a specialization of B, and B is a specialization of C, should one suppose that A *must* specialize C? Is it possible that a chain of such specializations might eventually fold back to its origin? Should one replace a partial order with a more local notion of order?

It is clear that we need a more precise understanding of the information flow from a given ensemble's conclusions to its specialization, as mentioned in Idea 1 above. For example, following upon the discussion after Idea 2, it may be possible to deduce the stationary measure of the instantiated ensemble from the set of the latter's conclusion measures, given that some or all of the participators enjoy true perception of their ambient dynamics. In any case, in order to formally develop the above ideas we will assume this, so that Idea 1 may be expressed in the following form:

Idea 1 bis. The premises of the specialized observer should be deducible in some manner from the stabilities of the dynamics of the participators in the instantiating ensemble.

In what follows we reintroduce these ideas in a more formal setting.

2. Hierarchical analytic strategies revisited

We now consider how to construct a formal model of a perceptual hierarchy. In **4**–5 we suggest that the hierarchy arises from an analytic strategy which decomposes the interactions of complex systems into strata, or levels, and which describes the passage of information between strata. Within each level the interaction appears to be homogeneous, i.e., to involve like entities. Within a given system, and at a given level, we say that the relevant entities together constitute the "representation" of that system at that level. Similarly, the total interaction of two complex systems "expresses" itself at a given level by means of the interaction of each system's representation at that level. But there is more to the total interaction than this: within each system information flows between strata. This flow determines the hierarchical relationship on the collection of strata.

When we introduced the notion of hierarchical analytic strategy in **4**–5 we spoke of "entities of like nature" which are irreducible or indecomposable at a given level. The fundamental hierarchical relation holds between this level and another "lower" level at which each entity has its own representation, a representation which provide a first order decomposition of the entity. The hierarchical connection between these two levels is expressed by a canonical form for the passage of information from the constituents of the lower level representation of the entity, to the entity itself at the higher level. And the information which propagates in this canonical way arises from the interactions between these constituents.

This is where, in a participator-dynamical model, the ideas of specialization fit in. In the model we develop here, reflexive observer frameworks represent the possible hierarchical levels, and participators on a framework are the "irreducible entities" at that level.

Specification 2.1. To give a model of a perceptual hierarchy based on participator dynamics is to specify the following:

(i) a form in which complex systems are represented by participators in given frameworks, i.e., at given levels of the hierarchy;
(ii) a form in which interaction of several such systems is expressed at a given level;
(iii) a canonical form for the passing of information between hierarchically related levels in a single system;
(iv) a manner in which an interaction (as described in (ii)) among several systems generates information which then propagates (within each of the separate systems) via the connection described in (iii).

Here is a more detailed proposal for such a model. First consider (i) of 2.1. We let the expression of a complex system **S** at the level of the hierarchy corresponding to the reflexive framework $\Theta = (X, Y, E, S, \pi_\bullet)$ be an ensemble of participators on Θ together with a τ-distribution on Θ, satisfying a *permissibility condition* (discussed below). We call these (participator, τ)-data the *level Θ expression of* **S**. It follows that to a complex system, when considered in isolation, are associated participator dynamics in various frameworks. These participator dynamics are the expressions of the system at the various levels of the hierarchy. Suppose that the level Θ expression of **S** is the participator ensemble $(\xi_i, \{Q_i(n)\}_n, \{\eta_i(n)\}_n)$ for $i = 1, \ldots, k$ together with a τ-distribution τ. These data can generate various Markov chains such as the augmented chain on $E^k \times \mathcal{I}(k)$ (7–3.1, 7–3.2) or the standard chain on E^k (7–4.3). However these chains contain less information than the collection of participators together with τ, for many distinct sets of k participators and choices of τ might give rise to the same chains. Moreover these chains omit the interpretation kernels $\eta_i(n)$ of the participators. For these reasons we equate the level Θ expression of **S** with the (participator, τ)-data even though, by an abuse of language, we sometimes speak of the "dynamical system which expresses **S**" in Θ.

We now consider (ii) of 2.1. Suppose that two complex systems $\mathbf{S}_1$ and $\mathbf{S}_2$ interact and that A_1 and A_2, respectively, are their level Θ expressions as (participator, τ)–ensembles.

$$\mathbf{S}_1: \; A_1 = \{(\xi_1, \{Q_1(n)\}_n, \{\eta_1(n)\}_n), \ldots, (\xi_k, \{Q_k(n)\}_n, \{\eta_k(n)\}_n); \; \tau_k\}$$

$$\mathbf{S}_2:\ A_2 = \{(\lambda_1, \{R_1(n)\}_n, \{\theta_1(n)\}_n), \ldots, (\lambda_j, \{R_j(n)\}_n, \{\theta_j(n)\}_n);\ \tau_j\}. \tag{2.2}$$

We stipulate that a precondition for the interaction is that τ_k and τ_j are compatible (i.e., are part of the same τ-distribution family $\{\tau_i\}_i$). We further stipulate that the interaction itself is expressed in the augmented dynamics of the *joint* participator ensemble. This is the Markov chain on $E^{k+j} \times \mathcal{I}(k+j)$ whose transition probability is

$$\widehat{\langle Q_1(n), \ldots, Q_k(n), R_1(n), \ldots, R_j(n) \rangle}_\tau, \tag{2.3}$$

and whose initial distribution is

$$(\xi_1 \otimes \ldots \xi_k \otimes \lambda_1 \otimes \ldots \otimes \lambda_j)_\tau, \tag{2.4}$$

with the notation of **7–3.4**. Thus the interaction of two systems at level Θ is expressed by the "running" of the participator dynamical chain generated by joining the ensembles representing the two systems separately at that level. Note that such an interaction is meaningful only when both systems employ compatible τ-distributions.

This description of the interaction at a level Θ is natural; it is consistent with the "interactive" character of participators: *any* ensemble of participators subject to the same τ-distribution generates markovian dynamics. It remains to give the specifications (iii) and (iv). For (iii) we must define what it means for two reflexive frameworks Θ and Θ' to be "hierarchically related." The definition must be given in terms of the way in which information flows between the level Θ and level Θ' expressions of a given system. This definition determines the hierarchy, i.e., the ordering of the analytical levels. For (iv) we must specify how information about a level Θ interaction among several systems as stipulated in (ii) is extracted for propagation through the levels of each system. And this specification must comport with the hierarchical relation between levels set forth in (iii).

We may view (iii) and (iv) as imposing constraints on the single-level interaction of (ii). In fact, the information that propagates according to (iii) will be encoded in a form which enables it to pass through the hierarchical connection. (iv) requires that the interaction itself, as specified in (ii), must permit the extraction of this kind of information. This restricts the participator ensembles which may be parties to the interaction. These restrictions constitute the "permissibility condition" on participator ensembles mentioned above, the fulfillment of which is the "form" referred to in (i).

To understand this more concretely, consider systems $\mathbf{S}_1$ and $\mathbf{S}_2$ whose level Θ expressions are as in 2.2, and whose interaction at that level is via the markovian dynamics described in 2.3 and 2.4. In this joint participator dynamics there is no reason why the identity of the original participator ensemble should be retained. By this is meant the following. Suppose that, in isolation, each ensemble has a stable dynamics. When the two ensembles are coupled, their individual stabilities will be disturbed by "cross channelings," i.e., channelings between participators not in the same ensemble. With no constraints on the original systems, we would expect this disturbance to be so great as to eliminate not only the original stabilities but also any possibility of a new pair of stabilities for the individual ensembles. But the interaction data propagated as in (iv) must be meaningful in terms of the individual asymptotics (c.f. Idea 4 of section 1). There must, of course, be a disturbance of these asymptotics in order that an interaction at level Θ of the complex systems $\mathbf{S}_1$ and $\mathbf{S}_2$ can be said to have taken place. But this disturbance should only *perturb* the stabilities, not annihilate them. For the individual stabilities are the very grounding of the propagated information.

Thus we suggest that the participator ensembles each need some cohesive stability so that, in this sense, each ensemble maintains its individuality in interaction and so that the resulting perturbations of the dynamics of each ensemble have sufficient regularity to be classified. Assuming this regularity, the perturbation of each system is the interaction data which propagates internally in that system in the sense of (iv). A cohesive stability property which is sufficiently strong in this sense can serve as a "permissibility condition" in 2.1 (i). The enunciation of such cohesive stability properties, and their matching to compatible notions of perturbation regularities, is a central problem in devising models of perceptual hierarchy.

We summarize these ideas in

Terminology 2.5. Let a reflexive framework Θ and a channeling distribution $\tau = \{\tau_k\}_{k=1}^{\infty}$ be fixed. Let $\mathcal{P}$ be a collection whose elements are finite ensembles of participators on Θ.

(i) A *stability type* for $\mathcal{P}$ is a class of asymptotic characteristics[1] of the dynamics satisfying the following conditions. The participator dynamics of each ensemble in $\mathcal{P}$ has asymptotic characteristics in the given class. Moreover, if the dynamics is perturbed by the presence of another ensemble in $\mathcal{P}$ (i.e., when we consider the new dynamics induced on the original ensemble by running

[1] We will not give a precise, general definition of the notion of "asymptotic characteristic." The terminology is intended to include properties of dynamics which can be stated in terms of stationary measures of the dynamics, and, more generally, in terms of "asymptotic" or periodic measures. See, e.g., Revuz chapters 4 and 6.

the joint participator dynamics generated by it together with another ensemble) then asymptotic characteristics remain in the class (although they may change within it).

(ii) The stability type for $\mathcal{P}$ is said to have a *perturbation regularity* if the following condition holds: The variation of the asymptotic characteristics within the class of the stability type, resulting from the perturbations as in (i), has sufficient regularity to be represented in a way which encodes dependency of the variation on the two interacting ensembles in $\mathcal{P}$.

(iii) In the presence of (i) and (ii), we say that $\mathcal{P}$ possesses a *strong stability type*.

(iv) A *permissibility condition* for a stability type is a condition on the ensembles in $\mathcal{P}$, expressible in terms of the action kernels and initial distributions of the constituent participators, which guarantees that the given stability type, with perturbation regularity, will hold for $\mathcal{P}$ (as in (i) and (ii) above). (In other words, it guarantees that $\mathcal{P}$ will have the given strong stability type.

We reiterate that the central idea for propagation between levels is that the information propagated consists in the regular perturbations of an ensemble's asymptotics. Given a framework Θ, the permissibility conditions on ensembles are conditions on the τ-distribution as well as on the data for the constituent participators. (It is expected that the interpretation kernels will play a role in the actual extraction of the data to be propagated—c.f. Idea 2 of section 1.) It seems likely that, even on a given framework, these considerations allow a wide variety of permissibility conditions.

3. Framework Specialization

In this section we discuss more formally how the specialization ideas of the section 1 give rise to canonical schemes for the representation of hierarchical relationships. In the subsequent sections we present two examples of such schemes, the first from computational vision and the second more abstract.

Terminology 3.1. A *specialization scheme* for a set $\mathcal{P}$ of participator ensembles together with a τ-distribution on a framework Θ, consists of a strong stability type and a corresponding permissibility condition (with the terminology of 2.5).

Intuitively the permissibility condition has two notable consequences. First, the dynamics generated by any ensemble in $\mathcal{P}$ has a stationary measure. Second, the dynamics induced on any such ensemble by running the joint chain generated by it and another ensemble in the set has asymptotic stability which is representable by a measure. The perturbation regularity expresses the relationship that holds, in general, between these latter measures and the original stationary measures. We need not make these intuitions more precise at this point; we only wish to here emphasize that they illustrate an assumption that the specialization scheme is, in some such manner, based on properties of asymptotics which can be expressed in terms of measures.

Any choice of specialization schemes leads to an explicit realization of a hierarchical analytic strategy for participator dynamics which models the stipulations of 2.1. This strategy includes a notion of an information connection between levels of the hierarchy in the sense of 2.1 (iii) and (iv). This connection does not exist between any pair of levels, but only between those which are "hierarchically related": information about perturbation regularities of systems at one level propagates canonically to the next. In this way, we think of the class of levels of the hierarchy, i.e., the class of reflexive frameworks, as having a *relation* defined on it: two frameworks are related if they are connected in this sense. We call the relation *specialization*; each specialization scheme gives rise to a specialization relation.

We now give a formal definition of specialization.

Definition 3.2. Let $\Theta' = (X', Y', E', S', \pi'_\bullet)$ and $\Theta = (X, Y, E, S, \pi_\bullet)$ be reflexive observer frameworks. Let τ be a fixed channeling distribution on Θ, and let a specialization scheme (as in 3.1) be given. Then Θ' is a *specialization* of Θ for τ and for the given specialization scheme if, for some environment $(\mathcal{B}, \Phi)$ supported by Θ' (5–2.6), the following hold:

(i)

(a) Let

$$\mathcal{Z} = \{\, (\text{participator}, \tau)\text{-ensembles on } \Theta \,\}$$

and

$$\bar{\mathcal{Z}} = \{\, (\text{preparticipator}, \tau)\text{-ensembles on } \Theta \,\}.$$

Let $p : \mathcal{Z} \to \bar{\mathcal{Z}}$ be induced by $(\xi, \{Q(n)\}_n, \{\eta(n)\}_n) \mapsto (\xi, \{Q(n)\}_n)$. Then there are maps $I : \mathcal{B} \to \mathcal{Z}$ and $\bar{I} : X' \to \bar{\mathcal{Z}}$ such that $p \circ I = \bar{I} \circ \Phi$.

In other words we have a commutative diagram:

$$\begin{array}{ccc} \mathcal{B} & \xrightarrow{I} & \mathcal{Z} \\ \downarrow \Phi & & \downarrow p \\ X' & \xrightarrow{\bar{I}} & \bar{\mathcal{Z}} \end{array}$$

(b) Let D denote the set of those preparticipator (6–2.6) ensembles on Θ having the strong stability property of the given specialization scheme. Then $\bar{I}^{-1}(D) = E'$.

(ii)

Let O_1 and O_2 be observers in Θ' (i.e., in $\mathcal{B}$). A channeling between O_1 and O_2 corresponds to the markovian dynamics in Θ resulting from the join of the two participator ensembles $I(O_1)$ and $I(O_2)$ on Θ.

(iii)

(a) The points of Y' parametrize variations of asymptotic characteristics that are meaningful for the preparticipator systems represented (via $\bar{I}$) by the points of X'.

(b) The distinguished premises S' of Θ' correspond to asymptotic variations which express the perturbation regularity provided by the specialization scheme (c.f. 2.5).

(iv)

(a) Given $e' \in E'$ and $x' \in X'$, then $\pi'_{e'}(x') \in Y'$ represents the perturbation of the preparticipator system $\bar{I}(e')$ on Θ which results from its interaction with the system $\bar{I}(x')$.

(b) If $x' \in E'$ then $\pi'_{e'}(x') \in S'$. (This just summarizes the effect of (i)(b) above, i.e., that points of E' correspond to preparticipator ensembles that have the given strong stability type.)

(i)–(iv) of this definition correspond (in toto) to (i)–(iv) of 2.1. The concept of specialization captures the notion of a hierarchical analytic strategy in the form of a relation on the class of reflexive observer frameworks. The environment $(\mathcal{B}, \Phi)$ supported by the framework Θ' (whose existence is required by the definition in order for Θ' to be a specialization) plays only a syntactical role in the definition: the issues which are most central to the question of the specialization of the frameworks themselves are issues of preparticipator dynamics.

Terminology 3.3. *Specialization and Instantiation.* Let Θ' be a specialization of

Θ, and let O be an observer in Θ'. If O is a distinguished observer with $\Phi(O) = e' \in E'$ we say that O is the *specialization* of the participator system $I(O)$, and that e' is a *specialization* of the preparticipator system $\bar{I}(e')$. Similarly, if A is an arbitrary participator (or preparticipator) system on Θ, we say that A *specializes* if it has the strong stability property of some specialization scheme. We do not say that $x' \in X'$ is a specialization of $\bar{I}(x')$, or that O is a specialization of $I(O)$ unless x' or O are *distinguished*, i.e., unless $x' \in E'$ or $\Phi(O) \in E'$.

The term *instantiation* denotes the opposite of specialization. For example, with notation as above we say that Θ is an *instantiation* of Θ'. However, we use the term "instantiation" to apply to arbitrary (including nondistinguished) configurations and observers, whereas we use the term "specialization" in the distinguished case alone. Thus, for $x' \in X'$, we say that the preparticipator system $\bar{I}(x')$ *instantiates* x'; for the observer O in Θ' we say that the participator system $I(O)$ *instantiates* O. The maps I and $\bar{I}$ are called *instantiation maps*. We also say that interactions of participator or preparticipator systems on Θ *instantiate* channelings on Θ'. Thus, for observers O_1 and O_2 with $\Phi(O_1) = x'_1$ and $\Phi(O_2) = x'_2$, we say that the markovian dynamics generated by joining the preparticipator ensembles $\bar{I}(x'_1)$ and $\bar{I}(x'_2)$ (or participator ensembles $I(O_1)$ and $I(O_2)$) *instantiates* the channeling between O_1 and O_2.

To fix these ideas, let us review how specialized observers make inferences. Let Θ' be a specialization of Θ. Let $e'_1, e'_2 \in E'$, and let $O_{e'_1}$ and $O_{e'_2}$ be observers whose perspectives are $\pi'_{e'_1}$ and $\pi'_{e'_2}$ respectively. Then $O_{e'_1}$ and $O_{e'_2}$ are associated respectively to participator ensembles A_1 and A_2 on Θ. A channeling between $O_{e'_1}$ and $O_{e'_2}$ is instantiated by the participator dynamics generated by joining A_1 and A_2. In the joint dynamics certain properties of the dynamics of the original, separate participator systems are modified, but the systems have sufficient cohesive stability so that these perturbations are not excessively chaotic; the perturbations possess a certain regularity. The distinguished premises S' of the observers in Θ' parametrize structure perturbations with this type of regularity. In particular, the perturbation of the participator dynamics generated in A_1 alone, as a result of A_1 being joined with A_2, corresponds to a point $s' \in S'$. In fact $s' = \pi'_{e'_1}(e'_2)$; it is $O_{e'_1}$'s premise from the channeling between $O_{e'_1}$ and $O_{e'_2}$. Now $O_{e'_1}$ makes an inference from this premise expressed as a conclusion measure, which is a probability measure on ${\pi'_{e'_1}}^{-1}(s') \cap E'$; if η' is $O_{e'_1}$'s interpretation kernel, the measure in question is $\eta'(s', \cdot)$. In terms of the specialization, for each subset C' of E', $\eta'(s', C')$ is the probability that the perturbation represented by s' resulted from joining A_1 with another participator system which instantiates an element of C'.

So far we have not taken notice of the role of the interpretation kernels in an instantiation. In fact, (i)(a) of 3.2 asserts that the role played by the interpretation kernels of the participators in the ensemble $I(O)$ is relevant to O itself only insofar as O's own interpretation kernel is concerned. Indeed, the environment $(\mathcal{B}, \Phi)$ is not uniquely determined by the definition; essentially distinct choices for $(\mathcal{B}, \Phi)$ correspond to essentially different ways for the interpretation kernel of the observers O in Θ' to relate to the interpretation kernels of the participators in $I(O)$.

The fibre $\pi'^{-1}_{e'_1}(s') \cap E'$ contains e'_2, the perspective of the observer which actually channeled with $O_{e'_1}$. But in general there will be many other points in the fibre, and the probability measure will not be concentrated at e'_2; a priori we can say only that the interpretation kernel η' of the specialized observer $O_{e'_1}$ is supported on E'. In fact E' expresses the bias of the specialized observer toward systems with the particular strong stability property specified in the specialization scheme. This means the following. Suppose the instantiation A_1 of $O_{e'_1}$ interacts with *any* participator system, say B, on Θ, in the sense of running the markovian participator dynamics generated by the join of the participator ensembles underlying A_1 and B. Suppose that the resulting perturbation of A_1 exhibits the regularity characteristic of the given specialization scheme, corresponding to a point $s' \in S'$. Then $O_{e'_1}$ will interpret the perturbation as having arisen due to an interaction of A_1 with a preparticipator system on Θ which is the instantiation of some point of E', i.e., a system which has the strong stability property. Thus, in order for $O_{e'_1}$'s inferences to be inductively strong the notion of perturbation regularity which distinguishes the premises S' must be substantially specific to the notion of strong stability which distinguishes the configurations E'. In other words, when a participator system satisfying the permissibility condition undergoes a perturbation with the given regularity, then the chances must be very good that this perturbation was caused by interaction with another permissible participator system.

In the same way we can discuss the instantiation of false objects. As usual, for $e' \in E'$ let $O_{e'}$ denote a distinguished observer in Θ', and let A be the stable participator system in Θ which instantiates $O_{e'}$. Suppose A interacts with an unstable participator system C for which $\bar{I}^{-1}(p(C))$ is in $X' - E'$. Suppose that the resulting perturbation of A exhibits the same regularity property as do perturbations of A resulting from its interaction with stable systems. Then C is an instantiation of a false object for $O_{e'}$. Note that in (iv) of (3.2) no stipulation is made about the premises of *nondistinguished* observers in Θ' which result from channelings with any other observer, distinguished or nondistinguished. This is so even though for nondistinguished as well as distinguished observers channelings are instantiated in the same way, namely by the interaction of the participator systems in Θ which correspond to the observers' configurations in X'. The difference is that for a nondistinguished observer in a reflexive framework there is no a priori relation between its configuration and its perspective map; thus, even though a channeling for a nondistinguished observer arises from an interaction of the instantiating participator system associated to the observer's configuration, and even though the premise resulting from the channeling is a point of Y' corresponding to a structure perturbation which is in principle meaningful for the participator system, yet in the absence of any information about the perspective map there is no basis from which to impute meaning to the premise of the nondistinguished observer *in terms of the interaction*.

Given that the permissibility condition and the perturbation regularity of a specialization scheme depend on stationary or asymptotic measures, it follows that the role of true perception in specialization is twofold. First, the existence of true perception is a step in the direction of stability in the sense that true perception requires stationary measures. Of course, the strong stability needed for specialization requires more than the simple existence of stationary or asymptotic measures for each instantiating system. For instance, these systems need to stabilize in the presence of other such systems in some way yet to be defined. Second, true perception—be it on the part of all or merely some of the participators in the instantiating system—is necessary for the conclusions of the specialized observer to be inductively strong. In fact, the distinguished specialized observer O infers the identity of the system which interacts with its instantiation $I(O)$; the premise for this inference is the perturbation of $I(O)$'s structure which results from the interaction.

Recall that 3.2 (i) states that in a given environment $(\mathcal{B}, \Phi)$ the interpretation kernels of the participators in the ensemble $I(O)$ functionally constrain the interpretation kernel of O itself. However, the definition does not stipulate any details about this constraint: the manner in which the specialized observers' interpretation kernels are related to those of the participators in the instantiations is a "free variable" in the specialization relation between frameworks. The various choices correspond to the various environments $(\mathcal{B}, \Phi)$ which fit in the definition 3.2. In particular there are many possibilities for formulating interpretation strategies for the specialized observers, whose principle is to exploit in some manner true perception down at the level of the instantiation. And it is such strategies which intuitively lie at the heart of the specialization idea.

There is not a unique way to specialize, nor to instantiate, a given framework. Beginning with the framework Θ we can consider various specialization schemes which make sense for Θ. But even if we fix the specialization scheme there is not a unique framework which is a specialization of Θ. For example one can restrict attention to various subclasses of all those participator systems which specialize in the sense of the given scheme, and then consider a framework Θ' whose distinguished configuration set E' parametrizes the participator ensembles in one such subclass. The parametrization itself can be made in various ways. Once this is done, however, the perspective maps $\pi'_{e'}$ in Θ' are essentially determined by the specialization scheme. In fact, $\pi'_{e'_1}(e')$ is the point of S' which represents the dynamical perturbation of the participator system on Θ which instantiates e'_1, resulting from the join of that system with the system which instantiates e'.

As we have remarked above, the concept of specialization of frameworks defines a relation on the set of all reflexive frameworks which we think of as a hierarchy relation $\dashv$. We do not prove here that specialization is transitive, but a few considerations make this plausible. Denoting specialization by $\dashv$, if $A \dashv B$ then the premises of A are perturbations of stationary measures for the dynamics of ensembles on B. If $B \dashv C$ then premises of B are perturbations of stationary measures for ensembles on C. For transitivity $A \dashv C$ must also be true; the premises of A must be perturbations of stationary measures for ensembles on C as well as on B. But, since $B \dashv C$, configurations (elements of X) of B correspond to ensembles on C. And at each instant each participator in an ensemble on B must manifest as a configuration of B, i.e., (via the map $\bar{I}$) as an ensemble on C. Thus, ensembles on B can be thought of as ensembles of ensembles on C. It is then at least plausible that the premises of A could correspond to perturbations of the stationary measures of ensembles on C.

We notice that for one framework to be a specialization of another does not imply that the intrinsic mathematical properties of the frameworks are different. For example, it is possible that two frameworks are abstractly isomorphic, yet one is a specialization of the other. Thus specialization provides a universal way to interpret frameworks in terms of others via the relation in the lattice, but does not constrain the intrinsic, purely mathematical, structure of the individual frameworks.

We have not discussed the way in which information propagates downward in the lattice, only upward. The downward propagation has to do with the effect that the presence of specialized systems have at the lower level. Intuitively, they propagate coherence. However, their effect (if one looks at dynamics down in Θ which are really joint dynamics with the specialized system, but are represented as though the specialized system is not there) may be described as a modification of the τ-distribution or of the action kernels in Θ. These two formulations of their effect may be equivalent, and the expression of that equivalence may be a "natural law," like Newton's law relating force and acceleration or more probably like the Einsteinian version relating metric geometry and force-acceleration. For remember that the τ-distribution is somehow intimately related to metric-like notions on

E, while changes in the action kernels of participators is intimately related to "acceleration" in the same spirit in which the action kernels themselves correspond to "velocity."

4. On Ullman's incremental rigidity procedure

4.1. Preliminary remarks and overview. We present an example of specialization inspired by Ullman's "incremental rigidity scheme," a procedure whereby a viewer can generate and update an internal three-dimensional model of an external object as the object moves in space relative to the viewer. One assumes that the object consists of, say, $n+1$ feature points and that the "correspondence problem" has been solved, i.e., that the viewer can track each point over time. We further assume that the viewer deploys a moving coordinate system in which the same one of these points is always at the origin. Then the vectors from this origin to the other n points describe at each instant of time. Finally we assume that the viewer has access only to two-dimensional orthographic projections (onto some fixed image plane) of these n vectors. The viewer updates its internal three-dimensional model based on

(i) its current model,

(ii) the latest two-dimensional projection of the object.

The viewer chooses that new model, from among all those compatible with the new information (ii), whose three-dimensional structure differs minimally from that of the current model. If the resulting sequence of models converges to a stable rigid structure then the viewer infers that the object has that same rigid structure. If, in the limit, the sequence of models exhibits some periodicity, then the viewer infers that the object has the type of quasi-rigidity expressed by the periodicity.

Ullman called this the "incremental recovery of 3-D structure from rigid and rubbery motion." The phrase "recovery of 3-D structure" here refers to the conclusion of an inference about the stable three-dimensional structure of the object, not about its instantaneous three-dimensional structure. One way an object might exhibit a stable or long-term 3-D structure is to forever move rigidly. Another way is to expand and contract periodically.

Just as the conclusion of the inference in Ullman's scheme refers to stability of structure, so also the premise of the inference depends upon a form of stability. An essential feature of Ullman's scheme is that the premise of the inference is derived from the long-term, i.e., asymptotic, behavior of a certain dynamical interaction. For

Ullman this is an interaction between viewer and physical object. For us all interactions are between observers; physical objects represent the conclusions observers reach in consequence of their interactions.

We now study an observer-theoretic treatment of this inference. We consider a symmetric observer framework Θ in which the observers' inferences regard *instantaneous* 3-D structure. On this framework we have a participator dynamics whose asymptotic stabilities give rise to premises for a "higher level" observer which infers a *long-term* structural regularity. This is a specialized observer, i.e., an observer in a framework Θ' which is a specialization of Θ in the sense of section three. Thus the observers in Θ' infer long-term stabilities; the observers in Θ infer instantaneous rigidity. Now, neglecting translation, instantaneous rigid motion is the same as instantaneous rotation, so we will take Θ to be the symmetric framework of instantaneous rotation observers studied in 5–6. Recall that a distinguished premise in this framework consists of two frames of n vectors, together with a reference axis, which are compatible with an interpretation that the frames are related by a rotation of $\mathbf{R}^3$ about that axis. In practice this means that, in our incremental rigidity procedure, two such consecutive frames of n vectors are required to trigger a step. This is in contradistinction to Ullman's original procedure, where any single frame of n vectors triggers a step.

We begin with the symmetric framework $\Theta = (X, Y, E, S, G, J, \pi)$ of instantaneous rotation observers. We will describe a specialization scheme and a framework $\Theta' = (X', Y', E', S', \pi'_{\bullet})$ which is a specialization of Θ for this scheme. This specialization is simple. Points of E' correspond (via $\bar{I}$ of 3.2, (i)) to preparticipator ensembles on Θ consisting of *one* preparticipator. Similarly, the distinguished observers in Θ' correspond (via I of 3.2, (i)) to participator ensembles consisting of one participator. For example, let O' be a distinguished observer in Θ' whose configuration $\Phi(O') \in E'$ corresponds to the ensemble consisting of the sole preparticipator A in Θ; we say "A instantiates O'." O' uses the incremental procedure to make inferences as follows. Suppose that A is involved in a participator dynamics on Θ with another participator B (or more generally some set of participators). The asymptotic behavior of this dynamical interaction instantiates a single channeling at the level of Θ' for O'. From this channeling O' infers, if possible, B's rigid or quasi-rigid structure. Here is how we think of this as an incremental rigidity scheme:

(i) At any time t (in the reference time for the dynamics in Θ) the state $e(t) \in E$ of A is the "current model" of the instantaneous structure of B.

(ii) A's action kernel is defined such that A executes the updating procedure associated with the scheme.

If this dynamics induces the right kind of asymptotic regularity on the trajectories of A, then O' infers that B has the appropriate stability. The existence of such an asymptotic regularity on A's trajectories corresponds to what Ullman calls the "convergence" of the incremental procedure. In our terminology it means that O''s premise resulting from the channeling is distinguished. In (i) above we used the quotes on "current model" to stress that it has no a priori perceptual status, even instantaneously, at the level of the specialized observer O'. Indeed, an instant of time for O' is that time in which a channeling occurs for O'; and this must correspond to sufficient time at the level of Θ for the entire participator dynamics involving A to reveal asymptotic stability. Thus an instant of reference time on Θ is not meaningful for O'. With this in mind we can present the situation in more detail.

4.2. We use the notation and terminology of 5–6 for the framework Θ of instantaneous rotation observers. Let us fix the point $c_0 \in E$, and henceforth denote the fundamental map π^{c_0} (5-6.20) simply by π. For example, for convenience of visualization we can take c_0 to be a configuration whose reference axis $\mathcal{A}$ is the positive z-axis, and whose $\mathbf{v}$ is the unit vector in the positive x direction.

We now discuss A's action kernel $\{Q_e\}_{e \in E}$. Recall that this is a family of markovian kernels on E, one for each $e \in E$ (7–1.1). The kernel Q_e describes how A moves in response to a channeling when A is at e. In our case the action kernel will be symmetric, i.e., $\{Q_e\}_{e \in E}$ is generated by a single markovian kernel $Q: J \times \mathcal{J} \to [0,1]$. Given Q, we define Q_e by $Q_e(e_1, \Delta) = Q(e_1 e^{-1}, \Delta e^{-1})$. This is the probability that A will move from e into the set $\Delta \subset E$ given that it received a channeling from e_1. The fact that the action kernel is symmetric means that this probability depends only on the position of e_1 relative to e, and of Δ relative to e (in the sense of the group action of J on E). Finally, we recall that $Q(\jmath, \cdot) = Q(\jmath', \cdot)$ if $\pi(\jmath) = \pi(\jmath')$.

Suppose that, at a particular time t, A is at e and A channels with another participator at e_1. This channeling results for A in the observation event $s = \pi(e_1 e^{-1}) \in S$. The updating procedure of (ii) above means, firstly, that A then moves so that its new state is a possible state of the participator which just channeled to him, i.e., A's new state will lie in $\pi^{-1}(s)$. Secondly, it means that the new state selected in $\pi^{-1}(s)$ will minimize the distortion of the underlying rigid structure entailed in the state change.

A's motion, then, is based on minimizing a certain nonnegative function ϕ on $\pi^{-1}(s)$, a function which measures the structural modification associated to the move. Now everything is already relativized with respect to A's perspective e; if $\jmath \in \pi^{-1}(s)$, the selection of $\jmath$ means that A will move from e to $\jmath e$. Thus the function in question is naturally a function on J, because the elements of J are intrinsically the "moves" whose structural effect we wish to measure.[2] We would expect, then, that the definition of the function ϕ itself is independent of both e and s; then, whenever a premise s is presented, the procedure is to minimize ϕ on the subset $\pi^{-1}(s) \subset J$. $\pi^{-1}(s)$ is a one-dimensional manifold with four connected components; this follows from the fact that the same is true for $p^{-1}(s)$ and that $\pi = f_{c_0} \circ p$ (5–6.20) where f_{c_0} is an isomorphism.

The function ϕ is by no means uniquely specified, for one may conceive of many different ways of testing "rigidity." However, the representation 5–6.17 of J leads naturally to a description of a class of reasonable ϕ's. In fact, in terms of this representation, and of the expression for $\jmath e$ in 5–6.19, it is easy to see that it is precisely the nonzero γ_i's, ζ_i's and λ_i's which contribute nonrigidity to the transformation $e \mapsto \jmath e$. δ simply augments the magnitude of the angular velocity of the instantaneous rotation embodied in e; β rotates the entire structure e. More specifically, the α's and ζ's perturb the structure additively while the λ's perturb it multiplicatively. Hence, we should require that

4.3. ϕ is a monotone function of $|\gamma_i|$, $|\zeta_i|$, and $|\lambda_{i-1}|$, where $|\gamma_i|$ denotes the distance (along the circumference) from γ_i to the identity element of the circle group $\mathbf{S}^1$.

Now given ϕ we can use it to define the action kernel Q of A. Intuitively, we want to minimize ϕ on $\pi^{-1}(s)$, and then let $Q(\jmath, \cdot)$ be Dirac measure concentrated at the minimum (when $\pi(\jmath) = s$). This is a deterministic action kernel; A's next state is uniquely determined by its current state and the observation event s which results from the channeling. But in general ϕ has a no unique minimum on each $\pi^{-1}(s)$. Therefore we consider nondeterministic action kernels for A. And we need not minimize ϕ. Instead we proceed as follows: Let μ denote some natural "unbiased" measure (such as Haar measure) on J and let

$$\mathcal{F} = \{\phi \text{ satisfying (4.3)} | \int_E \frac{1}{\phi} d\mu = 1\}. \tag{4.4}$$

[2] The identification of J with E simply gives a way to "visualize" the elements of J. In this sense the choice of c_0 in the definition of π means that A "thinks of itself" as c_0, and refers to an element of $j \in J$ in terms of what A would then become if it were modified by j (see 5–6.22 ff).

We identify functions in $\mathcal{F}$ that differ on a set of μ measure zero, i.e., we think of $1/\phi$ as an element of $L_1(J, \mu)$. We can then identify $\phi \in \mathcal{F}$ with the probability measure $\mu_\phi = (1/\phi)\, d\mu$ on J. Now there is a canonical way to generate the kernels Q given ϕ's:

4.5. To $\phi \in \mathcal{F}$ we associate the kernel defined by $Q(j, \cdot) = m_\pi^{\mu_\phi}(\pi(j), \cdot)$.

That is, Q is the rcpd of μ_ϕ with respect to π. (If we wish, we can replace $\mathcal{F}$ by a suitable completion. Then among the new limit measures we recover the Dirac measures of the deterministic case mentioned above.)

In this way any $\phi \in \mathcal{F}$ is associated with *an* incremental rigidity procedure, the one executed by the participator A whose action kernel is defined as in 4.5. Intuitively, if A interacts with a participator B then A converges asymptotically to the trajectory of B. The question of whether or not there is convergence in any particular case depends a priori on the choice of ϕ, on the initial distribution of A, and on the motion and shape of B. We do not consider this question in detail. The point of view we want to emphasize here is that of the "rigid object" as a *conclusion* of a specialized observer, not as an *object of perception* for that observer.

4.6. If $\{T_e\}_{e \in E}$ is B's action kernel then, for any e and e_1, the measures $T_e(e_1, \cdot)$ are supported on the orbit through the point e of the subgroup R of J given by $\alpha_j = 0, \zeta_j = 0, \lambda_j = 1$ (for all j). This subgroup of J, parametrized by β and δ, is isomorphic to $SO(3, \mathbf{R}) \times S^1$. Thus B will stay in a fixed R-orbit in any interaction.

There is another natural way to think about the ϕ's in terms of this subgroup R: each choice of ϕ as in 4.3 gives a "distance function" to R on J. To see what this means in terms of participator dynamics on E, consider a participator A on Θ whose action kernel Q is of the form of 4.5 for such a distance function ϕ. Suppose that at time t (reference time on Θ) A is at $e \in E$ and channels with an observer at $e_1 \in E$. Suppose $e_1 = j_1 e$, $j_1 \in J$. A then moves to je, where j is in the fibre $\pi^{-1}(\pi(j_1))$, with a probability that depends on the distance of j to R; the smaller the distance, the greater the probability. Thus, the effect of the action kernel Q is to make A tend to move on R-orbits in E.

We now give a sample definition for the specialized framework Θ', and for the specialization scheme that leads to it. We start with the specialization scheme; we use the terminology of 3.1. Let R be the subgroup of J defined in 4.6. The strong stability condition on participator ensembles is the following *asymptotic R-orbit property*: the dynamics admits a stationary measure which is supported, say, on a finite union of R orbits in E^k, where k is the number of participators in the ensemble. Recall that the strong stability condition must hold not only for the dynamics of each permissible participator ensemble individually, but must also hold for the dynamics induced on it by the joint system it generates with any other permissible ensemble. In our case this is part of the definition of the condition. Thus the strong stability condition is really a condition on *sets* of ensembles, not just on individual ensembles: any condition which defines a set of participator ensembles with these properties can serve as a "permissibility condition." The perturbation regularity is that the R orbit property of the asymptotics is preserved under perturbation, i.e., under interaction with another permissible ensemble.

We now describe one possible specialized framework Θ' for this specialization scheme, one which is especially (and artificially) simple. We assume that we have a fixed τ-distribution on Θ. We can let X' be a set of (preparticipator, τ)-ensembles each consisting of only one preparticipator (and the τ is the fixed one); the map $\bar{I}$ of 3.2 is then just the inclusion map. The elements of E' involve preparticipators whose action kernel is like the one given in 4.5 for a particular choice of ϕ. We assume that the functions ϕ and the initial measures of these preparticipators have been chosen so that the set E' has the following property:

4.7. The dynamics generated by a preparticipator in E' with any other preparticipator in X' has a stationary measure in E^2; the dynamics generated by two preparticipators in E' has a stationary measure supported on a finite union of R-orbits in E^2.

By saying that the dynamics "has" a stationary measure we mean that the initial measure converges to the stationary measure under the action of the dynamics. Also, when we say a "preparticipator in E'" we mean the ensemble in E' consisting of that one preparticipator. It may require work to show that there exist ϕ's and initial measures such that the resulting E' has this property. However, since our objective here is just to illustrate the basic ideas of specialization, we simply assume they exist.

Let $pr_1 \colon E^2 \to E$ be projection on the first factor. Let Y'' denote the set of measures on E^2 which are stationary measures of the joint dynamics generated by some $e' \in E'$ and some $x' \in X'$; we here use the property of E' in italics in the preceding paragraph. Now let Y' denote the set of all measures on E which are of the form $pr_{1*}(\rho)$ for some $\rho \in Y''$. Let S' denote those measures in Y' which arise as above in the case where both e' and x' are in E'. Note that if a measure ρ on E^2 is supported on a finite union of R-orbits in E^2, then $pr_{1*}(\rho)$ is supported on a finite union of R-orbits in E. It follows that each measure in S' is supported on a finite union of R-orbits in E. We can now define $\pi'_{e'}(x')$: it is the element of Y' which represents $pr_{1*}(\rho)$, where ρ is the stationary measure on E^2 of the joint dynamics generated by e' and x'. We have thus defined the reflexive framework $\Theta' = (X', Y', E', S', \pi'_{\bullet})$; note that we have not shown this framework to be *symmetric*. Conditions (ii), (iii), (iv) of Definition 3.2 are satisfied for Θ' with respect to our given specialization scheme. And the map $\bar{I}$ of (i) of 3.2 is defined as the inclusion. We have not yet discussed the map I of 3.2(i) (and the significance of the commutative diagram there) for our present situation; we consider this briefly below.

We discuss the relevance of Θ' to the original problem of rigid object perception. The elements of E' do not represent rigid objects, because the action kernels of the preparticipators of E' are of the type of the Q of 4.5 for some ϕ, and not of the type of the T of 4.6. In other words, unlike a "rigid object," a preparticipator with an action kernel Q does not remain in a fixed R-orbit regardless of its channeling interactions. It is still possible that some elements of X' represent rigid objects since for such elements not in E' we have made no stipulation about the action kernel of the preparticipator. We regard a "rigid object" as being a *conclusion* of a specialized observer. In fact, it is the conclusion of a distinguished observer in Θ' resulting from a premise $s' \in S'$ which is a measure (a $pr_{1*}(\rho)$ as above) supported on a *single* R-orbit. In general, a point of S' is a measure supported on a finite union of such orbits; the conclusion resulting from such a premise is a "quasi-rigid" object which is a superposition of "rigid conclusions." These latter correspond to the components of the measure on the distinct orbits of the union. If O' is a distinguished observer in Θ' whose configuration is e' then the conclusion of O' in response to the premise s' is a probability measure on $\pi'^{-1}_{e'}(s')$; in fact it is the measure $\eta'(s', \cdot)$, where η' is the interpretation kernel of O'. The rigid (or quasi-rigid) object is O''s representation of this measure.

The definition of specialization (3.2) requires that we adduce a particular environment $(\mathcal{B}, \Phi)$ supported by Θ'. Then when we speak of an "observer in Θ'" having a property which shows some aspect of the specialization we mean an observer in this $\mathcal{B}$. To define an environment on Θ', or at least to define the distinguished part of it, we describe the interpretation kernels which are associated with various points of E'. The commutative diagram of (i) of 3.2 means that, for the environment $(\mathcal{B}, \Phi)$, there is some relationship between the interpretation kernels of the observers O' in $\mathcal{B}$ and the interpretation kernels of the participators in the ensemble $I(O')$. For example, consider the observer O' whose configuration $\Phi(O')$ is $e' \in E'$. e' is an ensemble consisting of a preparticipator (ξ, Q) on Θ. The commutative diagram then requires that O' itself is associated (via I) to an ensemble consisting of the one participator $A = (\xi, Q, \eta)$, for some η. Let η' denote the interpretation kernel of O'. A complete demonstration that Θ' is a specialization of Θ requires that we state a relationship between η' and η which holds for all the observers in a set $\mathcal{B}$. We will not analyze this further here; we will only reiterate the basic idea that *true perception* plays a major part in this relationship. Namely, the assumption that η truly reflects the asymptotic behavior of participator A alone is the basis of a strategy expressed by η', a strategy for the specialized perceiver O' to make inferences based on perturbations of those asymptotics.

5. Chain-bundle specialization

We now sketch one approach to specialization, called "chain bundle specialization," which can be applied to symmetric observer frameworks under certain conditions. Starting with a symmetric framework $\Theta = (X, Y, E, S, G, J, \pi)$, we use a specialization scheme (3.1) which exploits the group action of J on E to define the permissibility condition on participator ensembles *and* of the perturbation regularity. The scheme is valid under conditions which we make explicit below. The mathematical content of certain of these conditions (which pertain to the perturbation regularity) is not yet clarified; for this reason the approach is speculative. However, we believe that the scheme is valid for natural and nontrivial classes of examples; we discuss this after presenting more details.

5.1. We introduce notation for certain elementary constructions associated with measurable group actions. Let Γ be a measurable group and Z a measurable space; let a measurable left action $z \to \gamma z$ of Γ on Z be given. Then there is an induced left action of Γ on the set $\mathcal{Z}$ of measurable functions on Z, namely

$$f \to \gamma f, \quad (\gamma f)(z) = f(\gamma^{-1} z).$$

This action is linear, i.e., $\gamma(f_1 + f_2) = \gamma f_1 + \gamma f_2$. We also use the notation ${}^{\gamma}f$ in place of γf. Thus we will also write the action as

$$f \to {}^{\gamma}f.$$

In this manner we think of $\gamma \in \Gamma$ as a linear operator on $\mathcal{Z}$ or on the space $\mathcal{Z}_b$ of bounded measurable functions. Now let K be a kernel on Z. K may be viewed as a linear operator on $\mathcal{Z}$ via

$$Kf(z) = \int K(z, du) f(u).$$

We can then define a left action of Γ on kernels by

$$K \to {}^{\gamma}K = \gamma K \gamma^{-1};$$

the notation on the right means $\gamma \circ K \circ \gamma^{-1}$ in the sense of composition of linear operators on $\mathcal{Z}$. The notation ${}^{\gamma}K$ thus makes sense for *any* operator on $\mathcal{Z}$ (not only those associated to kernels). If K preserves bounded functions then so does ${}^{\gamma}K$. In terms of arguments, we have explicitly

$${}^{\gamma}K(z, A) = K(\gamma^{-1}z, \gamma^{-1}A).$$

where A is a measurable set in Z; this is easily checked.

Any measure μ on Z can be viewed as a linear functional on $\mathcal{Z}$. In this sense, for $\gamma \in \Gamma$ we can define ${}^{\gamma}\mu$ to be the composition $\mu \circ \gamma^{-1}$. This gives a left action of Γ on the space $\mathcal{M}$ of measures on Z:

$$\mu \to {}^{\gamma}\mu.$$

$${}^{\gamma}\mu(A) = \mu(\gamma^{-1}A).$$

Proposition 5.2. With the notation as above,

1. For any operator K and function f,

$${}^{\gamma}(Kf) = {}^{\gamma}K \, {}^{\gamma}f$$

2. If K is a kernel and μ is a stationary measure for K:

$$\mu K = \mu \Rightarrow {}^{\gamma}\mu \, {}^{\gamma}K = {}^{\gamma}\mu.$$

Proof. Straightforward.

Definition 5.3. Let Γ be a measurable group, and suppose Z and W are spaces on which Γ acts measurably. Let $p\colon Z \to W$ be a measurable map. p is called a Γ*-homomorphism* if $\gamma p(z) = p(\gamma z)$ for all $\gamma \in \Gamma$ and $z \in Z$. In this case the data

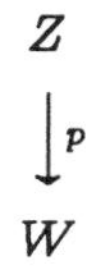

is called a Γ*-bundle* if p is surjective. If the action of Γ on Z (and hence on W) is transitive, it is called a *transitive* Γ*-bundle.* Z is called the "total space" of the bundle, p is called the "projection map," and W is called the "base space."

We will build bundles from participator systems on a given symmetric framework Θ. Under certain conditions we will be able to view the total space, base space, and projection map of the bundle as the distinguished configuration space, the distinguished premise space, and the perspective map of a new symmetric framework Θ' which is a specialization of Θ.

5.4. We begin with a symmetric observer framework $\Theta = (X, Y, E, S, G, J, \pi)$ with fixed τ-distribution τ. Let $k > 0$ be an integer, and consider k symmetric action kernels $Q_1, ..., Q_k$ on Θ. We can then construct the markovian kernels $\widehat{P_0} = \widehat{\langle Q_1, \ldots, Q_k \rangle_\tau}$ on $E^k \times \mathcal{I}(k)$, and $P_0 = \langle Q_1, \ldots, Q_k \rangle_\tau$ on E^k. $\widehat{P_0}$ and P_0 are, respectively, the transition probabilities for the augmented and standard dynamical Markov chains respectively, of an ensemble of k kinematical (i.e., time homogeneous) participators whose action kernels are $Q_1, ..., Q_k$. Now the properties of participator ensembles which are relevant to a specialization scheme may be best expressed in terms of the augmented dynamics of the ensemble, rather than the standard dynamics. Nevertheless for simplicity of exposition we restrict our attention to the standard dynamics.

The group J of the framework Θ acts measurably on E^k on the left via its given measurable action on E:

$$j(e_1, \ldots, e_k) = (je_1, \ldots, je_k).$$

More generally, let J' be a group which is a *measurable extension of a subgroup* of J. This means that we are given a group homomorphism $\alpha: J' \to L$ where $L \subset J$ is a subgroup; further, J', L, and α are measurable. In this case the action of J on E^k induces a measurable left action of J' on E^k by letting $\gamma e = \alpha(\gamma) e$ for $\gamma \in J', e \in E^k$.

Assume we are given such a J', which we view as acting on E^k in this manner. Suppose ν_0 is a stationary measure for the kernel P_0 on E^k. Then we can define ${}^\gamma P_0$ and ${}^\gamma \nu_0$ as in 5.1, and the conclusions of Proposition 5.2 hold, namely

5.5. For all $\gamma \in J'$, and measurable functions f on E^k,

$${}^\gamma(P_0 f) = {}^\gamma P_0 \, {}^\gamma f,$$

and ${}^\gamma \nu_0$ is a stationary measure for ${}^\gamma P_0$:

$${}^\gamma P_0 \, {}^\gamma \nu_0 = {}^\gamma \nu_0 .$$

Now we can describe our chain bundle. Let

$$E_1' = \{({}^\gamma P_0, {}^\gamma \nu_0) \mid \gamma \in J'\},$$

$$S' = \{{}^\gamma \nu_0 \mid \gamma \in J'\},$$

$$\pi_1' : E_1' \to S', \quad \pi_1'(P, \nu) = \nu. \tag{5.6}$$

The left action of J' on kernels and on measures gives a left action of J' on E_1', namely

$$\gamma_1({}^\gamma P_0, {}^\gamma \nu_0) = ({}^{\gamma_1}({}^\gamma P_0), {}^{\gamma_1}({}^\gamma \nu_0)) = ({}^{\gamma_1 \gamma} P_0, {}^{\gamma_1 \gamma} \nu_0).$$

It is then clear that

$$\begin{array}{c} E_1' \\ \downarrow \pi_1' \\ S' \end{array}$$

is a *transitive* J'*–bundle.*

The terminology "chain bundle" indicates that points in the total space E_1' are γ-homogeneous Markov chains on E^k. The chain is specified by its transition probability, namely ${}^{\gamma}P_0$ for some $\gamma \in J'$, and its starting measure ${}^{\gamma}\nu_0$. This starting measure is also a stationary measure for the chain by 5.5 since, by hypothesis, ν_0 is stationary for P_0. For $\nu \in S'$, ${\pi_1'}^{-1}(\nu)$ is the subset of E_1' consisting of all those chains whose specified starting (and stationary) measure is ν.

Consider a preobserver $O' = (X', Y', E_1', S', \pi_1')$, where X' is a set of Markov chains on E^k containing E_1', and Y' is a set of measures on E^k containing S'. The inferences of O' are at a "higher level" than the inferences of observers in Θ: each premise of O' represents a possible stability of a whole dynamical system in Θ, and a corresponding conclusion represents a Markov chain in E^k with that stability. This description of the meaning of O''s observations obtains because the group action on E_1' preserves stationarity of the measures, as in 5.5. However, the inferences of O' are not even *ascendants* of those of Θ. The reason for this is that while the initial Markov chain (P_0, ν_0) is a participator chain in the sense that $P_0 = \langle Q_1, \dots, Q_k \rangle_\tau$ for some action kernels $Q_1, \dots, Q_k$, the same is not necessarily true for $({}^{\gamma}P_0, {}^{\gamma}\nu_0)$ for arbitrary $\gamma \in J'$. This means that the premise ${}^{\gamma}\nu_0 \in S'$, while it is a stationary measure for *some* markovian dynamics in E^k, is in no meaningful way derived from conclusions of observers in Θ.

On the other hand, suppose

Assumption 5.7. For every $\gamma \in J'$ we can find action kernels ${}^{(\gamma)}R_1, \dots, {}^{(\gamma)}R_k$ on Θ such that

$$ {}^{\gamma}P_0 = \langle {}^{(\gamma)}R_1, \dots, {}^{(\gamma)}R_k \rangle_\tau. $$

(We may suppose that when γ is the identity element of J' the ${}^{(\gamma)}R_i$'s are the original Q_i's). Then for each γ we can imagine an ensemble ${}^{(\gamma)}A$ of kinematical participators,

$$ {}^{(\gamma)}A = \{ {}^{(\gamma)}A_i \}_{i=1}^{k}, \quad {}^{(\gamma)}A_i = (\xi_i, {}^{(\gamma)}R_i, \eta_i) \tag{5.8} $$

where the starting measure $\xi_1 \otimes \ldots \otimes \xi_k$, together with the transition probability ${}^{\gamma}P_0$, give rise to a chain on E^k with stationary measure ${}^{\gamma}\nu_0$. Let us also suppose that these participators have stably true perception (8–5.8), so that the interpretation kernels η_i are related to the stationary measure ${}^{\gamma}\nu_0$, via an rcpd construction similar to the one used with the "$\mathcal{D}$ operation" of 8–5.4 ff. We may even imagine that the situation at hand is sufficiently constrained so that the collection of η_i's is informationally equivalent to the stationary measure ${}^{\gamma}\nu_0$. Under these conditions we can say that the premises in S'—the various measures ${}^{\gamma}\nu_0$—are deduced from the conclusions of observers in Θ, namely the observer manifestations of all the participators ${}^{(\gamma)}A_i$ for $\gamma \in J'$. It follows that, in this context, elements of S' represent premises of inferences which are *ascendants* of the inferences in Θ.

Thus, assuming 5.7 and 5.8, let

$$E' = \{ {}^{(\gamma)}A \mid \gamma \in J' \}.$$

$$\pi_0' : E' \to S', \; \pi_0'({}^{(\gamma)}A) = {}^{\gamma}\nu_0. \tag{5.9}$$

J' acts on E' simply by acting from the left on the symbol ${}^{(\gamma)}$ in ${}^{(\gamma)}A$. In this way we can consider E' and E_1' to be isomorphic as measurable J'–spaces, and then the J'–bundles $\pi_0' : E' \to S'$ and $\pi_1' : E_1' \to S'$ are isomorphic. But in contrast to the inferences from S' to E_1', the inferences from S' to E' are now ascendants of inferences in Θ. And what is more, they have a chance to be inferences of observers in a *specialization* of Θ; for the configuration space of such a specialization consists by definition of participator ensembles in Θ. In other words, assuming 5.7 holds, we may be able to construct a specialization Θ' of Θ in which E' and S' are the distinguished configuration and premise spaces; we indicate, however, that 5.7 alone is not sufficient for the existence of Θ'. We will discuss this question below, but first we present an important class of examples where 5.7 holds.

The action of J' on E' described above is not intrinsic; it has been transported artificially to E'. We have indicated this by writing the superscript γ in parentheses in ${}^{(\gamma)}A$ and ${}^{(\gamma)}R_i$. The point is that these superscripts do not here refer to any well-defined mathematical operation, as they do in the case of the ${}^{\gamma}P_0$. In effect, in 5.7 we assume only that for each $\gamma \in J'$ an ${}^{(\gamma)}A$ exists; we have not assumed that the ${}^{(\gamma)}A$ are generated by some intrinsically defined group action on participator ensembles, starting from some such ensemble in which the action kernels are the original $Q_1, \ldots, Q_k$. However in the class of examples we now present there is such an intrinsic action which generates the ${}^{(\gamma)}A$.

Recall (5.4 ff) that we are starting with a group J' which is an extension of a subgroup L of J; J is the distinguished structure group of our original framework $\Theta = (X, Y, E, S, G, J, \pi)$.

Proposition 5.10. Suppose that (1) τ is a translation-invariant τ-distribution on Θ, and that (2)

$$\begin{array}{c} J \\ \downarrow \pi|_J \\ S \end{array}$$

is a bundle for the action of L on J by conjugation. Then there is a left action of J' on the set of symmetric action kernels on Θ; in terms of the generator Q of the action kernel (7–1.1) the J'-action is expressed by

$$Q(\cdot,\bullet) \rightarrow {}^{(\gamma)}Q(\cdot,\bullet) =_{def} Q(\gamma^{-1}\cdot\gamma, \gamma^{-1}\bullet\gamma),\ \gamma \in J'. \tag{5.11}$$

with the property: if $Q_1, ..., Q_k$ are any symmetric action kernel generators on Θ, then

$$^{\gamma}\langle Q_1, ..., Q_k\rangle_\tau = \langle\, {}^{(\gamma)}Q_1, ..., {}^{(\gamma)}Q_k\rangle_\tau. \tag{5.12}$$

Proof. To say that Q is the generator of a symmetric action kernel on Θ means that Q: $J \times \mathcal{J} \rightarrow [0,1]$ is a kernel with the property that if $\pi(j_1) = \pi(j_2)$ then $Q(j_1,\cdot) = Q(j_2,\cdot)$. Given such a kernel Q, ${}^{(\gamma)}Q = Q(\gamma\cdot\gamma^{-1}, \gamma\cdot\gamma^{-1})$ is clearly also a kernel on J; it remains to show that if $\pi(j_1) = \pi(j_2)$ then $Q(\gamma j_1\gamma^{-1},\cdot) = Q(\gamma j_2\gamma^{-1},\cdot)$. But to say that π is a bundle for L acting on J by conjugation means that $\pi(j_1) = \pi(j_2) \Rightarrow \pi(\gamma j_1\gamma^{-1}) = \pi(\gamma j_2\gamma^{-1})$, so the desired result follows from the property of Q.

Now, to prove 5.12, we begin with the kernel $^{\gamma}\langle Q_1, ..., Q_k\rangle_\tau$ on E^k. For $e = (e_1, .., e_k) \in E^k, \Delta = \Delta_1 \times ... \times \Delta_k \in \mathcal{E}^k$,

$$^{\gamma}\langle Q_1, ..., Q_k\rangle_\tau(e,\Delta) = \langle Q_1, ..., Q_k\rangle_\tau(\gamma^{-1}e, \gamma^{-1}\Delta)$$

by 5.1 and 7–4.1. This last expression is

$$\sum_{\chi\in\mathcal{I}(k)} \tau(\gamma^{-1}e_1, ..., \gamma^{-1}e_k; \chi)$$

$$\prod_{i\in D(\chi)} Q_i((\gamma^{-1}e_{\chi(i)})(\gamma^{-1}e_i)^{-1}, (\gamma^{-1}\Delta_i)(\gamma^{-1}e_i)^{-1}) \prod_{i\notin D(\chi)} \epsilon_{\gamma^{-1}e_i}(\gamma^{-1}\Delta_i)$$

$$= \sum_{\chi\in\mathcal{I}(k)} \tau(e_1, ..., e_k; \chi)$$

$$\prod_{i\in D(\chi)} Q_i((\gamma^{-1}e_{\chi(i)})(\gamma^{-1}e_i)^{-1}, (\gamma^{-1}\Delta_i)(\gamma^{-1}e_i)^{-1}) \prod_{i\notin D(\chi)} \epsilon_{\gamma^{-1}e_i}(\gamma^{-1}\Delta_i)$$

since τ is translation invariant. Recall that $(\gamma^{-1}e_{\chi(i)})(\gamma^{-1}e_i)^{-1}$ denotes that element $j \in J$ such that $j(\gamma^{-1}e_i) = \gamma^{-1}e_{\chi(i)}$. It is then evident that

$$(\gamma^{-1}e_{\chi(i)})(\gamma^{-1}e_i)^{-1} = \gamma^{-1}(e_{\chi(i)}e_i^{-1})\gamma,$$

and similarly

$$(\gamma^{-1}\Delta_i)(\gamma^{-1}e_i)^{-1} = \gamma^{-1}(\Delta_i e_i^{-1})\gamma.$$

Moreover $\gamma^{-1}e_i \in \gamma^{-1}\Delta_i \iff e_i \in \Delta_i$, so that

$$\epsilon_{\gamma^{-1}e_i}(\gamma^{-1}\Delta_i) = \epsilon_{e_i}(\Delta_i).$$

Thus, the last expression above may be written

$$\sum_{\chi \in \mathcal{I}(k)} \tau(e_1, \ldots, e_k; \chi) \prod_{i \in D(\chi)} Q_i(\gamma^{-1}(e_{\chi(i)}e_i^{-1})\gamma, \gamma^{-1}(\Delta_i e_i^{-1})\gamma) \prod_{i \notin D(\chi)} \epsilon_{e_i}(\Delta_i)$$

$$= \sum_{\chi \in \mathcal{I}(k)} \tau(e_1, \ldots, e_k; \chi) \prod_{i \in D(\chi)} {}^{(\gamma)}Q_i((e_{\chi(i)}e_i^{-1}), \Delta_i e_i^{-1}) \prod_{i \notin D(\chi)} \epsilon_{e_i}(\Delta_i)$$

$$= \langle {}^{(\gamma)}Q_1, \ldots, {}^{(\gamma)}Q_k \rangle_\tau (e, \Delta). \quad \blacksquare$$

Scholium 5.13. Let a group Γ act measurably on the left on a space Z. In 5.1, for $\gamma \in \Gamma$ we considered the linear operation on the function space $\mathcal{Z}$ induced by $z \to \gamma z$; we used the same symbol γ to denote this linear operator: $(\gamma f)(z) = f(\gamma^{-1}(z))$. Thus there is an induced left action of Γ on functions, namely $f \to \gamma f$ (or ${}^{\gamma}f$). Now suppose Γ acts on Z on the right. We can consider the linear operator on functions induced by $z \to z\gamma$, and we also get a left action on functions, namely $f \to \gamma f$, where now $(\gamma f)(z) = f(z\gamma)$. If Γ acts on Z both on the left and right, then we will use the notation $(\gamma_l f)(z) = f(\gamma^{-1}z)$. and $(\gamma_r f)(z) = f(z\gamma)$. For example we consider our group J' acting on itself by multiplication on both the left and right. γ_l and γ_r are distinct in general (unless J' is abelian), but they commute. If we view kernels $Q: J \times \mathcal{J} \to [0,1]$ as operators on functions in the usual way, then we can express the left action $Q \to {}^{(\gamma)}Q$ as follows:

$${}^{(\gamma)}Q = (\gamma_l\gamma_r)Q(\gamma_l\gamma_r)^{-1}.$$

Example 5.14. Suppose that in the framework $\boldsymbol{\Theta}$ we have $S = J/H$ for a subgroup H of J, and $\pi: J \to S$ is the canonical projection; these are frameworks like those of Example 5–4.1. Let $L \subset J$ be any subgroup contained in the normalizer of H in J, i.e., L is any subgroup of J in which H is normal. Then $\pi: J \to S$ is also a bundle for the action of L by conjugation. In fact, a fibre of π is a coset jH, and for $l \in L$ we have $l(jH)l^{-1} = (ljl^{-1})H$ (since $Hl^{-1} = l^{-1}H$) which is another coset. Thus conjugation by l permutes the fibres of π as claimed.

Suppose that we have a framework Θ with a τ-distribution which satisfies the hypotheses of Proposition 5.10. We would like to construct a framework Θ' which is a specialization of Θ, in which (with notation as in 5.8 through 5.11) E' and S' are the distinguished configuration and premise spaces, and J' is the distinguished symmetry group. We assume that the action of J' on the set E' of participator ensembles is compatible with the action of J' on action kernels given by 5.11. More explicitly, we can start with an "initial" participator ensemble

$$A = \{A_i\}_{i=1}^{k}, \quad A_i = (\xi_i, Q_i, \eta_i).$$

Then we assume that

$$^{\gamma}A = \{ ^{\gamma}A_i\}_{i=1}^{k}, \quad ^{(\gamma)}A_i = \left(^{(\gamma)}\xi_i, \ ^{(\gamma)}Q_i, \ ^{(\gamma)}\eta_i \right) \tag{5.15}$$

where $^{(\gamma)}Q_i$ is as in 5.11. The action of γ on the ξ_i and the η_i is assumed given, but we need not stipulate its properties now.

Now to build Θ', let us assume that we have chosen some set X' of (say k-fold) participator ensembles which contains E', and some set Y' of measures on E^k which contains S'. We further assume that we have a group G' which contains J' and acts on X' in a manner which extends the action of J' on E'. For simplicity, however, we will focus our attention only on the distinguished part of the structure, E', S', J'. We can define a fundamental map $\pi': J' \to S'$ using $\pi': E' \to S'$ and our "initial" element $A \in E'$:

$$\pi': J' \to S', \ \pi'(\gamma) = \pi'_0(^{(\gamma)}A) = \ ^{(\gamma)}\nu_0. \tag{5.16}$$

In this way we get a symmetric framework

$$\Theta' = (X', Y', E', S', G', J', \pi'). \tag{5.17}$$

We now discuss the question: Is Θ' is a specialization of Θ in the sense of 3.2? The primary issue here is the nature of the specialization scheme 3.1. Our distinguished configurations E' are already described as a set of participator ensembles on Θ, namely the set of all the ${}^{(\gamma)}A$. De facto, in any specialization scheme which applies to this situation, participator ensembles of this type must satisfy the permissibility condition of the scheme. Recall that the role of the permissibility condition is to ensure two things: first that the separate permissible participator ensembles have asymptotically stable dynamics; second that the perturbation of these stable asymptotic characteristics of one such ensemble by its interaction with another has sufficient regularity to encode information about the interaction in accessible form. Then, according to Definition 3.2, the possible regular perturbations which arise in this manner must be parametrized by S', and they must encode accessible information about the interactions in a very precise sense: Suppose the two ensembles ${}^{(\gamma_1)}A$, ${}^{(\gamma_2)}A$ correspond to points e_1', e_2' of E'. The interaction of these ensembles perturbs the asymptotics of ${}^{(\gamma_1)}A$ in a manner which is encoded by the element $\pi'_{e_1'}(e_2') = \pi'(\gamma_2\gamma_1^{-1})$.

We want to see what this means in our case. Using the same notation as in 5.4, let us denote the transition probability of the initial participator ensemble A by P_0, so that

$$P_0 = \langle Q_1, \ldots, Q_k \rangle_T.$$

We have fixed a stationary measure for P_0 on E^k, denoted ν_0, and

$$S' = \{ {}^{(\gamma)}\nu_0 \mid \gamma \in J' \}.$$

According to the definition of π' given in 5.16, $\pi'(\gamma) = {}^{(\gamma)}\nu_0$. Thus the perturbation regularity requirement may be stated as follows.

5.18. The interaction of the ensembles ${}^{(\gamma_1)}A$ and ${}^{(\gamma_2)}A$ perturbs the asymptotics of ${}^{(\gamma_1)}A$ in a manner which is encoded by the measure ${}^{\gamma_2\gamma_1^{-1}}\nu_0$.

Broadly speaking, there are two ways in which 5.18 might hold: concretely, and abstractly. In the concrete way the perturbation information is encoded in the properties of the measure ${}^{\gamma_2\gamma_1^{-1}}\nu_0$ *as a measure*. In the abstract way the information is simply encoded in the group element $\gamma_2\gamma_1^{-1}$ which is attached to the measure. How might the concrete way work? Recall that for every $\gamma \in J'$, ${}^{\gamma}\nu_0$ is stationary for ${}^{\gamma}P_0$; by 5.2 and 5.12 this kernel is the transition probability for the ensemble ${}^{(\gamma)}A$. Under suitable hypotheses (say on the initial ensemble A) the interaction in question may perturb ${}^{(\gamma_1)}A$ so that its stationary measure ${}^{\gamma_1}\nu_0$ is canonically deformed toward ${}^{\gamma_2}\nu_0$, and moreover so that the measure ${}^{\gamma_2\gamma_1^{-1}}\nu_0$ is some type of derivative of this deformation. This possibility is mathematically appealing. On the other hand, the abstract way for 5.18 to hold requires only that *some* canonically specified aspect of the total perturbation may be classified by the group-theoretic difference $\gamma_2\gamma_1^{-1}$ between the two interacting systems. We do not analyze these questions further here, and in fact no definitive analysis is now available. In the next chapter, when necessary, we will simply assume 5.18 is satisfied, so that we have a bona fide specialization scheme for which $\boldsymbol{\Theta}'$ is a specialization of $\boldsymbol{\Theta}$.

CHAPTER TEN

RELATION TO QUANTUM MECHANICS

In this chapter we begin a study of the relationship between observer theory and quantum mechanics. The first section presents an overview of the characterization of quantum systems initiated by von Neumann, Weyl, Wigner, and Mackey. For this section we have relied heavily on the book by V.S. Varadarajan (1985). The second section discusses the appearance of vector bundles in this context. In the third section we explore possible connections between these vector bundles and linearizations of the specialized chain bundles of 9–5.

Our approach is based on the idea that theories of measurement, which form the basis of quantum formalism, must have a large overlap with theories of perception. Quantum interpretations rest entirely on the interaction between observer and observed, and on the irreducible effects on both of them subsequent to such interaction. Conversely, it is reasonable to require of a theory of perception that it provide some illumination on the paradoxes that have dogged measurement theory to date. We must, however, make clear that in this chapter our intention is to provide neither a scholarly treatment of quantum measurement theory, nor a full and rigorous grounding of that theory in observer mechanics. Rather, we initiate a line of enquiry into their relationship, making a first attempt at setting up a language within which quantum measurement and perception-in-general may both be discussed.

There are other stochastic-foundational formalisms which seek to ground quantum theory, such as those of Nelson (1985) and Prugovecki (1984). We here make no comparisons with these theories.

1. Quantum systems and imprimitivity

The description of a "physical system" involves various constituents. First is a "set of propositions," or empirically verifiable statements. On this set is a "logic" obeyed by its elements. There is a notion of the possible "states" of the system and of the "dynamical evolution" of these states. There is a group of "symmetries" compatible with the logic and leaving the dynamics of the system invariant. There is usually a "configuration space" on which this group also acts. Finally, there is a specification of the possible "observables" of the system. In this section we discuss these concepts, and how they lead to the idea of a system of imprimitivity.

For our purposes, a logic $\mathcal{L}$ is a set Π of propositions together with a syntax in which the notions of "implies," "and," "or," and "not" are given, along with rules for their application. Quantum systems are distinguished from classical ones by their logics: a classical system obeys a "Boolean" logic, while a quantum system obeys a "standard logic."

More precisely, let Π be the set of propositions of a physical system. We call the system *classical* if there is a measurable space $(Y, \mathcal{Y})$ and a bijective function $\Phi : \Pi \rightarrow \mathcal{Y}$, such that the logic $\mathcal{L}$ on Π is that induced by Φ from the Boolean algebra $\mathcal{Y}$. That is, if we denote "implies" by $\Rightarrow$, "and" by $\wedge$, "or" by $\vee$ and "not" by $-$, we have $\mathcal{L} = (\Pi, \Rightarrow, \wedge, \vee, -)$, where for $a, b \in \Pi$,

$$
\begin{aligned}
a \Rightarrow b &\text{ iff } \Phi(a) \subset \Phi(b), \\
a \wedge b &\equiv \Phi^{-1}(\Phi(a) \cap \Phi(b)), \\
a \vee b &\equiv \Phi^{-1}(\Phi(a) \cup \Phi(b)), \\
-a &\equiv \Phi^{-1}(Y - \Phi(a)).
\end{aligned}
\tag{1.1}
$$

Here "$\equiv$" means "defined by." For the partial order $\Rightarrow$ on Π there is a least element $0 = \Phi^{-1}(\emptyset)$ and a greatest element $1 = \Phi^{-1}(Y)$. A logic is called a σ*-logic* if it is closed under countable applications of $\wedge$ and $\vee$.

The peculiarity of quantum systems is that their logics are non-distributive: e.g., the proposition "a and (b or c)" need not have the same truth value as "(a and b) or (a and c)." Hence the distributive, or "de Morgan," laws valid in Boolean logic must be abandoned in favor of weaker laws. It turns out that an appropriate logic, called a *standard* or *quantum* logic, may be described as follows. There is a separable Hilbert space $\mathcal{H}$ over $\mathbf{C}$. Denote the set of closed subspaces of $\mathcal{H}$ by

$\mathcal{S}(\mathcal{H})$. There is a bijective function $\Phi : \Pi \to \mathcal{S}(\mathcal{H})$ such that, for $a, b \in \Pi$

$$\begin{aligned} a \Rightarrow b &\text{ iff } \Phi(a) < \Phi(b) \quad (\text{ i.e., } \Phi(a) \text{ is a subspace of } \Phi(b)), \\ a \wedge b &\equiv \Phi^{-1}(\Phi(a) \cap \Phi(b)), \\ a \vee b &\equiv \Phi^{-1}(\Phi(a) \bigvee \Phi(b)), \\ -a &\equiv \Phi^{-1}(\Phi(a)^{\perp}). \end{aligned} \tag{1.2}$$

Here $\bigvee$ means "join": the join of a collection of subspaces is their joint closed linear span. $\perp$ denotes orthogonal complement. We set $0 = \Phi^{-1}(\{0\})$ and $1 = \Phi^{-1}(\mathcal{H})$.

It is easy to see that this is a σ-logic, and that if the Hilbert space $\mathcal{H}$ is of dimension ≥ 2 then the standard logic is non-distributive. For any $\mathcal{H}$, the standard logic is a σ-logic. Since there is a bijective correspondence $V \leftrightarrow P_V$ between closed subspaces in $\mathcal{S}(\mathcal{H})$ and orthogonal projections, we may also model the standard logic in terms of these projections. From now on we simply identify Π with $\mathcal{P}(\mathcal{H})$, the set of orthogonal projections on $\mathcal{H}$, or with $\mathcal{S}(\mathcal{H})$, whichever is convenient.

Assumption 1.3. We restrict our discussion of quantum systems to those obeying a standard logic.[1]

In section three we consider how these systems might be naturally associated to specializations of symmetric frameworks.

We may now define a *state* of a physical system. It is a mapping $\sigma : \mathcal{P}(\mathcal{H}) \to [0,1]$, the unit interval, such that

(i) $\sigma(0) = 0$, $\sigma(I) = 1$.

(ii) If $\{P_{U_i}\}_{i=1}^{\infty}$ is a pairwise orthogonal sequence of projections then

$$\sigma(P_{\bigvee_{i=1}^{\infty} U_i}) = \sum_{i=1}^{\infty} \sigma(P_{U_i}).$$

Intuitively, a state is a way to assign a likelihood to each proposition in the logic.

The set of all states, denoted by Σ, is a convex subset of the space of all mappings $\mathcal{P}(\mathcal{H}) \to [0,1]$. The *pure states* are the extremal elements of Σ as a convex set. Nonpure states are termed *mixtures*. If the dimension of $\mathcal{H}$ is greater than 2, a

[1] Some systems studied in physics obey logics which are (non-Boolean) sublogics of standard logics. We do not treat such systems here.

theorem of Gleason says that states are in one-to-one correspondence with nonnegative selfadjoint operators on $\mathcal{H}$ of trace unity, as follows. Let σ be a state. Then there exists such an operator D_σ such that

$$\sigma(P_V) = \mathrm{Tr}(D_\sigma P_V), \quad V \in \mathcal{S}(\mathcal{H}). \tag{1.4}$$

D_σ is called the *density operator* of the state σ. If σ is a pure state, D_σ is orthogonal projection onto a one-dimensional subspace V of $\mathcal{H}$. That is, to σ there corresponds a unit vector ψ in V such that $D_\sigma\phi = P_{[\psi]}\phi = \langle\psi, \phi\rangle\psi$ for all $\phi \in \mathcal{H}$ ($\langle\cdot,\cdot\rangle$ being the inner product of $\mathcal{H}$).

The states of a physical system change, in general, with time. Let us write the state at time t as σ_t, assuming it was σ at time 0. It is reasonable to assume that this change is linear: if $\{c_i\}_{i=1}^n$ are positive numbers whose sum is unity, and if $\{\sigma^i\}_{i=1}^n$ are states, then

$$\left(\sum_{i=1}^n c_i\sigma^i\right)_t = \sum_{i=1}^n c_i\sigma_t^i. \tag{1.5i}$$

It is also reasonable to suppose that, for any $V \in \mathcal{S}(\mathcal{H})$,

$$t \longrightarrow \sigma_t(P_V) \text{ is a Borel function} \tag{1.5ii}$$

from $\mathbf{R}$ to $[0, 1]$. Finally, it is clear that the evolution has the structure of a one-parameter group:

$$\sigma_{t_1+t_2} = (\sigma_{t_1})_{t_2}, \tag{1.5iii}$$

called the *dynamical group* of the system. The conditions in 1.5 are summarized by saying that $t \longrightarrow \sigma_t$ is a *representation* of the additive group of real numbers in $\mathrm{Aut}(\Sigma)$, the group of convex automorphisms of Σ. By Stone's theorem, to this evolution there corresponds a selfadjoint operator H on $\mathcal{H}$, unique up to additive constants, such that the density operator D_{σ_t} is related to D_σ by

$$D_{\sigma_t} = e^{-itH} D_\sigma e^{itH}. \tag{1.6}$$

If σ is a pure state with density operator $P_{[\Psi]}$, this reduces to

$$D_{\sigma_t} = P_{[e^{-itH}\Psi]}, \quad D_\sigma = P_{[\Psi]}.$$

The operator H, which determines the evolution of states, is called the *hamiltonian* of the system.

The result of a "physical measurement" is a proposition stating that a certain quantity takes values in some subset of, say, the real numbers. An *observable* of a quantum system is, then, the association of a projection to each (Borel) subset of the real numbers in a manner consistent with such measurements. Precisely, an observable is a *projection-valued measure,* i.e., a mapping χ from the Borel σ-algebra $\mathcal{B}$ of $\mathbf{R}$ into $\mathcal{P}(\mathcal{H})$, such that

(i) $\chi(\emptyset) = 0, \chi(\mathbf{R}) = I.$

(ii) If $E, F \in \mathcal{B}$ and $E \cap F = \emptyset$ then $\chi(E) \perp \chi(F)$.

(iii) If $\{E_i\}_{i=1}^{\infty}$ is a sequence of pairwise disjoint sets in $\mathcal{B}$,

$$\chi(\bigcup_{i=1}^{\infty} E_i) = \sum_{i=1}^{\infty} \chi(E_i).$$

The meaning of (i) is clear. The second condition is the requirement that the propositions

$\mathcal{E}$: The observation takes a value in E and

$\mathcal{F}$: The observation takes a value in F,

are logically contradictory statements if $E \cap F = \emptyset$. The third condition states that the proposition "the observable quantity takes value in at least one of the E_i" corresponds, in the logic, to the join of the subspaces corresponding to the E_i.

More generally, given a measurable space Y, a *Y-valued observable* of the system is a projection-valued measure based on Y (i.e., satisfying (i), (ii), and (iii) above, with $\mathbf{R}$ replaced by Y).

If σ is a state and χ is an observable, $\sigma \circ \chi$ is a Borel probability measure on $\mathbf{R}$. Quantum theory prescribes for $\sigma \circ \chi$ the interpretation that it is the distribution of observed values for the observable χ in the state σ. A customary way of saying this employs the spectral calculus to associate to χ the selfadjoint operator A_χ given by

$$A_\chi = \int_{\mathbf{R}} \chi(d\lambda)\lambda. \tag{1.7}$$

It follows that the *expected value of the observable χ in the state σ* is then

$$\langle\chi\rangle_\sigma \equiv \mathrm{Tr}(D_\sigma A_\chi). \tag{1.8}$$

In particular, for a pure state with $D_\sigma = P_{[\Psi]}$,

$$\langle\chi\rangle_\sigma = \langle\Psi, A_\chi \Psi\rangle \tag{1.9}$$

where $\langle,\rangle$ is the inner product in $\mathcal{H}$.

This is the point at which the theory makes contact with experiment.

We have seen above how a group representing the "time-axis" defines the dynamics of a system. Physical systems have, however, a deeper geometrical character arising out of the requirement of the "objectivity" of experimental results. This requirement is framed, within the scientific paradigm, in terms of the *relativity* of conclusions arrived at by different experimenters viewing the same phenomenon, as follows.

Consider a physical system, together with a class of "experimenters" which take measurements in the system. Suppose that the set of meaningful statements (with its given syntax) is, for each of these experimenters, the same: namely, the given logic $\mathcal{L}$. Intuitively, this means that each conceivable "physical" phenomenon for any one experimenter is a conceivable phenomenon for any other. However, at each instant of time the various experimenters have different *ways* to use the propositions of Π to describe these phenomena. Let us call a particular experimenter's way of doing this his "frame of reference" at time t. Let Ω denote the set of all the frames of reference for these experimenters. (We allow different experimenters to have the same frame of reference.) In looking at a phenomenon, an experimenter with frame of reference ω_i would describe it with a proposition, say $p(\omega_i) \in \Pi$; an experimenter looking at the same phenomenon, but with frame of reference ω_j, would describe it with a proposition $p(\omega_j)$. If $\omega_i \neq \omega_j$ then, in general, $p(\omega_i) \neq p(\omega_j)$. In order to objectively relate propositions in ω_i to those in ω_j we would expect that there exist bijective mappings

$$T_{\omega_j,\omega_i}: \Pi \to \Pi, \quad \forall \omega_i, \omega_j \in \Omega, \tag{1.10}$$

such that $T_{\omega_j,\omega_i}(p(\omega_i)) = p(\omega_j)$. Thus T_{ω_j,ω_i} provides a dictionary that translates propositions about any phenomenon made with frame of reference ω_i into propositions about that phenomenon made with frame of reference ω_j. Now what makes Π useful is the logic $\mathcal{L}$; thus these T_{ω_j,ω_i} should preserve the syntax of the logic, i.e., the operations of 1.2. Such a bijective mapping is called an *automorphism of the logic* $\mathcal{L}$. Notice that the identity automorphism of $\mathcal{L}$ is included: $T_{\omega,\omega}$ is the identity mapping of Π, for any $\omega \in \Omega$. Also, T_{ω_i,ω_j} is the inverse automorphism of T_{ω_j,ω_i}. The requirement of objectivity may then be expressed as follows:

Assumption 1.11. (*Objectivity*). The set

$$J = \{T_{\omega,\omega'} \mid \omega, \omega' \in \Omega\}$$

is a subgroup of the group of automorphisms of $\mathcal{L}$. Given $g \in J$ and $\omega \in \Omega$, there exists a unique $\omega' \in \Omega$ such that $g = T_{\omega',\omega}$. If we denote this ω' by $g\omega$, then $\omega \to g\omega$

is a transitive action of the group J on the set Ω. The automorphisms $T_{\omega',\omega}$ depend only on the frames ω and ω' and, in particular, have no explicit dependence on time.

We call J the *group of (physical) symmetries* of the system (for the given class of experimenters). The transitivity of the action means that no pair of frames of reference are isolated from each other, i.e., T_{ω_i,ω_j} exists for each pair (ω_i, ω_j). Furthermore, the transitivity on Ω implies that the dictionary translation between ω_i and ω_j can be effected through any intermediary ω_k: $T_{\omega_i,\omega_j} = T_{\omega_i,\omega_k}T_{\omega_k,\omega_j}$, $\forall \omega_i, \omega_j, \omega_k \in \Omega$.

Objectivity is a property of a class of experimenters on the system; it expresses the mutual consistency of descriptions of the system by the various experimenters in the class. At this level of analysis, the group J is associated to the class of experimenters; one does not need to have a "configuration space" for the system (see below) in order to make sense of the group.

At this point we note some connections with observer theory. The situation we have been discussing corresponds to a symmetric framework (X, Y, E, S, G, J, π). The "experimenters" are participators in the framework; the class of experimenters under consideration are the participators in a particular environment supported by the framework. The "frame of reference" of an experimenter at time t is the perspective of the participator at time t; thus we can think of the set Ω of frames of reference as being isomorphic to the set of distinguished perspectives $\{\pi_e \mid e \in E\}$ (or isomorphic to E itself). The group J is the distinguished structure group of the framework; the action of J on E in the framework corresponds to the action of J on Ω in 1.11. Notice that the logic $\mathcal{L}$ of the physical system is not explicitly in evidence at this level of description. However, recall that the original meaning of a frame of reference is a "way of using the propositions of the logic to describe physical phenomena." Such a way, then, corresponds to a way of mapping E to S. We should expect, therefore, that the logic $\mathcal{L}$ itself has meaning in the observer theory and, conversely, that the fundamental map π and the premise space S have meaning in the quantum mechanics. And the quantum mechanical notion of *state* must have an observer-theoretic interpretation consistent with these meanings. These interpretations will emerge most clearly when we realize the framework above as a *specialization*. The goal of the chapter is to lay some groundwork for this level of connection between the two theories. In this section, however, we continue to use the terminology "experimenter," "frame of reference" and "physical symmetry group" rather than "participator," "perspective" and "framework group."

Returning to our overview of quantum mechanics, we assume that 1.11 is satisfied. We denote the action of J on $\mathcal{S}(\mathcal{H})$ by $(g, V) \mapsto gV$ and its action on $\mathcal{P}(\mathcal{H})$ by $(g, P_V) \mapsto {}^gP_V \equiv P_{gV}$.

Thus J may be viewed as a subgroup of the *projective group* Aut$\mathcal{P}(\mathcal{H})$ of automorphisms of $\mathcal{P}(\mathcal{H})$. We assume henceforth that J satisfies the following assumptions.

Assumption 1.12.

(i) J has a locally compact, second-countable (lcsc) topology; the corresponding standard Borel structure will be denoted $\mathcal{J}$, and J is a measurable group with this structure.

(ii) If $\mathcal{P}(\mathcal{H})$ is given the *strong* topology, i.e., if $\{P_n\}_{n=1}^{\infty} \subset \mathcal{P}(\mathcal{H})$ then $P_n \to P \in \mathcal{P}(\mathcal{H})$ iff $P_n u \to Pu$ in $\mathcal{H}$ for all $u \in \mathcal{H}$, then J acts measurably on $\mathcal{P}(\mathcal{H})$.

These assumptions are summarized by saying that the action of J on $\mathcal{P}(\mathcal{H})$ gives a *representation* of J in Aut$\mathcal{P}(\mathcal{H})$.

Let $\mathcal{U}$ be the group of *unitary* automorphisms of $\mathcal{H}$ (i.e., $B \in \mathcal{U}$ iff $B: \mathcal{H} \to \mathcal{H}$ is a surjective isometry). We have the following result from representation theory.

Theorem 1.13. Under Assumption 1.12, the action of J on $\mathcal{P}(\mathcal{H})$ arises from a *unitary* representation in the following manner. Let J^* be the *universal covering group* of J. Let $\delta: J^* \to J$ be the covering homomorphism. Then there exists a unique unitary representation of J^* in $\mathcal{U}$, say $g^* \mapsto U_{g^*}$, such that for any $V \in \mathcal{S}(\mathcal{H})$ and $g \in J$,

$$gV = U_{g^*}V \quad \text{for any } g^* \text{ with } \delta(g^*) = g, \quad \text{or equivalently}$$

$${}^gP_V = U_{g^*}P_V U_{g^*}^{-1} \quad \text{for any } g^* \text{ with } \delta(g^*) = g.$$

Since we assume that our symmetry group J satisfies (i) and (ii) of 1.12, it also satisfies the conclusions of 1.13. Examples of such a J include the group of additive reals (leading to the dynamical group above) and the groups of Galilean and Einsteinian relativity.

We imagine that to each experimenter, at each time t, is associated a state of the system (which describes the way the experimenter assigns probabilities to propositions). We think of this as the experimenter's *description* of the system at time t. This is distinct from the experimenter's frame of reference. In particular, consider two experimenters whose frames of reference at time t are ω and ω', where $\omega' = g\omega$ for some $g \in J$. Suppose that at time t the state associated to the first experimenter is $\sigma \in \Sigma$. Let σ^g denote the state that expresses in terms of the frame of reference $g\omega$ the same underlying probabilities that are expressed by the state σ of the first experimenter in terms of its frame of reference ω. In this way the action of J on $\mathcal{L}$ gives rise to an action on Σ. By definition this action has the property that, for any $P \in \mathcal{P}(\mathcal{H})$,

$$\sigma(P) = \sigma^g({}^gP)\,, \text{i.e.,}$$
$$\sigma^g(\cdot) = \sigma({}^{g^{-1}}\cdot)\,. \tag{1.14}$$

It is clear that $\sigma \rightarrow \sigma^g$ is in fact a *convex* automorphism of Σ (i.e., preserving convex combinations of states). We assume that, for each $\sigma \in \Sigma$ and $P \in \mathcal{P}(\mathcal{H})$, $g \mapsto \sigma^g(P)$ is a Borel map from J to $\mathbf{R}$. We then say that we have a representation of J in the collection of all convex automorphisms $\mathrm{Aut}(\Sigma)$ of states, a representation which is *covariant* with the representation in $\mathrm{Aut}(\mathcal{P}(\mathcal{H}))$, as indicated in 1.14.

Henceforth we assume that, at all times t, the descriptions of the system by the various experimenters are in agreement; we say that their descriptions are *covariant* with J:

Assumption 1.15. *Descriptive Covariance with* J. Let A and A' be any two experimenters (in the given class) whose frames of reference at time t are ω and $\omega' = g\omega$ respectively. Then the states σ and σ' associated to A and A' at time t are related by $\sigma' = \sigma^g$.

To relate this type of covariance to the dynamics given in 1.6 we first note that the requirement of time independence of the $T_{\omega,\omega'}$ (in Assumption 1.11) may be expressed as follows: for any $\sigma \in \Sigma$, $g \in J$, and $t \in \mathbf{R}$,

$$(\sigma^g)_t = (\sigma_t)^g\,.$$

This implies that the hamiltonian H commutes with the unitary action of J of 1.13: if we write for $g \in J$, $U_g = U_{g^*}$ for any $g^* \in J^*$ with $\delta(g^*) = g$, then

$$[H, U_g] = HU_g - U_gH = 0\,. \tag{1.16}$$

That is, the dynamical law is the same for each experimenter.

We have now described the essential features of quantum systems we shall need in the sequel. A useful characterization of such a system arises if it possesses a "configuration space." We say that a transitive measurable J-space Y is a *configuration space* for the quantum system if there exists a Y-valued observable, i.e., a projection-valued measure $P(\bullet)$ based on Y with the following property.[2] If we denote the action of J on Y by $x \to g \cdot x$,

$$P(g \cdot F) = U_g P(F) U_g^{-1}, \quad g \in J, F \in \mathcal{Y}, \text{ or equivalently}$$

$$P(F) = P_V \Rightarrow P(gF) = P_{gV}. \tag{1.17}$$

The word "covariant" is also used here: we say that the Y-valued observable $P(\bullet)$ is *covariant* with respect to the unitary representation of J. We note that a configuration space is not part of the intrinsic structure of the quantum system and class of experimenters, in contrast to the type of covariance expressed in 1.15.

If this situation obtains for $Y = \mathbf{R}^3$, we say that the system is *localizable*: the position in space is an observable. Relativistic particles are localizable if they have nonzero mass; photons, e.g., are not localizable.

Given the understanding of observables, states, and their dynamics as above, we may capture the kinematical aspects of a quantum system with a configuration space by means of the following definition, due to G. W. Mackey:

Definition 1.18. Let $(Y, \mathcal{Y})$ be a standard Borel G-space, G an lcsc group, acting measurably on Y. Let $\mathcal{H}$ be a separable Hilbert space. A *system of imprimitivity for G acting in $\mathcal{H}$ and based on Y* is a pair (U, P), where

(i) U is a unitary representation of G on $\mathcal{H}$;

(ii) P is a projection-valued measure on $\mathcal{Y}$ with values in $\mathcal{P}(\mathcal{H})$;

(iii) $P(g \cdot E) = U_g P(E) U_g^{-1}, \quad \forall g \in G$ and $E \in \mathcal{Y}$.

We abbreviate "system of imprimitivity" by SOI.

Example 1.19. *Koopman system of imprimitivity.* Let α be a positive, σ-finite measure on Y. Assume that α is *quasi-G-invariant,* i.e., the null sets of α form an

[2] We use the notation $P(\bullet)$ for the projection-valued measure, and $P_\bullet$ for the projections themselves. For example, for $F \in \mathcal{Y}$, $P(F) = P_V$ for a suitable closed subspace V of $\mathcal{H}$.

invariant subset of $\mathcal{Y}$ for the action of G (equivalently, the measure class of α is G-invariant). Then it follows that the measures $\alpha(dx)$ and $\alpha^g(dx) = \alpha(d(g^{-1}x))$ are mutually absolutely continuous. Suppose

$$r_g(x) \text{ is a version of } \frac{\alpha(dx)}{\alpha^{g^{-1}}(dx)}. \tag{1.20}$$

Let $\mathcal{K}$ be a complex separable Hilbert space with inner product $\langle\langle , \rangle\rangle$. Let $\mathcal{H} = L^2(Y, \alpha; \mathcal{K})$, i.e., the Hilbert space of measurable functions $f: Y \to \mathcal{K}$ with finite norm, given the inner product

$$\langle f_1, f_2 \rangle = \int_Y \alpha(dx) \langle\langle f_1(x), f_2(x) \rangle\rangle. \tag{1.21}$$

For each $g \in G$, define U_g by

$$U_g f(x) = \sqrt{r_g(g^{-1}x)}\, f(g^{-1}x), \quad f \in \mathcal{H}. \tag{1.22}$$

Then $g \to U_g$ is a unitary representation of G in $\mathcal{H}$. Let the projection-valued measure P based on Y and taking values in $\mathcal{P}(\mathcal{H})$ be defined by

$$(P_E f)(x) = 1_E(x) f(x), \quad E \in \mathcal{Y}, f \in \mathcal{H}. \tag{1.23}$$

Then (U, P) is a system of imprimitivity for G acting in $\mathcal{H}$ and based on Y, called the Koopman system of imprimitivity. Systems of imprimitivity more general than the Koopman system may be constructed using the concept of "cocycles," discussed in the next section.

2. Cocycles and bundles

In this section we examine the one-to-one correspondence between systems of imprimitivity and certain "cohomology classes of cocycles." This correspondence leads to a classification of all SOI's based on a given space X and acting in a given Hilbert space $\mathcal{H}$; this is part of the theory of Mackey. We go on to discuss the one-to-one correspondence between cohomology classes and equivalence classes of "transitive G-bundles." This allows us to describe SOI's based on X in terms of unitary Hilbert-space bundles on X and to consider the way in which SOI's arise in the "linearization" of arbitrary G-bundles.

Aside from its intrinsic interest, our reason for presenting this theory is that it provides some support for a bridge between observer theory and physics. We have noted that the mathematical structure of a system of imprimitivity embodies the kinematical aspects of a quantum system with a configuration space and a physical symmetry group J (c.f. section one). We want to realize some general principles according to which this structure arises from observer theory. One approach is as follows. We consider a chain bundle symmetric framework as in **9–5**, with distinguished framework group J. Now a chain bundle is a principal bundle, not a unitary Hilbert space bundle, but it gives rise to a collection of Hilbert bundles by linearization; we discuss bundle linearization in this section. Among all linearizations of the given chain bundle there are certain *canonical linearizations* which contain information about the asymptotics of the participator-dynamical chains which appear in the chain bundle; we describe this in section three. We can then consider the systems of imprimitivity which are embodied in these canonical linearizations. We may view the quantum systems associated to these systems of imprimitivity as being "linearizations" of the specialized perception expressed in the original chain-bundle observer framework. We emphasize that while the primary meaning of the group J in physics is as the group of symmetries of the configuration space, in observer theory it is as the group of symmetries of the set of observer perspectives in the specialized framework. The role of physical configuration space itself is not primary in observer theory. As a matter of terminology note that the *physical configuration space* is not the same as the *observer theoretic configuration space* (e.g., the spaces E or X of the specialized framework). In fact, the physical configuration space, or at least the orbits of J in it, corresponds to the distinguished premise space S of the specialized framework.

In what follows we assume that G is an lcsc group. For such a group there exists a (nonzero, σ-finite) *left-invariant*, or *Haar*, measure λ on G:

$$\lambda(gA) = \lambda(A), \quad g \in G, A \in \mathcal{G}.$$

Denote the measure class of λ (cf. **2–1**) by C_G. Suppose G acts measurably on a measurable space $(X, \mathcal{X})$. Let C be a measure class on $(X, \mathcal{X})$.

Definition 2.1.

(a) If M is a measurable group, a (G, X, M)*-cocycle related to* C is a measurable function $\varphi\colon G \times X \to M$, such that

(i) $\varphi(e, x) = 1$ for almost all $x \in X$ (e is the identity of G and 1 is the identity of M);

(ii)

$$\varphi(g_1 g_2, x) = \varphi(g_1, g_2 x)\varphi(g_2, x) \tag{2.2}$$

for almost all $(g_1, g_2, x) \in G \times G \times X$. (Here the null set is determined by $\mathcal{C}_G \times \mathcal{C}_G \times \mathcal{C}$.)

(b) Two (G, X, M)-cocycles φ and φ' are *cohomologous* if there exists a measurable function $b\colon X \to M$ such that, for almost all $(g, x) \in G \times X$,

$$\varphi'(g, x) = b(gx)\varphi(g, x)b(x)^{-1}. \tag{2.3}$$

This is an equivalence relation on the set of (G, X, M)-cocycles. Its equivalence classes are called *cohomology* classes. The collection of all (G, X, M) cohomology classes is denoted $\mathbf{H}^1(G, X, M, \mathcal{C})$, or simply $\mathbf{H}^1$ when there is no danger of confusion. Cocycles cohomologous to the trivial cocycle $\varphi(g, x) \equiv 1$ are called *coboundaries*.

(c) If the cocycle φ satisfies (i) and (ii) of (a) for *all* values of the arguments, we call φ a *strict cocycle*. If φ and φ' are strict cocycles satisfying (b) for all (g, x), we call them *strictly cohomologous*.[3]

As an example of a $(G, X, \mathbf{R}^+)$-cocycle ($\mathbf{R}^+$ is the multiplicative group of positive reals) we have

$$\varphi(g, x) = r_g(x)$$

where $r_g(x)$ is as in 1.19.

Definition 2.4.

(a) A SOI (U, P) for G acting in $\mathcal{H}$ is *equivalent* to an SOI (U', P') for G acting in $\mathcal{H}'$ if

(i) They are both based on the same space X;

---

[3] If there are invariant measure classes on G and X, we have the cocycles defined in 2.1, as well as strict cocycles. Mackey showed how the cohomology classes (with respect to the measure classes) are in one-to-one correspondence with strict cohomology classes. For details, see Varadarajan chapter five. In what follows, we are not careful to distinguish between strict cocycles and cocycles related to measure classes.

(ii) There exists a unitary isomorphism $W: \mathcal{H} \to \mathcal{H}'$ such that for all $g \in G$ and $E \in \mathcal{X}$,

$$U'_g = WU_gW^{-1}$$

and

$$P'(E) = WP(E)W^{-1}.$$

(b) A projection-valued measure P based on X and with values in $\mathcal{H}$ is *homogeneous* if it is unitarily equivalent to the projection-valued measure $\bar{P}$ based on X acting in $L^2(X, \mathcal{K}; \alpha)$, ($\mathcal{K}$ is a separable Hilbert space, α is a σ-finite measure on X) given by

$$\bar{P}(E)f = 1_E f, \quad f \in L^2(X, \mathcal{K}; \alpha).$$

If (U, P) is a SOI and P is homogeneous, we say that (U, P) is *homogeneous.*

(c) For a SOI (U, P) the set

$$\{E \in \mathcal{X} \mid P(E) \text{ is the 0 operator}\}$$

is G-invariant and so defines a G-invariant measure class. We call this the *measure class of P*.

Suppose we have a homogeneous SOI (U, P). Then every SOI equivalent to it is also homogeneous. Let us suppose that $L^2(x, \mathcal{K}; \alpha)$ is as given in Definition 2.4(b) and denote by $\mathcal{U}$ the group of unitary transformation of $\mathcal{K}$. The following theorem is proved in Varadarajan, section 6.5.

Theorem 2.5. The SOI (U, P) for G, based on X and acting in $\mathcal{H}$ is homogeneous iff it is unitarily equivalent to an SOI $(\bar{U}, \bar{P})$ acting in some $L^2(X, \mathcal{K}; \alpha)$ where

$$\bar{P}(E)f(x) = 1_e(x)f(x) \quad \text{a.e. } x$$

and

$$\bar{U}_g f(x) = \sqrt{r_g(g^{-1}x)}\varphi(g, g^{-1}x)f(g^{-1}x) \quad \text{a.e. } x$$

for almost all g, every $f \in L^2(X, \mathcal{K}; \alpha)$ and where φ is a $(G, X, \mathcal{U})$-cocycle. This gives a one-to-one correspondence between, on the one hand, equivalence classes of homogeneous SOI's and, on the other hand, the set $\mathbf{H}^1$ of $(G, X, \mathcal{U})$-cohomology classes.

With this correspondence between homogeneous systems of imprimitivity and cohomology classes it is possible (using Hahn-Hellinger spectral multiplicity theory) to build up *any* SOI from inequivalent homogeneous ones. This is done by means of a direct sum construction; for details see Varadarajan, sections 6.4 and 6.5.

We turn now to a discussion of the relevance of cocycles to the structure of G-bundles. Recall the definition (given in 9–5.3) of a *G-bundle* (Z, p, W, G), where Z and W are sets, $p: Z \to W$ is a surjective function and G is a group acting on Z and W in such a way that p is a G-homomorphism, i.e., for $g \in G$ and $z \in Z$, $p(gz) = gp(z)$. (We write all actions as left actions, and assume that all sets, functions, groups, and actions are measurable.) Recall that (Z, p, W, G) is a *transitive* G-bundle if Z is a transitive G-space.

Definition 2.6. A *G-bundle homomorphism* from the G-bundle $\mathcal{A} = (Z, p, W, G)$ into the G-bundle $\mathcal{A}' = (Z', p', W', G)$ is a measurable map $\Phi: Z \to Z'$ such that

(i) Φ preserves the G-actions: $\Phi(g(z)) = g\Phi(z)$, for $g \in G$ and $z \in Z$.
(ii) Φ respects fibres: $\Phi(p^{-1}\{w\})$ is contained in a single fibre of p'.

(We say that Φ is a *G-bundle isomorphism* if it is bijective and bimeasurable.)

Given such a Φ, there exists a well-defined function $\Psi: W \to W'$ such that $p' \circ \Phi = \Psi \circ p$. Also, $(\Phi(Z), p'|_{\Phi(Z)}, \Psi(Z), G)$ is then a G-bundle. If $\mathcal{A}'$ is transitive then a G-bundle homomorphism from $\mathcal{A}$ to $\mathcal{A}'$ is surjective.

By means of cocycles, every transitive G-bundle may be viewed as a "twisting" of a trivial bundle (i.e., one whose total space Z is a product space $W \times F$, with p = projection onto the first coordinate). To understand how this is so, we shall need some terminology. Let us suppose that (Z, p, W, G) is a transitive G-bundle. The fibre over $w \in W$ is called Z_w, and the stability subgroup of G for $w \in W$ is G_w. Then Z_w is a transitive G_w-space for each w and the fibres Z_w are mutually isomorphic. Fix $w_0 \in W$ and let $G_0 = G_{w_0}$. We expect that our bundle (Z, p, W, G) is isomorphic to $(W \times Z_0, \mathrm{pr}_1, W, G)$ for a suitable action defined on the latter. The pursuit of this aim leads us to the association of (G, W, G_0)-cohomology classes to transitive G-bundles.

Definition 2.7. Let X, Y be measurable spaces and $f: X \to Y$ a measurable function. A measurable function $g: Y \to X$ is a *section of* f if $f \circ g = \mathrm{id}_Y$.

Because W is transitive, G/G_0 is in a one-to-one correspondence with W: $w \in W$ iff the set of elements of G transporting w_0 to w is a left coset gG_0. Define $\pi'\colon G \to W$ in terms of the canonical mapping $\pi\colon G \to G/G_0$ by

$$G \ni g \to \pi'(g) = \pi(g)w_0 \in W. \tag{2.8}$$

Then a section

$$\sigma\colon W \to G \tag{2.9}$$

of π' exists if G is lcsc and G_0 is a closed subgroup (Varadarajan, Theorem 5.1).

Lemma 2.10. Let W, G, w_0, and G_0 be as above. Let σ be a section as in 2.9. The function φ_σ, where

$$\varphi_\sigma(j, w) = \sigma(jw)^{-1} j\sigma(w) \tag{2.11}$$

is a (G, W, G_0)-cocycle. Moreover,

$$\sigma \longrightarrow \varphi_\sigma$$

is a one-to-one correspondence between the set of sections and a (G, W, G_0)-cohomology class (the latter being determined solely by the action of G on W).

Proof. The set of group elements taking w_0 to jw is precisely the coset $\sigma(jw)G_0$. But $j\sigma(w)$ takes w_0 to jw. Hence $j\sigma(w) = \sigma(jw)g_0$ for some $g_0 \in G$. Thus $\varphi_\sigma\colon G \times W \to G_0$. The measurability of φ_σ is clear and it is immediate that $\varphi_\sigma(e, w) = e$ and $\varphi_\sigma(j_1 j_2, w) = \varphi(j_1, j_2 w)\varphi(j_2, w)$.

Now if σ' and σ are two sections, they define a measurable function $\alpha\colon W \to G_0$ by

$$\alpha(w) = \sigma'(w)^{-1}\sigma(w). \tag{2.12}$$

2.11 then gives

$$\varphi_{\sigma'}(j, w) = \alpha(jw)\varphi_\sigma(j, w)\alpha(w)^{-1},$$

so that φ_σ and $\varphi_{\sigma'}$ are cohomologous. Conversely, if $\varphi \approx \varphi_\sigma$, we have

$$\varphi(j, w) = \beta(jw)\varphi_\sigma(j, w)\beta(w)^{-1}$$

for some measurable $\beta\colon W \to G_0$. Then $\varphi = \varphi_{\sigma'}$, where $\sigma' = \beta\sigma$. ∎

Definition 2.13. Let the group G act transitively on W. Let $w_0 \in W$ and let G_0 be the stabilizer of w_0. Let Z_0 be a space on which G_0 acts transitively. Let φ be a

(G, W, G_0)-cocycle. Then the G-bundle $\mathbf{B}^{\varphi}$ is defined to be $(W \times Z_0, \mathrm{pr}_1, W, G)$, with group actions given by

$$(g, w) \to gw \in W \text{ as before}$$

$$(g, (w, b_0)) \to (gw, \varphi(g, w) \cdot b_0) \in W \times Z_0. \qquad (2.14)$$

The reader may check that 2.14 indeed defines an action, and that $\mathbf{B}^{\varphi}$ is G-bundle isomorphic to $\mathbf{B}^{\varphi'}$ iff φ and φ' are cohomologous.

Theorem 2.15. Let $\mathcal{A} = (Z, p, W, G)$ be a transitive G-bundle. Let $w_0 \in W$ and G_0 be the stabilizer of w_0. Then there exists a unique (G, W, G_0)-cohomology class $\xi_{\mathcal{A}}$ such that $\mathcal{A}$ is bundle isomorphic to any $\mathbf{B}^{\varphi}$ (as in Definition 2.13), $\varphi \in \xi_{\mathcal{A}}$.
Proof. Let σ be any section of G/G_0 and let φ_σ be the (G, W, G_0)-cocycle defined in 2.11. We may lift φ_σ to a (G, Z, G_0)-cocycle by the projection p: define $\varphi^*(g, \cdot)$ to be $p^*\varphi(g, \cdot)$, i.e.,

$$\varphi^*(g, z) = \varphi(g, p(z)). \qquad (2.16)$$

$\sigma^*(z)^{-1}$ transports z to the fibre B_0, φ_σ^* moves the resulting point within that fibre, and $\sigma^*(gz)$ transports to the fibre B_{gz}.

We now define a map $\Phi: Z \to W \times Z_0$ that effects an isomorphism of $\mathcal{A}$ with $\mathbf{B}^{\varphi}$. Let

$$\Phi(z) = (p(z), \sigma^*(z)^{-1} \cdot z), \qquad (2.17)$$

It may be checked that the transitivity of the action of G on Z implies that Φ is an isomorphism.

Thus $\mathcal{A}$ is bundle-isomorphic to $\mathbf{B}^{\varphi'}$ for any φ' in the cohomology class $\xi_{\mathcal{A}}$ associated to $\mathcal{A}$ by Lemma 2.10; $\{\mathbf{B}^{\varphi}; \varphi \in \xi_{\mathcal{A}}\}$ is thus an isomorphism class among the "trivial" bundles of this form, as mentioned after Definition 2.13. ∎

Definition 2.18. Let $\mathbf{A} = (B, p, Y, G)$ be a transitive G-bundle. We denote the action of G on Y by $(g, y) \to gy$, and that of G on B by $(g, b) \to D(g)b$. Then $\mathbf{A}$ is called a *Hilbert bundle* (or a *unitary bundle*) if

(i) Each fibre $B_x = p^{-1}\{y\}$ is a separable Hilbert space, with inner product $\langle\cdot,\cdot\rangle_y$ and inner-product topology identical to that induced by B;
(ii) For each $g \in G$, $D(g)\colon B_y \to B_{gy}$ is a unitary isomorphism.

We can now discuss the linearizations of a given G-bundle. Suppose that $\mathcal{A}$ and $\mathbf{A}$ are G-bundles, with $\mathbf{A}$ Hilbert. Let $y_0 \in Y$ with stabilizer $G_0 < G$. Denote the fibre over y_0 in $\mathbf{A}$ by B_0, and the group of unitary transformations of B_0 by $\mathcal{U}$. As we have seen, to $\mathcal{A}$ is associated a (G, Y, G_0)-cohomology class $\xi_{\mathcal{A}}$, while to $\mathbf{A}$ is associated a $(G,Y,\mathcal{U})$-cohomology class $\zeta_{\mathbf{A}}$. If $\varphi \in \xi_{\mathcal{A}}$, then

$$g_0 \mapsto \varphi(g_0, y_0) \tag{2.19}$$

is a (measurable group-) homomorphism of G_0 into itself. Similarly, if $\Psi \in \zeta_{\mathbf{A}}$,

$$g_0 \mapsto \Psi(g_0, y_0) \tag{2.20}$$

is a unitary representation of G_0 in $\mathcal{U}$. Conversely, it was shown by Mackey[4] that every homomorphism class $G_0 \to M$ (M a group) corresponds to a unique (G_0, Y, M)-cohomology class. It is reasonable to call $\mathbf{A}$ a linearization of $\mathcal{A}$ only if the homomorphism 2.20 arises from 2.19 in a specified manner. Namely, there is a third homomorphism m from G_0 to $\mathcal{U}$, such that $\Psi(g_0, y_0) = m(\varphi(g_0, y_0))$. Recalling Definition 2.1, suppose that M, M' are measurable groups. Then every homomorphism $m\colon M \to M'$ induces a map from $\mathbf{H}^1(G,Y,M)$ to $\mathbf{H}^1(G,Y,M')$.

These considerations motivate the following definition.

Definition 2.21.
(i) Let ξ be a (G,Y,M)-cohomology class and ζ a $(G,Y,\mathcal{U})$-cohomology class for some group $\mathcal{U}$ of unitary operators on a Hilbert space. We say that ζ is a *linearization* of ξ if there is a Borel homomorphism $m\colon M \to \mathcal{U}$ such that ζ is the cohomology class of the $(G,Y,\mathcal{U})$-cocycle $m(\varphi(\cdot,\cdot))$, for each $\varphi \in \xi$.
(ii) If $\mathcal{A}$, $\mathbf{A}$ are transitive G-bundles over the same base space Y, we say that $\mathbf{A}$ is a *linearization* of $\mathcal{A}$ if the associated cohomology class $\zeta_{\mathbf{A}}$ associated to $\mathbf{A}$ (by Theorem 2.15) linearizes the cohomology class $\xi_{\mathcal{A}}$ (associated to $\mathcal{A}$).

---

[4] See Varadarajan, Theorem 5.27.

It is straightforward to verify that $\zeta_{\mathbf{A}}$ is well-defined by the above procedure; in fact

$$\zeta_{\mathbf{A}} = \{(G, Y, \mathcal{U})\text{-cocycles } \Psi \mid \exists \varphi \in \xi_{\mathcal{A}} \text{ and } \exists k \in \mathcal{U} \text{ s.t. } k\Psi k^{-1} = m(\varphi)\}. \tag{2.22}$$

We stated above the correspondence between homogeneous SOI's and $(G, Y, \mathcal{U})$-cohomology classes ($\mathcal{U}$ a group of unitary operators on some Hilbert space B_0). We also saw that such cohomology classes are in correspondence with equivalence classes of transitive G-bundles with total space $Y \times B_0$, which we now recognize as Hilbert bundles. Thus to Hilbert bundles are associated SOI's and vice versa. To complete the circle of ideas we ask: given a homogeneous SOI, what relationship obtains between the Hilbert space it acts in and the Hilbert bundle to which it is associated? The answer is given in Theorem 2.30 below.

We assume, as usual, that G is a lcsc group with (left) Haar measure. The projection of this measure to Y is σ-finite and G-invariant; we denote it λ. If a measure α on Y is quasi-G-invariant, it is in the same measure class as λ, as long as Y is a homogeneous G-space.

Definition 2.24. Let f be a measurable section of the Hilbert bundle $\mathbf{A}$ (notation as in 2.18). Let α be a quasi-G-invariant measure on Y. Define

$$||f||^2 = \int_Y \langle f(y), f(y)\rangle_y \alpha(dy). \tag{2.25}$$

The *Hilbert space* $\mathcal{H}_{\mathbf{A}}$ *associated to* $\mathbf{A}$ (and α) is the collection of all α-equivalence classes of sections f with $||f|| < \infty$ and with inner product

$$\langle f_1, f_2\rangle = \int_Y \langle f_1(y), f_2(y)\rangle_y \alpha(dy). \tag{2.26}$$

The measurability of the integrands in 2.25 and 2.26 follows from the existence of a measurable section σ of $\pi\colon G \to G/G_0$, where G_0 is the stabilizer of $y_0 \in Y$. We have

$$\langle f_1(y), f_2(y)\rangle_y = \langle D(\sigma(y))^{-1} f_1(y), D(\sigma(y))^{-1} f_2(y)\rangle_{y_0},$$

which is clearly a measurable complex-valued function on Y. It is straightforward to verify that

$$V_\sigma\colon \mathcal{H}_{\mathbf{A}} \to L^2(Y, B_0; \alpha) \text{ by}$$

$$(V_\sigma f)(y) = D(\sigma(y))^{-1} f(y), \quad y \in X, f \in \mathcal{H} \tag{2.27}$$

is a unitary isomorphism.

If the $(G, X, \mathcal{U})$-cocycle φ_σ is defined by

$$\varphi_\sigma(g, y) = D[\sigma(gy)^{-1} g\sigma(y)], \tag{2.28}$$

then there is a corresponding G-bundle isomorphism $\Phi\colon \mathbf{A} \to \mathbf{B}^{\varphi_\sigma}$ (as in Theorem 2.15, where the total space of $\mathbf{B}^\varphi$ is $Y \times B_0$). We have the diagram:

$$\begin{array}{ccc} \mathbf{A} & \longrightarrow & \mathcal{H}_\mathbf{A} \\ \downarrow{\scriptstyle \Phi_\sigma} & & \downarrow{\scriptstyle V_\sigma} \\ \mathbf{B}^{\varphi_\sigma} & \longrightarrow & L^2(Y, B_0; \alpha) = \mathcal{H}_{\mathbf{B}^{\varphi_\sigma}} \end{array}$$

DIAGRAM 2.29. *The horizontal arrows are associations of Hilbert spaces of sections to bundles; the vertical arrows are isomorphisms of the relevant structures.*

Theorem 2.30. Let $\mathbf{A} = (B, p, Y, G)$ be a Hilbert bundle. Let $\mathcal{H} = \mathcal{H}_\mathbf{A}$ be the Hilbert space (of square-integrable sections) associated to $\mathbf{A}$ and α. Let the projection-valued measure P in $\mathcal{H}$ and the unitary representation U of G on $\mathcal{H}$ be defined by

$$P(E)f(y) = 1_E(y)f(y) \quad \text{and} \tag{2.31i}$$

$$U_g f(y) = \sqrt{r_g(g^{-1}y)}\, f(g^{-1} \cdot y), \tag{2.31ii}$$

for $y \in Y, E \in \mathcal{Y}, g \in G$, and $f \in \mathcal{H}$; r_g is as in 1.19. Then (U, P) is a SOI acting in $\mathcal{H}$. Furthermore, if $\zeta_\mathbf{A}$ is the unique $(G, Y, \mathcal{U})$-cohomology class associated to $\mathbf{A}$, then for each $\Psi \in \zeta_\mathbf{A}$, the SOI (U, P) is equivalent to the SOI (U^Ψ, P^Ψ) acting in $L^2(Y, B_0, \alpha)$, where

$$P^\Psi(E)h(y) = 1_E(y)h(y), \tag{2.32i}$$

and

$$U_g^\Psi h(y) = \sqrt{r_g(g^{-1}y)}\,\Psi(g, g^{-1}y)\, h(g^{-1}y), \tag{2.32ii}$$

for $y \in Y, E \in \mathcal{Y}, g \in G$, and $h \in L^2(Y, B_0, \alpha)$.

Conversely, let $(\bar{U}, \bar{P})$ be a SOI based on Y and acting in $\bar{\mathcal{H}}$. Suppose $\bar{P}$ is homogeneous (as in Definition 1.26 (c)). Then there exists a Hilbert bundle $\mathbf{A}$ such that $(\bar{U}, \bar{P})$ is equivalent to the (U, P) of $\mathbf{A}$ given in 2.32.

Proof. That $\{U_g\}_{g \in G}$ is a unitary representation follows from Definition 2.18 and Equation 1.20. Moreover, it is straightforward to compute that

$$U_g P(E) U_g^{-1} = P(g \cdot E).$$

Hence 2.25 defines a SOI.

Now suppose that $V_\sigma : \mathcal{H} \to L^2(Y, B_0; \lambda)$ is as given in 2.22. The corresponding $(G, Y, \mathcal{U})$-cocycle is

$$\varphi_\sigma(g, y) = D[\sigma(gy)^{-1} \cdot g \cdot \sigma(y)]$$

(recalling 2.11). We claim that

$$\text{(a) } P^{\varphi_\sigma}(E) = V_\sigma P(E) V_\sigma^{-1};$$
$$\text{(b) } \quad U_g^{\varphi_\sigma} = V_\sigma U_g V_\sigma^{-1}.$$

(a) holds since $P(E)$ is a (scalar) multiplication operator. As for (b), we have by 2.26 and 2.27 that

$$\begin{aligned} U_g^{\varphi_\sigma} h(y) &= \sqrt{r_g(g^{-1}y)}\, D(\sigma(y))^{-1} \cdot D(g) \cdot D(\sigma(g^{-1}y))\, h(g^{-1}y) \\ &= \sqrt{r_g(g^{-1}y)}\, D(\sigma(y))^{-1} \cdot D(g) \cdot (V_\sigma^{-1} h)(g^{-1}y) \\ &= (V_\sigma U_g V_\sigma^{-1}) h(y). \end{aligned}$$

For a general $\Psi \in \zeta_{\mathbf{A}}$ we have $\Psi = k^{-1} \varphi_\sigma k$, where $k \in M$ and φ_σ is as in 2.27. Then $P^\Psi = k^{-1} P^{\varphi_\sigma} k = P^{\varphi_\sigma}$ and $U_g^\Psi = k^{-1} U_g^{\varphi_\sigma} k$. For the converse, note that by definition of homogeneity for $\bar{P}$, we may assume $(\bar{U}, \bar{P})$ is of the form 2.12. $\mathbf{A}$ may then be taken to be $\mathbf{B}^\Psi$, with action

$$D(g)(y, b_0) = (gy, \Psi(g, y) b_0). \quad \blacksquare$$

Thus vector bundle structures are in turn naturally associated to physical systems (of the sort we have been considering). On the other hand, as we show in section three, vector bundles arise in the "canonical linearization" of the chain bundles of chapter nine (structures associated to the asymptotics of participator dynamical chains). This is, in our opinion, the nexus of the two theories of observer mechanics and quantum mechanics, the conceptual point at which our observer-theoretic allusions to systems of experimenters may be concretely realized. We give more indications of this in section three.

We conclude this section with a few remarks about bundle linearization in terms of the "induced representation" theory of G. W. Mackey. Mackey's classification of the irreducible unitary representations of a lcsc group G may be summarized as follows:

2.33. Let Y be a standard Borel G-space on which G acts transitively. Let $y_0 \in Y$, and let G_0 be the stabilizer of y_0. Then the equivalence classes of irreducible unitary representations of G_0 are in one-one correspondence with the equivalence classes of irreducible systems of imprimitivity for (U, P) for G based on Y. Moreover, all representations U arise in this manner, up to equivalence.

In this theory, which has come to be called the "Mackey machine," G_0 is called the "little group," G the "big group." Thus 2.33 may be paraphrased by saying that all the unitary representations of the big group are associated with systems of imprimitivity (for that group), which are induced by unitary representations of the little group. Note that both the system of imprimitivity and the corresponding representation of G are said to be "induced" by the given representation of the little group.

One of the main technical components of this theory is a result about the description of (G, Y, M)-cocycles for an arbitrary lcsc group M, in terms of representations of G_0 in M. First note that if $\gamma: G \times Y \to M$ is a cocycle, then the restriction of γ to $G_0 \times \{y_0\}$, when viewed as a map $\tilde{\gamma}: G_0 \to M$ is in fact a group homomorphism. We can now state the result:

2.34. (c.f. Varadarajan, Theorem 5.27): With the assumptions of 2.33, the correspondence $\gamma \to \tilde{\gamma}$ induces a 1-1 correspondence between (G, Y, M)-cohomology classes and conjugacy equivalence classes of homomorphisms $G_0 \to M$.

One proves 2.33 by applying 2.34 in the case where $M = \mathcal{U}$ is group of unitary transformations of some Hilbert space $\mathcal{K}$, and using the representation of systems of imprimitivity by cocycles (Theorem 2.5).

Since we know that cocycles also classify bundles (2.15), the above theory can also be described in terms of bundles. The interpretation of bundle linearization in this context is given in the following result, which is obtained by applying 2.34 to the linearization definition 2.21.

Theorem 2.35. Let $\mathcal{A}$ be a transitive G-bundle with base Y, where Y is as above. Then $\mathcal{A}$ corresponds to a unique (G, Y, G_0)-cohomology class $\xi_{\mathcal{A}}$ as in Theorem 2.15. Consider the set $L_{[\mathcal{U}]}(\mathcal{A})$ of all linearizations of $\mathcal{A}$ such that the unitary group of their fibres over y_0 is isomorphic to $\mathcal{U}$. Then the distinct (G-bundle) equivalence classes in $L_{[\mathcal{U}]}(\mathcal{A})$ are indexed by the distinct equivalence classes of representations $\alpha\colon G_0 \to \mathcal{U}$ which factor through $\tilde{\gamma}$ for some $\gamma \in \xi_{\mathcal{A}}$. (This means that $\alpha = \alpha' \circ \tilde{\gamma}$ for some $\alpha'\colon G_0 \to \mathcal{U}$.)

Equivalently, we can then say that A is a *linearization* of $\mathcal{A}$ if the SOI on $\mathcal{H}_A$ associated by Theorem 2.30 is induced from a unitary representation of G_0 which factors through a $\tilde{\gamma}$.

3. Canonical Linearization

We have seen that quantum systems with configuration space Y and symmetry group J correspond to systems of imprimitivity, which in turn correspond to unitary Hilbert J-bundles with base Y. We propose that these "physical" bundles arise as linearizations of specialized chain bundles (c.f. **9–5**). This means that the phenomenology of the physical system is a linearized version of information about the asymptotics of a family of participator-dynamical chains on some "lower level" observer framework, which may itself have no evident physical interpretation. In fact, according to this viewpoint, the physics resides in the specialized perception of the asymptotics of these lower level dynamical systems, not in the systems themselves. We may take the proposal as representing a mathematical strategy for the embedding of certain aspects of physics in a more general hierarchical analytic context. Since examples have not been worked out in detail the ideas are speculative. Nevertheless we believe that the viewpoint is of sufficient interest to present at top level.

In particular, we may describe the essential mathematical idea as follows. Let be given a J-bundle (Z, p, W, J). Represent Z as a family of dynamical systems, say homogeneous Markov chains (on a fixed state space **E**). Represent W as a family of "asymptotic characteristics" (such as stationary measures) of those systems, in such a way that $p(z)$ is an asymptotic characteristic of z. Choose a complex number m, and construct a unitary Hilbert bundle B_m over W, which we might call the "m-linearization" of (Z, p, W, J), as follows. Each fibre $B_{m,w}$ of B_m is the subspace of functions on the state space **E**, generated by the eigenfunctions for eigenvalue m of the transition probability operators (i.e., the Markovian kernels) associated with the various Markov chains in the fibre Z_w of the original bundle. Thus we can think of the Hilbert bundle B_m as providing a canonical linearized picture of the "m-part" of the asymptotics of our J-family of dynamical systems. One thinks of the collection of all the linearizations B_m (as m varies) as giving a picture of the entire asymptotic structure of the dynamics. (Intuitively, the eigenvalue m corresponds to a characteristic frequency of the asymptotic behavior).

Notice that the family $\{B_m\}_m$ of linearizations is canonically associated to the bundle (Z, p, W, J) *together with* the particular representation of Z as a family of dynamical systems. In this section we consider this procedure for the case of the specialized chain bundles. In fact the chain bundle is, abstractly, the principal bundle $(Z, p, W, J) = (J, p, J/J_0, J)$, where J_0 is a subgroup of J, and $p \colon J \to J/J_0$ is the canonical map. To call it a "chain bundle" signifies precisely that we are representing Z as a particular family of participator-dynamical Markov chains, so that in principal we may consider the associated family of canonical linearizations.

Imagine that we are in the situation of the specialized chain bundle of **9–5**. Such a bundle, representing a specialized preobserver, arises from certain asymptotic regularities of an instantiation. Namely, a group J' acts on a class of stationary measures, as well as on a class of participator dynamical kernels, as in **9–5.6**. We now sketch the procedure which gives the canonical linearization, or "quantal description" of the chain bundle.

Let us first recall some definitions.

Notation 3.1. Let P_0 be a markovian kernel with state space **E** and let ν_0 be a stationary measure for P_0. Let J' be a group acting on **E**, with induced actions on kernels and measures as described in **9–5.1**. Let $\mathcal{A}$ be the J'-bundle (E_1', π_1', S', J') where

$$E_1' = \{({}^{\gamma}P_0, {}^{\gamma}\nu_0) \mid \gamma \in J'\},$$

$$S' = \{{}^{\gamma}\nu_0 \mid \gamma \in J'\} \quad \text{and}$$

$$\pi_1'(P,\nu) = \nu.$$

$\mathcal{A}$ is a chain bundle if it arises from a participator dynamical system with sufficient regularities, as described in **9–5**. In that instance $\mathbf{E} = E^k$ for some natural number k, and E is the configuration space at the instantiated level.

Henceforth we assume that everything has all the topological and measurable properties assumed in section two of this chapter.

Now suppose μ is a quasi-J-invariant measure on E. P_0 is then a selfadjoint operator on $L^2(\mathbf{E},\mu)$. If P_0 has an eigenvalue m with eigenfunctions g,

$$P_0 g = mg, \tag{3.2}$$

then for any $\gamma \in \Gamma$, ${}^\gamma g$ is an m-eigenfunction of ${}^\gamma P_0$:

$${}^\gamma P_0 \; {}^\gamma g = m \; {}^\gamma g. \tag{3.3}$$

moreover, ${}^\gamma g$ lies in $L^2(\mathbf{E},\mu)$ since μ is quasi-invariant.

We chose for μ the following measure. Suppose J' has a (left)-invariant Haar measure λ. Let

$$\mu = \int_{J'} \lambda(d\gamma)\; {}^\gamma\nu_0 \tag{3.4}$$

(note that $K(\gamma, de) = {}^\gamma\nu_0(de)$ is a kernel on $J' \times \mathcal{E}$, so that this integral is well-defined).

Definition 3.5. For each unimodular eigenvalue m of P_0, with μ as in 3.4 and ν_0 a stationary measure for P_0, let $\mathbf{B}_m = \mathbf{B}_m(\mu, \nu_0, P_0)$ be the J'-bundle with

base space $= S'$

total space $= \{[\,{}^\gamma f;\, P_0 f = mf, f \in L^2(\mathbf{E},\mu)] \times \{\,{}^\gamma\nu_0\}; \gamma \in J'\}$

projection $\pi: (\,{}^\gamma f,\, {}^\gamma\nu_0) \to {}^\gamma\nu_0.$

Here $[\cdot]$ means closed linear span in $L^2(\mathbf{E},\mu)$. $\mathbf{B}_m$ is called the *canonical m-linearization* of the chain bundle $\mathcal{A}$ of 3.1.

The fibres of $\mathbf{B}_m$ may be described simply. For $\nu \in S'$, let

$$J^{(\nu)} = \{\gamma \in J' : \; {}^\gamma\nu_0 = \nu\}. \tag{3.6}$$

Then the fibre $B_{m,\nu}$ over $\nu \in S'$ is

$$\begin{aligned} B_{m,\nu} &= [g \in L^2(\mathbf{E},\mu) : {}^{\gamma}P_0 g = mg \text{ for some } \gamma \in J^{(\nu)}] \\ &= \{ {}^{\gamma}f : f \in L^2(\mathbf{E},\mu), P_0 f = mf \text{ and } \gamma \in J^{(\nu)} \}. \end{aligned} \tag{3.7}$$

To justify the designation "canonical linearization" for $\mathbf{B}_m$, note that if f_0 is any m-eigenfunction of P_0, a mapping $\Phi : \mathcal{A} \to \mathbf{B}_m$ can be defined by

$$\Phi({}^{\gamma}P_0, {}^{\gamma}\nu_0) = ({}^{\gamma}f_0, {}^{\gamma}\nu_0),$$

and that this is a J'-bundle homomorphism.

The unimodular eigenvalues of P_0 play a fundamental role in the asymptotics of the Markov chain with T.P. P_0, in the instance where P_0 is a so-called *quasi-compact* operator. Specifically, to each such eigenvalue m is associated an asymptotic behavior of the dynamics (m is a root of unity). For details see Revuz, chapter six. The part of the spectrum of P_0 lying inside the open unit disk does not survive asymptotically: repeated iterations of P_0 send that part to zero. Hence our interest in the unimodular spectrum. We remark here that, for our present purposes, it is not important whether the spectrum of P_0 is pure point or not. A canonical "C-linearization" can be described analogously, where C is any measurable subset of the unit circle which intersects the spectrum of P_0.

EPILOGUE

After a marathon colloquium on observer mechanics we were approached by Matthew and Ida. Rumor had it that their relationship was stormy: they were quite contentious, each frequently found the other's point of view entirely unintelligible, and neither hesitated to say so. We expected the worst. However the ensuing conversation proved, to our relief, to be relatively free of hostilities and at points even edifying. Matthew had recently enjoyed the upper hand in his arguments with Ida, and he led off.

Matthew: Quite an interesting, albeit long, colloquium. Ida and I agree on little, but we both agree that you've left a lot of questions unanswered. Can we talk?

One of us: Most certainly. What's on your minds?

Ida: Lots. But for starters I'll be blunt: Is a fork an observer? When you say things like "the objects of perception are other observers" it sure sounds like you're saying something of the sort.

O: Not at all. A fork is a conclusion, not an observer.

M: You did say that the objects of perception are other observers, didn't you?

O: To a first approximation, yes.

M: Well if a fork isn't an object of perception, I don't know what is. And from the statements "forks are objects of perception" and "objects of perception are other observers" it surely follows that forks are observers.

O: It certainly does. But we don't buy the first statement. Forks aren't objects of perception under our definition of that term.

I: Could you remind us of your definition?

O: Surely. The objects of perception for an observer or a participator are those entities with which it interacts in an act of perception.

M: Then you deny that when I look at a fork I am interacting with the fork?

O: That's right. But what about you? Would you want to assert that when you look at a fork, the entity you're really interacting with is the fork itself?

M: Not really. I guess I'd say that the entities I'm interacting with are the fundamental constituents of the fork—it's quarks and leptons and whatnot. But I don't think this'll buy you much. If my true objects of perception, the things I'm really interacting with when I perceive, are quarks, then it seems that you're committed to saying that quarks are observers, aren't you?

O: Not at all. What goes for forks goes for quarks. Quarks and leptons aren't what we're interacting with in perception any more than forks are. And since we don't think quarks are objects of perception we're not committed to saying that quarks are observers. In fact, we think they're not.

I: That sounds fine to me. But that's because ...

M: That's because you don't keep a respectable ontology.

I: Do you want to get into it now?

M: Sorry. No. Let's continue to discuss with them.

I: Fine.

M: How can you say that elementary particles aren't the objects of perception, given all that we know about the physics of light, the optics of the eye, and the physiology of the visual system? There's a known causal path beginning with distal elementary particles, continuing with emitted photons, followed by absorption of the photons by rods and cones, and concluding, after some complicated neural processing, with perception. It would seem that you're contradicting some well-established scientific facts.

O: We see no contradiction. An observer, given some premise s, perceives that interpretation or those interpretations which are given nonzero weight by its conclusion measure $\eta(s, \cdot)$. These interpretations are encoded in a systematic representational scheme that we call X. If some physical objects or physical properties are among the symbols employed by this scheme, then these may be perceived. But the observer isn't interacting with its own symbols, it's interacting with other observers. The conclusions an observer reaches are tied to statistical properties of the dynamics of this interaction. In short, observers interact with observers; physical properties are among the symbols employed by observers to represent aspects of this interaction. The scientific story you just told is fine as far as it goes. But, so to speak, "behind" the physical symbols is the dynamics of observers those symbols represent.

M: Your ontology is no more respectable than Ida's.

I: I warned you.

O: Is there something amiss in our definitions? We've endeavored to define observers, participators, reflexive frameworks and all of our participator dynamics in a manner free of formal errors. But perhaps we've failed somewhere.

M: I don't know if you have. I've not had a chance to examine it carefully.

O: But then what's wrong with our ontology? Our commitments are restricted to those of logic and set theory. Set theory has problems, certainly, but we are no more in trouble on this count than is contemporary physics.

M: The problem is that your account isn't naturalized, nor does it seem amenable to naturalization. Look, physicists are going about finding and listing the fundamental categories and properties of the world. The list needs work, no doubt, but when they're all through it'll contain things like charge, spin, mass, and charm, but not things like observers and participators. But you're making observers and such fundamental categories in your theory. That is *prima facie* implausible.

O: If we were taking the terms "observer" and "participator" as ill-defined or undefined primitives we might agree with you. Such primitives would be poor foundations for a theory of anything. The appropriate move would be to try to naturalize them at best, and completely abandon them at worst. But we take observer and participator as technical terms with rigorous definitions. And we don't share your ontological bias. Rather than naturalize these technical terms our project is to "perceptualize" the technical terms of physical theories. That is, we want to show rigorously how the categories and properties employed in physics could arise (1) from statistical properties of certain dynamics of observers and (2) as aspects of the representational schemes employed by certain observers to describe these statistical properties.

M: Good luck. Go "perceptualize" quantum field theory and then let's have dinner.

O: We might need a rain check. Things take time, but we have some interesting leads. It happens that many physical properties, like spin and mass, turn out to be properties of the representations of algebraic groups. We mentioned, you'll recall, groups, Hilbert bundles, systems of imprimitivity and the like in our colloquium. Well our bet is that the groups that crop up in physics are intimately related to the groups that crop up in our reflexive observer frameworks and to the symmetry groups of the transition probabilities of observer dynamical systems. And it appears that the Hilbert spaces so ubiquitous in quantum theory might arise from the linearization of specialized reflexive frameworks. If so, then the notion of a physical state—namely a measure on the logic of subspaces of an appropriate Hilbert space—might be grounded in observer theory. And then quantum measurement theorists and perceptual theorists might have something substantial to talk about.

I: Sounds like an interesting direction to me. I was going to ask whether, although you deny that forks are observers, you would at any rate assert that forks are composed of observers. But what you just said suggests otherwise.

O: That's right. Physical objects are symbols employed by observers to represent aspects of their interactions with other observers. Physical objects aren't conglomerates of observers. Forks are no more composed of observers than a newspaper is composed of the people and events it describes. We don't endorse panpsychism.

M: Do you deny the existence of quarks or forks?

O: Not at all. Nor would we deny the existence of the symbols used by a Turing machine in its computations. Both forks and quarks are symbols employed by observers. Our view on forks and quarks shares something in common with the "internal realism" of Putnam. We agree with Putnam's rejection, on the one hand, of the metaphysical Realist view, say as put forward by Sellars, that denies the real existence of "middle-sized" physical objects such as ice cubes, and that grants existence only to the particles of physics and their occurrent properties. Putnam rejects it as embodying untenable dichotomies, for example a dichotomy between properties physical objects have "in themselves" versus properties projected on them by the mind. We also agree with Putnam's rejection, on the other hand, of complete relativism— relativism that goes beyond the acknowledgement of different "versions" of the world to the claim that truth is just consensus or some such. And we agree with Putnam that a quark, no less than a fork, is a version-relative notion; and that this impugns the ontological status of neither. Where we differ with Putnam, of course, is our specific proposal that quarks and forks are symbols employed by observers to represent properties of the dynamics of *participators*.

I: If matter isn't composed of observers, what about the converse? Would you say that observers are composed of matter?

O: No. According to our definition, an observer is composed of six parts: X, Y, E, S, π, and η.

I: Certainly. But although I have no trouble with this, I imagine Matthew would not be comfortable without some assurance of token physicalism regarding observers. I mean, he'd say it might be fine to have an abstract definition of observers, but any particular instance must somehow be physically instantiated. Maybe you endorse some kind of property dualism: matter has physical properties and observer-theoretic properties.

O: We do have a notion of the instantiation of an observer or a participator, but it doesn't amount to token physicalism or property dualism.

M: This doesn't sound good. What was your notion of instantiation again?

O: Recall that each observer is an inferential system. It gets certain premises and reaches certain conclusions. If O is some observer, where does O get its premises? Well from other observers. There is some collection of observers, say T, whose conclusions or their deductive consequences are the premises for O. We called these observers "transducers" for O. They are the first level of instantiation of O. Of course each observer in the collection T has, in turn, its own transducers. And so on ad infinitum, presumably. You can picture the instantiation of O something like an infinite cone with its tip at O and getting wider and wider as one goes through successive levels of transducers.

M: Fine and dandy. But if there's no matter in the instantiation, how can you see one? I for one have never encountered a perambulating cone.

O: In an interesting way, matter is involved in our notion of instantiation.

M: Pulling in your horns pretty quickly, sounds to me.

O: Not really. The idea is that there are many levels—infinitely many levels—of observer dynamics taking place in the instantiation cone of O. The way O represents the statistical properties of the dynamics of observers in its instantiation depends on how far down in the cone that dynamics is taking place. For dynamics near the top of the cone, close to O itself, the representation tends to be more "psychological" whereas as one goes down the cone the representation becomes more "neurobiological" and then more "physical" and then . . ., well there's no bottom that we know of.

I: Then you would deny a principled distinction between mind and body?

O: Yes. "Mind" and "body" are convenient terms to distinguish between levels of the instantiation cone for a given observer. Higher levels, or rather an observer's representation of the dynamics at these higher levels, are "mental."

Somewhat lower levels are its "body." Even lower levels, unrepresented and as yet unexplored, presumably also exist. And since what is mind and what is body are relativized to the observer, a dynamics which is mental relative to one observer may be physical relative to another, and vice versa.

M: This sounds worse all the time. Physical properties and physical entities must be the ontological bedrock. Any theory of mind must be built upon these, or at least be compatible with these.

I: Actually, I like this observer story. I've always felt that the physical could be reduced to the mental, or eliminated entirely.

O: Let's be careful here. We don't really claim to be reducing the physical to the mental. We're saying that both the physical and the mental are derivative upon something more fundamental, namely an infinite "hierarchy" of levels of observers/participators in dynamical interaction. And we certainly don't claim to be eliminating the physical. If anything, we're proliferating the physical. Since what's physical depends on which level of the observer hierarchy you're talking about, there's no such thing as *the* physical world, but rather there are infinitely many "physical worlds."

I: This is starting to sound rather like the monadology of Leibniz, what with hierarchies of perceivers and all.

O: There is some resemblance, but there are important differences. First, monads are rather loosely defined. Certainly not well enough to attempt to build a quantitative science on them. Observers and participators, on the other hand, have precise mathematical definitions. Second, whereas Leibniz postulates a preestablished harmony between the activities of noninteracting monads, observer theory postulates a stochastic dynamics of interacting participators, with markovian kernels that have been characterized precisely. Third, as one goes down the levels of monads, one encounters successively impoverished modes of perception. Whereas it is completely compatible with the observer-theoretic hierarchy that different levels are, in some sense, equally rich—just different. And finally, we don't yet know if our hierarchy reaches to the City of God.

I: And I take it, given your account of mind and body that, *pace* Berkeley, you would not want to say that physical objects, elementary particles, and so on are existentially dependent on one's mind?

O: There are a couple of reasons why we wouldn't say that. First, there is no mathematically precise definition of mind that is generally accepted, functionalist accounts not withstanding. So such a statement would not, for now, be at a level of precision required for dialogue with, say, a quantum measurement theorist. Second, whatever notion of mind eventually does emerge, we anticipate that it will be derivative upon the notion of hierarchies of dynamical systems of observers. So that the more fundamental issue is the existential dependence of physical objects on observers and participators. And third, here the relationship isn't one of simple existential dependence. Physical objects and properties are, we have claimed, among the symbols or representations employed by observers and participators, so that they are in some sense "parts" of these observers/participators. But that's not the whole story. Each participator is not alone. There are dynamical interactions among participators, and although a given participator contributes to its own dynamics and, indirectly, to the dynamics in its instantiation, there is much more to these dynamics than just the contribution of this participator. Something "independent" of or only partially dependent on this participator is going on, as is clear from that fact that the other participators are governed by their own action kernels. But since, on our story, it is statistical properties of this dynamics that are represented by the given participator's symbols, and since this dynamics is partially "independent" of that participator, it follows that the tokening of particular symbols by the participator depends in part on the participator and in part on its "environment." The statement that such symbols are existentially dependent upon the participator is just too simple. It only catches one part of the whole elephant.

I: This sounds a bit Kantian, the idea of having a supersensible realm which is behind the realm of experience and which, in some fashion, drives that realm of experience.

O: Perhaps a bit. But the differences are crucial. For Kant the supersensible thing-in-itself is unknowable and not a potential subject of scientific enquiry. For us the supersensible realm of participators in dynamical interactions is, although perhaps not directly knowable, still a subject of scientific enquiry. There is nothing unusual about exploring the unobservable through science. That's how we know about quarks and thermonuclear processes in the sun. Similarly for participators and observers. We can't see them directly, but we can legitimately construct theories of participators and their dynamics, and then look for empirical consequences that can be checked.

I: I take it then that you don't embrace phenomenalism?

O: Right. We don't take "elementary sensations" such as colors, sounds, spaces, and times as the constituents out of which physical objects are constructed or as the foundation, incorrigible or otherwise, upon which all else is built. Quite to the contrary, we take unobservable entities—observers and participators—as the (far from incorrigible) foundation. Sensations no less than physical objects are, for us, the corrigible conclusions of the nondemonstrative inferences of observers. This view of sensations is, by the way, one reason why we took time to point out the problems in defining transduction. By rejecting the widely held notion that one can point to a distinguished single stage of transduction in, say, vision, we were rejecting even the more recent (and nonphenomenalist) suggestions of a demure foundational status for sensations. Instead, we relativize the definition of transduction to the observer, so that what is "directly detected" relative to one observer is, relative to another, the conclusion of a nondemonstrative inference. If there are epistemological foundations, they are not to be found in sensations.

I: Can perception, then, yield knowledge? Say knowledge in the traditional sense of justified true belief?

O: For a specific premise s, the conclusion $\eta(s, \cdot)$ of a participator is true if the probabilities it assigns to the interpretations in $\pi^{-1}(s) \cap E$ match the actual probabilities generated by the dynamics in which it participates. The conclusion is justified if η is a regular conditional probability distribution (rcpd) with respect to π of the stationary measure of this dynamics. Justified true conclusions are, perhaps, knowledge.

I: It would seem, then, that your participators could have perceptual knowledge without being certain that they have it?

O: That's right. In fact it seems they can't be certain. A participator cannot determine if it's interpretation kernel η is the appropriate rcpd.

I: How then can it happen that η turns out to be the appropriate rcpd? This seems a rather unlikely coincidence.

O: For this to happen there must be an appropriate relationship between the action kernels and the interpretation kernels of the various interacting participators. The action kernels, you see, determine the transition probability of the participator dynamics, and it's the stationary measures of this stochastic dynamics for which the interpretation kernels must be rcpd's. Whether there are particular strategies that participators could adopt (for example, special kinds of action kernels) to enhance their chances of true conclusions is a topic for further research. But it is clear that a participator P "wants" not only its own conclusions to be true, but also the conclusions of participators at the various levels of its instantiation to be true as well—for these conclusions eventually become P's premises. This means that at the various levels of dynamics in the instantiation cone of P the conclusions of the instantiating participators should also be the appropriate rcpd's of the stationary measures of their respective levels. At the "biological" levels of the instantiation cone of P this matching of rcpd's to measures might appear, relative to P, as an appropriate "adaptation" of the instantiation of P. Thus on this particular point we apparently agree with evolutionary epistemologists such as Popper and Campbell: there is a continuity, a formal similarity, between the processes which eventuate in knowledge and those which eventuate in biological adaptation.

I: But you don't seem to buy their representationalism.

O: Not to the extent that they take the external world, the world that is to be in some fashion represented, as a physical world—a world of forks and quarks. For us the represented world, the "World 1" in Popper's terminology, is the world of observers and participators in hierarchies of dynamics. The world of forks and quarks is a world of representations, not the world to be represented.

M: You seem to put a lot of weight on the dynamics of participators, and I'm not sure I have an intuitive grasp of this dynamics. Can you help with an example?

O: We can try. But remember, there are three kinds of dynamics of relevance to a given participator P. First, there's the dynamics on the reflexive framework of P itself. Here P is interacting with other participators that are on the same framework with it. Second, there are the various dynamics going on in P's instantiation. The asymptotic properties of these dynamics eventuate as premises for P. And third, there are the various dynamics "above" P. For P is itself involved in the instantiations of higher observers and participators.

I: This just follows from the hierarchy of participator dynamics you mentioned before, right?

O: Exactly. Now let's look at an analogue of the second type of dynamics, the dynamics of P's instantiation leading to a premise for P's own inferences. We say "analogue" because this example isn't really a participator dynamics at all, but an example drawn from the physical realm to help intuitions. We discussed a real example, you'll recall, when we talked about instantaneous rotation observers and the incremental rigidity scheme. So if the analogue doesn't help, forget it and think about the real example.

M: Enough caveats. Do proceed.

O: Consider your perception of pressure and shape when you press your fingertip on a corner of a table. The physiologists tell us that your sensory experience is dependent upon various cutaneous mechanoreceptors, such as Pacinian corpuscles and Merkel cells. The physicists tell us that at an even more microscopic level your sensory experience is dependent upon the dynamics of many atomic and subatomic particles. Both the table and your finger are composed of such particles and, before touching your finger to the table, the dynamical systems of particles for the finger and for the table have each their own kind of stability—as evidenced by the fact that each retains its own shape over time. But now when you place your finger on the table corner you are bringing these two dynamical systems into contact and letting them interact, with the consequence that a new stability of the table/finger system of particles is reached. Of course the new stability requires more give and take on the part of the finger system than on the part of the table system, with the result that the original stability of the finger system becomes quite perturbed and gives way to a new, quite different, stability. This is evidenced by the new dented shape of the finger. It is this change in the stability of the dynamics for the finger system that is picked up by the mechanoreceptors and eventually experienced as pressure and shape. So here we get a glimpse of how stabilities of dynamical systems at a "lower" level can be premises for perceptual inferences at a "higher" one.

I: We aren't to infer from this example, however, that dynamical systems of physical particles are the same thing as dynamical systems of participators?

O: Right. Physical particles are not participators.

M: What leads you to suggest that the objects of perception are other observers or participators?

O: Chronologically the definition of observer came first. As early as 1980 we tried to write down a formal structure common to the theories of (e.g.) structure from motion, stereo, and shape from shading that had, at that time, recently been developed. This structure was refined over a period of seven or eight years, as we continued to study new theories of specific perceptual capacities and to develop our own theories of structure from motion and shape recognition. When we finally had in hand a formal definition of observer that we were reasonably comfortable with, the question naturally arose whether the same could be done for the objects of observation. It seemed we had a fundamental choice of strategies. We could either propose that the objects of perception have a formal description that is fundamentally distinct from that of observers, or we could propose that they have the same, or related, formal descriptions. Proposing a fundamental distinction seemed problematic: it would introduce a dualism, it would require a new formalism for the objects of perception together with a justification for this formalism, and it would require a new formalism to interrelate observers with these objects. So too did the alternative—proposing that objects of perception are observers. It would require us to figure out a formalism to relate observers with other observers so that mutual observation became possible. And it required us to face the obvious objections of the "Is a fork an observer?" variety. When we discovered the possibility of constructing reflexive observer frameworks, and thereby the possibility of mutual observation between observers, we decided to further pursue the nondualistic alternative. The vindication or rejection of this approach must await the further development of the resulting theory and the testing of its empirical consequences.

M: Your nondualistic approach seems to have the unsavory consequence that physical events do not cause other physical events. Is that a correct reading?

O: So it would seem. Physical events are employed by observers to represent properties of the dynamics of participators. Any notion of cause must derive from this dynamics, not from the symbols used to represent this dynamics.

I: Perceptual learning was conspicuous by its absence from your colloquium. Does observer mechanics have anything to say about it?

O: Actually it was absent only in name. Our entire development of participator dynamics can be viewed as dealing with perceptual learning. As a result of observations a participator updates its perspective π and its class of possible perceptual conclusions η, all under the dictates of its action kernel.

I: But the participator dynamics you develop is markovian—one can make the best possible prediction about the future behavior of the dynamics based only on knowledge of its current state. Isn't this a rather special case, not really suited to be a general theory of perceptual learning? What about the possibility of learning that depends on a past history, not merely on the current state?

O: It is true that the participator dynamics is markovian, and that this means that the present state is the best possible predictor of future behavior. However, the dynamics of various subsets of the participator system are typically quite nonmarkovian. And the markovian formalism is far more general than at first it might seem. For if, in one formulation of the notion of a dynamical state, it happens that predictions of the future are best conditioned not just on the current state, but on a finite history of states, then it is always possible to reconstruct the notion of state and the description of the dynamics such that it is markovian. Thus by formulating participator dynamics as markovian we include learning that depends on finite past histories of any length.

I: Also conspicuous by its absence was introspection. If you intend to extend observer theory beyond perception to include cognition as well, as it appears you do in your attempts to define the notion "cognitive" in terms of observer theory, then you can't ignore introspection.

O: Most certainly. We don't see a principled distinction between cognition and perception. The considerations that have led Fodor, for instance, to suggest that there is a distinction—namely, the relative isotropy and unencapsulation of cognitive or "central" processors, on the one hand, and the domain specificity and encapsulation of perceptual "input analyzers," on the other—can all be satisfied by the relativized notion of "cognitive" and "transductive" that we introduced in discussing the issue of theory neutrality of observation. So we do face the task of interpreting such activities as introspection in terms of observer theory. We have no detailed account of introspection at present. But perhaps introspection on a given reflexive framework is performed by participators on another framework which take as their premises finite sequences of dynamical states (or of conclusions) of the given framework. On this provisional construal of introspection, it is a finitary precursor of specialization.

M: Is observer theory falsifiable?

O: Certainly. Take, for instance, our "observer thesis"—that every single perceptual capacity has a natural description that is an instance of the definition of observer. This thesis can be disconfirmed by counterexample. And were a counterexample to appear, we would have to rework or abandon the theory.

M: If you say physical entities are symbols employed by observers to represent aspects of participator dynamics, then what do you say about spacetime itself?

O: Roughly, our ideas are like this. There is not one global time, but different times at different levels of the hierarchy of participator dynamics. As one goes down the instantiation cone, for instance, of a participator one finds that at each successively lower level the time scale "speeds up." This is because typically it is properties of the *asymptotic* behavior at the lower level that serve as premises for observers and participators at the next level up. At a given level of the hierarchy, moreover, there is not just one time either. Rather each participator has its own "proper time" which increases with every "channeling" in which it participates. In short, the unit of time for a participator is a discrete act of observation. A single unit of time for one participator will correspond to many, perhaps infinitely many, units of time for each participator in its instantiation. Now the rate at which a participator channels with others depends on the "τ-distribution" and the group difference-in-perspective of the other participators with which it interacts. The τ-distribution, then, governs the way in which time and "distance" trade off, and it is the key to an observer-theoretic account of the relativity of physical spacetime. Much is yet to be worked out, but the big picture is again that spacetime is part of the scheme employed by participators to represent properties of their interactions with other participators.

I: What other areas for further development do you see in observer theory?

O: Many. Here's an abbreviated shopping list. We have already mentioned introspection, and the project of perceptualizing physical theory (but not, of course, in any phenomenalist or idealist sense of "perceptualizing"). It would be interesting to develop the notion that physical properties are properties of the dynamics of interacting participators, and that therefore these properties hold only so long as the dynamics continues. Pursuing this may lead to an observer-theoretic understanding of the Aspect experiments. We need to develop further the theory of specialization and to understand the flow of information up and down between the different levels of participator dynamics. Information flows up as the conclusions from below become premises above. And information flows down as the participators above move under the guidance of their action kernels and "carry with them" their instantiations as they move. But more theory and examples, in addition to the incremental scheme we already discussed, are clearly required here. We need to understand strategies by which the interpretation kernels of participators can become rcpd's of the appropriate stationary measures. Here perhaps some benefit will derive from study of formal models of natural selection. Perhaps also we should explore more "cooperative" models, models in which the participators don't compete but choose action kernels which maximize the likelihood of true perception for all participators in their dynamics. We must develop more explicitly the epistemological and ontological implications of observer theory. And . . ., well there's much left to do. This is just a start.

REFERENCES

Ballard, D. and **Brown, C.** (1982). *Computer vision,* New Jersey: Prentice-Hall.

Bennett, B., Hoffman, D. and **Prakash, C.** (1987). "Perception and computation," *Proc. IEEE First International Conf. Computer Vis.,* 356–364.

Bennett, B., Hoffman, D. and **Prakash, C.** (1989). "Structure from two orthographic views of rigid motion," *J. Opt. Soc. Am. A,* in press.

Bhat, U. N. (1984). *Elements of applied stochastic processes,* New York: Wiley & Sons.

Billingsley, P. (1979). *Probability and measure,* New York: Wiley & Sons.

Breiman, L. (1969). *Probability and stochastic processes,* Boston: Houghton Mifflin.

Brindley, G. and **Lewin, W.** (1968). "The visual sensations produced by electrical stimulation of the medial occipital cortex," *J. Physiol., 194,* 54–55.

Brindley, G. and **Lewin, W.** (1971). "The sensations produced by electrical stimulation of the visual cortex," in *Visual prosthesis* (eds Sterling, T., Bering, E., Pollack, S., and Vaughan, H.) 21–40, New York: Academic Press.

Bruner, J. (1973). "On perceptual readiness," in *Beyond the information given,* (ed Anglin, J.) New York: W. W. Norton & Co.

Button, J. and **Putnam, T.** (1962). "Visual responses to cortical stimulation in the blind," *Journal of the Iowa State Medical Society, 52,* 17–21.

Catalan, E. (1838). "Note sur une equation aux differences finies," *J. Math. Pures Appl.* 508–516.

Chung, K. (1974). *A course in probability theory,* New York: Academic Press.

Churchland, P. M. (1988). "Perceptual plasticity and theoretical neutrality: a reply to Jerry Fodor," *Philosophy of Science, 55,* 167–187.

Einstein, A. (1956). *The meaning of relativity,* Princeton: Princeton University Press.

Fodor, J. (1979). *The language of thought,* Cambridge: Harvard University Press.

Fodor, J. (1983). *Modularity of mind,* Cambridge, Massachusetts: MIT Press.

Fodor, J. (1984). "Observation reconsidered," *Philosophy of Science, 51,* 23–43.

Fodor, J. (1987). *Psychosemantics,* Cambridge, Massachusetts: MIT Press.

Fodor, J. (1988). "A reply to Churchland's "Perceptual plasticity and theoretical neutrality"," *Philosophy of Science, 55,* 188–198.

Fodor, J. and **Pylyshyn, Z.** (1981). "How direct is visual perception?: Some reflections on Gibson's 'Ecological Approach'," *Cognition, 9,* 139-196.

Gibson, J. J. (1966). *The senses considered as perceptual systems,* Boston: Houghton Mifflin.

Gibson, J. J. (1979). *The ecological approach to visual perception.* Boston: Houghton Mifflin.

Gibson, J. and **Gibson, E.** (1957). "Continuous perspective transformations and the perception of rigid motion," *J. Exp. Psych.,* 54, 2, 129-138.

Gilbert, W. (1976). *Modern algebra with applications,* New York: Wiley & Sons.

Green, B. (1961). "Figure coherence in the kinetic depth effect," *J. Exp. Psych.,* 62, 3, 272-282.

Greenberger, D. (1986). *New techniques and ideas in quantum measurement the-*

ory, New York: New York Academy of Sciences.

Gregory, R. (1966). *Eye and brain,* New York: McGraw-Hill.

Grimson, W. E. L. (1980). "A computer implementation of a theory of human stereo vision," *Phil. Trans. R. Soc. Lond.* B292, 217–253.

Hadamard, J. (1923). *Lectures on the Cauchy problem in linear partial differential equations,* New Haven: Yale University Press.

Hay, C. (1966). "Optical motions and space perception – an extention of Gibson's analysis," *Psych. Rev.,* 73, 550-565.

Helmholtz, H. L. F. von (1910). *Treatise on physiological optics,* Translated by J. Southal, 1925, New York: Dover.

Hildreth, E. (1984). *The measurement of visual motion,* Cambridge: MIT Press.

Hoffman, D. (1983). "The interpretation of visual illusions," *Sci. Am.,* 249, 6, 154-162.

Hoffman, D. and **Flinchbaugh, B.** (1982). "The interpretation of biological motion," *Biol. Cyb.,* 42, 195-204.

Hoffman, D. and **Bennett, B.** (1985). "Inferring the relative three-dimensional positions of two moving points," *J. Opt. Soc. Am. A,* 2, 2, 350–353.

Hoffman, D. and **Bennett, B.** (1986). "The computation of structure from fixed-axis motion: rigid structures," *Biol. Cyb.,* 54, 71-83.

Hopcroft, J. and **Ullman, J.** (1969). *Formal languages and their relation to automata.* Reading, Massachusetts: Addison-Wesley.

Horn, B. (1974). "Determining lightness from an image," *Comp. Graph. Im. Proc.,* 3, 4, 277–299.

Horn, B. (1975). "Obtaining shape from shading information," in *The Psychology* *of Computer Vision*, (ed Winston, P.) 115–155, New York: McGraw-Hill.

Horn, B. (1985). *Robot vision*, Cambridge: MIT Press.

Horn, B. and **Schunck, B.** (1981). "Determining optical flow," *Artif. Intell.*, 17, 185–203.

Ikeuchi, K. and **Horn, B.** (1981). "Numerical shape from shading and occluding boundaries," *Artif. Intell.*, 17, 141–184.

Jacobson, N. (1974). *Basic algebra*, San Francisco: Freeman.

Johansson, G. (1973). "Visual perception of biological motion and a model for its analysis," *Perception & Psychophysics*, 14, 201-211.

Johansson, G. (1975). "Visual motion perception," *Scientific American*, 232, 6, 76-88.

Koenderink, J. and **van Doorn, A.** (1975). "Invariant properties of the motion parallax field due to the movement of rigid bodies relative to an observer," *Opt. Acta*, 22, 773–791.

Koenderink, J. and **van Doorn, A.** (1976). "Geometry of binocular vision and a model for stereopsis," *Biol. Cyb.*, 21, 29–35.

Koenderink, J. and **van Doorn, A.** (1976)."Local structure of movement parallax of the plane," *J. Opt. Soc. Am.*, 66, 717–723.

Koenderink, J. and **van Doorn, A.** (1980). "Photometric invariants related to solid shape," *Opt. Acta*, 22, 773–791.

Koenderink, J. and **van Doorn, A.** (1981). "Exterospecific component of the motion parallax field," *J. Opt. Soc. Am.*, 71, 8, 953–957.

Koenderink, J. and **van Doorn, A.** (1986). "Depth and shape from differential perspective in the presence of bending deformations," *J. Opt. Soc. Am. A*, 3, 242–249.

Land, E. and **McCann, J.** (1971). "Lightness theory," *J. Opt. Soc. Am.*, 61, 1–11.

Longuet-Higgins, H. C. (1982). "The role of the vertical dimension in stereoscopic vision," *Perception*, 11, 377–386.

Longuet-Higgins, H. C. and **Prazdny, K.** (1980). "The interpretation of moving retinal images," *Proc. R. Soc. Lond.*, B208, 385–397.

Luenberger, D. (1963) "Determining the state of a linear system with observers of low dynamic order," Ph.D. dissertation, Stanford University.

Maloney, L. (1985) "Computational approaches to color constancy," Ph.D. dissertation, Stanford University.

Marr, D. (1982). *Vision*, San Francisco: Freeman.

Marr, D. and **Poggio, T.** (1979) "A computational theory of human stereo vision," *Proc. R. Soc.* B204, 301–328.

Marr, D. and **Ullman, S.** (1981). "Directional selectivity and its use in early visual processing," *Proc. R. Soc. Lond.* B211, 151–180.

Mayhew, J. (1982). "The interpretation of stereo-disparity information: the computation of surface orientation and depth," *Perception*, 11, 387–403.

Narayan Bhat, U. (1984). *Elements of applied stochastic processes*, New York: Wiley & Sons.

Nelson, E. (1985). *Quantum fluctuations*, Princeton: Princeton University Press.

O'Reilly, J. (1983). *Observers for linear systems*, New York: Academic Press.

Parthasarathy, K. (1968). *Introduction to probability and measure*, New Dehli: Macmillan.

Pentland, A. P. (1984). "Local shading analysis," *IEEE Trans. Patt. Anal. Mach. Intell., PAMI-6*, 170–187.

Pitman, J. and **Rogers, L.** (1981). "Markov functions," *Annals of Probability,* 9, 4, 573-582.

Poggio, T., Torre, V., and **Koch, C.** (1985). "Computational vision and regularization theory," *Nature,* 317, 314–319.

Prugovecki, E. (1984). *Quantum mechanics and quantum spacetime,* Boston: Reidel.

Richards, W. (1983). "Structure from stereo and motion," *Artif. Intell. Lab. Memo,* 731, Cambridge: MIT.

Revuz, D. (1984). *Markov chains,* Amsterdam: North-Holland.

Rubin, J. and **Richards, W.** (1987). "Spectral categorization of materials," in *Image Understanding 1985-1986* (eds Richards, W. and Ullman, S.) 20–44, New York: Ablex.

Skyrms, B. (1975). *Choice and chance,* Belmont, California: Wadsworth Publishing.

Tikhonov, A. (1963). *Sov. Math. Dokl.,* 4, 1035–1038.

Tikhonov, A. (1977). *Solutions of ill-posed problems,* Washington, DC: Winston.

Ullman, S. (1979). *The interpretation of visual motion,* Cambridge: MIT Press.

Ullman, S. (1981). "Analysis of visual motion by biological and computer systems," *IEEE Computer,* 14, 8, 57–69.

Ullman, S. (1984). "Maximizing rigidity: The incremental recovery of 3-D structure from rigid and rubbery motion," *Perception,* 13, 255–274.

Varadarajan, V. S. (1985). *Geometry of quantum theory,* New York: Springer-Verlag.

Wallach, H. and **O'Connell, D.** (1953). "The kinetic depth effect," *J. Exp. Psych.,*

45, 4, 205-217.

Waxman, A. and **Wohn, K.** (1987). "Contour evolution, neighborhood deformation, and image flow: textured surfaces in motion," in *Image Understanding 1985-86* (eds Richards, W. and Ullman, S.) 72–98, New Jersey: Ablex.

Webb, J. and **Aggarwal, J.** (1981). "Visually interpreting the motion of objects in space," *IEEE Computer,* 14, 8, 40–46.

Zucker, S. (1981). "Computer vision and human perception," *Technical Report 81-10,* Computer Vision and Graphics Laboratory, McGill University.

INDEX

NOTATION INDEX

Symbol	*Description*	*Page*
$\mathrm{Aut}\mathcal{P}(\mathcal{H})$	projective group of automorphisms of $\mathcal{P}(\mathcal{H})$	237
$*$	convolution of measures and functions	125
$\mathrm{b}\mathcal{E}$	bounded measurable functions on E	–
$\mathbf{B}^{\phi}$	bundle associated to a cocycle	246
$\mathbf{C}$	the complex numbers	–
$\mathcal{C}$	a measure class on $(X, \mathcal{X})$	241
$\mathcal{C}_G$	measure class of Haar measure on G	241
χ	a channeling, $\chi \in \mathcal{I}(k)$	88
$D(\chi)$	domain of χ	142
$D_q M$	decomposable descent of kernel M by q	160
$\mathcal{D}$	linear map of measures	194
E	configuration event of observer	23
$\hat{E}$, $\hat{E}^k$	state space of augmented dynamics	147
$\mathcal{E}$	σ-algebra on E	23
$\hat{\mathcal{E}}$	σ-algebra on $\hat{E}$	147
$\mathcal{E}_+$	nonnegative measurable functions on E	–
ϵ_x	Dirac measure on the point x	–
η	interpretation kernel of observer	23
$\mathcal{F}$	σ-algebra on Ω	109
ϕ	a cocycle	241
${}^{\gamma}f$	group element γ acting on function f	220
${}^{\gamma}K$	group element γ acting on kernel K	220
${}^{\gamma}\mu$	group element γ acting on measure μ	220
${}^{(\gamma)}R$	modification of action kernel	223
${}^{(\gamma)}A$	modification of participator	223
G	symmetry group of a symmetric framework	93
Gm	orbit of m under group G	80
G/E	quotient set of G by E	79
$\mathcal{H}$	Hilbert space	231
$\mathbf{H}^1$	collection of all (G, X, M) cohomology classes	242
$h_*\mu$	"pushdown" of measure μ	21
h^*f	"pullback" of function f	171

$h^*\mathcal{V}$	σ-algebra induced by h	159
Id_X	identity map on X	–
$\imath$	identity element of a group	80
$\mathcal{I}(k)$	set of involutions on subsets of k elements	142
J	the symmetry group of E, $J \subset G$	93
$\hat{J}^k$	$J^k \times \mathcal{I}(k)$	169
L	active perspectives in a channeling	87
$L^2(X, m)$	(or $L^2(m)$) square integrable functions	119
m_p^μ	rcpd of μ wrt p, a kernel	22
$M_\nu(A)$	probability measure on $(\Omega, \mathcal{F})$	162
$M_x(A)$	$= M_\nu(A)$ with $\nu(\cdot) = \epsilon_x(\cdot)$	162
$\mathbf{N}$	the natural numbers	–
N_t	markovian kernel, standard dynamics	145
$N_{t,X}$	markovian kernel, channeling dependent	143
$N^\dagger$	a kernel, $N^\dagger(e, A) = N(-e, -A)$	125
$\hat{N}$	markovian kernel, augmented dynamics	149
Ω	canonical probability space	109
$\hat{\Omega}$	augmented chain canonical probability space	151
$\otimes$	tensor product	–
1_A	characteristic function of set A	–
$\mathcal{P}(\mathcal{H})$	set of orthogonal projections on $\mathcal{H}$	232
pr_1	projection onto first factor	–
P_n	n-fold product of kernel P with itself	109
$p_*(\mu)$	distribution of p wrt measure μ	21
$p_*^\tau(\hat{N})$	a kernel, the bring down of $\hat{N}$	154
$\prod$	product	–
π	perspective map of observer	23
$\pi\vert_E$	restriction of map π to set E	–
Ψ	quantum mechanical wave function	233
$\mathbf{Q}$	the rational numbers	–
$Q(s, \cdot)$	action kernel	140
$\widehat{\langle Q_1, \ldots, Q_k \rangle}_\tau$	one step T.P. for k participators	149
$\mathbf{R}$	the real numbers	–
$R_q M$	respectful descent of kernel M by q	158
S	observation event of observer	23
σ	state of a physical system	232
Σ_m	stabilizer of m	80
$\mathcal{T}_q$	proper time of participator q	121

τ	kernel for channeling probabilities	145
$\theta(A)$	shift operator applied to event A	109
$\boldsymbol{\Theta}$	reflexive framework	–
$\mathcal{U}$	group of unitary automorphisms of $\mathcal{H}$	237
X	configuration space of observer	23
ξ	starting measure of participator	140
Y	observation space of observer	23
$\mathbf{Z}$	the integers	–